MUSLIM
FASHION

Contemporary Style Cultures

REINA LEWIS

Duke University Press | Durham and London | 2015

Library of Congress Cataloging-in-Publication Data
Lewis, Reina, [date]– author.
Muslim fashion : contemporary style cultures / Reina Lewis.
pages cm
Includes bibliographical references and index.
ISBN 978-0-8223-5914-2 (hardcover : alk. paper)
ISBN 978-0-8223-5934-0 (pbk. : alk. paper)
ISBN 978-0-8223-7534-0 (e-book)
1. Muslim women—Clothing—Turkey. 2. Muslim women—
Clothing—Great Britain. 3. Muslim women—Clothing—North
America. 4. Fashion—Turkey. 5. Fashion—Great Britain.
6. Fashion—North America. I. Title.
BP190.5.C6L49 2015
391′.2088297—dc23
2015012564

Cover art: © Alessia Gammarota / Crossing the street to meet
Dina Toki-O, Oxford Street, London, 2012.

MUSLIM FASHION

WITH LOVE
FOR
Áine Duffy

IN MEMORY OF MY MOTHER
Estelle Lewis
1930–2014
Loving and Beloved

CONTENTS

ACKNOWLEDGMENTS

Before I started this project on contemporary Muslim fashion I mostly wrote about dead people and their paintings and about dead people and their books. It has been an entirely different experience to be writing about live human subjects and what they wear, what they design, how they shop, and what they discuss as readers and writers of magazines, blogs, and social media. Because many preferred to keep their participation confidential I can't thank by name all the women and men, Muslim and non-Muslim, who so generously shared their personal and professional experiences with me, but I hope they will be able to see in the pages that follow just how much I learned from our discussions, though they may not always agree with my conclusions.

I am grateful to have received funding from the British Academy Small Research Grants scheme for the initial stages of this research from 2007 to 2009 and subsequently from the Arts and Humanities Research Council/Economic and Social Science Research Council as part of their Religion and Society Programme in 2010–11. I benefited from the range of colleagues and approaches that I encountered as part of the program in a lively community fostered by Rebecca Catto and Peta Ainsworth, and from working with my coinvestigator Emma Tarlo and the project research assistant Jane Cameron. Program director Linda Woodhead continues to expand my intellectual horizons with her sense of how fashion and religion fit together.

The London College of Fashion, University of the Arts London, has provided a uniquely creative and intellectual home for me and this project: I am grateful for the material support provided by the LCF Project Fund and by sabbatical leave from the college and university, and I thank vice chancellor Nigel Carrington for his interest in the research. Most especially I wish to acknowledge my head of college, pro-vice chancellor

Frances Corner, who has continued to encourage me to find new ways to bring research about religious and religio-ethnic fashion practices into the frame of arts education. My colleagues and students at LCF and at UAL have been extraordinarily open to my mix of materials and approaches, pushing me to think further and harder. I wish also to thank Charlotte Hodes and Helen Thomas for their sustained encouragement during the course of this project.

This book seems have to been more complicated to research and produce than any of my previous projects, but I have been better resourced with expert help than ever before, and I wish to thank at UAL Rita Clemente, Rachel Jillions, Peter Taylor, and, in particular, Luella Allen for research administration support; David Hardy for picture advice; Alastair Mucklow and David Revalgiatte for digital communications; and Ros Barbour and Linda Bevan on events. Grant administration has been aided by Sean Tonkin, Prema Mundiany, and Betty Woessner; my media interactions were guided by Hannah Clayton, Rebecca Munro, Agatha Connolly, Charlotte Gush, and Lynsey Fox, and tutored by Wendy Smith. In addition, Simin Eldem tracked legal materials; and Susan Nicholls has provided unparalleled rapid response transcription services. I thank also Vanessa Pope for invaluable research assistance in the final stages of manuscript completion. Most of all I am grateful to Jane Cameron, whose research assistance has been instrumental in the development of this project.

At Duke University Press, Ken Wissoker has been the kindest of editors, and Elizabeth Ault has been an expert and encouraging problem-solver; the proposal was improved by the insightful comments of two anonymous referees; and the book now before you would have been far harder to navigate without the excellent advice of the anonymous manuscript readers, whose incisiveness was matched only by the collegial warmth of their approach. I am grateful beyond words.

Most academic books get rehearsed at conferences, and I would like to thank all those who have kindly invited me to join their conversations. I have been fortunate to convene two sets of public talks that have brought new perspectives into my thinking: from 2007 to 2009 I collaborated with Jo Banham on the Fashion Matters series at the Victoria and Albert Museum, and since 2013 at LCF I have run talks under the banner Faith and Fashion; interactions with speakers and audience members at these events have been exciting and challenging, enriching my capacity to think and, I hope, to communicate.

Also instrumental to the development of the ideas in this book have been the opportunities to publish earlier versions of the material as journal articles and book chapters: parts of the introduction and chapter 1 appeared in 2007 in *Fashion Theory* 11:4, Berg Publishers, used by permission of Bloomsbury Publishing; and chapter 3 in 2011 in *Journal of Middle East Women's Studies* 6, no. 3, used by permission of Duke University Press; sections of chapter 4 first appeared in Stella Bruzzi and Pamela Church Gibson's *Fashion Cultures Revisited* (2013: 305–21), used by permission of Routledge, Taylor and Francis Group; chapter 5 in Emma Tarlo and Annelies Moors's *Islamic Fashion and Anti-Fashion: New Perspectives from Europe and America* (2013), used by permission of Bloomsbury Academic, an imprint of Bloomsbury Publishing Plc; and chapter 6 in Djurdja Bartlett, Shaun Cole, and Agnès Rocamora's *Fashion Media: Past and Present* (2013), used by permission of Bloomsbury Academic, an imprint of Bloomsbury Publishing Plc. I am grateful for permission to reproduce and for the feedback of book and journal editors and anonymous peer reviewers that so improved these initial iterations.

This research has benefited from the generous participation of editors and staff at *Emel, Muslim Girl, Sisters, Azizah, Alef,* and *Âlâ* magazines, not all of whom are quoted here by name, but without whom this research would not have been possible. I am indebted also to the several human relations professionals who agreed to speak to me, and whose names remain absent from the record. I received tremendous assistance from many shop staff in Istanbul, in the modest tesettür sector and the secular stores, none appearing under their names, to whom I am beholden. I was welcomed with the utmost kindness at several Turkish modest fashion brands: at Tekbir, Mustafa Karaduman and Necip Karaduman were supremely generous with their time; at Armine, I benefited from insights from Şevket Dursun, Mehmet Dursun, and Nilgün Tuncer; and at Aker, Türker Nart responded with great kindness to my enquiries; all shared marketing materials unstintingly. In Britain and North America designers and bloggers showed outstanding kindness, often granting a sequence of interviews from which I was able to gain insights into the developing life (and sometimes cessation) of what was still a very new media form. I am indebted to all those companies, magazines, bloggers, vloggers, and photographers who kindly granted permission to reproduce their material. Every effort has been made to trace the copyright holders of illustrations and text reprinted in this book. The publishers would be glad to hear from any copyright holders that they have not been able to contact and to print due acknowledgment in the next edition.

The completion of this book was assisted by the counsel of Agnès Roca-mora, Peter Morey, Amina Yaqin, Özlem Sandıkçı, Aliakbar Jafari, Caro-line Evans, Joanne Entwistle, and Clive Bane, and by their willingness to comment on chapter drafts, though they are not responsible for what re-sults. Neither are the many wise heads who have advised me on aspects of this project over its several years of gestation, though I remain obliged to David Purchase for guiding me through British equality legislation; Louise Carolin, Penny Martin, and Nilgin Yusuf for sharing insights on magazine production; Liz Hoggard for relaying the fashion media atti-tude to modesty; M. Y. Alam for insights on Bradford; and Chris Jones for the inside scoop on corporations and social media. On modest Mus-lim fashion I have been fortunate to share ideas and debate detail over several years with Zehra Arat, Banu Gökarıksel, Roshan Jahangeer, Carla Jones, Annelies Moors, Jonathan Wilson, and Jasmin Zine. I shall be for-ever indebted to Leylâ Pervizat for her translation help in Istanbul and her many years as guide to the cultural politics and shops of my favorite city. In Istanbul and around the world I am lucky to have been in dialogue with Allison Bennett, Miriam Cook, Davina Cooper, Claire Dwyer, Edhem Eldem, Carolyn Goffman, Jackie Goymour, Inderpal Grewal, Rosemary Hennessy, Didi Herman, Zeynep İnankur, Sumayya Kassamali, Donna Landry, Rachel Lifter, Gerald MacLean, Dina Matar, Nasar Meer, Tariq Modood, Richard Phillips, Sherene Razak, Mary Roberts, Don Slater, Meyda Yeğenoğlu, Elizabeth Wilson, and Sally Wyatt. In London, conver-sations about Turkey, Islamism, and fashion with my research students Serkan Delice and Senem Yazam have nuanced my understandings, while Nazlı Alimen, herself researching pious consumption in Turkey, has mu-nificently shared materials and reflections. In Puivert, where some of this book was written, I have been encouraged, fed, and entertained by Ang Dooley, Paul Bennett, Kris Wischenkamper, Therese Köhli, and the Saba-tier and Riquet families, all of whom I thank. In each of these locations, Teresa Heffernan has been, as ever, my beloved research buddy, inspiring and invigorating.

My friends have been patient, kind, and patient again as I struggled through to completion: I can't thank everyone by name, but I promise to be better next time . . . as, indeed, I should pledge to my loving and end-lessly supportive family: Hilly, Laura, Helena, Pete; and Reuben, Alexan-der, and Iona. Áine may never let me write another book, but I hope she likes this one.

INTRODUCTION
Veils and Sales

SATURDAY, AUGUST 6, 2005.

*O*ne month after the bombs in London on July 7, and Oxford Street
is buzzing with shoppers. Retail figures are down, and travel on the
tube has diminished by a third, but the sales are in full swing, and
bargain hunters are not to be deterred. Walking from Oxford Circus to Marble
Arch reveals a significant number of visibly "Muslim" women: girls in tight
jeans with patterned scarves over their hair cluster around the makeup counter
in Top Shop; older women in embroidered salwar kameez with filmy dupatta
thrown loosely over their heads mooch around Debenhams; hip twentysome-
things in black boot-cut trousers and skimpy T-shirts wear their black head
wraps tight with a fashionable ghetto-fabulous tail cascading down their backs
from their high topknots as they check out bargains in Mango; clusters of young

women in black jilbabs move around the accessories department of Selfridges looking at handbags, perhaps to augment the selection of bags worn on wrists and over shoulders; in Marks and Spencer at Marble Arch, mothers in black abayas with niqabs over their faces select children's clothes. On the street, at the cafés that now increasingly line the pavements of this and other British high streets, women in various forms of veiling are highly visible, bearing these (generally presumed to be) most easily recognizable and decodable signs of religious and cultural identity. And in their activities as consumers the women in hijab, and not in hijab, are likely to be served by shop assistants who also veil. A trawl down the street reveals women in British Home Stores in cream jilbabs working alongside female colleagues in uniform blouses; in Marks and Spencer, young women wear the uniform-issue long-sleeved shirt with a store-issued (nonbranded) black scarf pinned close about their heads; in New Look, young women keep the changing rooms under control in colored headscarves worn over the items from this season's selection that constitute the store's "feelgood fashion" uniform choices. All this in a month when assaults on Muslims, or those perceived as Muslim, have increased dramatically from the police figures of this time last year, and in a week when some Muslim "leaders" have been quoted in the press advising women that they should relinquish their veils if their public prominence makes them likely targets for abuse or attacks.

Ten years on, and the vibrancy of Muslim wardrobe display has not abated. The streets, workplaces, and leisure spaces of Britain have for some time been animated by ever proliferating versions of modest fashionable dress. But the media and mainstream political response to these manifestations of religiously related fashion continue to regard the veil, in all its forms, as controversial political symbol, not as fashion. With innovations in hijabi fashion excluded from celebrations of British street style, for the mainstream observer it remains remarkable to put faith and fashion in the same frame. Yet the fashion choices of the Muslim women in the Oxford Street consumptionscape, including those whose dress did not announce their faith, are increasingly likely to be served by a growing niche market in Muslim modest fashion and advised by a rapidly expanding Muslim style media in print magazines and on social media. In publisher speak, the strapline for this book could have been "Muslim fashion: underrepresented in the style media, overrepresented in the news media" because, seemingly unaware of these developments in Muslim fashion commerce and commentary and ignoring women's everyday wardrobe choices as they style public modesty, the mainstream media persists in utilizing images of veiled women to illustrate and symbolize the presumed alterity of Muslims, continuing historical Orientalist stereotypes within contemporary debates about social cohesion, and the perceived rifts between Islam and the West.

Simply to pitch shopping, fashion, and veils together generates immediate interest because veils are seen by those outside veiling communities, and sometimes by those inside, as inimical to fashion and outside the commercial circuits of the fashion industry. With shops, and fashion shopping, operating as an indicator of modernity, and with Islam often presented as resistant to modernity, the presence of veiled shoppers and shop assistants becomes a potent mix of two contrasting spatial and social codes, often interpreted as a temporal clash. This is why the Oxford Street shopping scene is so interesting: it highlights how religious and religio-ethnic diversity is enmeshed within the experience of selling and consuming fashion in the globally recognized fashion city of London, even as responses to the bombs four weeks earlier in 2005 were reactivating the perceived opposition between Islam and modernity that had flared across the non-Muslim world after the attacks on America on September 11, 2001. In the British context this lack of coevalness (Fabian 1983) between Muslims and modernity had come to the fore during the Rushdie affair of the late 1980s and in 2001 had been inflamed by the urban riots involving young working-class Muslim men in northern England that preceded September's events in the United States. After the London bombs politicians and commentators again focused debate on the apparent non-integration of Muslim populations. With the bombers (as with previous rioters) seen as representative of a globally youthful Muslim population (Pew 2010), anxious discussions about alienated Muslim youth homed in on the perceived threat posed by the "new folk devils" (Archer 2007: 74) of Muslim young men, yet the image of the veiled Muslim woman continued to be ubiquitous.

Arguing that Muslim fashion needs to be taken seriously *as* fashion, this book switches attention away from questions of alienation and extremism among young men to explore how and why young Muslim women are using their engagement with mainstream fashion to communicate their ideas and aspirations about modern Muslim identities to coreligionists and to majority non-Muslim observers alike. The trends in Muslim style that I cover in this book have originated as a youthful phenomenon: the inaugurating cohort of designers, bloggers, and social media hosts—

many of whom I interview here—were predominantly young women aged between eighteen and twenty-four, as were most of the other women who shared their stories of styling hijab at home, college, and work. These style practices and modes of dissemination and mediation, with microgenerational distinctions among younger dressers developing rapidly during the course of my research, can be regarded, as I argue in chapter 5, as a form of youth subculture. This is a subculture in which religiosity figures as one among other mutually constitutive terms of social differentiation alongside class, ethnicity, and gender; a subculture that defines itself in relation to and distinction from the social and cultural norms of both a dominant or mainstream (and often hostile) non-Muslim majority and parental cultures of religion and ethnicity that are themselves socially and politically minoritized; a subculture in which creative practices of bricolage appropriate and transform commodities from multiple intersecting fashion systems including mainstream, "ethnic," and new niche modest commercial cultures; and a subculture in which style and values transmit "up" from daughters to mothers as well as across spatial divisions between neighborhoods and nations.

To explore these generational and geographical transmissions of style this book situates Muslim style in Britain in relation to other selected Muslim modest commercial cultures. This includes designers, journalists, and bloggers in North America, whose Anglophone culture in a Muslim minority context links Muslims to coparticipants in modest fashion cultures from other religions (on Australia, see G. Jones 2012). I focus also on Turkey because, while Britain is today recognized as a style setter in Muslim fashion (Moors and Tarlo 2013), it was Turkey that led in the initial commercial development of Islamic fashion from the 1980s, its covered or *tesettür* industry an important antecedent to the modest fashion industries developing now around the world. Located in a Muslim majority secular state in which "religious" dress has been regulated by the state and regarded with hostility by secularists, the longer established Turkish companies were part of the rise of Islamic or green (as in the color of Islam rather than eco-) capitalism that emerged during the liberalization of the state economy in the 1980s and the subsequent incorporation, as I discuss in chapter 2, of large parts of the population into diverse consumer cultures (Gökarıksel and Secor 2010b; Kılıçbay and Binark 2002). Now demonstrating generational change in style and modes of consumption, the distinctive aesthetic of Turkish Muslim fashion continues to be a reference point in Britain and elsewhere, though likely, as I go to press, to face challenges from Indonesia, another Muslim majority nation, where the secular state has shifted from outlawing to sponsoring Muslim fashion as part of its economic development plan and national branding strategy (Arthur 2000b; C. Jones 2010).[1] These shifting power relations between globalized corporate capital, nation states, and supranational (capital, political, third sector, and religious) forces reconfigure people's experience of the intersectionalities of gender, ethnicity, class, sexuality, age, and religion (Ong 1999) that frame processes of identity formation, the context in which to understand the historical and contemporary transnational transmission of styles between Muslim populations around the world (on Europe, see Tarlo and Moors 2013; on Egypt, see Abaza 2007; and on Yemen, see Moors 2007).

To examine the changing relationships between religion, gender, and society this book follows Appadurai's call to recognize the "relations of disjuncture" inherent in experiences of globalized capital "characterized by objects in motion," in which the "various flows we see—of objects, persons, images, and discourse—are not coeval, convergent, isomorphic, or spatially consistent" (Appadurai 2001: 5). Investigating the transnational movement of Muslim fashion objects—garments, images, discourses, people—I propose that commercial style cultures be seen as significant factors in the regulatory and liberatory "role of the imagination in social life," through which emerge "new patterns of dissent and new designs for collective life" (Appadurai 2001: 6).

I argue (following McRobbie 1998) that the significance of modest Muslim designs lies not only in sales but in their influence as image within discourses of female religious and religio-ethnic identity that achieve enhanced valency in the visually led digital and social media of which this youth population are notable early adopters. To explore the interconnections of production, distribution, and consumption, this book works thematically with selected examples from its constituent territories, providing historicized accounts of moments in the design, marketing, retailing, mediation, and consumption of self-consciously Muslim fashion and its reception. Here, I draw on the circuit of culture model (du Gay, Hall, Janes, Madsen, Mackay, and Negus 2013) that challenges the precedence conventionally given to production over consumption by linking both to representation, identity, and regulation as part of a mutually constitutive and interdependent set of relations through which commodities are brought into being and given meaning in the lives of human subjects. While this corrective conceptualizes the consumer as active rather than passive and emphasizes the significant role of businesses' own cultures, its emphasis on "meaning-making as an ongoing *process*" forged "through usage" (du Gay, Hall, Janes, Madsen, Mackay, and Negus 2013: 79–81) in particular times and places also foregrounds how regulation constrains what is produced and how it can be consumed. Regulating factors in production, from safety rules to component prices, are matched by economic constraints on consumer spending that are themselves culturally framed by historically specific variables of class, gender, location, and (I add) religion. Curbs on consumption may be overtly "moral," such as prohibitions on drugs or alcohol (for those "under" age). With religiously related practices in Muslim women's dress often designed, and serving, to regulate female and male sexuality, the field of contemporary Muslim modern fashion is immersed in a longer history of religiously regulated embodiment marked by forms of interpretation, contestation, accommodation, and imposition that vary across time and space. These intra-Muslim constraints intersect with external constraints such as school or workplace uniform codes or state bans on veiling that also impact unevenly and often unpredictably on the dressed experiences of Muslim women.

Susan Kaiser has adapted the circuit model for fashion, replacing representation with "distribution," a term preferred for its "connotations of both material and representational elements" (2012: 19). For my project this foregrounds the role of retail, bringing into critical view the physical spaces of the store and the bodies of those who labor and shop there as I discuss in chapters 2 and 5. Distribution also highlights fashion media and marketing as image and practice, as I discuss in chapters 4, 7, and 8. The mutually constitutive relationship between production and representation/distribution becomes even more embedded in the era of social media as the affordances of new hardware and software extend to the general population the experience of "prosuming" or "produsing" content initially the terrain of early adopter geeks (Jenkins 2006, noted in du Gay, Hall, Janes, Madsen, Mackay, and Negus 2013), itself restricted by the uneven global access to Internet infrastructure of the digital divide (Bunt 2009). Conditions for and constraints on the highly regulated practices of Muslim fashion thus can be understood as the "articulation" of "distinct processes . . . located in the contingencies of circumstance" (du Gay, Hall, Janes, Madsen, Mackay, and Negus 2013: xxx).

Attending to the enabling and restricting effects of spatio-temporal location (Hopkins and Gale 2009), my account locates Muslim fashion as contributory to a network of overlapping local, regional, national, transnational, religious, and diasporic fashion systems whose impact on Muslim design and dressing is always context specific and changeable. As Osella and Osella (2007) demonstrate in the context of rising Hindu nationalism in India, particular experiences of Muslim minority living produce Muslims as minoritized (rather than targeted/normative) consumers in particular ways: in Muslim-majority Turkey, the hostile reception of Islamic religiosity produces changes in women's style of covered dress and determines the modes of retailing and marketing available to modest fashion firms (chapters 3 and 4); just as in Britain, with a majority South Asian Muslim population, the diaspora fashion industry that I discuss in chapter 5 frames opportunities and limitations for hijabi designers and dressers regardless of their own family heritage.

In the locations covered in this book matters of Muslim self-presentation have come to operate as the limit case in debates about citizenship and belonging, secularity and modernity, for both the majority non-Muslim (or, in Turkey, nonreligious) public and often for Muslim (religious) communities themselves. In Britain the dress and demeanor of Muslims in public has taken on new significance, increasingly required post-9/11 and post-7/7 to declare themselves within a politically created dichotomy of good, moderate Muslims versus bad, extremist Muslims. With a historically immigrant Muslim population, the generational cycle of change and increasing acculturation and selective readoption of "traditional" practices common to most migrant communities has accelerated in a glare of often hostile publicity that puts a unique emphasis on the dressed behavior of Muslim bodies, often operationalizing a transnational civilizational discourse for localized political purposes. Elsewhere in Europe, legislation attempts to control Muslim women's dress with bans on face veils (niqabs, *burqas*) disproportionate to the small numbers of women actually wearing them in France, the Netherlands, and Belgium, upheld in July 2014 by the European Court of Human Rights. In Quebec, bans on the hijab and niqab (Zine 2006c, 2012) are matched with preemptive legislation to prohibit "Islamic" stoning (in a town with zero Muslim inhabitants), followed in 2013 by proposal for a province-wide French-style ban (see chapter 1) on all forms of religiously distinctive dress and adornment. In fact, completing this paragraph was becoming near impossible by autumn 2014, so constant was the stream of measures proposed to control Muslim female dress in Britain, Europe, and North America. Whether moral panics actually lead to legislation (always variably enforced and resisted), in all these instances the actual or presumed dress practices of some Muslim women impact discursively on their coreligionists who find their communities put in the spotlight over and again.

Secularities and Modernities: The Contested Emblem of the Veiled Body

In much of the non-Muslim-majority world Muslim women's dress, as with furors over the construction of new mosques, has become a flashpoint for controversy, understood by opponents and proponents to be an assertion of religion into the presumed secularity of modern public life. Challenging popular understandings of secular society as a religion-free zone, Talal Asad links the development of secularism to "the rise of a system of capitalist [and colonialist] nation-states," whose character he argues is inevitably mediated by the religious cultures (and conflicts) from which they emerged:

> Thus although in France both the highly centralized state and its citizens are secular, in Britain the state is linked to the Established Church and its inhabitants are largely nonreligous, and in America the population is largely religious but the federal state is secular. "Religion" has always been publicly present in both Britain and America. Consequently, although the secularism of these three countries has much in common, the mediating character of the modern imaginary in each of them differs significantly. The notion of toleration between religiously defined groups is differently inflected in each. There is a different sense of participation in the nation and access to the state among religious minorities in the three countries. (Asad 2003: 5–6)

With religion relegated to the domain of the private, in western European and North American (WENA) countries at the turn of the twenty-first century it has been demands in the name of Islam, a minority faith, that reveal and bring into crisis the normative Christian religious underpinnings of the secular nation-state. For France the priority of the secular state to protect citizens from religious intrusion has historically been melded onto a civilizing imperial mission that aims to assimilate migrants into a homogeneously unmarked secular national identity, *laïcité* has no scope for the sorts of hyphenated ethnic and religious identities that underwrite America's integrationist ideal of the multicultural melting pot (Scott 2007). In France, secular freedom from religious control has historically been equated with masculinist ideals of sexual freedom that, as Scott explains (following Foucault), positions veiling as a refusal of the male appraising gaze that defines modern (hetero)sexual liberty. Dating to 1989, French attempts to control Muslim women's dress through legal initiatives have impacted around the world, covered in Muslim lifestyle magazines and hijab fashion blogs as well as community news media. Centering on removing headscarves from the state secular school system, legislation expanded to include any religious symbol coded as "ostentatious" in 1994 and as "conspicuous" in 2004. Despite the civilizational rhetoric of protecting young Muslims from oppressive parents and communities (sometimes supported by French feminists and secularists), these developments were motivated, as Scott argues, by center Right politicians countering the rising power of the French Far Right post-9/11. Extending beyond schools, the ban on wearing the face veil (the practice of only a tiny minority of Muslims in France) in public in April 2011 prompted riots in summer 2013, while in the same period Belgium's niqab ban was challenged in the Constitutional Court (Donald 2012), and Germany devolved to federal courts decisions about controlling Muslim women's dress in municipal employment. With many French Muslims in favor of secular education (some having opposed religious Muslim rule abroad) and with Turkish secularists welcoming the early bans, and despite that in Europe as elsewhere the Muslim religious Right is joined by the Christian and Jewish religious Rights as cocombatants against laïcité (Helie-Lucas 2012; see also Killian 2003), it remains the case still that "Muslim fundamentalism appears in the media today as the primary progenitor of oppressive conditions for women when Christian, Jewish, Hindu, Confucian, and other forms of extreme fundamentalisms exert profound controls over women's lives" (Grewal and Kaplan 1994: 19).

In the context of the nation-state as an imagined community (Anderson 1983) formulated through and endorsed by self-representation in a free press, Asad (2003: 8) notes that "a secular state does not guarantee toleration"; rather, it creates a changing array of threats and guarantees. While much of this book is concerned with how Muslims as minorities are perceived as a threat within and to WENA countries, the minoritization of religion is not simply about numbers. In Muslim majority Turkey, the constitutional secularity of the modern state has been similarly, but differently, perceived to be under threat by manifestations of (Islamic) religiosity in the public domain. Established in 1923 as one of the successor states of the Ottoman Empire, the Turkish republic adapted from the multiple models of modernity already available in the West (Eisenstadt 2000) a version of secular and Westernizing modernity that was enshrined in the narrative of the new nation as a liberation from the despotism and religious obscurantism of the sultanic ancien régime. As Göle points out, in adopting from "French Jacobinism, a centralist [authoritarian] model of change, rather than Anglo-Saxon liberalism" as the rubric for the secular state, Turkey created a version of laïcité (*laiklik*) that "gives priority to 'freedom from religion' [rather than] priority to 'religious freedom'" (Göle [2005] 2011: 105). Abolishing the caliphate in 1928, Turkish secularity differed to the French separation of church and state by retaining control of the religious domain through the Ministry of Religious Affairs that regulated the official version of Sunni Islam at home and among migrant Turkish populations abroad.

From the early nineteenth century in the development and representation of modernities in what might broadly be called the Muslim world, the veil in particular and female dress in general were a source of continual tension in debates about modernity and its compatibility with Islam. As in subsequent and contemporary discussions, the figure of woman stood for both defense of tradition and the march of modernity. In Turkey, the unveiled, shingle-cut heads of the stylishly dressed "daughters of the republic" in the late 1920s and 1930s (Durakbaşa 1993) advertised secular modernity to the Turkish population and the world. Specifically positioning the veiled body as the opposite of modernity and, by inference, of civilization (Göle 1996), the veil was eventually banned in 1928. Like the temporal alterity ascribed by colonialism to "primitive" subject peoples, the veiled female body and the communities it represented were not seen as inhabiting the time of modernity, a lack of coevalness that was both spatial and temporal. As Gökarıksel and Mitchell propose, for both French and Turkish secular republics committed (differently, I would add) to neoliberal governmentality, the Islamicized female body is unassimilable because it challenges the norms that the "neoliberal individual must be free of any particularist spatial ties that prevent him or her from competing effectively in the global marketplace" (Gökarıksel and Mitchell 2005: 150). For France, the veiled woman is typified as a North African migrant from "outside the state's territorially defined borders," while for Turkey the presence of the veiled rural migrant in the modern city emblematizes the Islamic threat that derives from within the state's own borders, an alterity that is temporally as well as spatially intimate: "the 'dark and distant (Ottoman) past' when Muslim women's veiling was the norm" (Gökarıksel and Mitchell 2005: 148).

While part of the purpose of this book is to challenge the terms of the current hypervisibility accorded the veil within a post-9/11 securitizing discourse in the West, it would be incorrect to imagine that the veil's symbolic prominence is generated only externally to Muslim society. The heightened visibility of covered dressing as a *Muslim* phenomenon was also a desired aim of the global Islamic revival that from the 1950s and especially since the 1970s promoted veiling as both a form of religious observance and of religious distinction. The history of head covering as a mark of social distinction among women of diverse ethnic and religious communities in the Middle East and South Asia was reframed by Islamic revivalists as an exclusively Muslim marker, in a repositioning of Muslim daily practice intended as much as a counter to other forms of Muslim practice as it was as a riposte to the non-Muslim West (L. Ahmed 2011; Mahmood 2005; Moors 2009). For Göle, in 1996, the urban Islamist woman stood as emblem of a supranational Islamist collectivity and as evidence of the "latent individualism" emerging among the increasingly autonomous female elite cadres of the revivalist movements (Göle 1996: 22). Since then, vibrant Islamic consumer cultures have grown and diversified alongside the rising political power of Islamic politics and the growing alarm of secularists.

The Muslim character of the Turkish republic has been central to debates about religion in the present and future character of Europe at the turn of the twenty-first century. The perceived threat of Turkey's EU accession bid has, as Göle points out, "become a matter of identity for the Europeans (rather than, as was expected, for Turks)" (Göle 2011: 5). Responses to Turkey's EU bid reactivate the memory of the Ottoman assault on Vienna, a foundational moment in the construction of Europe as a supranational imaginary: it "was not Europe that the Turks threatened but Christendom, since Europe was not then distinct from Christendom" (Asad 2003: 162). For Muslims already in Europe, the framework for gaining minority protection demands assimilation to a naturalized Christian narrative: "Europe (and the nation-states of which it is constituted) is ideologically constructed in such a way that Muslim immigrants cannot be satisfactorily represented in it. [This has] less to do with 'absolute Faith' of Muslims living in a secular environment and more with European notions of 'culture' and 'civil' and 'the secular state,' and 'majority' and 'minority'" (Asad 2003: 159). In a world of global communication technologies news spreads quickly, and individual understandings of ethno-religious cultural identities as well as local community relations are conducted in a transnational frame, in which national, community, and religious politics combine with changing practices in Muslim dress increasingly encountered within and framed by consumer culture.

Multiple Modernities, Multiple Fashion Systems

Related to the recognition of and debate about multiple modernities is the transition from seeing fashion exclusively as a component of Western capitalist modernity to an approach that considers multiple fashion systems and style cultures. I started this introduction by saying that Muslim fashion was underrepresented in the style media not simply because new hijabi styles have been under the fashion radar: the entire concept of Muslim fashion has conventionally in the West been regarded as outside the worldview of the fashion industry and to studies of it. This derives from two related presumptions: that fashion is a Western experience and that Muslims are not part of the West. From this it follows that Muslims, even if "in" the West, will be wearing clothing that is "ethnic" or is "religious," categories outside the parameters of Western fashion. Until recently in fashion histories and popular parlance non-Western clothing was often relegated to the domain of costume that, as with the treatment of "folk'" costume at home, was regarded as the unchanging expression of essentialized collective cultural identities antithetical to the rapidly shifting self-creation of Western fashion; a temporal atavism matched by the spatial restriction of folk or ethnic clothing to "very precise places" in contrast to the "vast" "geographic remit" available to Western fashion styles and commodities (Riello and McNeil 2010: 358).

While all human societies mediate the naked body through body adornment and modification (from garments to tattoos) and are characterized by change over time, the pace and purpose of change that evolved in the context of Western modernity from the fourteenth century can be regarded, Joanne Entwistle argues, as a distinctive feature of today's now globalized fashion system, with fashion arising in situations of potential social mobility to offer the subject a technique of dressing with which "self consciously to construct an identity suitable for the modern stage" (Entwistle 2000: 75). Debate about the origins of fashion outside the West have centered on when originality came to be valued in non-Western contexts, and the pace of and extent to which ethnic dress while serving to demarcate group boundaries also interrelated with (Eicher and Sumberg 1995) and contributed to (Lemire and Riello 2006) "world" fashion.

Jennifer Craik argues that there are several coexisting and competing fashion systems of which "European high (elite designer) fashion [is] one specific variant," decentering the elite in favor of most people's experience of "everyday fashion" that has more in common with "other fashion systems, including those in non-European and non-capitalist cultures" (Craik 1993: x–xi). Although as Entwistle points out, it has long been the case that style derivation goes both ways, with trends trickling up from the street to couture, this characterization of syncretic everyday fashion practices has much in common with the blending of everyday religion that I discuss in chapter 1. Associated with a religious culture seen as non-Western and framed for some as the submission to transcendent religious truths, Muslim fashion is easily rendered outside the place and time of fashion; fabricated with garments from "other" clothing systems, or, even weirder to some, through the appropriation of items that would otherwise read as fashion into religiously demarcated ensembles. These articulations of style (Tulloch 2010) through the melding of diverse mainstream, non-Western, diaspora, and ethnic items are indicative of forms of (inevitably limited) human agency from designers and dressers that transcend binarisms of Western or non-Western, mainstream or ethnic, modern or traditional, authentic or inauthentic. As Kaiser argues, the contradictory and fluid experiences of participating in fashion need not be understood in terms of either/or when it is more realistic to conceptualize experiences as encompassing both/and, such as "dressing to belong *and* dressing to differentiate" (Kaiser 2012: 3).

For these reasons, my understanding of Muslim fashion practices situates them in relation to a web of multiple fashion systems seen within the frame of multiple modernities. This allows me to historicize and track the transmission over space and time of contemporary trends and modes of production and distribution in relation to their particular regional, national, and transnational geopolitical contexts and histories. For fashion, as with studies of other cultural forms and practices, repositioning Western modernity as one among a series of mutually constituting multiple modernities revises progressivist narratives of an "inexorable march forward," recognizing that "past-oriented traditionalism is as much a feature of modernity as modernisation" (S. Friedman 2007; see also L. Taylor 2002). This creates an opportunity to incorporate Western and other imperialisms into accounts of fashion history, recognizing that the generalized shift from "the reign of sumptuary law to the reign of fashion" relied on large-scale change and "socially organized forms of consumption" (Appadurai 1996: 72). As with imperial missionaries positioning "undressed" natives as nonfashionable recipients for outmoded Western fashion goods (Comaroff 1996), so too were Western observers (as I discuss in chapter 1) unable to recognize as fashion the diverse modes and temporalities through which Western garments or styles were indigenized in the nineteenth and twentieth centuries in the Ottoman Empire. Histories of fashion could similarly be cognizant of how in the Turkish republic in the 1920s and 1930s the imposition of Western clothing and headwear by the secular elite repurposed Ottoman Orientalism to picture as primitive and nonmodern the nonelite and rural Turkish population in terms previously applied to the Arab and provincial minority populations of the Ottoman Empire (Eldem 2007; Makdisi 2002).

Elizabeth Wilson's argument that "in modern western society no clothes are outside fashion; fashion sets the terms of *all* sartorial behaviour" (E. Wilson [1985] 2003: 3) can bring minoritized, disparaged fashion practices like Muslim fashion into view by emphasizing the relationality of dressed bodies. Even those who aim to be antifashion cannot entirely escape fashion, but neither do fashion participants escape antifashion. The mainstream and the alternative are mutually constitutive in ways that are socially, culturally, and historically specific: as I discuss in chapter 5, the apparently traditional styles of so-called ethnic dress are repositioned by their occasional adoption as mainstream fashion just as mainstream styles, like the layering of T-shirts under sleeveless dresses popular in the 2000s, can be kept *in* fashion for longer when adopted as part of hijabi cool. Similarly, Muslim fashion cultures are framed by their "mutual entanglement" with persistent Islamic antifashion discourse and practices (Moors and Tarlo 2013: 13).

Experiencing and contributing to dress practices at the intersection of diverse and differently valued fashion systems, Muslim modest dressers in Muslim minority contexts and (differently) in contexts of Muslim majority may both be frustrated that fashion trends do not allow for modest self-presentation and find ways to adapt them for hijabi fashion; they may deploy a neoliberal discourse of choice to counter stereotypes that Muslim women are forced to wear a headscarf and argue that hijab is a religious requirement; they may say that how women cover is up to them and feel intensely uncomfortable when women dress the "wrong" way; they may become famous as tastemakers giving guidance on how to achieve religiously appropriate modest styling and prefer not to regard this as a form of religious interpretation. And, above all, they are likely to be engaging with multiple fashion systems and clothing values, each system historically, socially, and spatially located and each variably both enabling and restricting individual women's wardrobe options and forms of expression. While the debate about Western and non-Western fashion and fashion norms continues, I note that for fashion and cultural studies the modest fashion practices of Muslim women and the growing market that supports them may be emerging as a paradigmatic diversity case study in books aimed at the classroom (Craik 2009; Kaiser 2012), incorporating religion within discussions of style, subject formation, and cultural regulation. Welcoming this, my study situates Muslim fashion within a wider frame of related circuits of faith-based and secular modest fashion and their constituent geographies.

Temporalities: Historicizing and Terminology

As with any book-length project on contemporary fashion and style, this book should be regarded not as a statement of the now but as a history of the present, written while it was happening. Writing about fashion is inevitably subject to problems of time; this year's trend is last year's retro, next decade's old news. The macropolitical events that frame, shape, and sometimes determine changes in, responses to, and recognition of Muslim women's self-presentation have also changed spectacularly and sometimes violently during the period covered. This book becomes therefore less a singular history of the present than a history of several presents: magazine editors speak of future plans in the now of their present, unaware that the title will have closed before this book is printed; designers may be full of creative plans that don't come to fruition, or unknowing that they will subsequently become the poster girls for new Islamic branding initiatives only recently waking up to the potential profits of fashion commodities; Turkish shopkeepers and modest fashion brands speak about the promotional advantages of association with the First Ladies of the Islamist Justice and Development (AKP) government before Prime Minister Erdoğan's antidemocratic responses to events in Gezi Park in 2013 discredit the party's claim of moderate Islam and highlight splits within the party and its international supporters, reframing previously established academic approaches to the sociopolitical significance of veiling fashion in the republic.

Muslim politics and cultural trends in the late twentieth and early twenty-first centuries have demonstrated astoundingly rapid development and ever wider transmission, rendering them a hot topic for academic enquiry, yet also dating rapidly. Less a problem than an opportunity, I seek to capture images, opinions, and dress practices in their moment, to situate them historically in relation to the transnational past of religious and cultural relations and clothing and material cultures, and to situate them contemporaneously as part of ongoing local and transnational dialogues whose forms and interlocutors are changing and growing as I write.

The commercial development of Muslim and modest fashion that I analyze in this book increases the variety of garments available to Muslim women and the pace of change in modest fashion. Like all fashion systems, the replacement and recycling of trends makes it impossible to tie down "the" look for Muslim cool. But battles over wardrobe definitions in the case of Muslim fashion are highly ideological, as different individuals, groups, and state agencies compete to patrol and control women's modesty. In all the territories covered by this book, the women I spoke to or whose blogs and journalism I followed are characterized by their emphasis on choice and variety in whether and how to cover, but they are surrounded by (and sometimes despite themselves participate in) forms of judgment about Muslim women's dress that most often center on the idea of "the" veil.

In my teaching and writing to date I had often used the term *veil* or *veiling* as the starting point for discussion, explaining that although the veil is today predominantly associated with (or claimed by or for) Islam, it is a practice that is pre-Islamic in origin and that has been adopted by diverse religious and ethnic communities, especially in the Middle East. I would also explain that in the Middle East, the veil often signified status rather than piety or ethnic allegiance and was more common among urban than rural women. For those women who did or do "cover," I would elaborate, there is no single garment that equates to the veil: different versions of clothing that are held suitably to preserve modesty in mixed-gender environments have been adopted by different communities (often with different names for the same garment). In recent years in non-Muslim-majority countries, controversies over the niqab or burqa have become more prevalent, shifting legal and popular definitions of veiling from head to face covering. This book does not focus on face veils, albeit there is now a developing fashion market. It does not focus on jilbabs and abayas either, because these robes are not the predominant garments used by the generation of young Muslim women studied here. While some young revivalists (male and female) living in Muslim minority WENA contexts prefer the long robes they regard as closer to the dress of the "ideal" society of the first Muslims of the Arabian Peninsula (Tarlo 2013a),[2] these garments are rarely adopted by the young women who make up my study. In contrast, their self-conscious creation of modest fashion, mostly but not always in a headscarf or hijab, is deliberately staged through participation in mainstream fashion. Combined with judicious use of offerings from the ethnic and modest sectors, the taste communities they develop with the bloggers, journalists, and designers featured in this book cannot be tied down to singular definitions. As for previous generations of women, the form and combination of garments that produce veiling changes over time, quite often within the lifespan of a single woman, rendering attempts to legislate which type of body covering is properly Islamic as only ever partial and located.

Historically, the veil has been intended primarily as outerwear, something that preserves modesty between the sexes when outside the gender-secluded space of the Islamically structured home (or when nonfamilial men are present in the domestic space, as may be the case more often in Muslim minority contexts). While the women in this book do cover in relation to who they are with or will be seen by, they have developed fashions in hijab that do not differentiate between spaces in the same way: assembled as part of their outfit for the day, more like a hairstyle than a hat, the hijab is not always so easily thrown on and off. These often quite complicated wraps are of a different order to the abaya, çarşaf, or chador that is left by the front door. Changes in the abaya fashion market have led to designer abayas (Al-Qasimi 2010; Belk and Sobh 2011) sometimes worn more as a dress rather than as outerwear, like those sold in the Gulf by Barjis Chohan (chapter 7). But this is not the predominant style of the women featured here, whose sometimes elaborate styles of hijab produce alterations in the conventional spatial relations of modest dressing; when hijab styles involve more than one piece of cloth, accessories, and difficult wrapping procedures (such as are demonstrated in the YouTube hijab tutorials of chapter 7), young women are more likely to keep them on when visiting environments in which hijab is not necessary (chatting in a friend's home when no men are present), rather than remove them at the door and don them again on leaving.

I still use the term *veil* or *veiling*, and when I refer to face covering I specify niqab or burqa. In the Turkish context, I refer to *headscarves* or *tesettür*, the commercially manufactured form of modest dressing associated with revivalist fashions (though this term is itself now repudiated as too limiting by some of the commercial brands discussed in chapter 2).

Other forms of Turkish covering are named and defined in context. In the other western European and North American territories of this book hijab remains the predominant term for head covering: there are fashions in hijab (different types of head covering arrangements) and there is hijabi fashion (the complete ensemble of which the head covering is part). Women might discuss how to "hijabify" an item of clothing to render it suitable for their modesty requirements. Women who wear a head covering in whatever style are often referred to as hijabis, not to be confused with niqabis, who cover also their faces, or "dejabis,"[3] whose decision to stop covering their hair, as I discuss in chapter 8, often marks a different stage in, rather than rejection of, their participation in modest fashion.

Many Muslim women rightly argue that the focus on what Muslim women are wearing takes away from thinking about what they might actually be doing (al Yafai 2010). This can be true of all women, and men, in a period when neoliberal enterprise culture presents "freedom and independence [as emanating] not from civil rights but from individual choices exercised in the market" (du Gay 1996: 77). But while the proliferation of neoliberal consumer culture into personal and community life creates and exploits ever more finely defined consumer segments, requiring a "choosing subject" (N. Rose 1999) for whom identity and self-worth is established and communicated through consumption, it also creates opportunities for the emergence of new social subjects and different articulations of existing power relationships. Akin to the conditions for the emergence of modern homosexual subjects created by the shift into capitalist wage labor from family household production units (D'Emilio 1993; Hennessy 2000), so too for Muslim women has the combination of neoliberalism and advances in information and communication technologies created opportunities for the development of a woman-led sector within Islamic cultures. In contrast to the masculinist jihadist modes most often seen to arise from this conjuncture (Bunt 2009), this book argues that the possibilities of Internet commerce and commentary combine with offline practices in modest fashion to foster women's agency in the making of new forms of Muslim habitus, those shared embodied values and dispositions of everyday life that cohere classes or communities (Goffman [1956] 1990; Mauss 1973; Bourdieu 1994). While for Bourdieu the values and tastes that make up subjective dispositions are unconsciously acquired and held—so embedded into class identity as to need no explanation—the conscious development of new Islamic revivalist habituses and especially the emphasis on women's embodied dress practices suggests (qua Mahmood 2005) a degree of agency in the cultivation of the pious self. It is at this nexus that I argue for the influence and significance of the range of women-led activities and practices cohered in this book: just as early feminist work in cultural studies had to argue that girls' "private" unspectacular "bedroom cultures" (McRobbie and Garber [1975] 2006) were as significant as what boys did on the public street, so too I propose that these design companies, magazines, blogs, and social media not be dismissed as small-scale or low-circulation, but be seen as a part of a shared (and internally contested and variable) new Muslim dress culture whose significance extends into other contemporary forms of Muslim habitus and beyond into relations with other faith and secular communities and societies.

The structural imperial racialized inequities of class, gender, and sexuality that underwrite the globalized relations of consumer culture in late capitalism so often disavowed in the celebration of consumer pleasure as agency (Comaroff 1996; Hennessy 2000; Ong 1995; Slater 1997) also inhere in the modes of production and dissemination on which these new Muslim style cultures depend. As I discuss in chapter 8's consideration of the development of Islamic branding, for a population that until recently did not enjoy the dubious privilege of being considered (constructed as) a marketable consumer segment (Sandıkçı 2011) in a marketized context where "those whose consumption does not matter for the successful reproduction of capital are virtually non-people" (du Gay 1996: 100), it not surprising that the development of Muslim consumer cultures produces its own panoply of marginalized others as failed consumers. Despite concerns that the predominance of "Islamic brand fetishism" may define nonparticipants as less pious Muslims (Süerdem 2013: 7), I see no reason why Muslim consumers or cultural entrepreneurs should be politically "pure," though I note how concerns with sustainability (a recent preoccupation of Euro-American consumer fashion discourse) meld with discourses of Islamic values of equity and redistribution. With the construction of marginalized nonconsumers inherent in the dynamic of consumer culture, as the Muslim lifestyle market diversifies women may simultaneously find themselves priced out by the ever more rapid turnover of styles (Sandıkçı and Ger 2005) or excluded by the new subcultural taste communities of Islamist "cool" (Boubekeur 2005), leading some modest fashion participants, as I discuss in chapter 8, to bewail the pernicious high-gloss unattainability of "halal celebrities" in a reactivation of earlier antifashion discourses.

Despite the significance of new hijabi fashions and discourse in the development and contestation of intra-Muslim distinctions, externally the veil in all its forms suffers from an almost generic illegibility in that the dress acts of most veiling women in the UK are observed by a majority nonveiling and non-Islamic audience who cannot adequately deduce the significance of their veiling choices. Women who veil are almost inevitably read as Muslim by a majority audience—even though, in Britain for example, there are substantial communities of Hindus and Sikhs, some of whose female members also sometimes veil. In a situation where the expression through dress of ethnicity and religion are often united in the minds of their practitioners, the likelihood of veiled women being presumed Muslim by those outside their communities is high, with noticeable increases in violence and abuse after 9/11 and 7/7 (WNC 2006). Islamophobic prejudice and violence or well-intentioned protectionism rain down on any woman who veils, regardless of her actual ethnic or religious identity.

In highlighting the contemporaneity of veiling fashions and distinguishing generational and microgenerational cycles of change, this book aims to challenge attitudes that read Muslim dress as signs of collective ahistorical community identities. Putting hijabi and modest dressing in the context of individuating fashion contributes to the political project of deexceptionalizing Muslim youth, an antidote to the alterity made common by securitizing discourses. This is also advanced by analyzing hijabi fashion within a subcultural frame that locates dress practices (on the body, in print, online, and in commerce) within overlapping local, national, and transnational contexts that are constitutive of and constituted by interlocking social factors including ethnicity, class, gender, sexuality, and faith. Given the essentializing effects of the Orientalist gaze it remains necessary to emphasize that Muslim women's styles documented here will change over their lifetime. While Muslim women's dress is politically conspicuous and contentious at present, and may remain so, with a globally youthful Muslim population it is salutary to be reminded that it is impossible to predict what they will be wearing twenty years' time.

How This Book Works

In compiling a cultural history of present practices and discourses in Muslim modest fashion I move back and forth between a number of themes and examples that, along with their related histories and methods for examination, I do not presume will be equally familiar to all my readers:

experts on Turkish Islamist politics may not be instinctively familiar with the structural logic of fashion magazines; fashion historians may know little about conventional modes of Islamic knowledge production and transmission. With elements of case studies—garments, images, media, people, spaces, theoretical approaches—recurring to elaborate new points, I provide explanations of specialist terms and theoretical approaches where they seem most useful, aware that historical and critical fields are unevenly developed and rarely connected in these particular ways. Although each chapter contains a chronological approach and introduction to its particular study, I hope my examples not only advance my case but also indicate how the ideas developed here might be applied elsewhere.

Chapter 1, therefore, introduces the key geographies of this book, with attention to the histories of their Muslim populations and the debates about secularity, ethnicity, religion, culture, politics, and gender with which they have engaged and through which they have been defined and define themselves. Arguing that current preoccupations reactivate and reframe previous Orientalist stereotypes and knowledges, this chapter traces the emergence of new discourses about Islam post-9/11 and post-7/7, in order to identify the ways in which the figure of the Muslim woman has become central in deliberations about citizenship and belonging across the political spectrum and round the world, including in the British context, the shift in multiculturalism from ideas of difference based on race and ethnicity to those conceptualized in terms of faith. Linked to histories of Islamic revivalism since the 1970s, the present revitalization of the *umma*, the supranational community of Muslim believers, which for many young Muslims has modified previous parental migrant affiliations, is situated in relation to the wider global increase in religious revivalism among young people. The ways in which dress, as part of Islamic consumer cultures, has become a key mode for the experience and expression of revivalist identities is identified as an example of everyday religion (Ammerman 2007; McGuire 2008), characterized by syncretism, by interaction with the market, and by a discourse of choice in the articulation of achieved rather than, or in addition to, ascribed inherited religious identities. The oft-discussed globalized relations of the fashion industry are thus linked to the cultural (and commercial) significance of the supranational umma. Proposing that majoritarian anxieties about encountering the covered female body outside of specifically religious spaces are based on the naturalization of secularized norms of body management, I argue that discussions about which garments constitute (acceptable forms of) the veil need to be reframed by an understanding of embodiment, challenging the tendency to focus on the veiled woman as static image by repositioning veiling as an embodied and located dress practice (Entwistle 2000). In the context of the development of the fashion industry as a feature of Western, and non-Western, modernities, the chapter combines cultural, fashion, and material culture studies understandings of body management (McRobbie 1998; Miller 1987; E. Wilson [1985] 2003) with Mahmood's argument (2005) that for adherents of modest dress the act of wearing the hijab is itself a process for creating a pious disposition.

Chapter 2 further elaborates how participation in mainstream fashion cultures can contribute to the creation of a devotional self. Historicizing and theorizing the commercial context in which the Turkish tesettür market emerged as market leader, I provide an international comparative account of the development of modest or Islamic fashion as a niche market, analyzing the creation of overlapping national and international customer bases at a time when many brands were switching their focus from European to Middle East and Central Asian territories in keeping with changing regional and global priorities of the AKP government since 2002. The commercial geography set out in this chapter is mapped politically in relation to disputes about religion, secularity, and modernity within and outside the EU, with Islamists using a discourse of rights to assert as consumer citizens a place within state and secular systems (Gökarıksel and Secor 2009; Göle 1996; Navaro-Yashin 2002). Interviews with directors at leading companies combine with visual analyses of ads, catalogues, and visual merchandising to chart the expansion and segmentation of this burgeoning market. I outline its complex interactions with, and impact on, the commercial and media norms of the global fashion industry, examining the significance of increased ethnic diversity among tesettür models within local discourse of ethno-national and religious identity. In a precursor to the focus on British fashion retail in chapter 5, this chapter also includes the agentive function (Sandıkçı and Ger 2010) of the tesettür shop in creating work environments for covered women (that in the religious district of Fatih extends to proximate non-tesettür shops).

Chapter 3 documents the content and production processes of Muslim fashion and lifestyle print media that in the mid-2000s inaugurated a new phase in the development of Islamic consumer cultures (the subsequent extension into digital and social media is covered in chapter 7), to examine the extent to which neoliberalism can incorporate the articulation of religious identities (Grewal 2005). This chapter's analysis of fashion editorial in Muslim lifestyle media is conducted through an examination of how content is generated, providing profiles of the working practices of journalists and aesthetic service providers (bloggers, photographers, stylists, and models) as they deal with the often conflicting demands of the mainstream and minority fashion industries without losing sight of the need to grow a new readership. Making links to the development of the lesbian/gay/queer niche media a decade earlier (R. Lewis 1996), this chapter explores how Muslim lifestyle media in seeking to meet the needs of an emergent international Muslim bourgeoisie (Ömer, Acar, and Toprak 2004) elaborates for Muslims a sense of identity through consumption parallel to that established for other minority cultures, such as gays and lesbians (Mort 1996). Focusing on magazines in Britain (*Emel* and *Sisters*), in the United States and Canada (*Azizah* and *Muslim Girl*), and in Turkey (*Âlâ*) as an example of minority media activity in a Muslim majority context, the chapter analyzes the profound controversy provoked by fashion photography in the Muslim style media, exploring how media and commercial image makers are creating new aesthetic strategies for the picturing of the presumed Muslim modest body.

Chapter 4 addresses the discourse of choice that predominates in discussions about, and justifications for, veiling and veiling practices. It argues that new taste communities based on modest fashion are emerging that create generational and social distinctions (Bourdieu [1984] 2010) for those with the cultural capital to engage in new modes of interaction with mainstream fashion cultures and religious practice. Proposing that these taste communities can be seen as a subcultural formation, the chapter situates the privileging of choice as one of the distinguishing factors of hijabi and modest subcultures, focusing on how the limitations of the neoliberal choice paradigm (N. Rose 1999) are recognized, managed, and negotiated through embodied dress practices and their representation. With ethnic and religious family and community norms about dress and comportment functioning as the grounds against which choice is often defined and/or contained, the chapter examines in the British context the changing relationship of contemporary hijabi fashion to South Asian dress cultures. Using interviews with designers, retailers, and consumers, I examine how Muslim, ethnic, and religious distinction is reframed by younger generations able to move between minority and mainstream fashion systems. The chapter identifies the range of styles that are being used by young women to achieve modesty (as defined by each wearer) and fashionability, relating these new trends to national, diasporic, and transnational fashion developments (Bhachu 2004; Breward, Crang, and Crill 2010; El Guindi 1999; Jones and Leshkowich 2003; Puwar and Raghuram 2003; Tarlo 2010). As with Schulz's account of the mix of garments and modes of acquisition that make up a contestatory "political economy of propriety" in Mali (2007: 274), my study challenges commonplace concepts of a polarized mainstream/Muslim fashion binary by arguing for a network of overlapping, mutually constituting — secular, religious, ethnic, alternative, mainstream — fashion circuits.

Chapter 5 connects the experiences of hijabis shopping for fashion with their experiences of selling it, elaborating further the scale of Muslim participation within the fashion industry by examining the contribution of hijabi shop workers to British high street fashion retail in the context of British (2003) and EU (2000) legislation protecting the expression of religion or belief at work, a development of previous provision for race and ethnicity to which Muslims were unable to appeal. Providing a still rare qualitative account (Bowlby and Lloyd-Evans 2009) of Muslim employment experience, the chapter examines how Muslim women combine their need to dress modestly with the requirements of employers that shop staff represent the brand by wearing a store uniform. Asking what happens when the branded body wears a veil, my research matches employee accounts with employer responses to the visibility of faith on the shop floor to add religious embodiment into considerations of aesthetic labor — "the mobilization, development and commodification of [employees'] embodied 'dispositions'" (Witz, Warhurst, and Nickson 2003: 37) — that retailers require for delivery of their preferred service mode. Based on interviews with Human Relations and Employee Relations directors of major high street multiples and department stores, I establish the extent to which, in the transition from equal opportunities to diversity, private sector companies incorporate faith overtly into codes of conduct, including the potential to commodify diversity for internal and external reputation management. Studies on service sector employment have moved beyond an initial focus on emotional labor to a concern with how the spread of demands for aesthetic labor may restrict employment opportunities for those without middle-class dispositions (Witz, Warhurst, and Nickson 2003), while also exploring how corporate branding is responsive to (constrained by) the embodied capacities available within the local workforce (du Gay 1996; Pettinger 2005a). At this juncture, my research suggests circumstances in which Muslim religio-ethnic dispositions and forms of cultural, ethnic, and religious capital may allow hijabi women to preserve (in some cases enhance) the value of their aesthetic labor.

Chapter 6 focuses on how digital information communication technologies have been used by hijabi bloggers and designers to create new forms and understandings of modest fashion. Interviews with bloggers and social media hosts as well as designers and entrepreneurs bring new agents into discussions about the significance of the Internet for the reactivation of contemporary understandings of the umma (Bunt 2009). Situating this historically in relation to discussions about religion and communications technology, the chapter also deexceptionalizes Muslim youth cultures by locating hijabi bloggers within a wider account of the development of the fashion blog genre. The opportunities for Muslim fashion start-ups offered by e-commerce are similarly located in relation to previous forms of diaspora ethnic fashion and the lifestyle media. In a context where the deethnicization of Islam and the revitalization of the umma provide spiritual and political opportunities for transnational Muslim affiliations, designers find themselves dealing with national and regional taste distinctions between Muslim consumers. The chapter concludes by arguing that in the mode of everyday religion the blending between commerce and commentary seen in online modest fashion discourse creates new forms of religious knowledge production and transmission through which are developed new forms of religious authority for women.

The potential of new forms of religious and spiritual capital in the actualization of diaspora Muslim identities for marketing professionals is investigated in chapter 7's discussion of Muslim branding, adding faith to previous market segmentation focused on ethnicity (Grewal 2005; Halter 2000). Responding to Sandıkçı's (2011) call for more research on Muslim entrepreneurs within a "situated understanding of Muslim consumers," I combine interview material about the building of Ogilvy & Mather's Noor Islamic branding initiative with examination of how the uneven interest in Muslim consumers affects modest designers and cultural entrepreneurs in the context of the development in mass-market apparel of South Asian ethnic fashion at Walmart and Asda. The impact of new taste communities in Muslim fashion is explored in relation to the international development of modest fashion commerce and commentary in the other Abrahamic faiths and among secular consumers, in which transreligious consumer activity on- and offline brings new forms of interfaith and suprafaith contact. As well as extending into interfaith dress practice, hijab fashion has also widened to include the growing demographic of dejabi women, whose decision to uncover their heads does not take them outside the wider zone of modest self-presentation and fashion. Drawing together and extending the interviews and textual materials used throughout the book, the chapter concludes by examining how this form of Muslim self-presentation is rendered visible, invisible, or offensive to Muslim and majority viewers.

Notes on Method and Sources

Styles change, what *styles* mean changes, and how women interpret religion in their lives changes. It should be clear by now that I am not in the business of arbitrating which, if any, form of covering is most correct or authentic. Neither do I distinguish between orthodox or heterodox Muslim affiliations or practices. This book is not concerned with religious doctrine. When respondents advance definitions of religious doctrine I do not challenge: everyone who agreed to participate was made aware that I am not Muslim or working from a religious perspective.

Muslims, especially young Muslims, complain about being over-researched, or researched for the wrong reasons (S. Ahmed 2009): youth workers report calls from think tanks wanting potentially radicalized young men;[4] women made, or presumed, visible by their dress are likely to be stopped by journalists for vox pops on almost any story with a Muslim angle; individuals are asked by members of the public about their clothes, sometimes with great hostility, sometimes with more neutral interest. Potential participants often checked if I was hostile to hijab before agreeing to take part, to which I answered that I am not hostile to hijab, neither am I advocating it. In taking this line, I am aware that my engagement with participants is not without impact, and is made harder or easier by various elements of my own social positioning. It is not simply that the neutrality of the unmarked masculinist "objective" ethnographic researcher has been debunked (Clifford 1986; Geertz 1984, 2000), but that the presumption that particularity will itself produce authentic results has also been shown to be erroneous (Archer 2002).

Not being Muslim was sometimes a benefit because it took me outside the nuances of spiritual or political judgment faced by coreligionist researchers (Ger and Sandıkçı 2006). Declaring myself (sometimes) as a (nonreligiously observant) Jew could provide points of affinity on growing up (white) in the third generation of an ethnicized religious minority in Britain. Being an older (to them!) woman who is interested in fashion (with teenage years of part-time shop work) credited me with sufficient fashion capital to recognize nuances of style and opportunities to bond over the serious pleasures of caring about clothes. Being at the London College of Fashion brought desirable glamor through association for non-professional respondents and gave me industry insider status with brands and designers (whom I realized needed assurance that I was not engaged in potentially competitive commercial research).

None of this stops my participation in this research having an impact on the field that it studies, which for studies of youth subcultures, as Sarah Thornton points out (1995), means that by validating hijabi fashion as an object for intellectual enquiry I, like journalists and in-group cultural mediators, am contributing to the production and promotion of knowledge about it. This is also why women agreed to speak to me. Those who were not promoting their own magazine, brand, or blog wanted to contribute positive information about Muslims. I found participants in several ways. Those I met in their professional capacity (whether their work was waged or, like bloggers, unwaged) were contacted directly; this included all media professionals, designers, and brand representatives in Britain, North America, and Turkey, and store HR managers in Britain. Shop workers in Britain came initially from a request posted for me by Jana Kossaibati on her blog *Hijab Style* that also brought some respondents on personal dress. Other personal dress narratives came from my personal and professional contacts, and from snowballing introductions from existing participants. Hijab fashion is a small, if growing field, and people were generous in sharing their contacts. This also means that some of the companies and individuals with whom I spoke have gone on to become "faces," the usual suspects for academics and journalist alike. This overlap can be productive, widening the archive and range of interpretation in what is still an underdocumented field of fashion practice.

To some extent I also became a face in the field of Muslim and modest fashion. Writing pre-Internet, Thornton could not have predicted how doing subcultural research in the mid-2000s would increase the means and modes by which the researcher could be incorporated into the field. Acting in accordance with research ethics concerning privacy and aware that online interactions have offline consequences (Buchanan 2011), I chose not to seek access to any online or offline discussions that might be closed to non-Muslims or the nonreligious. I also chose not to post responses or directly ask questions: except for the callout to shop staff that Kossaibati posted on my behalf, I "lurked" (Hine 2000) on digital and social media platforms in the public domain, supplemented by interviews with bloggers and social media operatives, as with print journalists. As I began to publish in this area, and to embark on a linked project on modest fashion in the Abrahamic faiths,[5] academic conference talks were augmented by requests to talk to youth and women's groups in churches, synagogues, and interfaith groups. The research was press-worthy, and I more than once found myself sharing radio discussions or newspaper pages with Kossaibati and other bloggers and designers featured here. I also convened public-facing discussions in which many of them participated. The digital and social media that I analyze here as indispensable to the development of modest fashion commerce and discourse also circulated news of my research. This brought more respondents and began to shape a space for me as a friend to the field that I was studying. Strangers contacted me, connecting themselves to the validating potential of my research, and cross promoting my publications or media appearances on transnational blogs, social media, and commercial websites. Sometimes I was placed front row at modest fashion shows (I am just visible in figure 3.25), and name-checked in blog write-ups. Gratifying as this might be to my inner fashionista, this kudos, plus my fondness for many of the bright creative women I met during this research, has to be balanced with a willingness to arrive at conclusions they may not share. This is especially a concern for those participants who appear with their real names, the bloggers, journalists, designers, and brand representatives who I spoke to in their professional capacity.[6]

I tried to be discreet in how I approached participants. While engaging in shopper observation (Pettinger 2004, 2005b) in all sites, in Britain I avoided approaching shop staff in their place of work, or asking to advertise on the staff notice board, in case this made Muslims uncomfortably conspicuous to coworkers. In Turkey my only occasional presence meant that shop assistants were recruited informally on repeat store visits, and conversations took place with varying degrees of privacy in store or in local cafés during meal breaks, either in English or in Turkish through a translator, and were recorded only in note form. Mostly I was able to interview people on tape in their offices, my office, cafés, or their homes, with few interviews done by phone or Skype, and, while I have sought to preserve idiom, I have tidied up excessive use of "you know," "like," and "kinda" where it impedes the flow of narrative. I chose not to ask to take photos of respondents to avoid inhibiting the interaction, especially in a zone of enquiry where some Muslim women don't want their image to circulate beyond their control. This means that I could not make my own visual record of what everyone was wearing, except in public events like the hijabi street fashion shoot in chapter 7.

The visual record of hijab and modest styles seen in this book derives from magazine fashion editorial, brand advertising, and blog posts considered public domain (Cavanagh 1999), plus my own photos where identification of subjects would not result. Just as in chapter 2 I apply theories of embodiment to consider how clothes acquire meaning when worn and seen on the body, so too in the book as a whole do I consider how images acquire meaning through their modes of production and circulation. The convergence (H. Jenkins 2008) of photographic images of hijabi fashion across media platforms also involved readers as coproducers or cocurators, whose remediation of image and text through reposting and retweeting provides the researcher with elements of reception history. Given the inherent mobility of the digital platforms that make up so much of my source material (Bunt 2009), my digital "archive" is understood to be a "unique version" rather than a definitive copy (Brügger 2011): liable to change within seconds, digital material should be seen as a snapshot of when it was captured in contrast to other sources such as print editions of magazines that can be regarded as a permanent record.

Across media forms professional and amateur images (to the extent that one can still make that distinction) are considered to be part of a wider domain of visual culture, the suffusion and saturation of image seen as characteristic of postmodernity made possible by increasingly available visual technologies (Mirzeoff 2002). This includes in this instance: the ways in which the presence of billboards advertising Turkish tesettür brands is treated as an incursion into the secular visuality of the Turkish republic; or what it means for British Muslim lifestyle magazine *Emel* to be displayed on the newsstand in major supermarkets; or how women who start to wear the hijab find themselves differently hailed (and regulated) by other Muslims to whom they are now differently visible. For the variety of majoritarian audiences who encounter the styled bodies of Muslim fashion participants, with dress serving as "a medium of communication and expression," the material fact of their presence in the visual world is itself an intervention into knowledges about Muslims (Moors and Tarlo 2013): young adherents in this book consciously use fashion to challenge stereotypes of Muslims as primitive and nonmodern, despite that the responses to their carefully designed self-presentation will inevitably escape their control.[7]

While my book is premised on the hypervisibility accorded to women in discernibly Muslim clothing, my understanding of visuality also includes what is, or is rendered, invisible:[8] the nuances of hijabi style changes that cannot be detected by observers without sufficient cultural competency (sometimes because observers are not Muslim, sometimes, as might be the case with any youth cultural dress form, because they are not young); the ways that the fact of hijabi fashion itself is made illegible by an Orientalizing gaze that cannot encompass Islam in the frame of modernity; and the ways that women's decision to dejab renders them subject to a scopic Orientalist fascination at the same time as their uncovered head sends them into selective invisibility for Muslim and non-Muslim viewers.

Just as the immersive visual world is always experienced in particular times and places (and connections between places), so too does my consideration of the processes by which visual images are produced and consumed attend to the variably determining impact of spatial as well as temporal location: in chapter 3 I evaluate how the editorial team at *Muslim Girl* magazine negotiate the fact that consumption of content by teen readers will likely be monitored by older relatives; in chapter 6 I explore how the capacities of social media produce an onslaught of hostile comments from men all over the world that threatens to disrupt the netiquette of mutual respect developed in previous years on the hijabi blogosphere; and in chapters 6 and 7 I attend to how the locatedness of Muslim and revivalist taste cultures can advance or hinder designers' international sales.

To track these myriad relationships, my treatment of visual culture sources is broadly discursive with detailed readings provided of different elements of material and the processes by which it reaches audiences in each section. Social relations in the visual world include consumptionscapes in which are located the Muslim dressed bodies under discussion: street scenes and store atmospherics are rendered through my own observational vignettes that, necessarily partial, give an impression of the sociality in which Muslim fashion is acquired and displayed. Still images in tesettür catalogues are animated by information from tesettür brands. Other images encountered only in print or online are given detailed compositional analysis (G. Rose 2012) accompanied by indication of reader response through their remediation history. Magazine fashion editorial benefits from the recollections of creative staff (photographers, stylists, and art directors) that foreground attention to the social relations through which fashion mediators acquire garments and access models for their staging of recommended Muslim fashion. My analysis of visual images or products combines with attention to the role of cultural mediators in their production and circulation that qua Nixon (2003) incorporates not only "creatives" but also the determining impact of their relations with brand executives and publishers, as is seen in the new forms of minority cultural capital made possible by the development of ethnic (Mazzarella 2003) and latterly Islamic branding.

One of the recurrent discussions in the nascent field of Islamic branding concerns terminology, the difficulties of working out whether a product or brand might best be described as Islamic or Muslim, as well as a growing awareness that Muslims are not a homogenous market (Jafari 2012). My book too faces a number of related difficulties with terms, not least "East" and "West." The imaginary geography of historical Orientalism (Said 1978), has been revitalized by notions of clashing civilizations at the turn of the twenty-first century bringing into popular usage terms such as "the Muslim world." Despite its inherent problems (not least the numbers of non-Muslims living in the presumed territories of the Muslim world; see also L. Ahmed 2011), I make selected use of this framing concept and others, regarding them as working definitions, approximations, and shorthands, never as neutral descriptions of anterior realities or of homogeneous populations. I follow current usage in reportage, with the emergence of WENA (western Europe and North America) as a complement to the longer standing MENA (Middle East and North Africa). The productive effects of these classification processes are seen in the perpetually uncertain status of Turkey; with the Ottoman Empire long pivotal to the Orientalist and imperialist imagination as the interstitial space between East and West, so too has the identity of "Europe" been called into question and reconstituted by Turkey's EU accession process (Asad 2003; Göle 2011), with Turkey figuring in demographic and attitudinal reports variously as part of Europe, Central Asia, and Asia Pacific depending on the purview and purpose of the investigation.

The hegemony of U.S. discourse (I realize that America is a continent not a country, hence my specifications of "North America" when I am referring to the Canadian and U.S. operation of *Muslim Girl* magazine in chapter 3), extends to the naming of events, most pertinently here 9/11 as the reference for the bombings on September 11, 2001. Having retained popular currency in the Anglophone world as a signal for the date of the attacks and their aftermath, I have decided to continue to use "9/11" and also "7/7" as referents for historical discursive events still active in the present. For similar reasons I refer to the "Arab Spring" rather than to the revolts and revolutions of 2011.

The contested place of Muslims as residents in and citizens of nation-states (as I discuss in relation to the gathering of demographic data in chapter 1) also leads to ideologically delicate descriptors. While many Muslims in America favor the conjoined "American Muslim" (as with the previously popular hyphenated "Muslim American") that underwrites the national narrative of the immigrant melting pot, others resist religio-national naturalization and the implied suppression of intra-Muslim differences of ethnicity and class (Wadud 2003). The hyphen itself—an initially resistant challenge to the unmarked white norm of American identity—selectively disappeared in the aftermath of 9/11 as minority Americans, wrapped in the national flag (as on the launch cover of *Muslim Girl* magazine in 2007; see plate 6), strove to embed themselves *as* Americans (producing in turn other categories of unassimilable others; see Grewal 2005). In Britain, hyphens have been less popular and I am more inclined to refer to Muslims in Britain than to British Muslims, though at times the political intent of the latter is appropriate. In Turkey, the religiously observant and revivalist population tends to be identified as "Islamist," rendering the commodities of religious revivalist consumer cultures as "Islamic," though in Muslim minority Britain or North America, as in Australia, many Muslim designers or journalists prefer to identify themselves or/and their products within the implicitly open-ended category of Muslim rather than the ideology-loaded and potentially more prescriptive Islamic.

Academic researchers deploy a variety of categorizations to denote the commodities, discourses, and practices that render this group visible to themselves and onlookers, from a wide-ranging vision of "Islamic fashion" (Tarlo and Moors 2013) to the more specific "veiling-fashion" in the Turkish context (Gökarıksel and Secor 2013). In this book I try to refer to "Muslim" and "Muslim modest fashion": I prefer *Muslim* to *Islamic* because what one person considers religiously appropriate may be judged as insufficiently Islamic by another; and I include the category "modest" because many of the designers, dressers, and fashion mediators covered in this book see their practices as part of a wider frame of fashion activity concerned with modesty that crosses between faith and secularities with brands often keen to find a commercial category that can capture the widest market (R. Lewis 2013a). But if some participants like to present themselves as part of a transnational modesty movement that creates links between women of different or no (discernible) faith, others have come to avoid the term altogether, finding that *modest* like *Muslim* hinders sales in the mainstream fashion market. The history of why these different terms of religious and community identification have become so significant in their adoption, projection, and repudiation by the cohorts of designers, mediators, and dressers that I met is explored in chapter 1.

CHAPTER 1

FROM MULTICULTURE TO MULTIFAITH

Consumer Culture and the Organization of Rights and Resources

I'm not trying to shy away from any aspect of who I am.
Some people dress in Arabian or Pakistani styles, but I'm
British and Caribbean, so my national dress is Primark and
Topshop, layered with colourful charity-shop scarves.
—SUKINA DOUGLAS, twenty-eight, spoken-word poet,
London Poetic Pilgrimage

This quote from a British Afro-Caribbean convert to Islam went viral after it appeared in the British newspaper the *Times* in 2010 and beautifully encapsulates the themes of this book. In using fashion to declare her faith, Sukina Douglas is typical of the youthful Muslim demographic that is coming to prominence in the UK and across the world. Trouncing the presumption that Muslims are somehow not part of the British body politic, she clads herself in the nation's favorite fashion retailers, ironically claiming as part of her collective religious and national heritage the two stores seen at the time as key to British high street style (now available around the world). These stores, like other high street retailers, loom large in the fashionscapes of the young women in this book, as a source of clothes and employment. Suddenly in the late 2000s the darling of the fash-pack, budget retailer Primark, dubbed "Prada-mark," had been appearing in glossy magazines, while Topshop was never out of the press as the most prominent fashion-forward store among the multi-chain Arcadia group. Forcing fashion and faith into the same frame via consumption Sukina Douglas renders Topshop and Primark, purveyors of fast fashion, in the timeless category of "national dress," or costume. For if, as I discussed in the introduction, fashion is frequently understood as a facet of Western individuating modernity, then the collective, communal unchanging costume of "ethnic" or traditional clothing is popularly positioned as its opposite. In claiming mass-market high street fashion as her native (British) and ethnic (Afro-Caribbean) birthright of secular shopping culture, she asserts her fashionable individuality as part of her membership of a religious (Muslim) collectivity, staking a claim to inhabit several worlds simultaneously and to redefine each of them.

Clothing herself Islamically in Topshop and Primark is not only a clever riposte to those non-Muslims who would see her as insufficiently British by virtue of her now visible faith. It also asserts her rights to define her fashionable clothing as Islamic to the wider Muslim community, setting her apart from those who regard appropriate Islamic dress as outside of consumer culture or as something to be achieved through dress conventional to their ethnic cultures. For an Afro-Caribbean convert the equation of Islamic behavior with community norms is not an experiential heritage. She may be a minority ethnically among the largely South Asian British Muslim population, but she is entirely typical in terms of her age, her immersion in consumer culture, and her understanding of Islam within the framework of a personal spiritual quest that may, in its doctrinal leanings, challenge other more conventional ethno-Muslim practices.

This young convert demonstrates the switch to alternative fashionings of Muslim dress and behavior characteristic of her generation. Her activities with the poetry performance duo Poetic Pilgrimage also link her to the fusion cultures developed by others in her age group (making her a frequent interviewee [Tarlo 2010]). Sukina Douglas is typical of many young Muslims around the world, in Muslim majority and nonmajority contexts, whose embodied presentation of Muslim identifications challenges cultural norms within their family and ethnic group with innovative combinations of mainstream and specialist modest fashion offerings. While, as Moors (2009) points out, Europe came late to the Islamic fashion industry, the vibrant Muslim fashion scene of western Europe is now internationally recognized, with Britain acknowledged as the style setter with new brands and influential social media. To understand the significance of revivalist innovations in Muslim style, this chapter provides a synoptic history of the Muslim populations in Europe and North America. I first attend to how the different religious underpinnings of secularity in Europe, America, and Turkey provide the context for the shift in minority politics from identifications based on "race" or ethnicity to those based on faith. From there I move on to how the reactivation of the concept of the transnational umma, or community of Muslim believers, by a younger generation is contributing to new forms of "European" or "global" Islam. These new forms are then shown to have much in common with the syncretic practices of everyday religion as the individuated expression of personal spiritual choice. The politicization of veiling as an embodied practice in the spaces of modernity is connected, finally, to the enmeshment of religion in the development of consumer cultures, East and West, and the valorization of the unveiled female body as emblem of Turkish republican modernity.

Counting Muslims, Counting as Muslim: Histories and Demographics

In the UK and elsewhere it has historically been difficult and contentious to obtain statistics about the Muslim population.[1] In the UK, the national census had not asked about religious affiliation since 1851, except in Scotland and Northern Ireland, until a voluntary question about religious identity was reintroduced in 2001, possibly "driven by the question: 'How many Muslims?'" (Peach 2006: 630). In the context of government support for increased faith presence in public life (Woodhead and Catto 2012), the Muslim community had lobbied (along with other faith groups) for religion to be included, perceiving the value of having an evidence base from which to argue for rights and resources as Muslims rather than as ethnics as has previously been the case. In the United States, where it remains illegal to ask for information about religious affiliation in census material under the constitution's protection for freedom of religious expression, it is only recently that estimates have been available (Pew 2007, 2011b, 2011c), with Muslim organizations also combining forces to generate data (Somers 2014). As I discuss in chapter 7, marketers developing Islamic branding strategies also see the value in statistics, with leading proponent Paul Temporal harnessing the same recently available reports that I use here to predict that the "huge" and "growing" Muslim market "represents some of the best global marketing opportunities for decades to come" (Temporal 2011b: 47). While different interest groups may want statistics on the Muslim population, it is never possible to establish clearly what individuals mean when they report themselves Muslim nor to predict or control the productive effects of inviting, or compelling, individuals and groups to recognize themselves within particular social categories.[2] In the British census, religious identification can be regarded more as "cultural background" than evidence of personal piety (Peach 2006), as in other countries that are not Muslim majority (Pew 2009b), with ethnic or national origin terms used in data collection understood to be also relational and variable (P. Lewis 2007).

However contentious the statistics, it is now apparent that the UK Muslim population is the third largest in western Europe, following Germany (the greatest number of Muslims in one country) and France (the greatest percentage of Muslims in the national population). The Muslim population in England and Wales in 2011 was 2.7 million, or 5 percent of the population,[3] showing a significant rise since the first figures in the 2001 census of 1.6 million, or 2.7 percent. This rapid increase of over 50 percent in a decade (see also Field 2011; Perfect 2011) continues a longer-standing pattern of growth from pre-2001 estimates, and it makes Muslims the largest religious minority in the country. Notably youthful with 48 percent under age twenty-five in 2011 compared to 30 percent under twenty-five in the general population, the numbers of Muslims in Britain are expected to almost double to a total of 5.6 million or 8.2 percent of population by 2030, the largest predicted increase in Europe and likely to bring the number of Muslims in Britain equal with those in Germany (Pew 2011b). In Britain, as across western Europe and North America (WENA), the increase in the numbers of Muslims is not because of conversion, which remains numerically static with those leaving or no longer identifying with the faith (Pew 2011b), but because of immigration and high fertility rates (Pew 2011d) in the context of a strongly heteronormative culture (Field 2011) that regards family as central to religious and community life.

Islam is not an ethnicity, but in the UK as in other non-Muslim-majority states in WENA, historical population movements have brought certain national and ethnic heritages to the fore in the Muslim demographic. While there has been a Muslim presence in Britain since the seventeenth century (Gilliat-Ray 2010), the biggest wave of Muslim migration to the UK came in the 1950s, when the British government recruited mainly rural unskilled single male laborers from its then South Asian colonies to the industrial textile towns of central and northern England and in London. By the 1970s Muslim migrants were establishing the structures and services essential to the vitality of a community beginning to think of itself as settled rather than as on the point of imminent return to "home" (Werbner 2002). Although close ties continued with families and kinship networks in South Asia (especially through localized *biraderi* or clan networks organized through male elder leadership), the migrant Muslim population embedded in their British locales, establishing, along with Sikh and Hindu South Asian migrant populations, areas of pronounced South Asian residency in parts of the UK. Overwhelmingly urban rather than rural and often located in particular and often poorer parts of larger cities, this initial geography set the pattern for the concentrated picture of South Asian and Muslim habitation that continues in the UK today. The Muslim population is centered unevenly in certain towns, notably in the West Midlands (especially Birmingham), West Yorkshire (around Bradford and Leeds), Greater Manchester, and London (Peach 2006; Perfect 2011; Poulsen and Johnston 2008). South Asians remain the largest group of British Muslims (making up 68 percent of the Muslim population in Britain), of which 38 percent are Pakistani, 15 percent Bangladeshi, and 8 percent Indian. Some towns or city sectors are reaching Muslim majority population density, often clustered in national/ethnic masses, overspilling by 2011 into adjacent boroughs (Jivraj 2013). In Bradford, South Asian Muslim neighborhoods might be populated by households of not only the same Pakistani ethnicity but from the same rural village, often connected by kin. Though London as a whole became home to a Muslim population of ethnic, regional, national, and denominational diversity, monoethnic South Asian clustering is marked in some areas: South Asian Muslims predominate in the east London boroughs of Tower Hamlets (of which most are Bangladeshi) and Newham, where designer Mani Kohli had her flagship store as part of the Green Street Asian fashion parade. Many of the women featured in this book live and work, or were raised, in these South Asian enclaves.

While Muslims nationally report lower than average incomes and many live in areas of multiple deprivation, some sectors are and have been for some time wealthier, immersed, like many Arab and Ismaili East African Asians, in middle-class professional life. Class segmentation is emerging within the South Asian Muslim population as first-generation businesspeople achieve sufficient wealth to move to middle-class suburbs in

Manchester, Bradford,[4] and London, where Muslim Arabs from the Gulf form a discernible cohort among the semiresident superrich (Salamandra 2005). Educational achievements among the second and now third generations of South Asian and other migrant Muslims also brings more professionally qualified people into the community. The Muslim population follows previous migrant community trends in which second- and third-generation educational achievement outstrips the parental and grand-parental generation: with family educational aspiration for daughters as well as sons (Basit 1997) now an ethnic cultural norm (Shah, Dwyer, and Modood 2010), Muslim students are often the first in their families to go to college or university. Girls' education especially can confer status and prestige on their parents and relatives (F. Ahmad 2001), with enhanced earning potential regarded as protection in case of divorce (Dwyer and Shah 2009), though Muslims, and Muslim women the most, still face discrimination in the labor market (chapter 5). Significantly for this project, Muslims, like other immigrants, have preferred vocational professional training for their children (in medicine, pharmacy, law, and business) rather than education in the arts and humanities. Though media careers are becoming more widespread, the preference is for the "harder" areas of business or political journalism rather than "soft" arts commentary. In contrast to the overwhelming contribution of Muslims to the British textile and fashion manufacturing industries (initially as laborers, latterly as owners), very few of the Muslims involved in fashion design and mediation have a creative arts fashion-based training—which is beginning to change with the crop of young designers I discuss in chapter 6.

Overall in Europe the Muslim population has risen from 29.6 million in 1990 to 44.1 million in 2010 and is projected to rise to over 58 million in 2030 (Pew 2011b). With Muslims constituting 6 percent of the total European population in 2010 and set to rise to 8 percent in 2030, the rate of increase for Europe remains static with the previous two decades as does Europe's overall significance as home to only 3 percent of the world's population. The majority of Muslims in Europe live in eastern and central Europe and in Russia, heirs to Muslim communities that are often centuries old, as with Muslim populations in parts of southern Europe (including the Balkans) now regarded as important emerging markets by the Turkish modest fashion industry (chapter 2), though their largest European market remains Germany (Gökarıksel and Secor 2013). Projected to rise from 4.1 percent to 5 percent of the total population between 2010 and 2030 (Pew 2011d), Muslim, mainly Turkish, migrants were recruited as "guest workers" by (then West) Germany in the 1960s and denied citizenship until the late 1990s. If Muslims in Germany are significant as consumers on the map of Muslim fashion, the experiences and treatment of Muslims in France are writ large on the related map of hijab activism because of the state's long-running attempts to control Muslim women's clothing through legislation. France's Muslim population was estimated at 4.7 million in 2010 and is predicted to rise to 6.8 million by 2030 (Pew 2011d). Like the UK's South Asian Muslim migrant population, the North African Muslim population in France is youthful, poorer, less well educated and less involved in the waged economy than the rest of the French population.

In contrast, the Muslim population in America is relatively well-off and proportionately represented in college-level education and the waged economy and is predicted to increase at a faster rate than in Europe, where the rate of increase is set to slow down (Pew 2011b, 2011d). Estimated at 2.75 million in 2011, the Muslim population is predicted to double to 6.2 million in 2030. This rise from 0.8 percent to 1.7 percent of the total population will bring Muslims in the United States into equal numbers with Jews and Episcopalians. Muslim Americans will however not become more than a "tiny" part of the global Muslim demographic (Pew 2011d: 137).

The first significant cohort of Muslims to America arrived as slaves from Africa in the Atlantic slave trade from the sixteenth century, forced like those of other African faiths to suppress or relinquish the practice of their religion (J. Smith 1999; Wadud 2003; also I. Malik 2004). Mass Muslim immigration to the United States came later than in most of Europe, with an influx of émigrés from the worldwide Islamic revival of the 1970s and 1980s and the Iranian Revolution (Morey and Yaqin 2011), followed by a steady flow since the 1990s, increasing rapidly since 2000. Unlike Europe, in the United States no one nation of origin accounts for more than 12 percent of Muslim immigration (Pew 2007), with Pakistan the largest single national demographic (Pew 2011b). Conversion remains at about the national average for those changing faith, 20 percent, most prevalent among African Americans and, latterly, Hispanic Americans (J. Smith 1999). While immigration is likely to remain the main cause of growth, the percentage of American Muslims who are native born is increasing, especially among African Americans (Pew 2011b: 8), projected to rise from a 2010 average of 35 percent to 44.9 percent in 2030 (Pew 2011d: 147). The American Muslim population is distinguished from those in Europe by its links to historically black forms of the faith, notably the Nation of Islam and Garveyism, regarded as heterodox by some Muslim communities (Morey and Yaqin 2011; J. Smith 1999). Originally a black-only organization, and known for its conservative and strictly enforced dress code for women and men, the Nation under the leadership of Warith Dean Mohammed (son of Nation of Islam founder Elijah Muhammed) was dissolved in favor of greater racial and theological integration with orthodox Sunni Islam, though subsequently reformed and continuing as a black-only organization under Louis Farrakhan.

The Muslim population is both more ethnically diverse than the American population as a whole and younger. In 2011, 59 percent of Muslims were age eighteen to thirty-nine compared to 40 percent in the general U.S. population (Pew 2011b, 2011d). The numbers of Muslims under the age of fifteen is expected to more than triple by 2030, giving enormous cultural, economic, and political significance to an anticipated native born and acculturated second and third generations that will be maturing in the United States in the first half of this century (Pew 2011d: 150). However, in terms of wealth and education, native-born African American Muslims, both converts and those born into the faith, mirror patterns of racial and ethnic deprivation among the black American population more broadly and reported the highest levels of discrimination experienced by Muslim Americans in the wake of 9/11 (Pew 2011b: 45–47). The Muslim American population is located across the country with regional demographics reflecting ethnic migration patterns of foreign-born Muslims and historic patterns of racial clustering for black Muslims, as seen in the many local African American designers featured in Atlanta-based *Azizah* magazine discussed in chapter 4.

In Canada, where *Muslim Girl* magazine is based, Muslims make up a much higher percentage of the overall population than in the United States, numbering 940,000 or 2.8 percent of the total population in 2010 and predicted to nearly triple by 2030 to 2.7 million or 6.6 percent (Pew 2011d), the result of steadily increasing post-1945 immigration, especially since the 1990s from Pakistan, Iran, Lebanon, Morocco, Afghanistan, and Bangladesh (Pew 2011d: 146). With nearly a third of Muslims under age fourteen, they are also a younger population than other religions in Canada (Pew 2011d: 152).

The young demographic is characteristic of the Muslim population globally, though the "youth bulge" peaked at the start of the twenty-first century, and rates of growth are anticipated to slow. The Pew Research

Center estimates the global Muslim population in 2010 to be 1.6 billion, or 23.4 percent of the world's population, and projects that it will increase at 35 percent or twice the rate of non-Muslim populations to 2.2 billion, or 26.4 percent, in 2030, still a slower rate of increase than in the previous two decades. The bulk of the Muslim population will remain concentrated in the Asia Pacific region (which includes China and Turkey), but Pakistan will replace Indonesia as the single country having the largest Muslim population. Turkey is projected to remain stable as the world's eighth-largest Muslim population, augmented by a predicted inflow of immigrants and diaspora returnees. In WENA the Muslim population is projected to grow with nearly a one-third increase expected in western Europe and a doubling of the U.S. Muslim population. By the 2030s the United States is predicted to have more Muslims than anywhere in WENA except for Russia and France.

From Migrants to Muslims: Shifting Terms in Multicultural and Minority Politics

In Britain, the Rushdie affair in 1988–89 over the perceived blasphemies in *The Satanic Verses* is generally seen to have marked the emergence of a politicized Muslim sensibility able to argue for minority rights on religious rather than racial or ethnic grounds. Demonstrating a new diasporic religious transnationality (Appadurai 1996) with Sunni South Asian Muslims responding to an Iranian Shia fatwa, Bradford led the way with public demonstrations and book burnings, demanding an extension of the British Christian blasphemy laws. Prior to the implementation of EU directives (2000) protecting religious expression in employment and training in 2003 that I discuss in chapter 5, British legislation under the series of Race Discrimination Acts could not cover Muslims, extending only to those faith communities that had managed to establish themselves in law as an ethnic group, such as Jews or Sikhs. For Muslims, Werbner argues, the affair "revealed a potentially powerful capacity for cross-sectarian mobilization on a national scale [that was] both empowering and disempowering: it alienated Muslims [from majority British public opinion] while anchoring them more firmly in their adopted society . . . creat[ing] new agendas for active citizenship" (Werbner 2002: 51).

The switch of attention to Muslim politics in Britain, rather than ethnic or national politics at "home," and the ability to forge alliances with disparate coreligionists was to be a precursor to the transnational politics of the umma embraced by their children. This new imaginary geography departed from the mental maps of their parents or grandparents who had largely been immersed in religious life structured by the South Asian Sunni schools of Deobandi and Barelwi Islam, respectively characterized as conservative (to some, puritan) and spiritual (charismatic) (Gilliat-Ray 2010). With most imams recruited from abroad via biraderi connections, neither school was preparing religious practitioners to meet the needs of second- and third-generation Muslims experiencing Islam as a minority faith in a mixed secular world. This became particularly acute after 9/11 and 7/7, when young people especially felt the need to learn about Islam because the "wider community [was] watching and scrutinizing both Islam and Muslims" but did not feel that they had been sufficiently equipped by their education in the madrassas (S. Ahmed 2009: 42).

In Britain the new significance of religion made prominent during the Rushdie affair had an enormous impact on official, popular, and activist discourse about minority relations. This, as Ceri Peach summarizes, had developed from a concern with "color" in the 1950s and 1960s, to one focused on "race" in the 1960s, 1970s, and 1980s, to a discourse of ethnicity in the 1990s, and from 2000 to a concern with religion and most specifically with Islamophobia, culminating in a "change in political discourse in Britain from multiculturalism to social cohesion" (Peach 2006: 631). Understanding minority cultural rights in terms of race and ethnicity, liberal multiculturalism was inherently secular, replicating, Modood and Ahmad argue, the secular exclusion of religion from the public domain by regarding ethnicity and race relations as a matter for the state while marginalizing religion to the private; "religious assertiveness, especially on the part of Muslims [was regarded as] a problem not as a strand within equality struggles" (Modood and Ahmad 2007: 189). Rushdie and the aftermath marked a split within British antiracist and multicultural politics, effectively ending the use of "Asian" (that had followed "black") as a mobilizing political category, except in relation to forms of pan-Asian consumer culture (chapter 4) popular with young Muslims (Werbner 2002).

Responses to events after the pivotal moment of 9/11 in 2001 further entrenched the focus in WENA countries on their Muslim populations. In Britain, the attacks in America had been preceded in the spring and summer of 2001 by the urban riots in Bradford and other northern English towns that sparked a flurry of media and policy reports about a crisis in multiculturalism, reading the riots as the result of lack of social cohesion rather than as the result of racism and sustained social inequality (Meer and Modood 2008; Yuval-Davis, Anthias, and Kofman 2005). With London established as a haven for political refugees and émigrés that facilitated (especially Arab) Muslim intellectual and political life, the presumption of the British government during the 1990s that Islamic "extremists" would restrict their potentially violent focus to their countries of origin was challenged by the events of September 11, 2001. The realization in 2005 that those responsible for the London bombs on 7/7 were British born and educated shifted modes of governmentality, making urgent the need to have "Muslim" representatives through whom to influence their apparently troublesome communities. This was combined with an extension of notions of Muslim culpability from the collective to the individual that was to have a major impact on the experiences of much of the Muslim population and especially on young people. In the street, in school, at work, in the media, Muslims were required to dissociate themselves publically from the acts of the bombers in ways not seen during the Rushdie affair in the 1980s. For individuals and groups this was framed within a new binarized terminology of good "moderate" Muslim versus bad "extremist" Muslim[5] with faith "a newfound surrogate for race and ethnicity in erecting barriers to equality of rights and entitlements for many citizens" (Afshar 2012: 23). Demonized as a potential terror threat, many of the stereotypes attached to other religious minorities in previous moral panics were now transferred to Muslims (Nye and Weller 2012).

The Prevent program launched by Tony Blair and relaunched by the coalition government in 2011 addressed the perceived risk of radicalization (jihadization) among Muslim (mostly male) youth, with government policy wanting mosques and religious and community leaders to steer young Muslims away from extremism. With a home-born Muslim population reaching nearly 50 percent by 2011, the inability of imams to reach young British Muslims, alongside the exclusion of women from mosque spaces, became a matter of urgent concern after 2001, while diverting resources from social and educational projects seen as more important by many grassroots and women's groups (F. Ahmed 2013; Patel 2012).

Though posed in terms of a perceived crisis of authority within British Islam, the focus of the state on the previously privatized spaces of Muslim religiosity since 9/11 and 7/7 has, like the Rushdie affair, created the potential for new forms of regulation and opportunity, with the tendency to favor the religious Right over secular or Left organizations (Bhatt 2012) and to reinforce power and biraderi inequities (Kariapper 2009) facing ongoing challenge. While many resented having to position themselves within this dichotomizing worldview, the demand for community representatives did create opportunities for Muslims to develop more sophisticated roles as interlocutors with governments across WENA (Pew 2010) and for new types of Muslim leaders, intellectuals, and opinion formers to become prominent within and as spokespeople for Muslim communities. New organizations and *quangos* emerged. Some, like the Muslim Council of Britain, founded in 1997 after invitations from the Conservative government, were in and out of favor as governments and priorities changed (Morey and Yaqin 2011). The MCB's recent role as provider of expert advice on the new faith and belief employment jurisdiction brings them into play in my discussion of store uniform policies in chapter 5.

In terms of gender, demands for minority legal religious rights during the Rushdie affair immediately raised feminist concerns that accommodations would endorse the inequities of religious patriarchies,[6] based on existing critiques that ethnicity-based multiculturalism reinforces elite and male "representatives" as able to speak for the entire community (Yuval-Davis, Anthias, and Kofman 2005). This, for Susan Okin (1999), is an inevitable consequence of liberal multicultural toleration of diversity: while liberal society is based on the protection of individual rights, minorities are offered protection as a group, meaning that minority women may find that their individual rights are attenuated by state protection of or collusion with perceived community norms based on essentializing notions of minority cultures as monolithic and unchanging.

The ongoing tendency to regard minority cultures as homogeneous fuels moral panics about Muslims that within the securitizing discourse post-9/11 presents Islam as uniquely oppressive to women, demonizing Muslims qua Muslims as a danger to society and, for women, to themselves. Refocusing long-standing Orientalist and colonial stereotypes onto Islam, the figure of the "imperiled Muslim woman" paired with that of the "dangerous Muslim man" (Razack 2008) emerge as tropes through which can be demonstrated Western civilizational superiority. Recalibrating, like others, Gayatri Spivak's famous comment on colonial attempts to regulate sati, that "white men are saving brown women from brown men" (Spivak 1988), in religiously civilizational terms, Razack proposes that the focus on Islam is an extension of the West's "*ongoing* management of racial populations" in which as "a practice of governance, the idea of the imperiled Muslim woman is unparalleled in its capacity to regulate" (Razack 2008: 6; see also Abu-Lughod 2002, 2013). This was exemplified by popular female and feminist support for war in Afghanistan to liberate

Afghan women from their (presumed Taliban-imposed) burqas (Hirsch-kind and Mahmood 2002), and subsequently in creating "practices of exception" that remove Muslims as a civilizational threat from the protection of liberal human rights (incarceration, rendition). As with the media scrum to obtain the photograph of the "first" Afghan woman "liberated" from her burqa, the scopic Orientalist desire to penetrate behind the veil reinforces a highly sexualized discourse of Western superiority (R. Lewis 1996; Macdonald 2006; Yeğenoğlu 1998) that in seeking to rescue Muslim (as with "Oriental") women is also available to women and feminists in the West, Muslim and non-Muslim. This exceptionalism underwrites the worst forms of multiculturalism that regard minority women as belonging to their group, rather than as liberal sovereign individuals with rights. To counter this, Maleiha Malik (2010; see also chapter 4) argues for a "progressive multiculturalism" that by enshrining the primacy of women's civil and human rights over collectivist religious accommodations can more effectively secure equal rights to autonomy for minority women (see also Max Farrar [2012] on "critical multiculturalism").

The increasing focus on Muslims as a religious rather than primarily ethnic minority occurs in the context of and has contributed to (Pew 2010) the rising significance of religion within public life in the UK and internationally. While Muslims may be numerically a minority in Western non-Muslim-majority countries, those of majority religions like Catholics in France and evangelical Protestants in the United States also present themselves as minoritized in the face of modern secular society (as per the enthusiastic adoption of new EU religious rights legislation by Christian lobby groups in Britain that I discuss in chapter 5). In Britain the postwar characterization of public and political life as nonreligious (despite religious organizations providing ideological and material resources for the welfare state [Woodhead 2012]) has altered as successive Labour and Coalition governments have encouraged the participation of faith groups in public life as providers of education and welfare services and as opinion formers: though, as Woodhead observes, "religion never really went away, so that talk of its 're-emergence' or 'returns' or of 'post-secularity' is misleading" (Woodhead 2012: 7).

Among Muslims in Britain the tendency to prioritize a faith identity over a national identity is growing. Young Muslims in 2011 were "remarkably" more religious (however so defined) than the rest of the population and significantly more likely than their parents to see their religious identity as more important than their British identity (Field 2011). The incidence of identifying as Muslim is common across the world and occurs in the context of widespread revivalism in other faiths (Pew 2011c). Though Americans overall are "considerably more religious than Western Europeans," for both Muslims and Christians, the higher a person's degree of religiosity the more likely are his or her primary identifications to be religious rather than national (Pew 2011c). At the same time, in Britain and the United States many of the Muslim modest designers I spoke with were keen to emphasize their nationality, seeing it as integral to their design philosophy and brand communications.

In light of this growing youthful religiosity it should not be surprising that hijab and hijab rights recur as a key issue for British Muslims under thirty-five, especially for the sixteen-to-twenty-four age group, who overwhelmingly (three-quarters) in 2011 thought that women should wear hijab and supported the right to wear religious dress at work and at school (Field 2011). In America, young Muslims are inclined to be less dogmatic than their parents and more open to multiple interpretations of faith and practice (Pew 2011b: 27), but although there has been a discernible increase in veil wearing among young women it remains a less prevalent practice in the country generally as has historically been the case. When Leila Ahmed (2011) writes about the impact of revivalist hijab wearing among conservative Muslim women in America (chapter 7), this occurs in the context of the overall lower rate of hijab wearing in America. Muslim women in the United States are less likely to cover than women in other non-Muslim-majority countries, with 40 percent never wearing hijab, 36 percent wearing it all the time, and 24 percent wearing it most or some of the time (Pew 2011b). While as elsewhere hijab wearing most often correlates to high levels of religious commitment, the distinctive forms of covering prominent in the United States, especially the turban wraps favored by African American women, have impacted on the development of Muslim style media and entrepreneurship as I discuss in chapters 3 and 6.

Correlating to the young Muslims' decreasing sense of attachment to national identities is a decrease in attachments to inherited ethnoreligious community norms underwritten by a growing identification with coreligionists who are not coethnics within the revivalist geographies of the transnational umma whether in Bosnia, Chechnya, or Palestine. The staging of Muslim as an ethno-religious identity is part of a long developing shift in networks between Muslims, and the direction and modes of ideas, resources, and leadership, a "process of inculturation" that by the early 2000s was steering away from a "narrow" focus on local or "home" issues (Niessen 2003: 39–40). Typically, by the late 2000s in Britain, many young people and women considered existing bodies and forms of Muslim leadership unrepresentative and irrelevant (S. Ahmed 2009; Field 2011), bypassing localized male and elder dominated publics to seek alternative spiritual and cultural guidance in the development of new Muslim publics.

New Generations, New Definitions:
"European" or "Global" Islam

Unlike their parents or grandparents, many in the second and third generation of migrant Muslims in Europe are native speakers of a European language and have grown up as digital natives. Their generational confidence with the Internet and new communications technologies combines with familiarity with majority cultural forms (Din and Cullingford 2004) to produce innovative forms of cultural and religious expression and new modes for communicating them. In the United States also the youthful Muslim population shows similar participation rates in consumer and leisure cultures to the rest of the population, with higher than average use of social media (Pew 2011b: 41). The importance of English as the initial language of the Internet has given a special opportunity for South Asian Muslims in Britain and English speakers internationally to forge links that do not owe allegiances to local kinship networks or deference to Arabic-based spiritual teachings. While young Muslims in deprived areas often have only partial access to the formal versions of European languages essential for employment and social mobility (P. Lewis 2007: 43), the prevalence of English in text speak plus visually led social media ensure participation for a wider social demographic. Giving prominence to actions perceived to be by, for, or against Muslims around the world, digital communication technologies have promoted a transnational imaginary for young Muslims that displaces the international affiliations of the parental generation.

The new geographies of the umma fostered by young people's facility with information and communication technologies (ICT) create transnational networks often regarded with suspicion by majority populations and governments fearful of radicalizations and social segregation, though extremism (and jihadism) is far rarer than public panics would suggest (Field 2011), with some organizations tainted by (an often fleeting) association with violent individuals (Pew 2010). Islamist movements have often been especially influential among the college-age Muslim population and play a (sometimes unwelcome) role in the student and peer group experiences of the young women in this book.

In Britain, the insularity of conventional Deobandi and Barelwi imams and mosques is often cited as one of the reasons why young Muslims are drawn toward radical, and jihadist, Islamist groups such as Hizb ut-Tahrir. Hizb ut-Tahrir, small in actual membership but large in influence and media profile, is one of the several groups and organizations that follow a Salafi, or Wahabi, approach to Islam, an exclusivist and strict reading of Islam from Saudi Arabia that advocates literalist readings of the holy texts and disparages other forms of Islam as inauthentic. Gaining significant hold in some British university Muslim associations in the 1990s, Hizb ut-Tahrir's core membership consisted of young men, though many women were also drawn to their version of "pure" Islam, finding scope for female agency in the conspicuous piety of dress codes whose stringent understanding of modesty supersedes the combinations of hijab plus Western clothing already popular with young British Muslim women by favoring Islamic clothing such as jilbabs, extended by some to include a face veil (or niqab) and gloves (Tarlo 2010). Not surprising, in relation to hyperbolic displays of ever increasing strictness in modest presentation, Hizb ut-Tahrir acted as "advisors" to teenager Shabina Begum, whose case against her school over wearing a jilbab in 2002 became pivotal to British legal debates covered in chapter 5.

Longer established Islamist movements influential in WENA include the Muslim Brotherhood and Jama'at-i Islami. The Muslim Brotherhood, founded in Egypt in 1928, dispersed to Europe and North America when the organization was banned in 1952 after a campaign of violence. Becoming an umbrella organization of affiliated groups and thinkers, the movement by the 1980s had adapted to life in Muslim minority contexts; the quest for an Islamic state was deemphasized, and Muslims were encouraged to contribute to wider civil society (Gilliat-Ray 2010; Pew 2010), including in Britain Muslim involvement in the Stop the War Coalition in 2002 (Philips and Iqbal 2009). The impact on affiliates of the Brotherhood's temporary rise to government and subsequent suppression in post–Arab Spring Egypt remains to be seen. The South Asian counterpart to the historically Arab-dominated Muslim Brotherhood is Jama'at-i Islami, established by Maulana Mawdudi in India in 1941. Also aimed initially at the establishment of an Islamic political system, Mawdudi challenged Deobandi and Barelwi ulema by arguing for ongoing *itjihad*, interpretation of the holy texts, for contemporary life, developing in Britain through its Islamic Foundation a reputation for liberal inclusivism and interfaith dialogue (chapter 7).

In North America, Jama'at-i Islami and the Brotherhood were prominent in the formation of the Muslim Student Association (MSA) in 1963, which brought together the early mosque associations and welfare organizations of the post–Second World War period. The annual MSA conference remains a central focal point for Muslims across the continent (with most of the designers featured here hosting a stall) and is now organized by the Islamic Society of North America (ISNA). Established in 1981, ISNA serves as an umbrella organization for the proliferating specialist associations devoted variously to Islamic finance (NAIT), and to Muslim professionals in medicine (IMA), education (ICS), or youth service (MYNA) (J. Smith 1999). Though ISNA aims to represent all Muslims in North America and includes Warith Dean Mohammed on its Shura council, it continues to be criticized as unwelcoming by African Americans who hold their own Warith Dean Mohammed conference each year (J. Smith 1999; Wadud 2003), where *Azizah* magazine maintains a presence.

With Muslim student life organized by ISNA, the Muslim Brotherhood and Jama'at-i Islami retain an impact on campus, though their Wahabist approach is often found unwelcoming by less doctrinaire Muslims. In contrast to the Saudi-backed Salafi Islamism influential elsewhere, Turkish Islamism (despite some Saudi money [Köni 2012]) is more interested in developing specifically Turkish versions of Islamism and regional influence, grounded in Sufi associations or *tariqats*. Banned in 1925 (G. Jenkins 2012), clandestine tariqats predominated in rural regions, moving into the cities with mass rural migration as to Europe (Argun 2003). There, especially in Germany (Blaschke and Sabanovic 2000), tariqats proved essential to the ideological development and financing of Islamists politics in Turkey, prompting interventions from the Ministry of Religious Affairs to appoint "moderate" imams to German mosques (I. Malik 2004). Among the several tariqat-style organizations (some preferring the term *cemaat* or faith-inspired community) many have developed distinct, if variably and selectively legible, dress and consumer cultures for women and men.[7] In the twenty-first century it is followers of Fethullah Gülen who have become the most influential group. Not declaring themselves members of a tariqats, followers of Gülen (in self-imposed exile in the United States) pledge time and money to the international network of education and welfare facilities that, like the Muslim Brotherhood in Egypt, constitute a parallel civil society (Davis and Robinson 2012) viewed with alarm by many in Turkey and seen by 2013 to be overtly intervening in national politics and jurisprudence. As with Salafi-style organizations elsewhere, Gülen features large in Muslim student life, running schools and outreach programs around the world, and in Turkey providing student housing and guidance with attempts at incorporation sometimes found oppressive by nonaligned pious students.

Despite this common student dilemma, North American and British governments continue to perceive university Islamic societies as potential centers for "radicalization" and jihadi recruitment, failing to realize that for many young Muslims affiliation with groups is fluid and partial and may be more about class and gender than radical religious politics (Samad 1998). Many young Muslims "see these movements and networks as generically 'Islamic' and may not care about or even be aware of their political ideologies and social agendas" (Pew 2010: 8), let alone the nuances between different versions of the umma (that for some "hankers back to the days of Islamic glory" [Afshar 2012: 35]) and its real or projected relationship to territory. The mainstream media seldom explicates the differences between groups, giving radical movements and clerics undue prominence. Despite evidence of "Salafi burnout" across WENA (Gilliat-Ray 2010: 81), the participation of young Muslims in forms of religious radicalization is rarely seen in terms of the often temporary affiliation to radical ideas and social movements generic to youth. In contrast to the sometimes tolerant understanding of other mobilizing movements or ideas that animate youthful rebellion and character formation, whether pontificating vegetarianism or righteous middle-class anarchism, majority culture demonstrates little scope to regard youthful Muslim zealotry as something that may mellow with time and maturity.

The younger generation's decoupling of individuated personal faith from inherited community patterns of customary religion is widely referred to as a "de-ethnicization" of Islam (see Göle 2011), separating it from the ethnic cultures of their parents and favoring thinkers and leaders who stress plural interpretations. These new affiliations and practices, given labels such as global or European Islam (on Italy, see Salih 2004), are developed in relation to, rather than direct rejection of, existing forms of Islamic knowledge development and transmission. The growth since the late 1980s of "critical Islam" (Mandaville 2003) is inextricably linked to the development of European-language Muslim print and digital media with popular religious intellectuals like Tariq Ramadam, Yusuf

Islam, and Ziauddin Sardar contributing to journals like *Q News* and *Emel*, which I discuss in chapter 4. In contrast to the parental generation's ethnic allegiances to particular schools of jurisprudence (*fiqh*) arising from contexts of Muslim majority, this intellectual cohort see school affiliation as a personal choice, in which interpretation (*ijtihad*) is open and flexible (Mandaville 2003). Sadar's new quarterly *Critical Muslim* in 2012 welcomed contributors and readers who "may define their Muslim belonging religiously, culturally or civilizationally." Outside Europe the banner of "progressive Muslims" unites those for whom "progressive itjihad *is* our jihad" (Safi 2003: 8).

Young women are significant in the development of these new digital and popular Islamic cultures. The innovations in dress, fashion, and style entrepreneurship that I discuss in chapters 4 and 6, plus the Muslim lifestyle mediation in chapter 3, are new forms of religious discourse that create opportunities for the development, as I discuss in chapter 7, of women as religious interpreters and authorities. Converts have played a significant role, with three of the magazines in chapter 3 established by women who chose to join Islam: Sarah Joseph at *Emel*, Tayyibah Taylor at *Azizah*, and Na'ima Robert at *Sisters*. Raised without allegiances to ethnic Muslim community norms, it is often easier for those new to the faith to articulate the revivalist distinction between culture and religion, as seen in Robert's biography and echoed on the street by the young Afro-Caribbean convert niqabi women in Brixton who reported to Sughra Ahmed that they "felt they were among the most engaged members of their local [Muslim] societies. A key basis for their view was the lack of cultural baggage, which they felt held back other more typical (Asian) Muslim communities whom they perceived to be culturally entrenched rather than religiously conscious . . . an obstacle to integration" (S. Ahmed 2009: 50).

In Britain, the public articulation of Muslim demands for religious rights in a securitizing context has often been read as the death or failure of (ethnicity-based) multiculturalism. In contrast, Modood recasts politicized affiliations to the transnational umma as a form of "Muslim power" with "provenance [in] anti-racism and feminism" comparable to the Afrocentrism of American black power movements (Modood and Ahmad 2007: 196). In America, the pervasive myth that multicultural plurality is both a uniquely "American genius *and* that there is an Americanness that somehow contains and transcends plurality" has historically naturalized whiteness as the national norm (Appadurai 1996: 171), but is also open to young revivalist Muslims who claim a unique ability to assert modern Muslim identities on the basis of their American heritage of civil liberties. Contextualizing them historically as part of a "multi-ethnic Muslim American generation," Ahmed finds they are "the product of the convergence of key elements in the teachings of Islamism with the ideals and understanding of justice in America in these very specific decades" (L. Ahmed 2011: 286–94). The racializing impact of Islamophobia (Franks 2000) prompts Meer also to reconceptualize Muslim as a "quasi-ethnic sociological" rather than "scripturally informed" formation (Meer 2008: 66), though Salvatore cautions against extrapolating from one context of anti-Islamic prejudice that there will be widespread support for "European Islam": "Disputes about Islam and Muslims may have taken on a racialized vocabulary in the UK but similar disputes on the continent, though certainly not devoid of racist overtones, have been somewhat different. There, the secularly minded stigmatize 'insurgent Islam' as a kind of anti-modern mobilization. Many perceive Islam less as the backward culture of the 'other' than as a 'return to the Middle Ages,' an egregious form of authoritarianism lacking the clear separation between religion and politics" (Salvatore 2004: 1014), a relegation of Islam to the nonmodern that has historically predominated in the Muslim secularity of Turkey.

That more Muslims are identifying via a group belonging framed in ethno-religious terms does not mean that "Muslim" is a settled, coherent, stable, or homogeneous identity. Like all forms of social subjectification, religious identities are shifting relational terms, contested within as well as without and subject to change over time. Just as secularities are framed by the religious cultures that they define themselves against (see introduction), so too are transnational "discourses of religious community" like the umma "constituted by the forms they appear to subvert, particularly the nation-state": the utopian ideal of the umma does not always translate into social facts on the ground, with the umma's presumed inclusiveness liable to be undercut by definitions of "an 'Islamic world' [that] reproduce exclusionary practices positioning particular places [and their populations] as peripheral to the true, authentic, originary authority of a single religion" (Jones and Mars 2011: 2–3). Thus, British Arabs aver the term British Muslim as an unwelcome "politicalization of Islam" synonymous with the interests of British Pakistanis (Nagel and Staeheli 2008: 101–5); kinship loyalties continue to inhibit social mixing between ethnic/national groups (P. Lewis 2007); and, in the United States, African American Jameelah Xochitl Medina asks herself "'what ummah?!'"; reporting that when "I am not perceived [externally] as an oppressed Muslim women in need of liberation, I am seen [internally] as an ignorant and potentially unruly black woman who cannot possibly be true to the din" (Medina 2011: 60).

The possibility of rising to prominence without the previous markers of religious distinction or community or biraderi seniority has seen the development of vibrant and pluralist Muslim publics bringing to the fore the voices of women and young people, many of whom populate this book. But, in the mishmash of ideas that make up radical Islamist political discourse, the umma can become a "community of equals, where charisma and not knowledge brings leaders to the fore," with an attendant "diminution" of learning (Roy [2002] 2004: 166–67). The challenges facing younger Muslims are not only of asserting themselves against elements of established religious frameworks and elder community norms that they find repressive or inappropriate, but also of arbitrating between the different interpretations and authority claims of diverse Islamic, Islamist, and radical youth Muslim formations.

Everyday Religion: Blending and Syncretism in Muslim Revivalist Cultures

The globalized vision of the new umma facilitates a model of personal spiritual quest that replaces structures of habitual religion and addresses the perceived failures of previous modes of religious authority and leadership. In this, Muslim revivalism (for Roy, neofundamentalism) shares in the individuating religious ideology of Christian (especially evangelical) revivalism (seen also among Jewish revivalists) with a "shift of emphasis from religion to religiosity" ([2002] 2004: 9). The resurgence of Islam as the basis for minority demands is sometimes seen as a belated attempt at a "Muslim reformation." But this would be to inscribe a religious evolutionary scale with a stagnant Islam belatedly catching up with Christianity. Unlike the desired, not achieved, model of centralized control that characterized post-Reformation Western Protestantism and Catholicism (McGuire 2008), for Islam, like Judaism, spiritual authority has historically been achieved through displays of learned disputation (Eickelman and Anderson 2003; see also chapter 6) that are themselves historically and socially contingent in their construction and power: "interventions must be authorized and the procedures of authorization are subject to ever-deeper changes related to the dynamics of social processes related to class, gender, and generation. Change and reform do not erase authority but redistribute it and might change its nature . . . in which, for example, women and youth acquire authority but where authority is not obliterated" (Salvatore 2004: 1016–23).

Accounts of Islam as a minority culture emphasize the individuation of faith, emblematized by the uptake of veiling as an expression of personal religiosity over an allegiance to Muslim parental cultures. That modern Islamists "campaign not for the compulsory wearing of a headscarf or hijab, but for the right to do so, playing on the modern concept of personal freedom rather than that of submission to God's law" illustrates for Roy how Islamists have adapted a discourse of choice deriving from a Christian reformation model of free religious will (Roy [2002] 2004: 192), though women's right to choose not to veil may rarely be equally defended (Sahgal 2012). Göle also reads the modern hijabi as typical of the performative nature of modern Muslim identities that, being deterritorialized in lands where Muslims are a minority, rely on everyday acts to bring into being "a new collective Muslim imagination" in which "it is not the imposition of sharia by seizing state power that defines the Islamist movement but rather these 'performative' and opposed practices that seek to create a place for religion in the public sphere" (Göle 2011: 86). The ability of the veil to read as distinctive is variable and situated. The challenge to existing Muslim norms is "only possible in relation to a certain, however contested, living tradition . . . neither a strictly individual choice nor the marker of an exclusive Muslim subjectivity" (Salvatore 2004: 1023). As Ahmed notes, the veil's potential "to signal resistance or protest . . . arises from and even depends on the fact that it is the dress of a minority," visibly challenging mainstream society, whether "material and economic injustices in the case of Egypt [in the 1970s, or] racial and religious in the West [today]" (L. Ahmed 2011: 210).

The emphasis on Muslim practices and identities as mutable and historically inscribed accords with developments in the sociology of religion that focus on everyday religion to challenge conventional thinking about religious boundaries, countering the presumption that people have become less religious. Despite the increase in historically black churches (Perfect 2011) and faith groups like Islam connected to postcolonial migration (Donald 2012), there is an increase in numbers defining themselves as having no religion; but religion has not so much disappeared as gone somewhere else and must be sought in the folk rather than the ecclesiastical.[8] Popular with younger generations (Pew 2009a), practices of everyday religion are characterized by blending and syncretism that, as

Nancy Ammerman (2007) and Meredith McGuire (2008) point out, disregard boundaries between denominations (Jews who do Buddhist meditation), and between the sacred and the profane (Latino Christian home shrines combining miniatures of the Virgin with commercial statuettes of angels). This does not make them inauthentic: it reveals the ideological work that goes into historical and contemporary boundary formation between denominations, between the sacred and the secular, and between sanctioned and outlawed forms of observation.

Often taking the United States (which never had an established church) as axiomatic, the experience of religious pluralism associated with post-Reformation Christian modernity in WENA is seen as a prerequisite for the choice and mobility exercised in new forms of religiosity. This emphasis on the voluntary membership of religious denominations naturalizes a culturally Protestant emphasis on religion as an achieved identity based on the individual's conscious embrace of God over an ascribed or religious identity inherited at birth, as with Jews (Davidman 2007). Now refuted, the "secularization thesis" considered that premodern ascribed social and religious identities would evolve into the achieved identities characteristic of modernity with religion becoming privatized and individuated. Religion though has not disappeared from public life in late modernity and is rarely fully privatized, often existing alongside shifting ascribed or "tribal" identifications with the incorporation into other faiths of a Protestant-derived presumption of voluntarism; Jews might feel themselves to be born Jewish (an ascribed identity) while also understanding themselves to exercise choice in their (achieved) mode of practice (Davidman 2007). As Ammerman (2007: 6–13) explains, "particular cultures and histories provide the materials out of which everyday religiosities and secularities emerge," whether established churches determining forms of American and European secularisms and religious cultures (Davie 2007) or histories and experiences of secularity impacting on Western minority faith traditions.

Against the presentation of denominationally sanctioned practices as the outcome of a discrete religious tradition, McGuire argues that most religious traditions come from a history of blending that continues in the eclectic mixes of everyday practices. That these might be identified by their adherents as "spiritual" rather than "religious" requires researchers to be "be alert to the social meanings between such distinctions" and their role in delineating "desirable from denigrated identities and statuses, and worthy from unworthy ideals and values" (McGuire 2008: 6).

Thus, while my project attends to the everyday practices of Muslim modest fashion as valid religious expression, it does so in the context of ongoing debates and disputes about changing definitions of Muslim identity as ascribed or achieved. While the normatization of religion as an individuated voluntary achieved identity has in the past often skewed the way that other faith traditions are studied and popularly understood, it is also the case that the extension of the voluntarist worldview beyond America (especially in its Christian revivalist and popular cultural forms) has impacted on the understanding and practices of younger Muslims raised elsewhere. While their identity as Muslim may be ascribed through birth, the increasing refusal of their communities' ethno-religious norms in favor of new different forms of practice and presentation is supported by a view of religious identity as achieved, and individuated (exemplified by the chosen identities of prominent converts). Just as blending can be regarded as integral to the development of religious traditions so too do individuals—in historically and socially contingent contexts—blend approaches to religious, and ethnic, identity itself. For young Muslims in WENA it is negotiation between parental and "new" forms of Islam that produces identity, not simply one or the other.

In my research I see evidence of both perspectives: young people do, for a host of reasons, feel that many of the religio-ethnic community norms of their parents (if they are not converts) do not straightforwardly work for them. But they are also adroit, like most young people, at making compromises, often recognizing the historical and social reasons behind the development of practices they may wish to dispense with as custom rather than religion. In arguing for their "pure" interpretations of Islamic practice, a certain level of rejectionism is displayed, but like most youth (and sub-) cultures, the relational dynamic to dominant and parental cultures is intrinsic to the formation of new practices. So too are intragenerational distinctions between microcohorts of different Muslim youth cultures, such as the rapid redefinition of hijab fashions and Islamic body management modes already developed by respondents' younger sisters over the few years of this study (chapter 4).

Sughra Ahmed's research draws out the fast changing intragenerational gaps between young people in which Muslims like any youth demographic can live in a very different pop cultural world from their older siblings, not just their parents. Keen to deexceptionalize the young Muslims she researched, Ahmed emphasizes the congruent experiences of young Muslims with young people from other faiths, quoting Robin Rolls, director of Christian Youth Ministry in Leicester: "Generation X who grew up in the Kylie-Jason era had links with faith that connected them to a sense of identity. Compare this generation to the next generation known as Generation Y. These are young people who are now growing up with faith as a leisure option" (S. Ahmed 2009: 66).

The experience of faith as part of identity framed through leisure and shared with like-minded others who may not come from the same background or territory links the revivalist identity with the transnational in the context of neoliberal consumer culture. As Morey and Yaqin discuss, today's version of the umma may draw links to earlier Ottoman models (of international trade and transnational loyalty) but in the context of globalization and free market economies: "a new global Islamic cosmopolitanism is surfacing, mediated through a diversity of ethnic identities among a disaporic Muslim population settled in the West" in which "dialogically constructed cosmopolitanism" plays out "through material culture and manifests itself in the marketing and branding of Islamic goods such as Ummah chocolate, Islamic fashions, lifestyle magazines such as *Emel*, *Q News*, and Islamic comedy, films and music" (Morey and Yaqin 2011: 181).

Embodiment and Spatiality: Veiling in Public and in Politics

Garments used for all varieties of veiling can, like all dress, best be understood as what Joanne Entwistle calls a "situated bodily practice" (2000: 3). Clothes and fashions acquire social meaning through being worn on dressed bodies, whose ability to present in socially appropriate ways relies on the internalization of learned "techniques of the body," literally how to hold oneself, to walk, to dress (Mauss 1973). Nobody is born knowing how to walk in high heels, but many women learn the body management necessary to enact this particular gender-related and socially sanctioned embodied practice. Although "the" veil is often fetishized as a thing in itself, wearing any form of veil similarly requires the development of particular techniques of body management, such as the processes by which Hindu girls in an Indian village "learn" to wear the veil, progressing from the lighter half-sari adopted in late childhood to the complex techniques demanded by stricter forms of face and head covering as they grow toward "marriageable" age (Tarlo 1996). Rather than see clothes as simply symbolic, a matter only of external form or representation, their activation on the body mediates the subjects' experiences of themselves and situates them in a social world, subject to and intervening in forms of regulation and surveillance.

Dress is not only an embodied practice, it is also spatialized and temporal, with dressed bodies given meaning through their location in specific times and places that have their own rules of dress and comportment. Space is not an inert entity in which things just happen; it is dynamic, and the different places that dressed bodies inhabit are relational, acquiring distinction and meaning from their relationship to what lies "beyond" (Massey 1994). Individuals, therefore, never belong to only one spatial community: they engage with overlapping sets of spatial relations whose socializing effects produce differences of gender, sexuality, class, race, ethnicity, and faith.

For veiled bodies, the diverse audiences that witness their spatialized dress practices provide additional complications. The veiled body in the contemporary world travels across what Anna Secor names different "veiling regimes": "spatially realized sets of hegemonic rules and norms regarding women's veiling, which are themselves produced by specific constellations of power" and which vary in terms of "formality, enforcement, stability, and contestation" (Secor 2002: 8). These regimes of veiling, which also include the normatization of nonveiling, inhere in different spaces and are enforced and challenged to varying extents, officially by state police in Saudi Arabia, or unofficially by the regulatory role of gossip and elders in close-knit minority ethnic communities in Bradford, Detroit, and Paris: "To say that moral subjects (and, I would add, spaces) are not only controlled but also created through (religious) dress is to move away from an idea of religious dress as either merely a symbol or an instantiation of 'social control'" (Secor 2007: x).

The veil is not just a garment that is worn in particular locations: it can itself be regarded as a spatializing device for communities that adhere to codes of gender segregation and/or seclusion. Fatima Mernissi (1985) argues that the veil can be understood as a sartorial mechanism by which the gender seclusion of the harem (or *purdah*) system, the Islamic organization of domestic space that keeps distance between women and those men to whom they are not closely related, is extended beyond the harem walls. Based on the presumption of an active female sexuality, harem seclusion and the veil serve to keep men and women separated to protect the community from the chaos of *fitna*, or uncontrolled sexual energy (itself variably defined historically [Mir-Hosseini 2011]), which some hold would follow from inappropriate sexual contact.

Though concepts of modesty, and attendant codes of honor and shame, logically require modesty from both genders, it is most often women who have borne the burden of representing and protecting family and by extension community morality, especially as mothers charged with transmitting Muslim/community values to the next generation. In the past and today for women in territories largely governed by Muslim habits of body management, the wearing of a veil may constitute a legible display that should prompt similarly respectful performances from male bodies in her vicinity, such as not staring at her face. In a contemporary non-Muslim-majority environment of mixed religions, genders, and ethnicities, there is no such social contract. (Ironically, a behavior held retrospectively to mark out the "extremist" tendencies of one of the London bombers in 2005 was his habit in his recent ultraorthodox incarnation of refusing to meet the eyes of any woman in public. This practice, when repositioned to postcolonial, postindustrial northern England, read as misplaced zealotry to others in his community, rather than as good modest manners.) For migrant Muslims, adaptation to diaspora life heightens control of female sexuality, with dress and body management acquiring new prominence as a guarantor of traditional values (Afshar 1994).

In the Middle East and elsewhere since the late 1970s, the presumed exile of the veiled woman from the spaces of modernity has been challenged by what have now become a range of politicized Islamist dress practices and a related and growing industry. As with all social and political developments, people's participation derives from a range of overlapping and sometimes conflicting motivations. Many women in the first wave of Islamic revivalists in Egypt and elsewhere in the Arab world in the 1970s were part of a piety movement that opposed the growing secularization of the newly independent postcolonial states, while others were attached with a looser "affinity to Islamist movements and their cultural politics" combining a general opposition to Western influence and local authoritarianism (Moors 2009: 178). The first generation of revivalist activists mostly made their new Islamic clothing at home (El Guindi 1999). Plain and sober in color, the "new veiling" (MacLeod 1991) was a change in style from traditional forms of covered dress worn by older and rural women and a change in spatial and social relations when seen on the confident youthful forms of educated urban dwellers. Sewn in inexpensive fabrics, the uniformity and affordability of the style provided an antidote to fashion and a leveling out of class distinctions in what some saw as an increasingly materialist society. In contrast, in Turkey in the 1960s, Şule

Yüksel Şenler commandeered mainstream fashion and American movies to create intrarevivalist distinction with a new veiling style, dubbed the "Şulebaş," that enabled participation for a cadre of young women within the Nurculuk religious sect (Altınay 2013b). By the 1980s and 1990s revivalist dress in varied styles was available commercially, replacing earlier anticonsumerism with the new Islamic lifestyle consumption habits of an emergent Islamist bourgeoisie (Kılıçbay and Binark 2002).

Studying women in the mosque movement in Cairo in the 1990s, Saba Mahmood (2005) found that for many the initial and repeated experience of dressing in hijab was fundamental to the construction of the pious self. Extending Mauss, Mahmood argues that the subject is not faithful a priori to donning the clothing, which might then merely clad the physical self, but that the pious disposition is cultivated and exercised through the act of wearing, being seen in, and comporting appropriately the veiled body. Like prayer, veiling "is both a *means* to pious conduct and an *end*" (Mahmood 2005: 136). While it is hard, as I discuss in chapter 4, for proponents and opponents of hijab to accommodate the idea of agency through submission into the neoliberal discourses of choice that predominate hijabi discourse, the revivalist emphasis on body management in the achievement of a moral disposition does offer broader points of contact for Muslims raised within an embodied faith-based habitus.

For Muslims, Mahmood and Talal Asad suggest, morality is not conceptualized as exterior to the body (a rational quality of mind that can be imposed on bodily behaviors) but as embedded in physical expression. Discussing the religiously distinct underpinnings of modern secularity, Asad adds to theories of embodiment, "that human actions and experience are sited in a material body," the concept of ensoulment, "the idea that the living body is an integrated totality having developable capacities for activity and experience unique to it, the capacities for sensing, imagining, and doing that are culturally mediating" (Asad 2003: 89). Differences between societies based on different religious and cultural antecedents matter, as do differences within any given faith-based social structure, including those invisible to outsiders.

The biggest change since the 1990s in practices of covered dressing is that today women are most often achieving hijab through an overt engagement with consumer culture and the fashion industry. As designers, bloggers, and as discerning consumers, young Muslims in WENA and in many Muslim majority countries are cocreating fashion-literate forms of visibly Muslim embodiment whose presence in the spaces of secular modernity challenges both majoritarian presumptions and community norms. New taste communities based on modest fashion are emerging. Forms of generational and social distinctions (Bourdieu 1984) are being forged for those with the cultural capital to engage in new modes of interaction with mainstream fashion cultures and religious practice. It is no longer sufficient to talk about the new veiling in the singular, so myriad are the range of styles created by young hijabis. There are more permutations of veiling fashion, and they are changing faster in a cycle of change whose pace matches globalized "fast" fashion, producing microdistinctions within as well as between generations of young women.

In Britain veil wearing serves to differentiate many of its young exponents from parental culture and from non-Muslims in the majority British and minority ethnic populations. This, Werbner argues (2004) has been especially significant for South Asians (the largest component of the British Muslim population), whose development of their own forms of veiling (or, for men, beards) allows young Muslims to assert and validate their values in relation to new forms of transnational Islam over the biraderi- or clan-dominated religious cultures of their parents. Seeking alternative religious scholarship, and engaging in firsthand study of the holy texts, has been especially important for young women in Britain in the 2000s (as for earlier generations of revivalist women in the Middle East), who are able to counter parental or community expectations about appropriate female behavior with scriptural arguments.

In France similarly in the 2000s, as Göle points out, young hijabis who unlike their immigrant mothers have mastery of the French language "enjoy a double cultural capital, to paraphrase Bourdieu, at once religious and also secular and scientific" (Göle 2011: 136). If, for previous generations of Muslim women access to modernity was often framed through processes of deveiling (in response to the stigmatization of veiling as primitive by the modernizing elites of the Middle East) then, for Göle, contemporary hijabis can be regarded as engaged in processes of reveiling in which "they seek to re-adopt the stigma and turn it into a sign of prestige" (Göle 2011: 14; see also Sandıkçı and Ger 2010). Whereas their mothers, wearing the marginal "traditional" dress of economically and socially marginal migrant subjects in the spaces of the ethnic enclave could remain invisible, young women in headscarves in France (as in Turkey) bring innovative forms of Muslim dress into mainstream spaces, making a temporal, spatial, and stylistic incursion into Westernized secular modernity. This "self-conscious intrusion of hybrid subjects" (Göle 2011: 24), which posits as coeval the Muslim and non-Muslim world, is achieved by new style cultures of Islamic dress created aesthetically through selective participation in mainstream fashion. This de-ethnicized Islam is validated intellectually and spiritually through personal interaction with scriptural sources, a process facilitated and transmitted by the media forms and commodities of global consumer culture.

Creating and Regulating Consumers: Gender, Faith, and Place

In the West, in white settler colonies, and in the modernizing cities of the Middle East, the development from the second half of the nineteenth century of the department store as a space for respectable female luxury expenditure (Benson 1988; Lancaster 2000; Nava 2007; Reekie 1993; Wilson [1985] 2003) fostered the blossoming of consumption as a facet of female subjectivity. The creation of women as gender distinctive and morally judged consumers (Slater 1997) and especially as consumers of fashion has long been regarded as a central element of Western modernity. The more recent incorporation into world fashion history (Riello and McNeil 2010) of the gendered development of consumer cultures in the Middle East and other locations outside the "Euromodern" provides a chance to emphasize the imbrication of religion in the development of diverse consumer cultures as in related moral debates and forms of social regulation (Barton 1989).

From the 1850s the development of the department store (in Britain and North America the same companies that dress and employ the young women featured in this book) as a space for respectable female labor and female consumption went hand in hand with the commercialization of Christian religious culture. American manufacturers and retailers operationalized Christian festivals for product development and marketing, from Easter bonnets to Christmas fairs, within the spectacle of secular visual merchandising and advertising (Leach 1980, 1989). With the commercialization of religion centered on fashion commodities, Domosh (1996) argues that consumption itself became a form of middle-class women's religious duty, melding their responsibility for household piety with their obligation to parade conspicuous consumption in the establishment of family social standing. Developments in consumer culture were rolled out to rural and less affluent populations through mail order, with catalogues more than mere "mediums of accumulation": serving as etiquette manuals on how to use the commodities, like the educational and political hyperlinks of the hijab webstores that I discuss in chapter 7, they "engendered a range of cultural behavior beyond [their] material manifestation" (Schlereth 1990: x; Wrigley and Lowe 2002).

The different play of religion in specific commercial cultures can be seen in the history of Walmart in America and Selfridges in Britain, both of which have a role in this book. Selfridges appears in chapter 4 as the location for Maleeha's transition into hijab while employed in shop work, and Walmart in chapter 7 as the parent company of British supermarket Asda (Fernie and Arnold 2002), which, with its "Asian" fashion range in 2009, was the first British apparel retailer to target Muslim and ethnic consumers. From its start in the rural American South in the 1960s, Walmart had drawn on white Southern Christian cultures to modify a previous habitus of frugal home-based production into a culture of commercial consumption. Marketed as an alternative to the prevailing consumer culture of the department and chain store, coded as Northern, Jewish, wasteful, luxury, Walmart legitimated nonluxury shopping as prudent Christian housekeeping and family improvement (Moreton 2009).[9] In contrast, in Britain in the nineteenth century, American entrepreneur Gordon Selfridge was resolutely cosmopolitan, advertising in the suffrage and Jewish media, and deploying an exoticized version of Orientalist foreignness in his creation of the London store as an immersive spectacle in which women of all classes were invited to participate (Nava 2007). For both companies, this participation rested on the relationship between women shop assistants and customers. Encouraged by retailers to forge bonds between customer and store (Benson 1988), women shop assistants were inculcated into a retail ideology based on the (heterosexual) seduction of female consumers, requiring training in appropriate behavior and self-presentation (Reekie 1993) that predated the commodification of staff personas in the lifestyle retail revolution of the 1980s discussed in chapter 5.

Shopping for the nonessential, and for clothing especially, was also significant for the constitution and performance of modern femininities in the Middle East (Lewis and Mickelwright 2006), though here, as in other non-Western modernities, consumer practices were often overtly politicized. In the nineteenth century, for modernizing rulers like Mohamad Ali in Egypt (reigned 1805–49) and successive Ottoman sultans who sought to harness the advantages of modern Western technologies (from railways to cameras), the social behaviors that accompanied Western commodities were not necessarily to be emulated. As with non-Western modernization processes elsewhere, the indigenization of Western technologies and goods was a process of selective adaptation rather than straightforward adoption (Frierson 2000) with Ottoman-style leaders adapting Western imports to suit local social mores (Göçek 1999).

Local fashion circuits evolved as part of indigenized consumer cultures (Durakbaşa and Cindoğlu 2002) in contexts unlikely to regard dress as outside of politics, especially in the Ottoman Empire, where sumptuary legislation continued long after it had fallen out of favor in Europe (O'Neil 2010). Dress reform was often concerned with men, such as the imposition by sultan Mahmud II in 1829 of the fez, which replaced the previously required distinctive headgear allocated to each religious community. The wide-ranging social reforms of the Tanzimat era (1839–76) further extended Western practices in the male domains of military and formal education, diffusing into women's lives as the century progressed. The arena where most people encountered Western goods was in the home, and most of this selective cross-cultural consumption was directed by women. Women of the Egyptian and Ottoman royal families and the progressive elites who surrounded them had access to Paris fashions from the mid-nineteenth century, ordering direct from Paris and commissioning copies from local seamstresses who visited the harems. Fashion designs were seen in the imported European press and the Ottoman and Egyptian women's press (Baron 1994; Frierson 2000). Apart from complete toilettes of the latest French styles, women altered conventional Ottoman garments to include elements of Western styling. But as these modifications were to indoor clothing rather than outerwear, curious Western observers did not see them, and if they did, were rarely equipped to understand their significance (Micklewright 2000). Western clothing and goods that were seen were most often bewailed by Westerners as a sad absence of picturesque local "costume" (Lewis and Micklewright 2006) in a version of "imperialist nostalgia" (Rosaldo 1993) that allowed Westerners to position themselves as the experts on and guardians of "real" Oriental dress and to sneer at the "vulgarity" of Ottoman cultural hybridity. By the turn of the twentieth century most sectors of the Ottoman urban population were regularly engaging with Western goods (Duben and Behar 1991). Relying on the social conventions of their veils, women from elite segregated households in Istanbul and Cairo and other major cities started to go out to shop in the bazaars of the old city quarters and, in Istanbul, to the shops of Pera (today's Beyoğlu), the international quarter.

Just as many young hijabis at the turn of the twenty-first century see their fashionable ensemble as a way to promote positive images of Islam in the West, so too were local wardrobe decisions understood to have international ramifications at the turn of the last century. Ottomans and Egyptians were well aware that the image of the veiled harem lady was seen by the West as an indicator of the state of civilization of their entire society and took pains to counter Orientalist stereotypes, often through attention to the dressed visibility of Muslim women. The temporal and spatial alterity that came increasingly to be projected onto those parts of the population not rendered modern extended generically to distant and minority imperial populations in a process of Ottoman Orientalism (Eldem 2007; Makdisi 2002) that reinforced for the modernizing elite a self-image as progressive modern sovereign subjects.

By the 1920s, in a version of modernity that was to become increasingly and aggressively secular, the new Turkish republic under Mustapha Kemal (Atatürk) promoted its modernity through the public presence of unveiled female bodies, specifically aiming to disassociate itself from the old-style image of the secluded *hanım* (lady). While secularity on the French model of laïcité was established as the basis of the republic, religion remained regulated by state authorities with Sunni Islam the default marker of social and institutional life. Initiating a program of top-down reforms, the Kemalist modernization project relied on the public performance of educated unveiled femininity as a route to national social emancipation through Westernizing secularization (Göle 1996). Building on Ottoman reforms, Kemalism aimed to export to the entire population the Westernized disposition of the late-Ottoman elite, using "clothing as a constitutive element in its establishment" of the secular republic (O'Neil 2010: 67).

In 1925 the Hat Law required all government officials to wear a hat with a brim, to be combined with Western lounge (business) suits and (for the then few women employees) skirts as an example to the nation designed to render obsolete the "Asian" salwar, baggy trousers, still prevalent among rural and nonelite dressers of both sexes (O'Neil 2010). Effectively banning the fez, the Hat Law impeded prayerful body management (hats with brims being unsuitable for the head-to-floor pose required in Muslim prayer). For women the shift from veiling to hats (as in the West, it was inconceivable that respectable men or women would go about in public with completely bare heads) was initially to be managed through propaganda and the inspiring example of young unveiled women teachers (Arat 1999b; Durakbaşa 1993). When social pressure proved insufficient, legislation banned the veil in 1928. Headscarves, tied loosely under the chin, referred to as *başörtüsü* continued to be worn with relative impunity by older women and by the rural poor in regions of Anatolia, regarded as antiquated or habitual rather than as signs of committed religiosity. Even when mass rural migration in the 1950s and 1960s made başörtüsü visible in the modernizing city, while restricted to the shanty towns of the urban poor representing "the migrants' lower class status and rural origins" (Gökarıksel and Secor 2010b: 3), it could be tolerated. This changed when the headscarf became a symbol in visibly Islamist cultural politics and concomitantly a key commodity of Islamic consumer culture, as I discuss in chapter 2.

CHAPTER 2

THE COMMERCIALIZATION
OF ISLAMIC DRESS

Selling and Marketing Tesettür
in Turkey and Beyond

I f the "new" veiling of the global Islamic revival in the 1950s and 1970s
was often antifashion and homemade, by the 1980s a new industry was
developing in Turkey for the commercial production and distribution
of Islamic dress. Emerging at the same time and as part of the liberalization of the Turkish economy, what came to be known as the tesettür
industry was and is controversial in a Muslim majority context. The distinctive styles of tesettür on the bodies of young women in urban environments distinguished them from women in the looser headscarf,
başörtüsü, associated with rural immigrants (Secor 2002) or the chador
of the ultraconservatives (Tepe 2011), contravening the spatial divisions
of the secular state by bringing into public displays of religiosity that had
been relegated to the private and by framing as modern (through fash-

ion) modes of body management that had been coded as old-fashioned or rural. With covered women a continuing political flashpoint, the tesettür industry in Turkey has grown and diversified, creating and meeting the needs of a population of modest dressers whose increase from 62.5 percent of the population in 2006 to 72 percent in 2008 was fueled by a spectacular rise among eighteen-to-twenty-eight-year-olds that bucked the national trend of youngsters becoming less religious than their parents (Aslanbay, Sanaktekin, and Ağırdır 2011).

This chapter focuses on the retail operation and marketing strategies of three pioneering firms in the tesettür sector, Tekbir Giyim, Armine, and Aker. Providing a snapshot of distribution practices in the late 2000s and early 2010s, the chapter analyzes marketing and retail strategies on the cusp of digital take-up, at a point when regional geopolitics appeared to be opening newly Islamicized markets in southeastern Europe and Central Asia. This was a moment before the Islamist Justice and Development (AKP) government, in power since 2002, faced widespread (Islamist and secularist) demonstrations in the wake of the violent suppression of environmentalist protests in Istanbul's Gezi Park in 2012, and subsequently lost its majority in 2015.

These long-standing companies play a significant role in the Turkish and international visualization of modest Muslim style through products that dress loyal and new consumers (including, at this point, high-profile members of the AKP political elite) and through the transnational reach of the tesettür industry's distinctive marketing. Unlike the other designers in this book whose e-commerce model relies on the Internet, in Turkey tesettür is historically purchased offline and relies for promotion on the glossy print catalogue, whose production and visuals (also including apparel company Kayra) I discuss here. For all these companies, the desire to be recognized as global brands while formally and informally regulated by the Turkish state's defended secularity unavoidably politicizes their products, their marketing materials, and their shop staff.[1]

Fashion and Politics: The Rise of the Islamic Bourgeoisie and the Development of Turkey's Tesettür Industry

The core constituency of the Islamic revivalist movement in Turkey in the 1980s and 1990s, as in other parts of the Muslim Middle East, were young newly urbanized rural migrants. These were augmented by a youthful population of already urban young lower-middle- and middle-class women (often college and university students) from families without a tradition of head covering (Secor 2005). For many young Islamist women then and now, that this sartorial choice marks them out as different from their mothers is precisely the point: like other forms of revivalist dress, their new form of veiling seeks to present itself as a doctrinal choice based on personal knowledge of the holy texts.

Producing new urban forms of Islamic dress, the tesettür wearer sported a distinctive combination of a long-sleeved and long, often ankle-length, raincoat (*pardesü*) with a large square scarf pinned close under the chin and cascading down to cover the hair, neck, and shoulders in their entirety, unlike the loosely tied başörtüsü (worn with mid-calf coats and stockings). The new head coverings were called *türban* by the Turkish press; that, for Göle, by referencing pious male headwear, acknowledged the women's "'power' [and] indicated their 'virilization' by religious politics" (2011: 95). Early styles of tesettür were international in their referents and inference, using, as Göle elaborates, the contemporaneous Western aesthetic of 1980s power dressing to produce a "muscular and tri-angular [silhouette], with accentuated shoulders," which, by contrasting with "the oriental silhouette of fluid femininity in the form of a 'bell' (as in the case of women wearing the chador)" disassociated Turkish Islamists from their counterparts in Iran. The new look was further distinguished from the chador by the satin or satin-like square scarves, *echarpe*, often in bright colors and patterns, that were to become the mainstay of the newly commercialized tesettür industry

The development of the commercial tesettür industry in Turkey is linked to the growing power of Islamic political parties and the concomitant rise of Islamic, or green, capital. Unlike the secularist business elite of Istanbul who, linked to the Kemalist Republican People's Party leadership, had previously dominated the Turkish economy, the new entrepreneurs of the green economy were an independent business elite. Based in the south and southwest of the country, the so-called Anatolian Lions (as they named one of their trade associations) were embedded in conservative communities that had remained religious and regional, culturally and politically distinct from the great families of Turkish business (Demir, Acar, and Toprak 2004). The green economy was aided by remittances from the Turkish diaspora, especially Germany, where the Sufi religious associations or tariqats were resignifying business as compatible with Islam. This was important in the Turkish context because in the Ottoman Empire trade had been a largely minority population enterprise, the province of the Jewish, Greek, and Armenian communities, with Muslims adhering to a cultural (if not necessarily devout) religious avoidance of interest-accumulating operations. The homogenization of the population that marked the last years of the Ottoman Empire and the formation of the Turkish nation-state (with the separation of European and Arab territories, population exchanges with Greece, and the decimation of the Armenians) meant that the newly constituted republic commenced with a deficit of business know-how (Demir, Acar, and Toprak 2004), compounded by Turkist policies seizing minority assets (White 2013). The Nationalists under Kemal instituted a state-controlled economy focusing on production for export, rather than internal consumption, which remained in place after the arrival of multiparty politics in 1950 until the liberalization of the economy in the 1980s in the wake of the 1980 military coup.

Prior to this, the impact of the 1928 ban on veiling had been variable and fluctuating. Many young women quietly bypassed the ban at school and university until the coup rendered women's head covering newly politicized. Altering conventional Kemalist approaches to Islam (Gökarıksel and Mitchell 2005), the military promoted Islam "as a socially cohesive force" to counter the perceived communist threat (G. Jenkins 2012), retaining Turgut Özal to run the economy. By 1983 Özal was prime minister with the moderately Islamic Motherland Party (ANAP) and oversaw the liberalization of the economy, replacing import substitution protectionist policies with export-focused reforms. This vastly increased the availability of foreign goods, introducing consumer culture to the average Turk for the first time. The opening of the economy under Özal was combined with increased openings for religious involvement in education and social and economic life: indeed, in "the context of Turkey, the rise and development of 'Islamic capitalism' has been directly associated with neoliberalism processes of the past two decades" (Gökarıksel and Secor 2009: 11). Opportunities for religious expression were accompanied by the means for monetizing and containing it (Gökarıksel and Mitchell 2005). In response to the increased visibility of young veiled women, bans on headscarves in schools and colleges were enforced with unprecedented stringency (causing many to withdraw from education) and while religious education became part of the school curriculum it was subject to state regulation. With the fluctuating fortunes of other Islamic political parties, the regulation of veiling in education and employment continued to be highly political and variable. This came to a head in 1999 when Merve Kavakçi was elected as an MP for the Islamist Virtue Party (FP) but was prevented because of her headscarf from taking her oath in the National Assembly (Göçek 1999). Described by her America-based sister, blogger Elif Kavakçi (see chapter 3) as the "Rosa Parks of Turkey,"[2] the politician eventually returned to America (Shively 2005). In contrast to much popular opinion in Britain that (certainly in the 1980s and 1990s) regarded French response to schoolgirls in veils as a massive overreaction (see also Werbner 2007), secularists in Turkey took comfort in French bans on Islamic dress.

The Kavakçi affair allowed the Constitutional Court to close the Virtue Party for undermining the secularity of the republic, and from the split that followed emerged the ostensibly moderate Islamist AKP led by Tayyip Erdoğan, previously mayor of Istanbul and like Özal a member of the Naqshbandi order. Whereas earlier Islamists like the Welfare Party were left leaning, the probusiness AKP presented themselves as center Right conservatives rather than as Islamists. Mobilizing a discourse of human rights to argue for religious freedom of expression, the AKP initially demonstrated some commitment to religious and ethnic diversity (lifting the ban on Kurdish language education in 2004), though their contradictory and selective stance on human rights rarely (even in the early years) convinced their opponents of their sincerity.

The AKP was repeatedly foiled in its attempts to revoke the headscarf ban. Secular and state insistence that public spaces like schools and universities be unmarked by faith won out in 2004 when Leyla Şahin (with shifting support from the AKP) lost her case at the European Court of Human Rights. The ECHR ruled that Sahin did not have a human right to wear her "Islamic" headscarf, presenting the court as protecting observant Muslim women from Muslim patriarchies and as protecting unveiled Turkish Muslim women from threats to their secularism (Gökarıksel and Mitchell 2005). The AKP's constitutional amendment to permit headscarves at university in 2008 was annulled after opposition from the secular national higher education authority. They eventually managed to repeal the ban in summer 2012.

During the AKP government Turkish attitudes to the EU accession process shifted, partly because the world economic recession made the EU a less attractive financial proposition and because of ongoing frustration at EU prevarication. Instead, the end of the Cold War and the ensuing War on Terror provided opportunities for the AKP to develop Turkey's profile as a regional leader. The decision in 2003 to refuse permission for American troops to launch attacks on Iraq from Turkish bases gained kudos for Turkey among the other Arab nations (important given the historical hostility between the Arab states and those that were seen as the heirs of their erstwhile Ottoman colonizers), without relinquishing U.S. and NATO alliances. Criticism of Israel became more prominent, with Turkey's participation in the 2010 peace flotilla to Gaza further raising Turkish credibility with Arab nations and with those committed to the politicized umma of transnational Islam. Seeking prominence as a negotiator between factions during the Arab Spring in 2011, taking a lead in organizing criticism of the Assad regime in Syria from 2011 (though facing criticism for a reluctance to act against the Islamic State of Iraq and Syria [ISIS] by mid-2014), the AKP sought to position Turkey as a regional superpower able to parlay its moderate Islamism into a mode of communication with even Iran, the font of demonized Islam to Western conservatives. In this the pious elite, Jenny White argues, have a different concept of the nation from the Kemalist elite, imagining "Turkey not as a nation embattled within its present political borders but as a flexibly bounded Turkey that is the self-confident successor to the Ottomans in a rediscovered (and reinvented) past" (2013: 9). Characterized by the nationalist Turkism that it shares with secularists, Islamism in Turkey demonstrates little affinity with Arab-inflected versions of the umma. Despite Kemalist fears of Saudi (Köni 2012) or Iranian influence, the Turkish Islamists prefer to imagine and reconstitute pan-Islamic affiliations on post-Ottoman lines focusing "less on a shared global umma" (White 2013: 48) and more on regional neo-Ottomanist leadership (G. Jenkins 2012). The AKP's potential PR advances looked set to be lost in June 2013 when Erdoğan's excessive attempts to suppress democratic opposition at home saw running battles in the streets. If by the early 2010s some commentators had already begun to predict that Gülen support for the AKP was waning,[3] by summer 2013 Gülen seemed to be shifting away from Erdoğan toward the less abrasive Abdullah Gül, with a public breach opening in winter 2014, and rumors that other tariqats were gaining ascendancy in the political arena.[4]

The end of the Cold War has opened access to the developing economies of the newly independent Central Asian republics, important to the Turkish economy not only as proximate new markets but also significant historically through previous Ottoman trade patterns and sentimentally as regions with significant Muslim populations now free from Soviet suppression. The Balkan states of the former Yugoslavia are similarly important. To avoid pretensions of empire building, the AKP (who do not all embrace the term) have fostered a form of neo-Ottomanism often manifested through a widespread nostalgia (developing since the 1980s [Eldem

2007]), available to be shared with secularists, for "a 'golden age' of communal solidarity and cosmopolitan civility in which moral values co-exist with affluence" (White 2013: 12). The desire to provide commodities for Muslim observance to coreligionists in the Balkans and Central Asia (and Iran) was cited by more than one of the tesettür companies I interviewed, linking sound business sense with religious solidarity on a patriotically neo-Ottomanist transnational scale.

This combination of justifications is typical of the Islamic business sector in Turkey. Historically, the Turkish business attitude has not privileged the accumulation of capital for its own sake, presenting business success in the guise of a service to the national economy with an attendant emphasis on public endowments that reformulates for the republic the Muslim and Ottoman basis of charitable works. The religious bourgeoisie convert this into two legitimacy bases, using "religious arguments to address their social support base" and "nationalist arguments when dealing with the government and secular elite" (Ömer, Acar, and Toprak 2004: 175).

The Turkish tesettür industry has contributed significantly to the textile and apparel sectors essential to the development of Turkey's boom economy. Initially focused on textile production and then apparel assembly for foreign companies, the division saw significant success until threatened by the global recession of 2007 and the increasing prominence of Chinese manufacture (see Gökarıksel and Secor 2010a). The Turkish industry has since the 1990s moved into its own brand design for domestic and export markets. Like other emerging markets (China or India) Turkey's success in creating foreign markets for its own brand products remains challenging and uneven (Mavi jeans name-checked in the Western fashion media, an Ipekyol store in London's Westfield shopping center). Istanbul is now developing itself as a fashion city with a critical mass of consumers and fashion operatives: by the late 1990s, 25 percent of Turkey's retail trade was estimated to be located in the greater Istanbul area, with other urban areas also developing as concentrated zones for post-1980s consumer culture (Durakbaşa and Cindoğlu 2002). While the ability to participate in consumer culture was and remains dependent on class and income, the growing urbanization of the Turkish population means that vast numbers are becoming newly imbricated in the practices of modern Western global retail.

Companies manufacturing garments for the tesettür sector are also heavily involved in export, with many having their headquarters and showrooms (and sometimes factory) in Istanbul (Gökarıksel and Secor

2010b). Developed and expanded post-Özal to be promoted as a regional hub for global capital, the erstwhile capital of the Ottoman Empire is also the Islamists' symbolic location of choice (Robins and Aksoy 1995; Stokes 2000), with Ankara seen as the power base of the secular political and business elite. While few companies manufacture exclusively for the tesettür market, those significantly involved in tesettür (mostly small- and medium-sized businesses) numbered 174 in 2009; of these, "over 80 per cent have half or more of their production in veiling-fashion, with half of the firms reporting that veiling-fashion comprises 90 per cent or more of their production" with 40 percent (twice the national average) manufacturing for export (Gökarıksel and Secor 2010b: 5–6). The success of tesettür manufacturers in the export market underlines the importance of Turkey in the commercialization of Islamic dress that is now almost routinely experienced through participation in an Islamic consumptionscape of global dimensions, in contrast to the anticonsumerism and homespun aesthetic of previous generations.

By the late 1990s tesettür had diversified in styles and increased in availability with a veritable explosion (Gökarıksel and Secor 2010a) of new companies opening between 1996 and 2008. The initial uniform of loose long raincoat and scarf spawned new variations that allowed for the expression of nuanced distinctions of class, age, and occupation. Early styles, and the *tesettür giyim*, or "pious," companies that manufactured them, were by the mid-2000s coming to be disdained as grandmotherly by younger adherents who, as in Britain and North America, crafted their ensembles from a mix of specialist and mainstream offerings. Raincoats became less plain in shape and color, with shorter versions to the knee sported over skinny jeans (that remained popular through the 2000s), while longer coats appeared in more form-fitting shapes and embellished with details that echoed the seasonal trends (frogging in line with the trend for military style overcoats in 2011, and so on). Coats of all styles were increasingly seen in brighter colors, available in a wider range of fabric qualities with an accordingly wider variation in price points. Scarves became smaller and tied more tightly, often tucked into the collar to produce a streamlined shape suitable for waged work outside the home, part of a shift into a "soft tesettür" (Sandıkçı and Ger 2010) more easily accommodated into the activities and spaces of secular life. With headscarf bans in municipal employment or education still in place, women wearing the softer tesettür presented a less confrontationally "Islamist" appearance, reporting that a more "modern" fashionable look incited less hostility than the long raincoat with its associations of unfashionable backwardness (Sandıkçı and Ger 2010).

Impression management is not confined to the secular viewer: as the tesettür market diversified and segmented it facilitated and made legible forms of distinction between covered women. If in the 1980s the early forms of tesettür were adopted by Islamists "to differentiate themselves from the secularists, [by the late 1990s] the initially homogenous Islamic identity appears to have fragmented, as various segments of Islamists attempt to differentiate themselves from each other" with the increasingly diverse Islamic consumptionscape making it possible for "Islamic moderns" to distinguish themselves from "the secularist moderns, the Islamist newly rich and the habitually religious lower classes," creating not one but a range of Islamic habituses (Sandıkçı and Ger 2002: 470). Jenny White (2002) also points out the contradiction for early cadres of Islamists whose promotion of Islam as inherently democratic and community-minded made wealth-based distinction more problematic. The valorization of tesettür as a signifier of elite status for Islamist women was, she suggests, under threat of erasure from women adopting tesettür style for social advancement rather than from religious conviction.

Introducing the Brands

One of the first and most prominent tesettür companies, Tekbir Giyim ("God is great"), began, tells CEO Mustafa Karaduman, because "there was a hole in the market. In 1982 when we started there were no tesettür shops."[5] Tesettür was being produced, he clarifies, "in private shops and private places," a reference to the religious associations characteristic of nonelite religious life and central to Turkish Islamist politics. Tekbir's mix of commercial manufacture and marketing moved tesettür beyond the purview of the tariqats to mainstream it as fashion within the broader religious community (Sandıkçı and Ger 2007). With management initially above their first store in Fatih, a conservative religious district on the European side of Istanbul, Tekbir now has ninety shops, including three in Fatih, and has moved its executive offices on-site with their showroom and factory in the Mahmutbey manufacturing district on the outskirts of the city. Across Turkey there are fifty franchises, and three hundred international franchise arrangements, with Germany its biggest market as for other tesettür firms (Gökarıksel and Secor 2013), followed by the Netherlands, Belgium, and Bosnia.

Tekbir started with a core of customers in their twenties, and while many have grown up with the company, the company was in 2009 reporting an increase in teenage consumers, possibly linked to the 2008 collection by German designer Heidi Beck (with whom one of Mustafa's daughters had interned during her British fashion design degree at Nottingham University). Tekbir offers clothes at price points for the varied customer base (identified as 45–50 percent middle income, 30 percent elite, 20 percent from lower socioeconomic classes). Emphasizing quality and price, Mustafa Karaduman points out that 40 percent of customers do not cover but buy the clothes because they are good value and a recognized brand, "so instead of buying one blouse from [high-end shopping district] Nişantaşı, they are probably buying three blouses from Tekbir, which is also an international brand name." Unlike the slower development of branding practices in Iran (Bălăşescu 2005), being identified as an international brand was important to all the tesettür companies I spoke to, aware that they compete with the global brands that have suffused the Turkish market since the 1980s.

Armine, established in 1982, the same year as Tekbir and therefore also part of the Özal-era liberalization of the economy, began as a wholesale export manufacturing operation, moving into the Turkish market in 2003, when it diversified into garment design and manufacture. A family firm, like Tebkir, the company is run by three brothers and a sister.[6] Director Mehmet Dursun trained initially in law and began his textile business by manufacturing scarves and selling direct to retailers. Brother Şevket Dursun is head of design, while another brother and their sister oversee scarf and garment design at their Bursa factory. Scarf designs are sometimes purchased from Italy but increasingly are produced in-house, often eighty designs for each six-month season. Product goes wholesale to Europe, finding its largest market among the Turkish migrant population in Germany, followed by Holland, then France, plus the UK, the United States, and Malaysia. In the Middle East they sell especially in Lebanon and in some Arab countries, for which they manufacture a different range. The Turkish tesettür scarf has conventionally been the large square of 90 × 90 cm, with Arabs favoring the rectangular *shayla* (usually 120 × 140 cm). For this market Armine (like other brands) manufactures to different dimensions in different materials (thinner silk for hotter climates), using "Arabian designs" of repeat pattern arabesques in abstract rather than figurative motifs. With twenty-four stores plus franchises, Armine scarves (all silk with hand-rolled edges) are at the higher end of the Turkish market, retailing in 2010 at eighty-one Turkish lira. Tekbir in contrast also offers a less expensive range with machine hemmed edges.

Armine and Tekbir are differentiated not only in price but also by the differences in their ideological approach to commercial tesettür. At Tekbir, as Gökarıksel and Secor (2010b) point out, the company sees itself as having an educative role to guide customers in the correct form of covering, producing only garments that fit its interpretation of suitable length and shape and making sure that all in-store visual merchandising accords with appropriate bodily display, whether on mannequins or staff (as discussed below). In contrast, at Armine, the range of garments lends itself to multiple versions of tesettür or non-tesettür dressing (shorter jackets and dresses, garments in "un-Islamic" colors like red, subsequently seen also at Tekbir), meaning that the attribution of Islamic values to the garments is up to the style and religious preferences of the customer: "in this way, Armine defers the question of the Islamnicness of its products to the moment of their use" (Gökarıksel and Secor 2010b: 15).

Unlike Tekbir with its Istanbul headquarters in an industrial zone, or Armine based in Sultanahmet near the grand bazaar, Aker has its showroom in Osmanbey, traditionally Istanbul's garment district. With twelve shops in Istanbul (of which the branch in Fatih is the busiest), the Aker showroom is located here to market coordinating scarves to the apparel buyers choosing their seasonal collections. The Aker showroom is currently the only scarf shop and showroom in the district; sales executive Türker Nart suspects that other brands (he hears rumors of Vakko) will likely follow to reach international clients making their twice yearly visits. (Several showrooms already have signage in Cyrillic.)[7] Like the other brands, Aker manufactures mainly the square 90 cm silk scarf, with some larger 120 cm squares for the Arab market, producing standard sizes in lighter fabrics for Iran and Syria. As well as its own Aker range the company has a house line of less expensive scarves under the Arancia label. Since 2008 Aker has held the regional (Turkey and Middle East) license to produce and distribute for Cacharel and Pierre Cardin, moving from manufacture to design after convincing the global brands that they could produce designs more suited to local taste. These two brands they oversee in the region but cannot sell in Europe, though their Aker and Arancia lines sell to Turkish customers in Germany, the Netherlands, and France, via their website. They produce on average 130 designs, each in four colorways, twice a year across the four brands: Cacharel remains their highest price point at sixty-five euros, with Cardin following at fifty, Aker at forty-two, and Arancia at thirty euros. Designing for customers of all ages, they also include a youth range, *onyedi serisi* or "seventeen."

It is not uncommon in discussions with tesettür brands in Turkey to find a global perspective informed by regional and Islamist politics, correlating the significance of modest fashion as a practice of visibility and an economic force to the AKP's changing regional and global priorities. Early foreign markets in European territories with significant Turkish migrant populations are augmented with attention to territories in the Middle East and Central Asia. Looking at the list of stores on Tekbir's promotional material I commented to Mustafa Karaduman in 2009 that retailers did not usually open shops in war zones such as Dagestan, to be told that where Chechnyan soldiers fight the stores will follow, as had been the case postconflict in the Balkans: "Before the war in Bosnia Muslims did not have tesettür. Now after the war ended, it has increased. . . . Bosnian people embrace Muslim values, Islamic values, and now they are asking for dresses and fashions that fit their understanding of this." New retail opportunities are depicted as a moral obligation to support the nascent Islamic consciousness developing in the former Yugoslavia, understood as the result of genocide: "Previously Bosnian women, Muslim women, would marry Serbian men in interethnic marriages. Bosnian women who were married to Serbians were murdered by Serbian families but nothing happened to Serbian women who married Bosnian men, [and so] marriage practices have changed."

The brutal dismantling of a previously secularized multicultural habitus marked Bosnian Muslims as Muslim, creating new minority identities (Appadurai 1996) that brought them into the purview of Muslims in the West and in the Middle East. As the special edition of *Emel* magazine "Remember Bosnia 20 Years On" in 2012 made clear, the shock of learning that "people in Europe who were native to their land were being murdered for being Muslims" was a wake-up call for many young British Muslims as elsewhere in WENA.[8] For successful businessman Naved Siddiqi, "like all Thatcher's children, . . . armed with credit cards," it was a shock to compare his reality with events taking place just hours away: "I was a European Muslim, so were my Bosnian countrymen; I was integrated, they were more so; I was systematically building my life, theirs were being systematically destroyed." For young Muslims in the West Bosnia brought into being a new sense of solidarity within the umma; many engaged in fundraising, a few volunteered as combatants. In some quarters the atrocities were received as evidence that Muslims could never find safety in secularized assimilationist identities. From around the world religious preachers and commodities moved in to educate Bosnian Muslims in Islamic observance.[9]

The willingness of tesettür firms to market in Central Asia and the Balkans reclaims the Muslim history of the region as part of a selective recuperation of the Ottoman past, reconnecting with previous European territories whose exit from the empire deprived the Ottoman state of the bulk of its non-Muslim population and signaled the fault lines in the multicultural ideal of Ottoman inclusivism. In seeking to nurture the Islamic identity of the contemporary Balkan Muslim population, the tesettür firms are involved in a reorganization of cultural memory that by reinstating the long history of Muslim residence within Europe simultaneously invokes the presence of non-Muslims within the Ottoman population, for these were the domains in which under Ottoman rule Muslims were historically the minority. At Armine, the geopolitical significance of the umma is not restricted to markets but finds its way through design into merchandise with a scarf featuring the iconic Mostar bridge. Standing as a painful symbol of the genocide against Bosnian Muslims, the destroyed bridge, now a UNESCO world heritage site, was eventually reopened in 2004 with the support of international funders that included the Turkish AKP government. To celebrate the restoration of this architectural gem with a scarf does more than provide a souvenir of the wonders of world architecture. It serves, in the Turkish Islamic context, to memorialize the attack on a European Muslim population and to celebrate the reinscription through masonry of the long-standing existence of a multiethnic multifaith sociality within Europe. In Europe the dismantling of the bridge is little commemorated, highlighting for Göle (2011) the ongoing alterity of Muslims as the other of Europe: while the fall of the Berlin wall facilitated the incorporation of former Communist states into the EU, the tragedy of the bridge and the destruction of a European Muslim population did not bring an equivalent willingness to reconceptualize the boundaries and characteristics of Europe.

As my colleague and translator Leylâ Pervizat pointed out when reviewing the Armine catalogue, the Mostar scarf was one among a range of topographical designs that, including scenes of Paris and Istanbul but not Aleppo or Damascus, focused on European connections rather than the Arab territories of the Ottoman Empire. This was before the Arab Spring and the opportunities this provided for AKP prime minister Recep Tayyip Erdoğan to build positive relations with Arab neighbors while promoting the image of a moderate Islamist government as a protector of democracy. In the same way as young Muslims in WENA now routinely care about Palestine or Chechnya rather than only the countries of their family origin, so too the AKP government builds on an affective sense of the Muslim transnational as part of national politics, repositioning Turkey as facing to the Muslim world rather than her erstwhile Western allies. The scarves of Istanbul are not just about touristic mobility; they also represent the Ottoman capital and the home of the last caliphate.

If the destruction of a secular Balkan lifestyle formed newly Muslim consumers in Bosnia and the fall of the Soviet Union foregrounded religiosity in Central Asian successor states to Turkey's north, the Iranian Islamic state to the east presents other opportunities. Reporting that "Iranian women are saying that they don't want to cover their heads because there is nothing fashionable," Mustafa Karaduman responded to an invitation from the governor of Tehran to "present fashionable clothing so these women will choose to cover their heads," winning awards in Iranian fashion shows in 2007 and 2008. The advent of fashion shows in Iran in 2001 also saw affluent women in Tehran making a "strong political statement" through their use of global fashion commodities, wearing designer headscarves with logos displayed to announce class distinction and signal choice in forms of covering (Bălăşescu 2003: 50) within state-imposed veiling regimes (Secor 2002). By the end of the decade, with local government encouragement, Tekbir was planning to open shops in Iran, "starting with Tehran" to test demand.

Armine also sells into Central Asia, with strong markets in Kazahkstan, Turkmenistan, and Azerbaijan, helped by advertising on television channels like the Gülen-linked Samanyolu. Similarly Ankara-based company Kayra, active since 1982 and producing garments since 1992, has stores in Palestine, Iraq, Saudi Arabia, and Syria, as well as Abu Dhabi, Qatar, and Kuwait, exporting to Denmark, France, Germany, Israel, and Australia.[10]

Marketing Tesettür: The Role of the Catalogues

One of the biggest changes on the global fashion scene since the mid-1980s has been the increasing diversity and prevalence of fashion mediation, so that consumers' encounters with garments are increasingly mediated by professionals (Wilson [1985] 2003). Born in this period commercial tesettür too has developed professionalized fashion mediation techniques, from catwalk shows to point-of-sale materials. This requires the existing professional expertise of secular aesthetic service providers (fashion models, graphic designers, stylists, and photographers) and creates opportunities for Islamist participants (often women) to develop professional-level skills in fashion mediation. Although this is true also of the modest fashion industry growing among faiths around the world (R. Lewis 2013b), the internal and external opportunities and constraints that affect fashion mediation for tesettür in Turkey impact on both the medium and aesthetics available for brand communication strategies. Externally, the still uneven penetration of Internet access couples with a nationally low take-up of Internet retail in apparel (especially among often lower income conservative groups [Aslanbay, Sanaktekin, and Ağırdır 2011]) to produce an emphasis on hard-copy marketing, with relatively underdeveloped websites (in contrast to the role of e-retail as a key enabler for the commercial development of modest fashion in the UK and North America [R. Lewis 2013c]).

While Mustafa Karaduman knows that customers use the Internet to follow international style trends, in 2009 it was not popularly a medium for shopping: "In Turkey we don't have an Internet culture of shopping. We want to see and touch and wear. The website is not for ordering, it's for promotion." Many tesettür websites are available only in Turkish, though other languages (often in rudimentary translation) are becoming incorporated: the Tekbir website offers options for Turkish and Arabic; Armine provides some web copy in English (presuming that customers in their developing Arab market can operate in English) as part of its mission to position the brand "among the trend setting companies [in] the world fashion centers."[11] While communication strategies prioritize other media platforms, websites will likely remain basic, but it is almost inevitable that they will become more sophisticated as the technology develops. By 2012 Tekbir's home page featured video of live catwalk action, Armine was extending catalogue poses into moving image, and Kayra was filming international shoots in South Africa in 2014 with a now complete English website option.[12] These instances of remediation and convergence (H. Jenkins 2008) are discussed in more detail in chapters 3 and 6 in relation to the development of Islamic lifestyle media and new modest designers and bloggers. Already in Turkey, evidence of developing Internet sales is seen on the Turkish-language Kayra website, where catalogue shots are the basis for product information and sales (in Turkish lira). Internally, the aesthetics of catalogue and marketing imagery are subject to rigorous evaluation within competing definitions of Islamically appropriate visual regimes.

FIGURE 2.1 CEO Mustafa Karaduman's office, press wall, Tekbir headquarters, Istanbul, 2009. Photo by Reina Lewis.

Externally, the presence of tesettür marketing is liable to be challenged as an assault on the republican secularity of the Turkish visual world.

The initiative by Tekbir in 1992 to hold a catwalk show was seen as nothing less than revolutionary, meriting heated responses from secularists who derided the clothing as failed fashion and from religionists who deplored the use of nonreligious models and the display of female bodies (Gökarıksel and Secor 2009; Sandıkçı and Ger 2007). This was matched by an Islamist anticommercialism that may have precipitated Tekbir's distancing from the anticapitalist Welfare Party in favor of the probusiness AKP (Tepe 2011). Tekbir has long sought media attention and the fashion show was (and is) especially press-worthy, with Mustafa Karaduman (who takes pride in showing his wall of framed cuttings; see figure 2.1), initially organizing the now annual catwalk himself before handing it over to fashion industry professionals. A vigorous public promoter of Islamic business, partly financing the company with Islamic banking, Mustafa Karaduman (prominent in Turkish Islamic business associations) is also notorious for his public defense of his polygamous marriage.

Armine is notoriously unwilling to talk to the press, who it is presumed will follow an aggressively secularist agenda, as seen in the hostile response to their 2007 billboard campaign (Gökarıksel and Secor 2009: 14). They also aver the catwalk as unsuitable bodily display for covered women. At Tekbir, though media presence is key to their vision to promoting the company as an international brand, they do not rely solely on billboards or advertising; Mustafa Karaduman turns the restricted opportunities for advertising into a positive, celebrating that in a recent (unnamed) survey on women's wear "even though we spent very little on advertisement, we came fourth" for brand recognition.

Brand recognition was being extended by the early 2010s: as tesettür companies began to post catalogue visuals on their websites they were re-mediated by bloggers as style tips (even if accompanied by complaints that import duties increase prices and restrict availability). While the Internet puts tesettür brands into the transnational digital modesty frame, in Turkey at the time of writing, the catalogue, not the website, remains the essential marketing tool for tesettür. As has long been the case for Tekbir, in Turkey and abroad women select from the catalogue for telephone orders or store purchase. Shop staff report that customers, not regular readers of fashion magazines, use the catalogue as a style guide, arriving in store with a copy. Younger customers also use the catalogue to find on-trend looks (florals in 2008, animal prints in 2011). The same applies at Armine, with the directorial team able to predict the most emulated scarf and garment ensembles (see, for instance, figure 2.2, which shows the black-and-white outfit with diamante trimmed coat shown in 2009 on the billboard above their Istanbul flagship store).

As with the Muslim lifestyle magazines in chapter 3, producing images for tesettür incorporates companies into debates about morality and ethics. As Kılıçbay and Binark noted in 2002, while tourism and fashion (along with food) were the initial mainstays of the nascent Islamic lifestyle market in Turkey, marketing fashion required careful coding to counter anticapitalist sentiments still then prevalent in much of the Islamic press as well as criticisms that spending on fashion contravened Islamic injunctions against waste (a perennial challenge faced by *Emel* magazine). If this first phase of tesettür marketing relied on line drawings, often not depicting the human face, phase two, with Tekbir's first fashion show in 1992, prompted adverts and catalogue visuals with full-face shots aiming, as Karaduman put it, to "use fashion as an instrument of tesettür."[13] Images showing the veiled model with mobile phones announced her participation in an Islamic form of modernity at the same time as it presented her as a spectacle for consumption. Sandıkçı and Ger

FIGURE 2.2 Armine billboard above flagship store, Istanbul, 2009.
Photo by Reina Lewis.

read changes in tesettür advertising as signs of market maturation: "over
time tesettür marketers learnt to be 'better' marketers: better in terms of
identifying new needs, designing new products, and communicating with
consumers. And covered women learnt to be 'better' consumers; better in
terms of demanding new products, crafting their identities through consumption, and competing in the status game" (Sandıkçı and Ger 2007:
202–3). Even better marketers face challenges as opportunities for visual
marketing outside of the Islamic press remain limited. Apart from billboards tesettür companies have little presence as advertisers in the mainstream press and none at all in the fashion and style press (who either

ignore or ridicule the wardrobes of the AKP First Ladies). The catalogue continues to demand staff expertise and company finance.

Just as Tekbir emphasizes the touching and wearing of the product, Nilgün Tuncer, public relations and production executive at Armine, emphasizes the materiality of the catalogue mailed to about forty thousand customers: "you can taste it, you see it, it's different from the Internet." The Armine catalogues and ad campaigns are designed by a secular Turkish agency with collaboration from Tuncer, who does the headscarf styling on the shoots, whereas Tekbir catalogues are produced entirely in-house by their own marketing team.

Conventionally catalogues display the brand's scarves and/or garments on models, with the entire seasonal scarf range laid out on the closing pages. Across the catalogue genre company staff and commercial designers concoct ingenious ways to arrange the scarf on models and props to best display new designs and tesettür wraps. Outside the studio, catalogue shoot locations variously signify aspirational travel, modernity (see figure 2.3), or tradition (see figure 2.4) (see also Gökarıksel and Secor 2013). Most tesettür catalogues are full color, printed on high-quality expensive paper stock with gloss laminate covers (Tekbir's autumn/winter 2007/2008 catalogue was even a hard-bound album), and running to between forty and seventy pages.

As I discuss in chapters 3 and 6, Muslim style magazines and designers in Britain and North America encounter difficulties not only obtaining professional models on their limited budgets, but also in briefing models on required body management that differs from the sexualized norms of industry standard posing (Evans 2013). The same considerations apply for tesettür brands, who additionally seek certain facial types for scarf modeling. To this end, Armine has built a relationship over six years with a favored Romanian model (on the 2009–10 cover; see plate 1), who, like the "long faces" cast by Tekbir for their fashion show, has the distinctive high forehead considered important for showing the scarf and "shinier, more attractive" green eyes preferred (like blue) to brown. The Armine model has also learned how to pose, which is, Tuncer explains, "very important. How you look, you know, it's different, because of the scarf. She has to be innocent also, not sexy." Of all the models reviewed, she impressed head of design Şevket Dursun with "the way she walks and the way she sits down and gets up, it's very demure and it's not like the others that we saw, it's not jumpy. She doesn't bounce."

While garments made by Armine might not be designed to prohibit

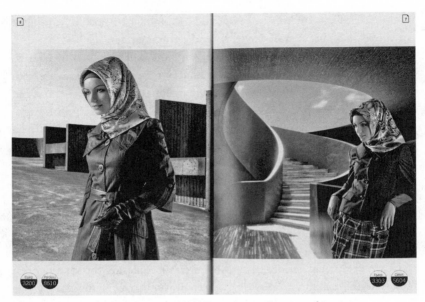

FIGURE 2.3 Armine, autumn/winter 2009–10 catalogue. Courtesy of Armine.

FIGURE 2.4 Armine, spring/summer 2006 catalogue. Courtesy of Armine.

immodest dressing, Islamic scruples do predominate in their visual merchandising. Pulling out a recent Aker catalogue where scarves are worn as accessories or arranged with hair still showing, Nilgün Tuncer points out that for the Armine catalogue she always styles the scarf as an effective hijab, incorporating a bonnet (or cap), a pull-on or tie undergarment that contains the hair and can serve to anchor a hijab wrap, manufactured to match seasonal trends (see Sandıkçı and Ger 2005). Models are shown appropriately posed in positions that do not jut hips or chest. In

FIGURE 2.5 Armine, spring/summer 2006 catalogue. Courtesy of Armine.

the spring/summer 2006 catalogue one can still discern the shape of the body in the curve of the breast in the white raincoat by the tiles (see figure 2.4), or the sheen of satin skirt that indicates the thigh against the grille (see figure 2.5). Set in Topkapı palace in Istanbul, the legendary "grande seraille" of Orientalist fantasy in art, literature, and music, the palace provides both backdrop and design reference, with the foliage of the famous Iznik wall tiles appearing to snake onto the Ottomanesque floral designs of the model's jacket and waistband. For the Islamist Turkish viewer, the location is more than simply gorgeous; it also invokes the importance of Istanbul as the home of the last caliphate, center of a powerful Muslim empire (Robins and Aksoy 1995; Stokes 2000). In contrast, the autumn/winter 2009/2010 catalogue selects a deliberately modernist architectural setting, their favorite Romanian model leaning against the clean lines of the balustrade in a check skirt whose wide front pleats produce the (then) fashionable tulip shape (see figure 2.3). While her hips are only slightly out of line, her head protrudes more markedly forward and down (as in other shots) to emphasize the high cone of the headscarf rising behind her. In a clingier pink jersey dress (see figure 2.6), the cowl detail and restrained pose minimize the shape of breast and thigh visible beneath the clothes. The head this time is posed with a slightly raised chin, creating a near straight horizontal along the top line of the elevated scarf, arranged to frame the face smoothly and symmetrically in the desired *düzgün* manner (Sandıkçı and Ger 2005). The catalogue features the square echarpe in both the classic tesettür style, cascading over chest and back, and in the more recent soft tesettür, tied into the neckline.

Always an expensive if not luxury item, by winter 2011/2012 Tekbir's

FIGURE 2.6 Armine, autumn/winter 2009–10 catalogue. Courtesy of Armine.

catalogue had transformed into a magazine-style format that broke with genre conventions. Announcing the change, the front cover migrates the Tekbir trademark logo to the center top of the page to serve as magazine masthead over which (*Vogue*-style) is superimposed the head of the tesettür-clad model (see figure 2.7). Her upright form (in on-trend animal-print coat) gazes out, surrounded by captions and titles indicating content as seen on fashion magazines the world over. Interior pages also depart from the standard contents and design of the catalogue, utilizing a fuller range of images and fashion mediation modes to create a mixed visual economy. Introduced with an editor's welcome (see figure 2.8), the usual studio shots of models now share the page with inserts from the catwalk, with the Tekbir logo visible as catwalk backdrop. Most radically, the catalogue replaces the product-shot scarf section with pages combining text and images in the mode of magazine "get the look" features (see plate 2) mixing outfits with designer mood board montages themed in English as "flowing sculpture," "avant-garde craft." This welter of information, designed to inspire rather than simply sell (selling through inspiring), echoes the established print fashion media and invokes the visuality of digital fashion mediation. Outfit combinations mimic the cut out and stick mode of polyvore outfit sets (Jacobs 2010) beloved of bloggers, or the virtual scrapbook "likes" of Pinterest that circulate images of (and links to

FIGURE 2.7 Tekbir, autumn/winter 2011–12 catalogue, cover. Courtesy of Tekbir.

FIGURE 2.8 Tekbir, "From the Editor," autumn/winter 2011–12 catalogue. Courtesy of Tekbir.

sales pages for) products and designers. These participatory forms of fashion mediation are of growing importance to fashion industry public relations (PR) internationally, and in Turkey were central to the launch of Âlâ magazine, for which, as I discuss in chapter 3, social media like Facebook were instrumentalized to recruit readers and generate content.

While catalogues in the style of magazines are not uncommon in the luxury and midmarket global fashion industry, the mixing of representational modes in this Tekbir catalogue has particular meanings in the evolution of tesettür as a validated form of fashion. The ability to present modest dressing in the modes of mainstream fashion mediation (made possible by affordable developments in digital photography, and sustained by a commitment to the costs of printing and distributing catalogues) is especially important in light of the moral judgments about images made by practitioners and detractors.

Although Aker's use of non-tesettür scarf styling had been criticized at Armine, when I raised the topic with Aker they reported that they presumed their Islamic clientele knew that the product was intended for tesettür. Popularly recognized as an Islamic brand, Aker was able to photograph the scarves in ways that showed more of the surface print, with brand staffers collaborating with external designers and professional models to style a variety of display modes. This is typified in the autumn/winter 2009/2010 scarf catalogue that shows the model's glossy fair hair in all of the thirty-six images, including the eight that show the scarf draped over head and neck: in these the scarf is worn without a bonnet, rendering the apparently modest wrap redundant in tesettür terms. In other shots, the scarf appears draped over one shoulder, folded as a cravat, and tied loosely about the neck with day, work, and eveningwear of understated elegance. Modesty does however regulate how the rest of the body appears: with the exception of one slightly deeper V-neck all tops button above the collar bone, and no sleeve rises higher than mid forearm. Short-sleeved dresses are layered over long sleeves, body management is restrained, and the maquillage neutral. Set against a nighttime backdrop of city lights seen from a chrome-fitted terrace, the catalogue immerses the Aker woman in a life of metropolitan modernity. In their Cacharel catalogue of 2010/2011, the scarf appears either as accessory or as nonfunctional hijab, set behind the hairline of a pale-skinned, freckled redhead in a domestic set of contemporary international Westernized bourgeois taste posed moodily against a shelf of prop books in European languages.

In Kayra's marketing the assumption that women will know when and how to cover extends beyond showing models with uncovered heads to include the depiction of the company's garments with bare arms and open necklines, as would be suitable for a non-hijab environment with family or other women. This presumes viewers able to make nonliteralist readings and indicates the development of more sophisticated modes of fashion mediation in the tesettür sector as are now developing among designers, bloggers, and magazines in Britain and North America. Kayra's 2011/2012 catalogue (and website) show a short-sleeved "jumpsuit dress" (their version of that year's boilersuit revival; see plate 3) without either long sleeves underneath or a jacket on top. Cinched at the waist and revealing arms, hair, and neckline, the tassel of the belt swings out toward the forward edge of the wide-legged palazzo pants, combining with the retro-cool baby blue Vespa to underline the carefree movement of the maxi's fluid draping across the model's lithe form; a bifurcated garment suitable for modestly mounting the moped that, when reposted on the English-language Turkish blog *Hijabi in the City*, was coveted by blog readers around the world.[14]

One of the distinctive microgenerational changes in tesettür fashion during the course of this research has been the advent of the rectangular scarf or şal, a chunkier heavier pashmina-style wrap that was by 2011 gaining ascendancy over the satin square (figure 2.9) (also Sandıkçı and Ger 2005).[15] Reflecting transnational hijab fashions—patterned or plain, in fabrics from jersey to linen, worn with ends draped or knotted ornamentally front or rear—the şal has become cool with teens and twenty-somethings yet was slow to appear in the tesettür catalogues. Of all the catalogues that year, Kayra featured the şal most often. Not at the time themselves scarf manufacturers (a credit appears for scarves from Ipekevi) they are not tied to existing stock of or client demand for the lighter echarpe square. In an updated version of the earlier tendency to feature mobile phones as a sign of tesettür technological modernity, Kayra shows a tesettür-clad woman holding an iPad (figure 2.10) in conversation with noncovered companion. The mix of trendy şal with the more conventional boxy jacket is styled with spectacles for both models in a novel twist on the popularity of sunglasses as an accessory in hijabi styling.

As seen in plate 4, worn atop the head sunglasses can anchor a scarf and enhance status; desirable as signifiers of international cool from the decades before cheap mass travel, designer shades are now ubiquitous among the spin-off accessories by which the global luxury brands expand

FIGURE 2.9 Şal, Fatih, Istanbul, October 2011. Photo by Reina Lewis.

their consumer base. Here, three items in toning shades of ecru (bonnet, şal, and sunglasses) combine to effect a complex headdress as part of a deceptively simple ensemble. The edge of the bonnet emphasizes the model's high forehead while the unpatterned şal curves in elaborate folds at the base of her slender neck echoing the horizontal ruffles on the breastplate of the knee-length trench. Shot from below, the model appears slightly above the viewer's eye line, jutting her chin forward to frame the face against the dark background. Her position also allows the camera to reveal under the jaw-line, accentuating the delicate beauty of her creamy skin surrounded by the swathes of scarf, sheening in the soft natural look-

FIGURE 2.10 Kayra, spring/summer 2012 catalogue. Courtesy of Kayra.

ing light that illuminates her from above left. Moving upward along her face, the line of her nose is mirrored in the sharp pleat that raises the front edge of the scarf into a wimple above the bonnet while the diagonal lenses of the sunglasses extend the plane of her prominent forehead upward and backward, emphasizing the sense of volume in the scarf behind her head. The elevation of the scarf at the front distinguishes the styling as Turkish, a variant on the crisply rigid face surrounds of the Turkish square headscarf. While volume is desirable in many styles of hijab in Britain and America, it is more usual to see the front of the scarf flat against the bonnet or headband that covers the hairline. On the streets and in the malls, the şal also appears casually wrapped, softer and closer to the shape of the head, in a move away from the formal high rigid beehive that previously defined Turkish hijab style. Catalogues bridge the two aesthetics. Here, perched high on her head, the arms of the glasses disappear into the vertical folds of the scarf above the hidden ears, their color echoed in the gleam of the chunky bangle and the two-tone weekend bag. The royal blue trench becomes urban chic when worn in conjunction with these pale denim skinny jeans and high heeled open-toe court shoes (referencing the current 1980s revival). Her body steps toward the viewer, yet her interrogative gaze (mouth slightly open) looks into the middle distance; with bag in hand, this woman is dressed to go.

Across brands, there is emerging a distinctive body type favored by the tesettür catalogue market: a light-skinned woman with high forehead and light-colored eyes. Models look to be in their twenties, not the teenagers who model for the global luxury brands, and show some variation in body size, rarely replicating the oft-criticized overly skinny underdeveloped bodies favored by high-fashion glossies and advertising campaigns.

Until recently models have remained resolutely Caucasian. While this is entirely in keeping with the disproportionate preponderance of "white" models in the global fashion industry, it has particular valence in Turkey and in the context of tesettür. The religious and ethnic homogenization of the population brought about during the end of the Ottoman Empire dramatically changed the complexion of a population previously known for its ethnic and cultural diversity and mixing, including the children of slaves from Europe, Central Asia, and Africa. External observers found this hybrid mix noteworthy, depicting it as inspirational, exotically bewildering, or a sign of Ottoman inferiority in keeping with their individual political response to prevalent codes of racial and religious difference within their own historical cultures (Heffernan 2011). With elite harems populated by women who arrived as slaves (a position not necessarily permanent [Toledano 1982] or without power [Peirce 1993]), many Westerners struggled to explain how elite men and women (including the sultan) might be the children of slaves or themselves have once been slaves (R. Lewis and Mickelwright 2006). For the West, the "white" slave of the harem was an especially potent figure of oppressed but eroticized Orientalist spectacle (R. Lewis 1996), proof of Oriental depravity and Western superiority.

The determination of men and women of the progressive Ottoman elite in the late nineteenth and early twentieth centuries to challenge the civilizational stereotype of the eroticized but backward harem woman (Lewis 2004; Roberts 2007) was taken up with renewed zeal under the early republic. Fashion and the display of the fashionable female body has not been incidental to this process, with state-sponsored beauty contests (Shissler 2004) and fashion shows (Altınay 2013a) organized in the early decades of the republic to demonstrate modern Westernized bodies for citizens to cultivate and to promote abroad the civilizational parity of the modern secular state. These politicized bodily aesthetics rested on and helped disseminate a racialized Turkish ethno-national identity to which many conservative Muslims also subscribed, even if the uncovered fashions remained culturally alien. This explains why, although tesettür companies are building export markets on the basis of transnational religious affinities, the diversity of the umma's bodies have not generally been a feature of their marketing.

The 2011 inclusion of black models in Tekbir's catwalk (remediated in their catalogue; see plate 2) and in the Tuğba & Venn summer 2012 catalogue and ad campaign (see plate 5) takes on a situational prominence. It transgresses strongly embedded national expectations about the homogeneity of the embodied Turkish nation at the same time as presenting the pious body as part of the nation. As I discuss in chapter 3, Muslim lifestyle magazines in Britain and North America consciously aim to show visible ethnic diversity in their fashion coverage to express the universality of the umma and reflect the ethnic variety of readers in Muslim minority contexts. In Turkey the politically minoritized status historically felt by the religious does not apply when attachment to the supranational supraethnic umma might undermine the need to register as authentically Turkish, played out here in relation to local racialized codes of beauty.

Retailing Tesettür: Shops, Bodies, Spaces

The shift from race and ethnicity to faith in employment regulations in Europe provides the context for my discussion of British hijabi shop workers in fashion retail in chapter 5. In Turkey, tesettür shops themselves can be seen as agentive, providing work for women who wear tesettür and combining with "restaurants, hotels, and sports and beauty clubs catering to the Islamist consumers" to provide "venues for tesettürlü women to parade in and intermingle with each other" (Sandıkçı and Ger 2010: 32). In this section I return to the consumptionscape of Fatih to explore how the market "routinization of tesettür" also incorporates non-tesettür retail into the commercial cultures of religious revivalism.

In the developing fashion city of Istanbul, the retail geography of Fatih melds high street stores with tesettür brands to provide a microcosm of the new Islamic habitus. Long established as the "paradigmatic Muslim *mahalle* (neighborhood)" in the eyes of religious and secular Istanbul residents and foreign observers (Gökarıksel 2012), the homogeneity of religious conservatism with which the district has been associated for several decades has recently been disrupted by the spatial segmentation of the quarter between new and old pious residents (White 2013). The extremes of uncovered fashion may have become consistently less visible over time, but the varieties of modest dress to be viewed on the streets, in the shop windows, and on the bodies of shop staff have multiplied: Fatih remains a prime location for the consumption of covered fashion as prod-

FIGURE 2.11 Çarşaf in Fatih, Istanbul, October 2011. Photo by Reina Lewis.

uct and as spectacle with all versions of covered dressing on display, and groups of covered and uncovered women shopping together. The critical mass of tesettür dressers and shops to supply them increase opportunities for covered women to obtain retail work with both tesettür and secular brands. Easily distinguishable from women in the enveloping çarşaf (figure 2.11) of the older or more conservative, the tesettür dresser manifests fashion savvy through personalized bricolage of different scarf and garment styles sourced from a mix of mainstream and tesettür suppliers (figure 2.12). With many stores providing free in-house alterations, consumers can customize skirt lengths and fit to meet their own interpretations of modest presentation.

FIGURE 2.12 Mix of styles on the street in Fatih, Istanbul, October 2011. Photo by Reina Lewis.

Tekbir has three flagship stores in Fatih, responsible in 2010 for 20 percent of total revenue. Many customers are brand loyal, some returning twice a year to buy a seasonal wardrobe, with international visitors from mainly Germany and Chechnya mirroring the Turkish guest worker demographic and the newly mobile and increasingly Islamist population of the new Central Asian states. The Fatih store has seen a change in local customers to a more elite demographic, with less affluent shoppers using the local open market except during the sales when "everyone" comes. Like all fashion retail in Turkey, personnel are mainly female and young, recruited locally, usually from ads in the store. Company director Necip Karaduman explains that Tekbir is seen by religious families as a safe place for their daughters to work, often employing several women from the same family in sequence or simultaneously.[16] Contra the oft-held idea that educated hijabis take lower-grade jobs, Necip Karaduman reports their workforce is no more educated than at other retailers. Staff turnover is high, with young women mostly leaving upon marriage. Unlike the increasingly casualized part-time nature of retail in the UK and North America, Tekbir does not offer part-time work. Unusual for the tesettür sector, Tekbir also manufactures menswear sold in 20 percent of their stores, in departments staffed by men who, working after marriage, are older than the eighteen-to-twenty-year-olds who characterize the female workforce. Men are "hired for life" and given a household wage, unlike women who receive differential pay rates and are not usually expected to forge a career. However, he notes, young women with ambition achieve greater success and higher salaries than the boys. This pattern of young women working before marriage is common across retail in Turkey, as is the low pay and status of shop work. But the expansion of consumer culture has also created opportunities for women to gain higher status roles as store managers with retail seen as "suitable for upwardly mobile women" and clothing retail especially demonstrating significant numbers of women in management positions (Durakbaşa and Cindoğlu 2002: 85). On my visits to Fatih and to tesettür stores elsewhere in Sultanahmet between 2008 and 2012 I more than once was recognized by, or recognized, women working in one shop whom I had originally met employed in another, as well as reencountering longer-serving staff members. Demonstrating increased employment power albeit in the generically poorly paid retail sector, women were moving between retailers to gain better pay (many work on commission) or more interesting duties.

While, as I discuss in chapter 5, store uniforms and dress codes are now a core part of global branding practice, in Tekbir uniforms were introduced in 2008 for operational reasons typical in the history of retail to make staff more recognizable and easier to regulate. Shop assistants wearing the (then new) uniform confirmed that their increased visibility meant that they were busier now that "everyone knows who the staff are." Female staff are given guidance against excessive makeup, but Necip Karaduman, who "doesn't let" his wife wear makeup, is aware that the store cannot interfere in the private lives of workers as long as their self-presentation is not "excessive."

Observing staff dress in Tekbir stores just before and then after the introduction of the uniform, it was clear that the uniform was more conservative than the style of some employees, which ranged from long black tesettür pardesü, through midthigh tunic over loose trousers with scarf, to a funkier street-style ensemble of midcalf colored denim skirt with high-top trainers. Officially, the uniform's scarf can be draped as they like, but employees did express concern that they would be told to wear the scarf in a style other than their personal preference.[17] The scarf itself is chosen by a staff member from each store: combining worker participation with customer feedback, store representatives are invited to Tekbir HQ twice a year to select the scarf and, as Mustafa Karaduman explains, to contribute to the "production process because they know what the customers want."

The young women who work in Tekbir's stores are indeed well placed to report on what customers want because, as in much fashion retail, they are themselves customers of the shop, often choosing to work in stores because they like the merchandise, one young woman spending nearly all her wages in the store.[18] Staff members advise customers on style, building up rapport with their special customers whom they might call with news of special offers and new lines. In the West this practice is now reserved for elite brands or independent boutiques, but personalized service remains common sales technique in Turkey. For tesettür retail, being able to gauge customer preference is essential because scarves are rarely available for customer self-service. In the often small shops devoted to scarves, as in the scarf section to be found in most tesettür stores, the walls are generally crammed with boxes of scarves on shelves or in drawers. Protruding strips of fabric indicate color and style, from which array the assistant must pull out a selection to be thrown open across the counter (often a vitrine within which sit folded scarves), deducing customer preference for color, motif, and style from appearance, augmented with reference to the catalogues displayed on the counter. While many Turkish retailers have moved into Western-style visual merchandising and self-service, the scarf-buying experience continues to require salesperson interaction; rarely would the entire range be available to be handled directly by the customer. The range and speed with which new styles emerge inflate both the costs and the level of technical skill needed for the "beauty work" entailed by veiling fashion, reinforcing the significance of staff expertise (Sandıkçı and Ger 2005) and emphasizing how their dressed presence contributes to the aesthetic service provision required by the store (as I discuss in chapter 5). In Armine, staff wear a store uniform tesettür, seen in figure 2.13, with the branded scarf worn to flow over the back of the longline coat in a more traditional tesettür style at odds with the often avantgarde styling of their catalogues. Though Aker started a clothing line in 2008, it did not immediately introduce a staff uniform, only requiring staff to model a scarf from the season's collection, but (as in their catalogues) not necessarily as a headscarf.

The range of modest and tesettür dressing on display in the retail spaces of Fatih expands into the secular stores on the bodies of staff and

FIGURE 2.13 Armine shop assistant in uniform, flagship store, Mahmutpaşa, Istanbul, October 2010. Photo by Reina Lewis.

shoppers. In non-tesettür fashion brand Pece, staff do not have a uniform but wear their own black clothes, some in headscarves, serving a mixed clientele ranging from uncovered women to consumers in conservative tesettür pardesü or scarves with fashionable but non-tesettür outfits. In tesettür chain Tuğba & Venn (a regular advertiser in *Âlâ* magazine), staff wore headscarves but no store uniform, selling modest versions of the current trends (skirts never shorter than mid-calf) set at low midrange price points. Hijab is incorporated into store visual merchandising (figure 2.14). In midprice boutique Tempo, smart businesswear is sold to an older age range of conservative and tesettür customers. Although several of their suits were similar to (but cheaper than) Tekbir products, the manager avowed that her clientele "would never shop in Tekbir."[19] Products might look the same, but the store feels very different with up-tempo pop music and bright lights creating a fashion atmospheric that contrasts to the staider environment down the road at Tekbir.

A stalwart of the mall, Turkish fashion brand Ipekyol was present on Fatih high street. Its standard bright, modern shop interior is staffed by "uncovered" women in store uniform black trousers and white blouse, but

FIGURE 2.14 Shop assistant styling hijab on mannequin in-store, Tuğba & Venn, Fatih, Istanbul, October 2009. Photo by Reina Lewis.

there are plenty of covered customers including some in conservative pardesü. Selling fashion-forward daywear, workwear, and eveningwear in the middle range of higher-end prices, Ipekyol is popular with secular professional and middle-income women in their thirties and above but is also willing to appeal to the covered consumer, with recent promotional collaborations with *Âlâ* magazine. The other secular brands employed a mix of uncovered and headscarved staff: in high street youth brands like Koton, Y-London, and Collezione, selling inexpensive casuals, jeans, and T-shirts, hijabi staff often substituted a long denim skirt for the otherwise ubiquitous jeans.

While the prevalence of hijabi shop workers in Fatih demonstrates that the tesettür habitus creates employment opportunities for religious women, it would be wrong to assume that the covered heads of staff always correlate to employee piety: sometimes the scarf is no more or less than a uniform requirement. In one store, Cengiz Arjurk, selling medium- to upscale tesettür women's wear, staff wear a uniform (of loosely flared trousers and long-sleeved, midthigh-length tunic) and a headscarf (a design of individual choice, mostly worn tucked into the neckline of the tunic top). One young woman staff member was not in uniform because she was a recent hire and her uniform had not arrived yet. Neither was she in a headscarf: for her the headscarf would be donned only as a part of the store uniform requirement. Just as the density of Islamic consumption in areas like Fatih creates spatial relations that foster employment for hijabis, so too does it incorporate other bodies into its veiling regime: the presence of headscarves in tesettür shops cannot in itself always be read as an indicator of staff religiosity, while the presence of headscarves in secular brands in this location can be seen as a sign of staff personal, spiritual choice as would be the case in high street shops in the UK. For some companies like Tekbir, the bodies of front-of-house staff are utilized in the promotion of tesettür while backstage staff in the factory, or the occasional female executive, are untrammeled by clothing regulation (though seating in the staff canteen is segregated; see also Gökarıksel and Secor 2010b). Creating employment and career opportunities for copietists is a motivation, but not to the exclusion of other justifiable/necessary hires: most of the showrooms and design offices of the brands I visited also included women not in headscarves.

The critical mass that advantages young tesettür women shop workers in areas like Fatih does not in general extend to fashion shops in other high streets or malls. Malls, as emblems of modernized consumer culture, are loaded territories in Turkey subject to overt politicization and covert discrimination against perceived signs of intruding religiosity. Like the department store in the nineteenth century (chapter 1), the mall in Turkey has been central to the development of respectable mixed-gender commercial spaces; in the Muslim context, household provisioning is moving away from its previous male associations as a prestige activity carried out in the sacralized homosocial spaces of the bazaar, often part of the mosque complex (Durakbaşa and Cindoğlu 2002). Directly linked to the development of neoliberal consumer culture, Turkey's first mall, Ataköy Galleria in Istanbul, was opened in 1988 by Özal himself (Gökarıksel 2007), marking a shift in Turkey's modernization process from a European emphasis on educational improvement to the "American dream" of "success in the economic sphere" (Akçaoğlu 2009: 55). The visible development of Islamic consumer culture exemplified by tesettür has prompted retaliatory Kemalist consumer practices, with newly commodified forms of Kemalist nostalgia seen since the 1990s in badges and T-shirts that facilitate personal and publically paraded forms of emphatically secular embodiment (Navaro-Yashin 2002; Özyürek 2006). The Ottoman nostalgia (Eldem 2007) that, as seen in the regeneration of restaurants and shops of Beyoğlu's arcades, is (differently) appealing to both secularists and Islamists, may support a trend for mall décor that blends Ottoman and nationalist motifs (Tunç 2009), but the mall spaces, like the outdoor shopping streets, are liable to be festooned with Turkish flags and images of Ataturk when secularity seems in need of defense.

This in part explains why to date tesettür-brand clothing is not on sale in the malls (with the exception of one mall in Istanbul devoted to tesettür retail). Tesettür firms may be excluded from the malls but tesettür fashion is present on the bodies of "covered" consumers who in increasing numbers are users of this commercialized civic space, and who purchase from non-tesettür brands scarves and other garments used to create their ensembles. Though reports of hostility from shop staff (Gökarıksel 2007, 2012) and other customers (Turam 2013) are legion, tesettür women can be found buying scarves across the price spectrum (from H&M to Hermès) and sourcing skirts and trousers just as in the UK. The privatized space of the mall has come to function here, as elsewhere (Shields 1992), as a duplicate of (sometimes replacement for) the erstwhile social spaces of the city. Those without money participate by hanging out at this key site for the new forms of urban sociality across the classes, perhaps parading with a totemic branded coffee cup from one of the international (and now Turkish) coffee chains available in the food court (Tunç 2009). Previously shunning the commercial impious spaces of secular society for a network of bookshops, tea gardens, and coffee houses, Islamist youth cultures have also incorporated the mall into their spatiality: the characteristic 1990s care "to display a serious, cool appearance in public places, especially when among non-Islamist people" (Saktanber 2002: 266) is reframed by increased mixing with other young people. Among young women, the high street and especially the mall have become important gendered spaces for shared consumption experiences. Including the entire range of styles of tesettür and covered dressing, in the malls as on the street, women in headscarves are seen socializing with those who are not. In Cevahir mall in the Şişli district of Istanbul on a hot spring day in 2008, the food hall was thronged with teenagers including tables of girls with and without headscarves. Dressed not in tesettür raincoats but in versions of global teen casual, the young women's behavior (deeply immersed in conversation punctuated by surveillance of and interaction with other groups of teens arriving and leaving other tables) was mall standard of international teen sociality. With middle-aged women in midrange fashion also strolling in mixes of headscarved and uncovered bodies, none of the women in the mall wore the black çarşaf seen in Fatih. In Metro City, on a Sunday in October 2009, by which time this older mall had been joined by the competing higher-end open-air Kanyon mall (famous as home to Turkey's first branch of Harvey Nichols), the midrange stores were full of women shoppers in headscarves. The fashion stores in Metro City include many of the British multiples like Topshop and Dorothy Perkins that employ the British hijabis I discuss in chapter 5, as well as European high street giants Zara and Benetton, plus Turkish midrange brands. Women in their twenties and thirties strolled around in small groups of veiled and unveiled friends, while the benches were often occupied by grandmothers in headscarves and dark coats sitting three abreast.

Multiple Tesettür Cultures and Affiliations

Ever more nuanced forms of distinction and judgement are an inevitable feature of the expansion of covered dressing. This was brought home to me in 2009 when I made the mistake of assuming that as sector leaders Tekbir and Armine would have a presence at the first tesettür trade fair in Istanbul. How wrong I was: the initiative designed to help establish Istanbul as a fashion city for modest fashion was not considered an appropriate place for either brand.

For Tekbir, the Istanbul fair was for small fry, likely to be populated by "new upcoming brands [who] want to introduce themselves." Asked about competitors, Mustafa Karaduman laughed that Tekbir "doesn't have a competitor even in the world," and, knowing that I had also spoken with Armine, he distinguished their mission thus: "Armine only does headscarves, they have a very small clothing line. But we do everything, we are a different scale." Armine similarly did not show at the Istanbul tesettür fair, also too established to be showing with start-ups. For Armine, avoiding the tesettür fair was about more than brand positioning: the company eschews the term *tesettür* itself for its associations with "something of lower quality," a phrase that might relate equally to people and to products. Armine prefers the word *muhafazakâr*, "which means conservative and denotes high quality," to describe the "people who buy our products, but who do not necessarily [dress] with tesettür, but have general conservative leanings."

As the Turkish Islamic bourgeoisie has grown in size and economic power, segmentation in style becomes an essential component of internal differentiation and status. Passing reference in Islamists' conversation to the "other Turkey" reappropriates a phrase used by urban, educated secularists to refer to the presumed alterity of rural and minority populations, religious and/or Kurdish alike. The "other Turkey" maps onto a popular division between the "white Turk" secularist Kemalist elite and those disparaged as "black Turks," the uncivilized, unmodern peasants (even if long urbanized) whose habitual religiosity is read as evidence of their lack of evolution. When the AKP came to power in 2002 the aversive response from the secularist press and public presented the AKP as interlopers, "not us." By 2003 Erdoğan was proudly proclaiming himself a black Turk, reversing the binarism to validate the cultural attitudes and expressions that previously denigrated the nonurban nonelite population (Demiralp 2012; White 2013). But where Erdoğan enthusiastically performed a macho masculinity in his role as man of the people, Armine as a tastemaker and purveyor of elegant contemporary fashion seeks to be positioned as part of the Islamic moderns, the "white Muslim" even, an educated Islamic elite whose advocacy of moderate participation in consumer culture is often linked to participation as entrepreneurs. Providing bespoke scarves to match the famously monocolored outfits of AKP style leader Hayrünnisa Gül, with stylists for political daughters pulling products from the clothing range, Armine like the other lead tesettür firms is engaged in the sorts of discrete status enhancing services that establish elite political women as ambassadors for indigenous design, whether national, ethnic, or, in this case, religious.

The pitfalls of supporting commerce became horribly clear in the violent suppression of demonstrations in Turkey in summer 2013. Prompted by campaigns to stop the destruction of Istanbul's Gezi Park (and the displacement of local residents) to build a high-end shopping and housing complex, the initially small environmental campaign became a vast national expression of mistrust in the AKP government. Following highly publicized attempts to restrict alcohol sales (even if unlikely to be enforced) the demonstrations became a focus for anxieties that the AKP were indeed bent on the Islamicization of the country, framed through the populist anticonsumerism associated with the youth-based Occupy movements recently seen around the world. With the demonstrations inaccurately represented in the international media as a clash between Islamists and secularists, the state's excessive and violent reprisals and Erdoğan's intemperate expressions of personal affront registered his macho posturing in civilizational terms as a politically primitive overreaction that, confirming Orientalist stereotypes, refigured AKP neo-Ottomanism as a return to despotic sultantic autocracy.

As the Islamic bourgeoisie expands and subdivides and as the cadres of Islamist politicians splinter with time in office, consumption practices come to demarcate ever more finely defined forms of distinction. For women, and for men, dress, behavior, and the spaces of their consumption simultaneously differentiate them externally from secular society (while also asserting rights of participation) and internally from the microdistinctions of Islamists from other classes, regions, tariqats, and political affiliations, sometimes through the judicious use of non-tesettür sourced garments in the crafting of class fusion fashion (Sandıkçı and Ger 2001). Acquiring respectability as Turkish Islamists also requires a tactical differentiation from foreign Islamists: with secularist rumors circulating that mosques and veiling are funded by Saudi Arabia or Iran, or the suspicion that apparently nonaligned Turkish Islamist organizations are fronts for shady tariqat conspiracies.

Armine, like Tekbir, Kayra, and Aker, is part of a growing Turkish industry that is itself constitutive of new types of consumers and new social identities reconceptualizing the "target consumer" from "a 'pious women'" reached through religious indoctrination to "a woman who is defined more by her taste and less by her religiosity. Religiosity equalized and homogenizes the Islamic identity: taste classifies it" (Sandıkçı and Ger 2007: 200–201). The ways in which these taste communities are supported and extended by opinion formers in the new Muslim lifestyle media is the project of chapter 3.

CHAPTER 3

MUSLIM LIFESTYLE MAGAZINES

A New Mediascape

This chapter is about the development of Muslim lifestyle media, a field that is changing rapidly in modes of production and address. Since I started documenting in 2004 what were then the new Muslim lifestyle magazines available in printed hard copy, the advent of widespread Internet accessibility followed by the global growth of social networking sites such as Facebook, Twitter, Instagram, and Tumblr has meant that there are now more ways than ever of receiving Muslim lifestyle media and more people and groups willing and able to participate in creating it. This example of what Jenkins calls convergence culture, by which consumers/readers can access content through more than one media platform, has implications for the type of content produced, who is able to produce it, and how it is used and reused, with the migration of content across media channels connected to "ever more complex relations between top-down corporate media and bottom-up participatory culture" (H. Jenkins [2006] 2008: 254). Convergence has become a daily factor in contemporary life; for the Muslim mediascape, as with the media generally, it is impossible to predict the course that media changes will take. Print publications augment with websites and digital editions; social media function as content in their own right and are used to drive readers to other platforms (whether print magazines, blog pages, or commercial websites). This chapter documents and analyzes moments in the development of Muslim lifestyle media: operating thematically and chronologically, it gives accounts of media developments as they emerged in what was then their present moment, with journalists and editors discussing future plans that do or don't work out as envisaged.

Lifestyle, Cultural Intermediaries, and Minority Cultures

The beginning of the twenty-first century saw the appearance of lifestyle media aimed at Muslim readers, heralded in its first iteration by print publications that remediated for Muslim purposes the form of the secular lifestyle magazine genre (see plate 6). Dating to the 1980s, lifestyle marked a shift in magazine publishing that created new reader groups based on shared consumption habits (from sports to travel) and redefined existing readerships who might otherwise have been served by previous publication genres such as women's magazines. The lifestyle publishing remit responded to and helped further to disseminate modes of social existence in which individual identity was based more on relationships to the consumption of commodities than to their production, with distinction through the exercise of taste, "the social organization of consumption" (Chaney 1996), replacing previous (often class-based) forms of status achieved through the social organization of production (Bourdieu [1984] 2010). Within networks of symbolic exchange, status comes not only from the ability to accumulate goods (economic capital), but in the exercise of expertise in knowing how to discriminate between goods, requiring what Bourdieu ([1984] 2010) calls cultural and aesthetic capital. The massification of consumer society in the second half of the twentieth century in western Europe and North America (WENA) extended habits of competitive consumption to the majority of the population (Slater 1997) as to the modernities of the Middle East (chapter 1). As the previously elite ability to "consecrate" taste came increasingly to be contested by less elite groups, a significant set of roles emerged for what Bourdieu in 1984 termed the new cultural intermediaries ([1984] 2010), themselves arguably heirs to longer established mediatory roles (Nixon 2003).

The term, now in popular usage, derived from Bourdieu's observations of 1970s France, where the young of the upper classes discovered that their inherited economic and cultural capital no longer guaranteed the best jobs, at the same time as the young of the rising petit bourgeoisie graduating from the new mass education system discovered that their qualifications no longer secured economic security. The result, he argued, was the emergence of new types of "fuzzy" jobs in which the demonstration of cultural capital became extremely significant, notably in "occupations involving presentation and representation (sales, marketing, advertising, public relations, fashion, decoration, and so forth) . . . [and] cultural production and organization (youth leaders . . . radio and TV producers and presenters, magazine journalists)" (Bourdieu [1984] 2010: 359). While at the time many of these roles were kept deliberately vague so that the maximum status could be extracted from quite lowly occupations, today many roles in cultural mediation have become recognized, sought after, and increasingly professionalized occupations. The emergence of fashion stylist as new tastemaker may have developed organically in the British style media of the 1980s (McRobbie 1998), and the fashion stylist continues to rely on personal contacts, but students in fashion education can now train for this professionalized role.

The cultural intermediary continues to be instrumental in consecrating new forms of aesthetic and symbolic capital and in challenging established hierarchies of taste with new forms of distinction. True then and now is that the apparently egalitarian position from which the cultural intermediary operates (part of the mystique of the role) relies on access to the advantages of established class habitus that, as Bourdieu pointed out, often emphasizes the physicality and management of the body (grooming, posture, etiquette, or access to dental treatment). While for Bourdieu competition is characterized by allegiance to the value of the field rather than desire for its dissolution, with competition within haute couture fashion regarded as a top-down model of emulation and aspiration (1994), today design inspiration is widely seen to trickle up from the street as well as down from couture, with cultural intermediaries likely to consecrate tastes as mass-market popular rather than elite culture (Rocamora 2012). Similarly, minority or nonelite groups may in particular moments be able to parlay expertise with previously disparaged cultural forms into aesthetic capital, though as I discuss in chapter 4, the ability of fashion to co-opt temporarily diaspora stylization does not necessarily transfer cultural capital to those who wear it habitually. In this chapter and again in chapter 5 I am concerned with how cultural intermediaries in minority cultures distinguished by faith are engaging in processes of consecration that endow particular styles and modes of presentation with forms of capital both aesthetic and Muslim. What challenges are particular to their version of lifestyle culture and media, what forms of internal disputation must they negotiate, and what are their markers of success?

Lifestyle as a relatively new media genre has malleable boundaries able to incorporate everything from obvious contenders like *Wallpaper*, the paradigmatic lifestyle title cofounded and published by Paul de Zwart (subsequently publisher and executive editor of *Alef*), to men's magazines, to the rebranding of previously unsexy hobby magazines. While all lifestyle magazines create a community of readers cohered by taste, Muslim titles are unusual in that they take faith as a basis for the consumption practices that form the inherent basis of lifestyle publishing.

It is not surprising that this upsurge in Muslim publishing is concerned with lifestyle in general and with fashion in particular. Lifestyle as a mode of social engagement often privileges bodily presentation and the achievement of distinction through the cultivation of the appropriately embodied self that was once a defining characteristic of the elite. Now, "body work" is a preoccupation of ever expanding constituencies with new groups of consumer subjects produced by the successful marketing of new products and gelled through mediation in the lifestyle press, as can be seen in the late twentieth-century commodification of men's bodies previously regarded as outside the purview of grooming, styling, and fashion (Jobling 1999; Mort 1996; Nixon 2003). As I discussed in chapter 1, clothes and associated codes of body management, especially women's, have long been integral to the experience and staging of faith-based identities. Now, in the context of the growing international Islamic bourgeoisie, the consumption of clothes alongside other goods and services provided by Islamically run businesses has meant that Muslim subjectivities can be formed, presented, and understood as modern and religious through Islamic lifestyle consumption.

With young people making up a large percentage of revivalists and converts, the new Muslim lifestyle media in print and on the web, alongside college Islamic societies, provide guidance in clothing etiquette and the body management necessary for modest dressing that might otherwise have been localized through older relatives and community observers. The previously secular role of style intermediary is filled by Muslim style setters representing new trends in modest dressing and veiling within the individuating discourse of modern lifestyle consumer culture (Kılıç-bay and Binark 2002). For Muslim lifestyle magazines fashion editorial is often the hardest content to produce and the most contentious component of the genre, bringing minority cultural intermediaries up against competing norms within the fashion industry and their own communities. These same problems were encountered by the new queer lifestyle magazines of the 1990s and the parallels are instructive. When titles are few, reader expectations are high, with readers often looking for points of identification and affirmation far in excess of those expected from other mainstream media.

For queer and Muslim lifestyle media the inclusion of fashion, an indispensable element of this consumption-focused genre, raised dilemmas for magazine producers and readers. It is often argued in relation to lesbian/gay/queer communities that "out" cultural forms have played a crucial role for individuals in finding or affirming their own identity, locating others, and communicating a minority sexual identity to the majority culture. When lesbian and gay lifestyle magazines emerged onto the market in the 1990s this was one of the factors that made them appealing, but that also fueled specific and conflicting reader demands, with readers wanting to see themselves mirrored on the magazine pages. This was especially the case with the fashion pages for the British lesbian magazine *Diva*: complaints about the cost and style of clothing were underwritten by a concern that the pictured bodies should look "lesbian" and affirm readers' own self-presentations (R. Lewis 1997). For Muslim lifestyle magazines fashion and the representation of the female body raise the greatest controversies among readers or commentators, with preferred modes of femininity nuanced by concerns about modesty, types of covering, and the spiritual dilemmas of picturing the human body.

Muslim lifestyle media then and now find themselves having to visualize, and to recommend, how their constituency might present themselves as dressed bodies recognizable as, and to, members of the given community. The question of what Muslim looks like, or what looks Muslim, brings to the fore many of the issues of collective and individual identity that underpin the very project of formulating a commercial version of Muslim lifestyle culture. More so than other regular consumption features (cars, gardening, food), fashion pages (most frequently focused on women's fashion) require journalists and readers to negotiate visual politics about representing the human form and, in particular, to deal with competing definitions of female modesty and concerns about the depiction of female bodies. Framed as internal debates but mounted in media that are also mined by the mainstream press for examples of "Muslim opinion," fashion pages become a site of struggle as editors and journalists strive to be stylistically innovative within the title's understanding of fashionable modesty, and to contain community or external censure without failing the conflicting demands of their target readership.

This chapter focuses on five titles that cover the range of English-language Muslim lifestyle magazines emerging in the first decade of the twenty-first century as a minority genre within Britain and North America and concludes with a study of Âlâ, the first Muslim lifestyle magazine to develop in the Muslim majority context of Turkey. My first study is the British magazine *Emel* (2003–2013), whose inclusive middle-market lifestyle pitch is compared to the short-lived luxury title *Alef*, which for the two years of its run (2006–8) was aimed primarily at the Gulf elite consumer and associated diaspora. Although originating from Kuwait but produced in New York and then London, *Alef* (paradoxically the title with the best links to the fashion industry) was positioned by the industry as a minority publication during its production processes, even though its minoritized status as Muslim ceased to apply once the magazine entered its primary distribution areas in Muslim majority countries. The diversification of the field is studied through Muslim lifestyle titles that specialize in terms of age (the now defunct North American *Muslim Girl*, 2006–8) and gender and degree of piety (the long-running American *Azizah* and the more recent British *Sisters*). Not all these magazines brand themselves as lifestyle—*Sisters* markets as a women's magazine—but they all structure themselves according to the components of the lifestyle genre. The redefinition of lifestyle brought about by new Muslim and regional magazines intervenes in the classificatory norms of the magazine industry at the same time as it constructs new forms of identity for readers.

The conditions of possibility for the development of Muslim lifestyle media in WENA rely on a number of interconnecting factors: the growing local and international Muslim bourgeoisies and associated goods and services; the now strongly established global reach of diaspora fashion circuits (chapter 4); the increasing political and cultural confidence of second- and third-generation Muslim migrants (chapter 1); and a widespread (though varied) revitalization of the concept of the umma, the supranational community of Muslim believers, as an adjunct to the regional and diaspora community affiliations that characterize many Muslim communities (see also chapter 1). The new magazines can rely on a young generation of readers familiar with popular culture and media, but they publish in a context where, especially for girls and young women, reading teen or fashion magazines may have been clandestine in the face of parental interdiction (Din and Cullingford 2004).

In magazine terms, the new faith-based lifestyle glossies depart from established niche publications that construct reader groups in terms of race/ethnicity (*Ebony*, *Black Beauty*, *Asian Bride*). Yet, while the Muslim lifestyle press is inherently multiethnic, it shares with the ethnic and community press a minoritized niche status, related in this instance to the majority secularized-Christian norm of their places of publication in the UK and North America. Muslim lifestyle relates not only to mainstream lifestyle and fashion media but also to Muslim community and ethnic media as well as to media generated by political, social, and religious organizations across a local, national, and transnational spectrum. When Muslim lifestyle media creates fashion content they must also be cognizant of prevailing global and local forms of fashion mediation. Ideas about Islamic fashion created and circulated in Muslim lifestyle media, while retaining (and forging new forms of) local taste distinction are therefore characterized by particular forms of global transmission. Journalists and editors are keenly aware of international developments, locating their titles in a transnational Muslim mediascape that, as C. Jones (2010) demonstrates in relation to Indonesia, encompasses different national Islamic and secular commercial and cultural forces. Just as fashion-forward consumers in the UK will peruse *Vogue Italia* for its more avant-garde fashion styling, Muslim readers who are not literate in, for example, Arabic also consume in print or online non-English-language magazines featuring modest fashion. Visuals require no translation and Internet marketing makes it possible for the determined consumer (willing to meet import costs) to obtain products from manufacturers in diverse territories, assisted by Islamic style mediators such as British fashion blogger Jana Kossaibati whose *Hijabstyle.co.uk* (chapter 6) regularly includes links to international Muslim designers and visuals from foreign-language fashion sites. In different geographic and ethnic contexts, lifestyle magazines were able to build on the achievements of existing community presses that had often provided the initial training grounds for lifestyle journalists, just as the lifestyle magazines have gone on to develop the next generation of cultural mediators.

In Britain, the events and aftermath of the Rushdie affair in 1989 (chapter 1) prompted an increase in Muslim media written in English, responding and contributing to the widespread repositioning of migrant identities as Muslim rather than Asian and meeting the linguistic needs of second-generation British Muslims not fully literate in community languages (T. Ahmed 2005; Masood 2006; Samad 1998). Notable among this new wave was *Q News*, established in 1992 by journalist Fuad Nahdi to provide nonsectarian community news and help young Muslim men and women into journalism. Its magazine format and feature-length human interest content (Moll 2007) included coverage of "women's issues," such as domestic violence, that were rarely aired in the Muslim public. *Q News* did not however include fashion editorial and is therefore not analyzed in detail in this chapter. In the United States, Muslim lifestyle magazines are heirs to the politicization of consumption in the black and minority press that included championing fashion as a route to social mobility for post-abolition rural migrants in early twentieth-century black women's periodicals (Rooks 2004), boycotts of discriminatory businesses organized by the civil rights movement, and criticisms of too much commercialism in black women's magazines (on *Essence*, see Woodard and Mastin 2005). On both continents, minority ethnic and religious presses have long sought to express and develop the political, social, and economic aspirations of their communities: by the mid-2000s this was likely to be articulated through the pages of lifestyle glossies.

The 2000s saw a veritable explosion of Muslim lifestyle magazines emitting from likely and unlikely sources. In the arts sector, the art gallery commissioned MSLM *Fashion Magazine* (Medium, Small, Large, Medium) and an exhibition appeared as a one-off title in the Netherlands (Heydra 2007). Also arts-focused but long-running, *Bidoun* magazine was established in 2004 with a mission to create "a platform for ideas and an open forum for exchange, dialogue and opinions about arts and culture from the Middle East,"[1] with team member Sameer Reddy serving as the editor in chief for the first three issues of *Alef*.

More surprising perhaps are forays into lifestyle magazines allegedly attributed to radical Islamist and jihadist organizations like Hizb ut-Tahrir and al-Qaida (chapter 1). Seen as a move to make Hizb ut-Tahrir more family friendly, in contrast to the previous mission of young men reaching young men, the short-lived *Salam Magazine* extended their adroit early adoption of communication media (P. Lewis 2007). In 2010 and 2011 British newspapers reported on two digital magazines purportedly launched by groups related to al-Qaida: *Inspire*, attributed to al-Qaida in the Arabian Peninsula, was aimed at the English-speaking would-be jihadi (Black 2010), while the alleged al-Qaida online Arabic-language magazine *Al-Shamikha* (*The Majestic Woman*), dubbed by commentators as "Jihad Cosmo," appeared to be utilizing the aspirational address of lifestyle media for jihadi recruitment (Cavendish 2011).[2]

That the framing of new Muslim identities is increasingly materialized through consumer lifestyle practices aimed at, and developed by, groups previously marginalized by normative consumer cultures fits with Inderpal Grewal's characterization of contemporary neoliberalism in which, "as new social movements created new identities in the United States, marketing practices were designed to understand these communities and to diversify and differentiate them to sell more and different products" (Grewal 2005: 7). Consumerist logic is, she argues, integral to the development of rights-based social movements that utilize a discourse of choice (as I discuss in chapter 4) whether for democracy, reproductive rights, or religious freedoms as evidence of agency, so that the right to consume becomes increasingly prevalent in the conceptualization and enactment of diverse modes of citizenship and belonging. Lifestyle magazines, in seeking to assert Muslims' ability to participate in specialist and mainstream consumer cultures *as* Muslims, are indeed part of this formulation, contributing to a model of minority identity through consumption seen previously in queer consumer politics (Mort 1996).

Unlike elements of the queer population, however, Muslims are not popularly associated with conspicuous consumption. In chapter 7 I discuss the industry in Islamic branding that began to gather pace during the latter period of this research, but for the establishing years of the English-language titles covered in this chapter it was the reluctance of mainstream companies to see Muslims as consumers that had an impact rather than the more recent desire to incorporate Muslims into marketing campaigns. Getting ad revenue was hard, available only from public or voluntary sector recruiters or welfare providers, or from Muslim brands offering "intellectual commodities" for Islamic schooling or devotional practice (Starrett 2003) or modest fashion. The impact of Islamic branding is likely behind the noticeable increase in ads in recent issues of *Sisters*, though this new advertising spend, so essential to magazines, is for parenting and family products rather than fashion. This reflects the ongoing ambivalence of the fashion industry to seeing Muslims as a consumer demographic, not helped when the production values and press pack of many of the magazines fail to meet industry standards (with the exception of *Alef*, and to a lesser extent *Muslim Girl*), further inhibiting early adopter advertisers whose validation was essential in establishing the economic and cultural capital of the early lifestyle magazines in the 1980s.[3] The difficulties faced by journalists in accessing fashion industry PR services butt up against readers' overinvestment in policing images of Muslims to reveal a fault line in the still only partial inclusion of Muslims in neoliberal consumer culture.

The Politics of Lifestyle: Fashion as a Component of Muslim Lifestyle Magazines

Intending to grow a community of readers for its version of progressive British Muslim identities, *Emel* led the way as the first lifestyle glossy in the British market, identifying itself fearlessly as a magazine of "ML" or Muslim Lifestyle (echoing *amal*, aspirations, in Arabic and Turkish) (see figure 3.1). Founded as a bimonthly in 2003, *Emel* went monthly in 2005, the first Muslim magazine to achieve mainstream bookstore and supermarket distribution. As with the British lesbian monthly *Diva* (founded 1994), availability outside specialist community venues helped indicate commercial viability to advertisers. With a consistent print run of twenty thousand (thirty thousand for popular issues by 2012) and a steadily growing subscription rate of just under 40 percent, *Emel* sold mainly to professionals in their early thirties, with a readership mirroring the British Muslim demographic: 40 percent of readers reside in London, the majority are South Asian, with a secondary Arab and slightly lower Turkish and African take-up. *Emel* distinguished itself by its lifestyle focus from news-oriented monthlies like *Q News* while continuing traditions of nonpartisan community coverage.

Emel editor Sarah Joseph (see figure 3.2), who converted to Islam at age sixteen, gained her publishing experience in the community sector editing Muslim youth magazine *Trends*, and then the *Common Good* for the Muslim Council for Britain. Determined to remain politically nonaligned, Joseph has developed a significant profile within the UK Muslim community and externally, awarded the state honor of Officer of the British Empire (OBE) in 2004 for services to interfaith dialogue (chap-

FIGURE 3.1 *Emel* magazine covers.

editorial

BEING FAITHFUL CITIZENS
Sarah Joseph, editor

FIGURE 3.2 *Emel*, editor's photo.

ter 7). Speaking in 2012, Joseph remained resolute that the magazine stay open spiritually and politically, refusing despite regular demands to align the magazine or herself with particular schools of Islam: "I became a Muslim, I didn't become a denomination, and that for me is my principle. . . . There wasn't a school of thought in the time of the Prophet, there wasn't a sect in the time of the Prophet, and so I just try and follow the Qur'an and the Sunnah as it was then."[4] Against readers' highly politicized spiritual judgments of content (for instance, Deobandi criticisms of music coverage), Joseph delineates the limits of *Emel*'s inclusivity, phlegmatic that

FIGURE 3.3 *Alef*, cover, winter 2007–8. Courtesy of photographer, Kai Z Feng.

the magazine will not meet the criteria of all Muslims: "at the end of the day we really do believe in freedom of choice as [the] divinely ordained principle from God and so if God has given us freedom of choice there's no compulsion in religion, there's no compulsion in reading *Emel*, if you don't want to read it, don't read it."

In 2006 *Emel* was joined on the racks of mainstream UK distributors for two years by the high-end glossy *Alef* (see figure 3.3). Visually led, with copy appended in Arabic, *Alef*'s editorial office moved at the end of their first year from New York to London, with staffers based in Dubai. *Alef* was backed by Kuwaiti Shaykh Majed al-Sabah, to build on his Villa Moda luxury brand retail operation in Kuwait and Dubai. Distributed largely through partners such as private banks, airlines, and retailers, *Alef*'s primary markets were in Kuwait, UAE, Dubai, and Lebanon. Publisher and editor Paul de Zwart identified three types of affluent reader: young Emiratis in their twenties to midthirties returning from education overseas who took new pride in local culture; the fashion reader for whom *Alef* was a reference point on luxury products; and a cross-generational group of the great and the good, power brokers in business and those who people the emergent cultural sphere, "the ones at the forefront of all things indigenous." Retailing in the EU and United States through mainstream bookstores and specialist outlets, *Alef* also reaches diaspora readers of Arab and non-Arab descent. Operating prior to the Arab Spring of 2011, de Zwart saw *Alef* as having a dual mission: "to be an ambassador for the Middle East, celebrating the region across the world and in its own backyard" (Wrelton 2007). While the need to challenge negative stereotypes is part of this mission, de Zwart was clear that "Alef is very much apolitical, it's lifestyle driven and it gives readers interested in fashion, culture and art a view into the Middle East through the people that are living here and also through the diaspora overseas" (de Zwart quoted in Wrelton 2007).

Unlike *Emel*, whose address to mainly middle-income readers means that consumer features include midprice options, *Alef* was located squarely in the luxury market, directed at a wealthy Gulf readership with the presumption of internationalism common to the global luxury consumer (Coleridge 1988). The only title in my survey that was not specifically faith-based, and distributing in nondemocratic territories governed by state censorship, *Alef* relied on intersecting transnational and regional consuming audiences, tied to the global reach of new luxury markets and the related spread of print capital. The growing awareness among luxury brands that their vitality in new markets is dependent on the development of distinctive local consumer cultures creates an opportunity for regional luxury lifestyle media at the same time as the newness of the media form in those markets makes the success of new media titles especially fragile. For *Alef*, the challenge was to tailor the mechanisms of lifestyle to incorporate regional characteristics without alienating readers in terms of age or location, as in the menswear feature on Tom Ford's new bespoke *dishdash* service (see figure 3.4). The dishdash (or *dishdasha*, also known as the *thobe*) is an ankle-length long-sleeved robe worn by men (and sometimes women) in the Arabian Peninsula and elsewhere that has particular valency in *Alef*'s Gulf territories, where it has been adopted as a marker of national identity and hence citizenship privileges in contrast to

FIGURE 3.4 *Alef*, Tom Ford dishdash, fashion feature, autumn 2007. Courtesy of *Alef*.

the often majority nonnational population of migrant workers. That this local garment was now included in the offering of Tom Ford, at the time the iconic menswear designer (only recently departed from global luxury brand Gucci), gave the article, de Zwart thought, the potential to speak "to the young who understand Tom Ford, [to] the older people who actually like to wear made-to-measure dishdashes, but also to a Western audience who is given a bit of a background on dishdashes generally. So this is transnational, cross generational."[5] The need to cater to a wider than usual reader demographic is typical of the early stages of a new media market. Like the queer lifestyle press then and still largely now, Muslim magazines are read by many whose social and political profiles range far beyond the target readership constructed by their content. This may help sales, but reader satisfaction is harder to ensure.

The vitality of a field can be indicated not only by longevity but by diversification, and in North America early signs of segmentation were shown by the quarterly *Muslim Girl* magazine targeting the youth market. Launched in 2006, *Muslim Girl* initially focused on Muslim young women age fourteen to eighteen, though content was soon adapted to appeal to the older college-age group (eighteen to twenty-four) with whom the magazine proved popular (see figures 3.5 and 3.6). Prepublication market research confirmed for editor Ausma Khan that while Muslim teens

FIGURES 3.5 AND 3.6
Muslim Girl, covers,
July–August 2007,
photographed by Paul
Perrier; April–May
2008, photographed
by May Truong.

shared many of the characteristics of other North American teens, they also experienced a specifically Muslim version of teen growing pains, feeling "alienated on questions such as boyfriends, relationships, drinking and having certain types of freedom."[6] To meet these needs the magazine offered advice on negotiating teen troubles and young adult dilemmas within an international positive images remit.

With readers mirroring the mainly African American and South Asian Muslim American demographic, *Muslim Girl* was available in mainstream North American bookstores. Produced in Toronto, *Muslim Girl* aimed for continental distribution and reach. The magazine was published by ExecuGo Media, a Toronto-based company usually producing bespoke media for clients, most often in business skills and education services. Searching for a new project with a social progress remit, but not intending specifically to enter into faith-based publishing, ExecuGo publisher Faye Kennedy's quest took her to the annual conference of ISNA (Islamic Society of North America), where she heard Ausma Khan speak about growing up excluded from American cultural life. Kennedy saw the potential for a new magazine with a "mission to educate, not just Muslim girls but to educate other girls about Muslim girls."[7] Khan, a lawyer and academic, seized the opportunity as a "continuation of [her] human rights work," with scope for "community empowerment" and interfaith relations by opening up "a different kind of dialogue and [showing] a different face of Muslims that [is] rarely presented in the media."[8] The genesis of *Muslim Girl* was exceptional; commissioned by corporate capital and not overtly funded from within the Muslim community, the result was a subsidized medium concerned with devotional lifestyles whose Muslim particularity was seen by the secular publishing company to have special significance for the majoritarian culture also perceived to be damaged by the demonization of Muslims post-9/11.

As part of its commitment to community development, the magazine strove to use only Muslim women writers (a policy that *Muslim Girl*, like other titles, was unable to pursue for visual and fashion content where there is still an insufficient skills base). As Khan explained, "we try to use young writers who are close to our constituency and who have a real feel for the kind of stories that we want to tell." The aspirational consumer mode often held as standard for teen/young women's magazines, focusing on "their lifestyle and the brands that they will purchase," was reinterpreted at *Muslim Girl* to include aspirations for self-development that connected to the magazine's social progress program while rendering

consumption cognizant of faith as well as fashion. In addition to providing a fashion fix for Muslim readers already accustomed to, but frustrated
by, the secular teen magazine market, fashion for Khan was integral to
how *Muslim Girl* challenged stereotypes of Muslim girls as inevitably
veiled, "very conservative and demure": "The majority of Muslim women
and girls in North America . . . don't dress that conservatively, but still
consider themselves Muslims and subscribe to those values. And in the
magazine we wanted to make sure that we included all of those girls. And
I've read other press from *Azizah* that says their policy is always to have
a woman in a headscarf on the cover as the appropriate model, and our
policy is exactly the opposite—to represent as many different girls as possible and all their different approaches to faith."

As has been the case for some time, Muslim women in the United
States continue to be less likely to cover than in other non-Muslim-
majority countries, with 40 percent never wearing hijab, 36 percent wearing it all the time, and 24 percent wearing it most or some of the time (Pew
2011c). The distinctive forms of covering prominent in the United States,
especially those favored among African American women, have impacted
on the development of American Muslim style media and entrepreneurship. As in Europe, the younger generation of Muslims in America are inclined to be less dogmatic than their parents and more open to multiple
interpretations of faith and practice (Pew 2011c: 27), providing a ready
appetite for Khan's deliberately open policy on hijab and critical engagement with religious scholarship.

Inspirational role models are provided with profiles of women "doing
things you would not typically expect a Muslim woman to do," alongside hard-hitting local and international news stories with a human
rights agenda connected to young Muslim women (interviews with teenage Muslim refugees from Srebrenica, and young women from Darfur).
Overtly politicized, the magazine was careful to remain bipartisan on
North American Muslim and national politics: accepting an invitation in
2007 to visit the White House during the Bush administration—"if opportunity for engagement arises, it's ridiculous not to take it"—Ausma Khan
carefully contextualized the photograph of herself with Condoleezza Rice
(see figure 3.7) with an editorial highly critical of U.S. policy in Iraq.

Azizah and *Sisters*, the two titles that focus specifically on women's
spirituality, also see fashion as an essential and politicized component
of the Muslim lifestyle magazine market. The American quarterly *Azizah*, founded in 2000 (see figures 3.8, 3.9, and 3.10) is the longest-running

editor's letter

The end of the year is a good time to take stock of the things we've accomplished and the goals we have yet to achieve. For *Muslim Girl*, that's meant publishing our first six issues and getting to meet girls from across North America and around the world.

From the moment we began, we heard from Muslim women worldwide wanting to know more about our endeavor and eager to connect with their sisters. In this, our Girls Around the World issue, we've responded to that desire for community and are proud to share some of the most inspiring stories of the year.

There's no question that life is different in the north as compared to the global south, a reality reflected in many of this issue's stories. Our privilege is immense, our luxuries too numerous to count. Meanwhile, huge divisions remain between East and West while the name of Islam continues to be associated with violence and despair. Muslims face disaster in Darfur at the hands of other Muslims. In a year of changes, nothing changes in Iraq except for the worse. Most relevant of all, so many girls across the globe never have the opportunity to develop their inner strength and live out their full potential. We've shed light on these subjects in the past and it's a challenge we'll take up again in the future.

Girls Around the World is our reality check but it's also an exploration of hope in dark circumstances. There is something to celebrate in a young woman like Zaynab Aden who works to bring the violence in Darfur to an end. There is something incalculably humane about Jenna Hage-Hassan who comes back from a summer of war in Lebanon focused on the best hope for the future.

And there is something completely humbling about a young woman like Merlinta Anggilia who lost her family in Indonesia's devastating tsunami then reached out in friendship to the Jewish doctors who came to her country in its aftermath.

At an *iftar* graciously hosted by the State Department, we recently had the opportunity to discuss the vision of *Muslim Girl* with Secretary of State Condoleezza Rice.

This is a time for engagement—a time when it could not matter more that Muslim voices be heard by those with the power to transform the grim realities facing the young women of our global community. The recent war in Lebanon, the Israel-Palestine conflict, Indonesia's recovery from overwhelming tragedy—all are understood very differently through the prism of lived experience. How fitting that the stories with the deepest resonance that evening were Shadya Zoabi's and Merlinta Anggilia's—both girls whose homelands have known decades of suffering, both girls who struggle to build a better world.

When the headlines resound with escalating war rhetoric and every day brings a new dose of despair from Iraq, it helps to remember that there are young women on the ground who are using their time and talents to defeat the relentless nihilism of the news. Their vision is tolerant, inclusive and compassionate. Their deeds speak back to those who argue for war and those who commit mindless acts of destruction in the name of our shared faith.

Our mission is to enlighten, celebrate and inspire Muslim girls. But as you reached out to us to share your courage and vision, we're the ones who have been inspired.

Ausma Zehanat Khan

①

FIGURE 3.7 *Muslim Girl*, editor's letter featuring Condoleezza Rice, November–December 2007.

FIGURES 3.8, 3.9, AND 3.10 *Clockwise from top: Azizah, cover, vol. 3, issue 3; Azizah, cover, vol. 6, issue 2; Azizah, vol. 6, issue 4. Courtesy of Azizah magazine.*

UPFRONT

As salaamu 'alaykum.

One way to gauge what is important to those around us is to take note of how people spend their time and money. Three hours spent volunteering at a food bank each week makes a bold statement about one's priorities. Three closets full of designer shoes make just as loud a statement, while saying something else.

As we look at the state of today's economy and its prolonged downturn, we wondered about the link between the money we spend and the values we hold. Is there a connection between spirituality and the economy? This issue's Special Report looks at the Islamic guidelines that govern our financial transactions and how they may (or may not) impact the economy.

In the Special Report, we also step away from the gloom and doom to look at one of the more positive economic developments – philanthropy in the community and the establishment of the Muslim Women's Fund. This fund promises to employ philanthropy all over the world, to empower Muslim women to walk on the road of economic independence and to enable them to propel their communities forward. This fund is another remarkable brick in the beautiful social edifice being constructed by Muslim American women.

Besides discussing money, we also look at our readers' favorite topic – marriage. Couples who have been married long enough to weather a variety of emotional storms let us know a joyful marriage is not just a romantic dream. They share their experience, showing that wedded bliss is definitely attainable, and they give us useful tips to that end.

God willing, we are creating strong, happy marriages and stable financial institutions. Love *and* money – let's celebrate!

Tayyibah Taylor & Marlina Soerakoeosoemah

FIGURE 3.11 *Azizah*, editor's picture, Tayyibah Taylor (*left*). Courtesy of *Azizah* magazine.

magazine in my sample and is more overtly devotional in its content than *Emel* or *Muslim Girl*, with whom it shares some readers. As publisher and editor in chief Tayyibah Taylor (see figure 3.11) states, "it's the magazine for the Muslim woman who puts Islam at the center of her life."[9] Designed to address the issues of Muslim American women, *Azizah* publishes only articles written by Muslim women—"we feel very strongly that in order to have a vehicle for her voice, that her voice is unfiltered"—and features only clothes designed by Muslim women or carried by Muslim businesses.

With a print run of five to ten thousand, *Azizah* made an ideological decision to avoid mainstream distribution for fear that the additional financial backing they would need to meet industry practice of printing more copies than are sold would compromise their independence. The magazine relies on minority traders for sales and takes stalls at key American Muslim conventions like ISNA and the annual African American Warith Deen Mohammed Convention (chapter 1). *Azizah* is unique in holding regular "celebrations" to bring together readers and community groups. Significant in an American context where the Muslim community has often been found to be ethnically fragmented, with mosques sometimes perceived as monocultural, the carefully nurtured inclusive character of *Azizah*'s celebrations is now well established (Karim 2005). Seeing off initial suspicions that it might be a "mouthpiece" for particular organizations, the magazine avoids official affiliations: "our publication was actually the first one that wasn't tied to an ethnic group or wasn't tied to a certain Islamic organization or an Islamic community."

In content and presentation the magazine aims for ethnic diversity, while also reflecting the African American Muslim demographic of its Atlanta location. Readers tend to be educated, from a range of age groups, and internationally traveled. *Azizah*'s largely U.S.-born readers (both those who are Muslim by heritage and those who have converted) have "grown up with magazines" and expect print media to be "part of their social lexicon." This creates an opportunity for Taylor's magazine to contribute to a broader process of "formulating a Muslim American culture . . . one that's going to be marked by critical thinking and one that is very inclusive of diversity, because that's what American society is, and [that] definitely [includes] women's participation."

Also directed at the pious Muslim woman is the UK-based *Sisters* magazine, established online in April 2007 and moving to print at the end of that year (see figure 3.12). The quarterly developed from editor Na'ima Robert's 2005 book, *From My Sisters' Lips*, which melded her account of conversion to Islam with stories of other international young adult converts. To build on the receptivity for conversion narratives—"I think all Muslims are always inspired by the stories of people who were not born into Islam becoming Muslim"—Robert considered starting a social network before settling on the magazine format. When *Sisters* launched, Robert faced immediate comparisons with *Emel*, by then established as the UK Muslim standard: "When we came out, people asked, are you like *Emel*, how are you different from *Emel*? So we didn't want to really cam-

FIGURE 3.12 *Sisters*, cover, May 2012, issue 33. Courtesy of *Sisters* magazine.

paign on an anti or a "we are not *Emel*" platform, although we are very different from *Emel* magazine." [10] Surveying the by then rapidly expanding Muslim media market, Robert was determined that her magazine should be distinctive on a local and international level: "The biggest difference between *Sisters* and all of those magazines is the strength of our Islamic ethos. . . . We are a very Islamic magazine, which is not actually something you find very often in general in any publication unless it's an Islamic book and certainly [not] in glossy magazines."

Referring to itself as a magazine for women, to differentiate itself from *Emel*'s lifestyle strapline, *Sisters* was for several years the only publication in my sample to avoid photographs of the human form (showing hands, but never faces). The text-heavy title reinterprets lifestyle conventions explicitly in relation to the spiritual preoccupations of its observant readership (articles on how to occupy your toddlers while you pray). Like *Azizah*, *Sisters* features writing only by Muslim women but is determinedly international in its address. Robert, who now lives in Cairo, prioritizes spiritual self-development over allegiances to community norms in a product committed to the international sisterhood of Muslimas: "We purposefully [choose Muslim] writers from all the over the world; we try to put content in that can apply to sisters all over the world, regardless of where they live. . . . The global sisterhood to us is more important than kind of adhering to a certain national identity."

Sisters's revivalist position uses the umma's supranational perspective to reclassify previously normative community practices as cultural (hence open to correction) rather than religious. *Muslim Girl*'s less doctrinal take on new definitions of the umma leaves matters of religious practice heterogeneous but adopts the umma's potential for politicized affective identifications to validate its young North American readers' international connections: on the website readers could nominate a Muslim Girl of the Month for inspirational community work and propose "interesting Muslim girls outside the United States" for their "Muslim Girl International" feature, producing a nuanced geographical axis atypical in the youth lifestyle market (especially in the United States).

In taking lifestyle as its vehicle for the development and promulgation of positive British Muslim identities, editor Sarah Joseph, when speaking of her magazine in September 2007, resisted the idea that *Emel* is political in the "narrow" sense. Although prompted in part by the negative fallout for Muslims after 9/11, she emphasized instead the need for a positive self-determined identity from which to contribute to society: "You can't keep framing your identity in an anti; so we're anti-terrorism, anti-violence, anti, you know, extremism. That's all very well [but], if and when terrorism, extremism ends . . . what are you for? . . . You need a positive identity . . . proactive as opposed to reactive."

For Joseph, lifestyle provides a means to make this political intervention. Promulgating a vision of faith-based identities in a Muslim minority context, *Emel*'s assertion that Islam is a faith that can inform every aspect of life is not just about empowering religious practice for Muslims, it is also about resituating how those practices are seen by an external world. Faith-based practices, especially those that make Muslims' lifestyles conspicuously different from the UK norm, need to be normalized in modern terms because otherwise, "we're defined externally and we define our-selves . . . in relation to [a set] of very narrow religious parameters." Facing "the reality that we're consumers in the twenty-first-century Western situation," *Emel*'s editor sees the transformative potential of lifestyle as a platform from which to make contributions from an Islamic and "ethi-cal perspective": "It was incredibly important to us that *Emel* represented those people who were actually contributing and inspired others to con-tribute and to position themselves and ourselves as stakeholders in the global dialogue."

Crucial in the early years of this politicized lifestyle mission, says Joseph, was for *Emel* to be assertive "about an ethical consumerism" and to reintegrate Muslims' role as consumers with their creative contribu-tion as cultural producers. Mixing consumption with ideology, the Mus-lim magazines share with the queer lifestyle publications the need to re-claim hidden histories and activate cultural heritages. For *Emel*, lifestyle has the potential to situate modern Muslim practices as part of contem-porary consumer culture while simultaneously celebrating Islam's histori-cal heritage. Yet the magazine faces an immediate tension between the consumption ethos of lifestyle publishing and Islamic principles about the fair distribution of resources. In mainstream British lifestyle and fashion media, sustainability has also become a popular topic (see blogger Jana Kossaibati's excellent post on why Muslim brands can't be as cheap as the high street).[11] But the potential conflict between articles on the environ-ment and fashion featuring the products of sweated labor is more easily contained in mainstream fashion magazines that can presume a reader accustomed to switching between the aspirational (couture fashion) and the practical (high street alternatives). At *Emel*, where a more literal mode of reading inheres, there is a need to square consumption with Islamic values; while "embedded" across the magazine's content, it is, predictably, the fashion pages that cause the most anxieties: "Because fashion can be ridiculously expensive . . . I ask people to be realistic and to be ethical about it and we have had massive debates in this office on whether it's ethical to, you know, profile a £3,000 pair of shoes. . . . [From an ethical] Muslim perspective, if you're earning that amount of money, you have that much disposable income, you're paying all of your charity things, you can, in theory, Islamically, spend it on what you like. Still, is it ethical?"

If for *Diva* fashion was a difficult subject because of a feminist inheri-tance of antifashion and anticapitalist opposition to consumerism (be-fore the no-logo campaigns), for *Emel* ethical consumption and conventions about modesty are similarly determining. Given the challenges of dealing with mainstream fashion brands discussed below, *Emel* would likely find it very hard to get much fashion advertising, but the decision to avoid high-end brands on ethical principles applies disproportionately to fashion (and not to the regular features on cars, for example) and takes the magazine outside of the direct, if unacknowledged, relationship between advertising and editorial coverage common to publishing protocols (Shinkle 2008).

Price was not the issue at luxury magazine *Alef*, but Paul de Zwart, like Sarah Joseph, wanted to avoid a restrictive definition of "political." Arguing that "*Alef* is very much apolitical," he too demonstrates a desire to use lifestyle as a vehicle for social change: "We only tend to see the negative thing, over-hyped Dubai [or] conflict zones. . . . But we don't really see the subtleties of Kuwaiti society that is . . . traditional and modern and semi-democratic, but also very conservative at the same time."

In contrast to *Emel* and most of the other titles here, *Alef* had no ideological problem focusing on luxury products and, thanks to the personal and professional contacts of de Zwart and his team, was able to call in (pull, in North American idiom) product to use in shoots as well as sell advertising. In this, *Alef* functioned far more like other lifestyle publications in its mix of, and relationship between, advertising and editorial, especially important as little income came from cover price. In creating a lifestyle product in its Gulf territories, *Alef* faced distinctive problems. Kuwait, where *Alef* was founded, "has a very small [magazine] market and certainly no upmarket magazine that brands can advertise in." Cognizant of its overlapping reading publics, *Alef* trod its way between existing models: "The magazine's designed to be stylish and elegant, [not] cutting edge. . . . That's not its remit because there isn't a market for it. . . . [It's] more in the mold of *Numero* [or] *Vanity Fair* and *Vogue* if you like. It's not meant to be *Fantastic Man* or a *Pop* or a *Dazed* [*and Confused*]." *Alef* being neither a trend title nor quite *Vogue*, de Zwart, having admitted that it "doesn't have enough fashion content to be an Arab *Vogue*" (Lucas 2007), ultimately characterized the magazine as a genre hybrid, "lifestyle as well as fashion."

The Politics of Pictures: Making Modesty
in Magazine Fashion Spreads

Framed by conventions of modesty and determined by an agenda against overconsumption, it is not surprising that when *Emel* was establishing its credentials the fashion coverage needed to be overtly attached to the magazine's mission. Early spreads directly link fabrics to faith, with stories on "Sleek in Silk" or "Comfort in Cashmere" accompanied by copy about the social histories and Islamic significance of the textiles. That spreads initially lacked precise product information is not uncommon for start-up titles not yet linked in with brands and designers (as was the case in early issues of *Diva*). After four issues the fashion in *Emel* got more assertive, progressing to trend and seasonally directed stories without the educational copy. The magazine continued to cover the Islamic roots of lifestyle commodities, but the fashion pages became more generic in their themes while aiming to be modest and Islamic in their selection and presentation. Where copy is overtly concerned with faith it is because the story is about special-occasion clothing (weddings or festivals; see figure 3.13) or focuses on design and textiles from regions of Muslim population. Brands are a mix of mainstream and ethnic designers, with several shoots presenting fusion styling.

For *Diva* there were two key factors that determined the commodities seen on the fashion pages: reader expectation about what could count as suitably lesbian and the challenge of calling in products to shoot. When *Diva* started in 1994 (at the same time as the UK gay men's glossy *Attitude*), and in the context of media excitement about the suddenly perceived spending power of the pink pound, lesbians were not favored as a consumer group to cultivate: many brands were (and still are) unwilling to be associated with a lesbian title. For *Emel*, as previously at *Diva*, when contributors include specialist fashion writers their personal contacts expanded the range of brands, but while access to PR image banks is relatively easy to acquire, calling in product can be difficult for a Muslim magazine.

Journalists and stylists working on the *Emel* fashion pages encountered responses from uniformly helpful to outright rejection. When brands refused access to image or product, *Emel*'s first stylist, Shapla Halim, in common with stylists on all the other magazines I spoke to, felt sure this was because brands wanted to avoid the Muslim connection, rather than that the magazine was too small or too new to be worthy of attention. The two

FIGURE 3.13 *Emel*, "Eid Style," fashion feature, issue 37, October 2007.

young interns who took over the fashion pages, Onjali Bodrul and Natasha Ali, also found a mixed set of responses from PR and brands. That *Emel* was relatively unknown was both a problem and a benefit, Bodrul admitting, "I actually cheat sometimes when I e-mail a big company; I just say lifestyle magazine. I don't actually say Muslim lifestyle magazine."[12] At *Muslim Girl* stylist Claire Murray honed her pitch to provide an industry comparison brands would recognize, emphasizing *Muslim Girl*'s mainstream distribution: "I have a standard thing, you know, it's a lot like *Teen Vogue* but for Muslim girls, and the editor has been interviewed in lots of different media outlets, CNN and the *New York [Times]* style section. [It's distributed] North America–wide, available anywhere."[13] By 2010 *Emel* lifestyle editor Fatema Zehra was able to source products from a wider range of brands but still encountered repeated unresponsiveness from some fashion brands that she knew were popular with *Emel*'s consumer demographic. In contrast to the active Islamic branding market for food and finance discussed in chapter 7, apparel companies seldom appreciate *Emel*'s commercial potential: "this is a niche market that they'd be hitting. . . . The brand is unique; it's Muslim lifestyle, and a lot of places don't cater for this so [it would be] to their benefit."

While many brands still need to be educated about their potential fit with *Emel* readers, the press officer at Tie Rack was immediately enthusiastic: "she said, of course we want to be on your pages; she was so excited about it. And I thought why hadn't they thought about this earlier, the Muslim market? Modest fashion is a huge market, and it's still waiting to be taken in. A lot of companies could make a lot of money from it." I knew that this accessories retailer of ties and scarves was a regular favorite with hijabis, and Zehra concurred, wondering to what extent the hijabi consumer was impacting on store offerings: "I think a lot of places do provide modest fashion, like you see in H&M when they started doing shirts that are longer sleeve and longer [length], and you think, they must have taken it into consideration because it's not necessarily a fashion trend, so they must be thinking about it but not saying that it is for modest fashion. Maybe that would stop people from buying it."

Mainstream fashion brands still have little understanding of the particular needs or tastes of Muslim (or modest-dressing) consumers and rarely see them as valuable customers. Like style intermediaries on lesbian titles, fashion stylists who are "outed" as Muslims when working on a Muslim magazine (likewise regardless of their own personal faith or sexual identity) have not only to determine trends for their readers, but to educate brands that their readers are even interested in style. However, as is typical across the fashion industry, personal relationships count for a great deal, and magazines can find that links with brands or shops come and go as their press personnel move from one company to another.

Concerns about modesty extend beyond the selection of clothing to decisions about how garments, and the bodies they clothe, are seen on the page. At *Emel*, Sarah Joseph wanted to differentiate between the representation of the body on the fashion pages and in other editorial content. Faces and full-body shots appeared when they belonged to named individuals in features or news items, but for the first seven years no faces were seen on the fashion pages except in "straight-ups," ostensibly unstyled street shots of real people (see figure 3.14). Joseph, whose mother ran a modeling agency, was determined to avoid the objectification she sees as typical of the fashion industry: "When you're dealing with a model . . . you're objectifying that person and presenting that person as you want them to be. . . . [It's] incredibly important that we present women [in features and interviews] according to what they have to say, what they're doing . . . not according to how they look. . . . We don't make any changes to that. They present themselves with a scarf . . . without a scarf, that's up to them." Printing most fashion shots as a full-body composition that was simply and obviously cropped at the chin (see figures 3.13 and 3.15),

FIGURE 3.14 *Emel*, "Hot off the High Street," street style feature, issue 35, August 2007.

FIGURE 3.15 *Emel*, "Noir, the New Black," fashion feature, issue 17, February 2006.

known around the office as the "French Revolution Approach" (Joseph 2013: 48), might have effectively announced the ideological slant of editorial visual policy. But it posed design problems for the two art directors who had to respond creatively to the challenge of creating a new Islamic visual vocabulary (see figure 3.15).

By 2010 Joseph had been persuaded to change her visual policy as fash-

FIGURE 3.16 *Emel,* "Recessionista Chic," fashion feature, January 2011.

ion shoots came increasingly to be themed around named individuals. For Joseph, admitting in 2012 that she had at first felt "a little bit uncomfortable," the key lay in finding a way to expand their visual repertoire while still avoiding the commodification of models' bodies inherent in fashion industry castings: "the whole point of not showing their faces was that with models you would have to [do] castings, and did you want a tall model or a thin model, a black model, an Asian model, a white model?" Maintaining Joseph's politicized opposition to this particular form of embodied aesthetic labor (Entwistle 2009), *Emel* initially recruited models through word of mouth, implementing their own casting priorities — "they're not chosen for their height, they're chosen for their volunteerism" — while also making efforts (easier now with social media) to avoid reproducing their own ethnic mix (see figure 3.16).

Lifestyle editor Zehra, not herself exercised about showing faces, recognized that for the magazine there was a value in avoiding professional models that went beyond labor relations or the sometimes gimmicky use of diverse "real" bodies in ad campaigns: "we don't need to do a Dove campaign where they show larger women, because we're going to show real people all the time. I don't want to promote modeling; it's not like I want people to come up and say I think I'm amazing, feature me as a model, no. It's more about if you have an interest in certain things or if you're keen on fashion. . . . They don't have to be perfect, that's the important thing; they're just normal people."

These real bodies are valuable not simply as differently shaped real people in fashionable clothing but as real *Muslims*: their diversity of size, ethnicity, body management, and grooming (men with and without beards) makes manifest *Emel*'s determination to validate as authentic multiple rather than single or doctrinaire understandings of Islam as a living faith. However, as Zehra knows, not all Muslim women and hijabis can incorporate modeling into their understanding of modesty and many would be reluctant to be displayed in a magazine. Although some readers complain about the new policy (and continue to complain about the fashion in general), showing fashion on real Muslim bodies rather than professional models helped to contain the regulatory attempts of critics. Realizing that "people actually like to be able to relate to the people that are on the pages [to know] that they're real-life Muslims," Zehra began to include a backstory with the models' names and occupations.

With the inclusion of faces comes the inclusion of hijab, demanding additional skills and time from fashion staff on Muslim magazines: "the difference between Muslim and non-Muslim fashion is that you have to think about things like is she covered, she has to have hijab that matches. . . . I notice when I look at fashion magazines, if there's a dress, there's just a dress. . . . [Hijabi fashion] takes a lot more clothes." Like the additional garments (and attendant costs) and technical skills that make up the beauty work of tesettür consumers and shop staff in Turkey (Sandıkçı and Ger 2005), so too fashion journalists in WENA face a tariff of difficulty not required by secular style intermediaries. Incorporating hijab when working with real Muslim women rather than models necessitates the development of participatory stylist etiquettes. While in secular fashion shoots with nonprofessionals, the makeover volunteer might expect to be entirely done over by the stylist, for women modeling hijab collaboration must be part of the process because "it's a bit different styling someone's hair from styling their hijab."

The extent and range of *Emel*'s fashion imagery expanded further in 2011 when they launched two digital supplements, *Modestyle* for fashion and *Embox* for students. Enhancing reader connectivity, and supported by a dedicated web worker, a digital version of the main magazine was by early 2012 reaching seventy-four thousand subscribers, with the *Emel* website averaging forty thousand unique hits per month, rising to eighty thousand "if there's something that's really buzzing out there" (Joseph).

FIGURE 3.17 *Embox*, student supplement, "What Makes a Muslim Student?," cover, September 20, 2011.

With social media attracting about 260,000 followers worldwide, fashion is consistently the biggest hitter for Internet traffic. The technological change from print to digital allows Zehra to make an ideological change in imagery from hijabi to non-hijabi fashion. Just as it "took a while for people to get used to going from no faces to faces," so too she predicts will the move to including non-hijabis have to come gradually. The range of digital platforms lets her try different versions of modesty, opening the "wider discussion" by including a woman without hijab on the cover of their student supplement *Embox* in 2011 (see figure 3.17), "a very conscious decision because we know that there are Muslim women who don't cover and that doesn't say any less about them."

At *Alef* too it was fashion in editorial and advertising that had to tread a delicate line, with features on architecture, arts, or prominent individuals less likely to fall foul of state censors. In editorial, said Paul de Zwart, photographers and stylists knew they were "shooting for a Middle Eastern audience" and were briefed to be considerate of "non-defined but general views on modesty" in the region, to be "judicious" in their use of skin and choice of poses. While in *Emel* it is clear that the garments are chosen to facilitate various versions of Muslim modesty, the range of garments in *Alef* might initially appear to have little in common with this. Given that local dress habits for the fashionable elite combine all-encompassing outerwear with the latest global fashion at home or in single-sex environments, the magazine was unrestricted in its choice of garments but took care to present them on the page in accordance with local representational codes, with lead stylist Beth Dadswell and photographer Jean François Carly posing models to camouflage flesh with the pleats of an upheld skirt (see figure 3.18) or combining thick tights to cover the legs under the dinner jacket worn as dress, though chest and arms were revealed on the spread's other page (see figure 3.19). The parameters of acceptability fluctuate unpredictably, both in relation to local taste codes and official censorship operating in some of *Alef*'s distribution territories: even when ministries had clear guidelines on what could be published there was still wriggle room if one could "be discreet," though, as Paul de Zwart laughingly pointed out, "we won't do a swim-suit issue." With few hard and fast rules, getting editorial past censors could be precarious (see also Salamandra 2005), though the decision to be printed abroad helped: "while we are indigenous we technically are importers because we ship in from overseas so I think that gives us some leeway, [whereas] a local magazine with a local printing licence would be even more cautious."

The range of images seen in the magazine often exceeded expectations. Unlike *Emel*, which has to accommodate a significant sector of older first-generation immigrant readers who are unfamiliar with English-language media and rarely participate in mainstream fashion cultures, *Alef* was largely addressed to members of a well-established market for global luxury brands who are *au fait* with the staging of luxury products in editorial and advertising outside of local regulated territories. Ads posed the biggest problem for *Alef*. De Zwart was often given permission to crop images in global advertising campaigns because brands knew, he said, that "the images as they are photographed as a campaign" won't get past censors: "apart from my magazine, they can't talk to their consumers." Interven-

FIGURE 3.18 *Alef*, "Always in Style," fashion feature, autumn 2007. Courtesy of photographer, Jean-François Carly.

FIGURE 3.19 *Alef*, "Always in Style," fashion feature, autumn 2007. Courtesy of photographer, Jean-François Carly.

ing in ad visuals at the point of magazine publication expands his role from editor to intermediary between brands and consumers: unlike in the smaller-scale tesettür sector in Turkey, where brand executives literally place the scarves on the models (chapter 2), the production of global ad campaigns does not foster intervention. It is not that brand managers responsible for the Middle East are unaware of localized visual cultures, knowledges soon to be rendered valuable in the development of Islamic branding marketing practices (chapter 7). Rather, executive input during the creative process might not hold sway when big-name photographers were midshoot: "[they] may tell the communications person, listen, I need you to shoot a spread image or point of sale images that I can use in the Middle East, [but] then it comes down to the shoot, [and] you're not going to say to the photographer, listen now, we're going to do a Middle East shot and I would like . . ." The inability of clients to control the advertising image is not restricted to fashion or to region. As Nixon (2003) points out, "creatives" at an advertising agency and the photographers with whom they collaborate are likely to be more motivated by the desire to produce innovative campaigns that will gain them kudos from others in the industry than to stick to a "dull" client brief when career progression rests on establishing distinction through displays of virtuoso creativity. A similar habitus applies to marketing executives selling ad space, who might find, as reported to Faye Kennedy, that taking on a magazine like *Muslim Girl* could be regarded by colleagues as "career death."

At *Muslim Girl*, features and fashion showed the whole body with and without hijab (see plate 7 and figures 3.20 and 3.21). With its own interpretation of modesty, the teen magazine reflected the range of styles seen in the dress of young Muslim women across the continent. Responsive to the lower rate of head covering among Muslims in North America, the magazine used its covers to signal an open policy on hijab: each issue featured a reader as cover girl, alternating between one with hijab and one without (see figures. 3.5 and 3.6). As is common across the sector, matters of dress generated the biggest mailbag of letters to the magazine, with readers complaining about makeup, lack or type of hijab, and even some criticism that features on sports encouraged immodest display. Editor Ausma Khan, who grew up "hearing lots of commentary like that," preferred to ignore it "because I think it really takes you away from the important things that you're trying to do," though the magazine had to reaffirm its dedication to hijab as a choice, not a mandate, more than once in responses on the letters page.

Keep working
volume for fall.
Cream linen dress,
H&M. Dark denim
jeans, **Cheap
Mondays.** Brown
leather pumps,
Aldo. Ring,
Claire's Jewelry.

FIGURES 3.20 AND 3.21 *Muslim Girl*, "Well-Dressed," September–October 2007, and "Long Days of Summer," May–June 2007, fashion features, both photographed by Rina Noto for *Muslim Girl*.

The magazine's commitment to ethnic diversity was especially demonstrated on the fashion pages, with a range of bodies and a wide variety of fashion and hijab styles corresponding to the taste communities and faith practices particular to the ethnic makeup of North America's Muslim population. Because they want the skills of professionals, models are unlikely to be themselves Muslim but knowing that "some people ask, are

An African inspired scarf finishes this flowing look. Dress, $60, **H&M.** Jacket, $30, **Old Navy.** Scarf, $48, **Echo.** Belt, $25, **Aldo.** Necklaces, $8, $13, Bangles, $8, **Claire's.** Earrings, $7, **Icing by Claire's.** OPPOSITE PAGE: Gauzy cotton and textured linen with tangerine zing. T-shirt, $11, blouse, $50, necklace, $10, **H&M.** Skirt, $30, belt, $19, **Old Navy.** Bracelets, $6, earrings, $7, **Claire's.** Bag, $118 **Roots.** Shoes, $20 **Payless.**

those girls real Muslims," the magazine, as creative director Elena Kovyr-zina explains, goes for full disclosure with "a disclaimer that we use professional models."[14] Persistence in crossing industry norms to achieve ethnically diverse casting was so unusual that local Toronto agencies would call when they signed new "ethnic" models.

Diversity extends to styling with *Muslim Girl*, like *Azizah*, showing versions of the turban favored by African American Muslims (see figures 3.6 and 3.21), though they aim to match hijab style to an ethnically appropriate body: stylist Claire Murray explains, "for black girls we do turbans. . . . typically though we wouldn't put an Asian girl in a turban." This visually inclusive policy, Khan noted, has had "such tremendous feedback from the African American community. [The] bulk of nominations we get for '"Muslim Girl' [the cover feature] will have come from that community."

Khan briefed the largely non-Muslim staff team on modesty issues, and the creative director and stylist would call from a shoot for guidance on outfits or pose. While fashion editorial and covers shot in Toronto (part of the treat for cover girls was to be flown in for a day of styling) could be organized in line with the magazine's policy, photo shoots for features on real girls from around the continent were commissioned from local agency photographers and could pose problems. As Kovyrzina explained, "girls who cover . . . know the boundaries" and so do not present any problems regarding modesty of dress or pose. But girls who did not cover sometimes had to be asked to adapt their outfit: if she "chooses to wear [something] sleeveless, so she could be wearing a tank top, she knows that if this is a Muslim magazine that she needs to cover." Despite itself the magazine becomes a regulatory force.

The economic and political as well as spiritual significance of Muslim women's dress is taken one stage further at *Azizah* magazine. In editor Tayyibah Taylor's words,

> *Azizah* is not only a vehicle for the voice [of Muslim American women], but it's also to accentuate our accomplishments, and part of that is our accomplishments in business and science and of course in fashion and arts. And so to me it doesn't seem that we're really moving our community forward if we're talking about fashion for Muslim women and we go to Macy's and the Gap. . . .
>
> I feel very strongly that this is part of creating the Muslim American culture and establishing the Muslim American community is supporting and giving voice and giving presence and giving visibility to what Muslim women are doing as far as their businesses are concerned. . . . I mean, is [a Muslim woman designer] going to get a page in *Vogue*, is she going to get a page in *Cosmopolitan* or *Glamour*?

Unlike *Emel*, *Azizah* does not make ethical decisions about price. Its ideological commitment to support Muslim women's creativity prompts selection based on quality but does not override Taylor's concerns for original content in the magazine: "We really try to be exclusive. For instance, if [a designer has been profiled elsewhere], then we'll say, well sorry, this is a very small market, we won't do a story on you."

At *Azizah*, a visual policy foregrounding diversity testifies to the supra-ethnic appeal of Islam, intentionally counteracting the oft-expressed reader demand that everyone in the magazine "should look like them." Taylor is resolved to "overturn" what she sees as a "homogenization of Muslim women" among Muslim readers and externally: "At the beginning we were very careful to balance the visual and afterwards I realized that I couldn't because somebody else would come up and say, you know, you have too many hijabis, you don't have enough hijabis, you've got too many African Americans, you don't have enough dark-skinned African Americans . . . or where are the Arabs, where are the Pakistanis? . . . [We are] trying to educate the community [that] Islam in general doesn't have to look exactly the way you're doing it, [that] unity doesn't dictate uniformity."

Cover shots bring home the message (see figures 3.8, 3.9, and 3.10), showing ethnically diverse women, all covered, but in the full gamut of American Muslim styles, while fashion editorial provides full-body shots of ethnic and mainstream or fusion dress, always with hijab (see figure 3.22). Reader style features demonstrate diversity of ethnicity and style ranging from urban cool, through casual, to high drama occasion wear (see figure 3.23). Ads for local and Muslim designers cover a similar range of styles and cater to a range of body types. Like *Emel*, *Azizah* aims to use nonprofessional models: "We use Muslim women of all ages, of all backgrounds, of all body types, and we try to be as inclusive as possible. We definitely take pains not to show [American small] size four," sourcing models through contacts or at conventions.

Although some shoots are provided by featured designers, *Azizah* produces most of their fashion editorial in Atlanta, where the long-standing Muslim women's annual fashion show means that "many of the women in the community [do] know a little bit about runway, even though they're not professional models." The forms of fashion capital available in Atlanta are now spreading with the proliferation of similar shows in other North American cities (surveyed in *Azizah* in 2012; see figure 3.24),[15] as also in Britain (see figure 3.25). Muslim and modest models from other faiths have set up modeling agencies (Dumas 2012; Thompson 2012), while other aesthetic service providers expand the skills base beyond modeling to include functions such as fashion styling and promotion (seen in the activities of several of UK bloggers in chapter 6). As in the mainstream indus-

FIGURE 3.22 *Azizah*, "Conservative Chic," fashion feature, vol. 4, issue 4. Courtesy of *Azizah* magazine.

FIGURE 3.23 *Azizah*, "Favorite Fashion Designers," reader style feature, vol. 6, issue 1. Courtesy of *Azizah* magazine.

FIGURE 3.24 *Azizah*, fashion feature, vol. 3, issue 3. Courtesy of *Azizah* magazine.

FIGURE 3.25 *Azizah*, "Modesty on the Runway," fashion feature, vol. 5, issue 3, 2009. Courtesy of *Azizah* magazine.

try, these roles often overlap: "We have someone who helps [with] styling the scarf and styling the hats. One of the models [has] been the stylist for the fashion show for years and years."

Fashion is also a key component of *Sisters*, where a hijab-wearing readership is presumed, including some who wear the niqab, or face veil. Going further than *Emel*'s early policy of not showing models' faces, *Sisters* initially restricted fashion coverage to product shots or graphics. For editor Na'ima Robert, this pictorial policy was almost its USP (unique selling point): "People expect to find more religious content in *Sisters*, and they expect us to follow religious guidelines much, much more than those other magazines. Just the fact that [they use] images and we don't use images, for example. That's one of the biggest differences between us." As with all the titles considered here, modesty structures fashion editorial; but the assumption of *Sisters* that readers adhere to stricter codes of gender segregation potentially gives it leeway to include more revealing clothing to be worn underneath modest outerwear or in domestic or single-sex environments (as in *Alef*'s Gulf territories). Nonetheless, some initial contextualization was needed, and the first print issue for winter 2007 (see figure 3.26) included a jokey riposte to anticipated criticism with the disclaimer, "PS. All fashion ideas on these pages are intended for hijab-free environments. Please use them responsibly! x x x The SISTERS team." References to context in subsequent spreads (coffee mornings, Eid party) signal the gendered spatiality of Muslim's women's dress, while others address the personal temporality of individual women's evolving wardrobe decisions about modesty: the winter 2008 fashion pages responded to an imagined letter seeking advice on whether items bought "before I started covering" are "destined for the charity shop" because they are too skimpy even to wear "in front of sisters and family members." Using creative combinations to rescue for modesty items such as skinny jeans or décolleté evening dresses, the fashion pages present practical style solutions, reframing wardrobe dilemmas as part of the development of individual spirituality.

In winter 2012, fashion spreads in *Sisters* started to show the body in the clothes but not the face (see figure 3.27). The first issue to reveal this new editorial approach included a style manifesto: "we at Sisters have strongly held views about fashion," asserting women's right to "create her own style and not become a slave to fashion" in the context of respecting the "wisdom of hijab and [its] conditions in keeping adornment private and moderation in all things. Bear this in mind as you browse

FIGURE 3.26 *Sisters*, "Dear Sisters . . . ," fashion feature, 2007.
Courtesy of *Sisters* magazine.

FIGURE 3.27 *Sisters*, "Enrobed Elegance," fashion feature, 2012.
Courtesy of *Sisters* magazine.

these pages."[16] This justification was likely well placed, as the same issue included a letter criticizing the "un-Islamic" nature of recent fashion posts on the *Sisters* Facebook page.[17] The magazine's new fashion pages (not labeled as advertorial) focus on individual designers or brands using a mix of editorial and PR images. Brands are sourced from around the world using the new Internet retail geography of an Islamic fashionscape (R. Lewis 2013a) and making *Sisters* part of a cross-referential world of Muslim fashion mediation.

Muslim Lifestyle Media in a Muslim Majority Context: Âlâ Magazine

The place of fashion and lifestyle within Muslim transnationalities and the continued vitality of lifestyle media as a mode for the expression and promulgation of Muslim identities was demonstrated with the launch in 2010 of *Âlâ* magazine, the first Islamic lifestyle magazine in Turkey. Inspired by an initial contact with Sarah Joseph (here as cover story; see figure 3.28), *Âlâ* built on the model provided by *Emel*, able to benefit from ICT developments not available to earlier titles.

Like *Alef* in the Gulf, *Âlâ*'s market is in a Muslim majority country, but one where religiosity has been culturally minoritized: in Turkey, just as in the UK or North America, *Âlâ*'s association of fashion and Islam is often perceived as bizarre. Like Muslim lifestyle media in Muslim minority territories, *Âlâ* speaks to and for religious readers and seeks a national and international ambassadorial role. In Turkey *Âlâ*'s launch gained much, often hostile, press, but internationally despite having no English-language platform it became a go-to source for stories on women and Islam in Turkey. Friends since childhood, Ibrahim Burak Birer and Volkan Atay, the two men who founded *Âlâ*, previously worked in multinational brand management and communications: Said Birer, "when Sarah Joseph sent the [copies of] *Emel*, we interrogated ourselves, how is that there are a hundred magazines in Turkey and none of them are for Muslim pious women [in] this the geography that is predominantly Muslim?" Since the ending of state media monopolies in the 1980s and the periodic loosening of restrictions on religious expression, there has been an increase in newspapers, periodicals, and women's magazines aimed at religious readers (Sandıkçı and Ger 2010). Initially associated with religious communities or tariqats (Gül and Gül 2000), features on veiled women served as moral antidote to the perceived evils of Westernized secularism. But in

FIGURE 3.28 *Âlâ*, cover featuring Sarah Joseph, April 2012.
Courtesy of *Âlâ* magazine.

a context where some Islamists criticized the commercial development of tesettür as the Americanization of Islam and others regarded consumption (fashion especially) as a contravention of Islamic principles forbidding waste (Kılıçbay and Binark 2002: 501), fashion editorial was rarely center stage and was often difficult to incorporate. America-based Turkish fashion blogger and designer Elif Kavakçi discovered this when commissioned to produce a weekly fashion feature for (Gülen-associated) *Zaman* newspaper. Aware that fashion would pull in readers, the male editorial team lacked sufficient fashion capital to grasp the relationship between "important world fashion topics" and Islamic fashion in Turkey.[18]

It was these insufficiencies of style in the religious media and insufficiencies of morality in the lifestyle media that Birer and Atay set out to remedy after their extensive market research confirmed a demographic of pious women who, while, as Birer put it, "they were buying the other lifestyle magazines to follow the trends [were extremely] ashamed to bring the magazine inside the house in front of their husbands because of the nudity." The *Âlâ* team knew that as well as cooking and child care these women wanted more fashion. Although hailed in some quarters as the "*Vogue* for the veiled," Birer was resolute about *Âlâ*'s genre classification: "This is not a fashion magazine; this is a lifestyle magazine, but you cannot sell any lifestyle magazine, it doesn't matter where, without putting some fashion in it." Readers were anticipated in the twenty-to-forty age bracket, but, as with *Muslim Girl*, early sales revealed an additional teen demographic of fifteen-to-twenty-year-olds. The print run started at ten thousand, selling through word of mouth, rapidly increasing to fifteen thousand for issue two, and twenty thousand for issue three. By issue four, this has risen to forty thousand, partly in response to the adversity of having the initial national distribution disrupted by a boycott by secularist franchise holders in Izmir. Brokering a supplementary national arrangement alongside existing orders from a conservative bookstore service, the magazine raised its print run faster than planned. Newsstand sales remain buoyant, with the largest numbers in Istanbul, with Turkish subscriptions of five thousand augmented by a further eight thousand sold by their Turkish-language European agent in Germany.

While pious women are increasingly well educated, employment opportunities in Turkey do not match their achievements, and providing suitable work is part of *Âlâ*'s mission: Said Birer, "This is the first and only company that embraces the veiled women openly, proudly. . . . [Since most often] veiled women are accountants or software writers or the IT people in the companies, they are kept in the back; they are not on display. Since *Âlâ* so openly showcases this [pious lifestyle], women want to come and feel a part of it." Unable to draw on a pool of professional media talent among tesettür women, *Âlâ* called for staffers on Twitter, finding their two hijabi photographers (working with a male professional art director). Contributors of written content respond to requests for topics posted on Facebook. Successful writers may be invited to contribute again with editorial advice to develop their journalistic skills. Repeat contributors may get a name-check on the masthead, to provide professional credits for résumé building. Like many start-up and established fashion/lifestyle titles (as across the media), *Âlâ* relies on interns and volunteers, often linking this to a commitment to community capacity development, though this benevolence is disputed by some, with Kavakçi concerned that *Âlâ*'s female staff rarely wield real power. The generic inequities of unpaid internships notwithstanding, training and support in media and fashion industry skills are provided across the sector, with internship programs at the other Muslim magazines, college work placements in the tesettür design companies in Turkey (chapter 2), and a nonprofit ethos of mutual support among Muslim (and non-Muslim modest) bloggers (chapter 6).

At *Âlâ*, given their advertising background, the two founders have strong views on the marketing strategies of the tesettür sector and the ads seen in the magazine. Selling ad space in *Âlâ* is now contracted out to a Turkish consortium, leaving Birer free to work with tesettür brands on improving their visual communications, essential community development, he explains, because the hostility of the Turkish press (chapter 2) meant that tesettür companies with little opportunity to place ads were untutored in the importance of producing quality campaigns. Brands buying advertising space in *Âlâ* may be offered free professional marketing consultancy—"there is a voluntary side to us"—that helps pious companies realize their potential and helps *Âlâ* achieve the high production values it wants on its pages. To my delight, the ads Birer pointed to as examples of this collaboration came from Kayra, the company whose (then) most recent catalogue had formed the basis of my examination of tesettür visual marketing in chapter 2.

Early ads from Kayra did not reflect the high quality of their products, Birer explained, but *Âlâ* did more than simply suggest to Kayra that they produce something better for the next edition: "We showed the way. You should work with this photographer. You should have a picture like this. You should have advertisements like this." Pointing approvingly to the more sophisticated visuals of Kayra ads in issue three (see figure 3.29), Birer presents the magazine's investment in brand development within the tradition of mutually beneficial relationships between magazines and designers, citing the role of *Vogue* in rebranding Gucci. *Âlâ*'s capacity development mission extends from jobs for pious women to the tesettür industry itself.

Âlâ, like Muslim lifestyle magazines in the UK and North America, faces challenges gaining ads from mainstream brands and, like *Alef* in the Middle East, in finding usable images from global ad campaigns. The publishers will not compromise the "honor" [*iffet*] of the title or their readers by running an unsuitable ad. This, they tell me, would apply even

FIGURE 3.29 Kayra brand advertising in *Âlâ*, April 2012. Courtesy of *Âlâ* magazine.

to a brand such as Burberry that they both like (drawing my attention to the distinctive check trim on Atay's shirt), but which had recently produced a campaign advertising scarves on a naked male model. Birer, like Paul de Zwart in 2008, argues that the global luxury market will have to adapt campaigns to reach the modest niche market: "They need conservative branding communication." Locally, *Âlâ* had managed to arrange with Mango for their fashion editor to preview new collections, agreeing to the brand's condition that a Mango ad appeared in the magazine. This became a deal breaker when the global campaign showed models dressed in miniskirts and sleeveless tops that *Âlâ* could not feature on its pages. It might be possible to render the garments themselves tesettür-friendly, but the way they were styled on the body for the ads ruled them out.

While "there is a distinctive tesettür style in Turkey" emulated by women in the Middle East, Malaysia, and Indonesia, both are concerned that, as is typical of the Turkish textile and apparel industry, tesettür remains focused on production to the detriment of design. Garment manufacture is excellent, but, Atay despairs, "for the design, for creating a brand name or for creating a position, zero . . . we are the copiers." The lack of infrastructure explains the short life of the much publicized collaboration between Armine and leading Turkish designer Rabia Yalçın, interviewed in *Âlâ* in October 2011. Birer elaborates that moving into a higher-end design-led sector would require companies to integrate production, mediation, and sales: "to create the brand name, they have to create the atelier; they have to invest in it." The Armine example is instructive: they are the "strongest headscarf company, but they cannot create any trend or style; they do not [yet have] a developed brand image." Though not renewed, the collaboration had a long media life, with the signature jacket design on the Armine catalogue cover and billboard remediated in the *Âlâ* profile (see plate 8) and appearing again worn in a reader style feature the following spring (see plate 9).

The *Âlâ* founders argue that style inspiration for modest fashion transcends the tesettür industry, citing the importance of the street in the development of covered style cultures: "The woman on the street has a culture of [taking ideas] from Seljuk Empire, Ottoman Empire, early republic and the current republic; this is the culture of development; they developed their pious distinctive conservative tesettür. So those women are the leaders; [the brands] just have to listen to them . . . not only the designer. [If] they follow the chat rooms they will realize that this is necessary."

Âlâ listens intently to the chat rooms, employing a dedicated Facebook team and having from the start used social media to build readership, recruit contributors, and generate fashion content. Their successful deployment of conversion culture harnesses reader participation to create copy for the print edition, such as their regular reader style feature in which readers appear in outfits of their choice, named (with short biographies), and a citation of garment sources (see figure 3.30). Social media are used to announce the date and location of the next reader photo shoot, and would-be models send a photo to the *Âlâ* Facebook page. Editors longlist the best twenty, inviting them to meet the photographer and stylist. Often using a branch of a foreign coffee shop brand (spaces of metropolitan chic, seen as safe for women, chapter 2) as their local base, the magazine team select four or five women to be posed and photographed in the style of the now well-established street style "straight-up."

Associated with the rise of the British style press in the 1980s, the straight-up was rendered iconic by magazines like *i-D* that presented apparently unmediated shots of real people in urban locations to demonstrate that style emanates from the streets, not just the catwalk. Now ubiquitous in fashion and news media, the straight-up, as Rocamora and O'Neill (2008) point out, is in fact carefully mediated to present "realness"; always connected to the fashion industry (the radicalism of street style registers only if the catwalk is there as a counterpoint) and always mediated by the fashion professionals who select which bodies are to be con-

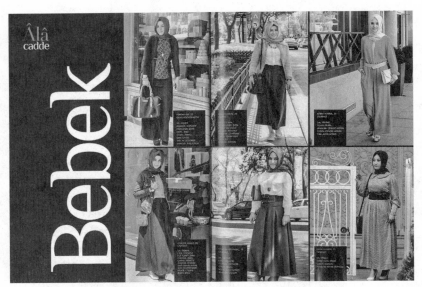

FIGURE 3.30 *Âlâ*, "*Âlâ* Cadde," reader street style feature, May 2012. Courtesy of *Âlâ* magazine.

secrated as style-worthy. Growing awareness on the part of photographic subjects of how to give the photographer what they want has now extended into the "citizen" journalism of the digital fashion blog (with cool urbanites springing into model-style body management when blogger-photographers appear). If at *Emel* magazine street shots are sometimes digitally tweaked postproduction, at *Âlâ* the mediation is evident from the start. Women arrive dressed to be photographed, their presentation and pose finessed by stylist and photographer, and (as was always the case) the final cut is made at editorial level. Given that many of *Âlâ*'s readers are Facebook followers, this process is not so much a deception (staging the "real") as a coproduction: readers collaborate with the magazine to picture pious bodies within the visual norms of the secularized fashion media. The straight-up was also instrumental in consecrating the street as a fashion space (Rocamora and O'Neill 2008).

Transposed to an Islamic magazine in Turkey, where the presence of tesettür-clad women in urban public spaces and institutions has long been regarded as an assault on the secular values of Westernized modernity as opposed to the toleration of traditional headscarves, başörtüsü, of rural women at home or in migrant enclaves (chapter 1), the straight-up's consecration of tesettür fashion as urban street style asserts a coevalness both spatial and temporal. The locations confirm that modestly dressed women are everywhere, while the up-to-the-minuteness of their styling confirms them as participants in (produsers of) a vibrant fashionscape encompassing secular global and modest local commercial fashion provision. Naming the feature "*Âlâcadessi*," literally "*Âlâ* Street," the innovativeness of these straight-ups here does not rest on the discovery of new fashion cities or edgy urban locations but on the attribution of fashion capital to covered bodies in the already iconic spaces of Turkish urbanity, with shoots in quarters of Istanbul and major regional cities rather than in the conservative heartlands of the Islamic bourgeoisie.

As the product credits on the reader style pages demonstrate, Turkish women create modest fashion by fusing products from high street and tesettür brands, with pious brands no longer able to presume on taking the lead. Birer argues that while the increasing numbers of (especially young) women in headscarves on the street "give the illusion that the tesettür market is growing," they "are not necessarily shopping from the tesettür brands, or they are only buying a few things because the tesettür brands are regarded by the young as too matronly." The young, he says, are "hating" the tesettür brands; instead, "these women are working extra time to get outfits out of Koton, Mango and Zara . . . but [the tesettür sector] is not responding to them because they are dressing them up as *sünnetçi*." Sünnetçi, the ornate, kitsch, outfits in which young boys are dressed for circumcision, favors an antiquated (often sultanic or arabesque) aesthetic that is the opposite of contemporaneity or fashion. This is "totally unacceptable" for modest dressing women who, "wanting to look stylish" and "individual," reject the aesthetic homogeneity of the tesettür "uniform." Reflecting the span of modest dressers' retail geographies, *Âlâ*'s promotional competitions (bringing readers in-store for styling with the *Âlâ* editor) feature collaborations with tesettür brands like Armine alongside high-quality "secular" fashion retailers like Ipekyol (see figure 3.31). Picturing their readers shopping in the malls of the city (chapter 2) demonstrates at a glance that the economic and fashion capital of the modest style community traverses the perceived divides between religious and secular, convention and fashion, tradition and modernity.

Negotiating Modesty, Managing Dissent

Common to all these titles is an understanding that wearing hijab, like other forms of sartorial modesty, is a choice for individual women. This emphasis on choice, inherent in the construction of the neoliberal con-

FIGURE 3.31 *Âlâ*, "*Âlâ* Goes Shopping," Ipekyol shop report, April 2012. Courtesy of *Âlâ* magazine.

sumer subject as I discuss in chapter 4, requires delicacy from style mediators who are alert to the nuances of how hijab is unlike other fashion choices. Speaking in 2007 when *Emel* still did not show faces and therefore had not included hijab in fashion editorial, *Emel*'s Onjali Bodrul reflected: "We don't want to be preachy; we don't want to offend people who don't wear the hijab but are Muslim. . . . So we don't want to say, look, these clothes will only look good if you wear it with a hijab. Or, you know, we don't want to say that if you're wearing hijab that means you're fashionable."

Demonstrating the complicated place of hijab in the frame of fashion, Bodrul's deliberations teased out the multivalent implications of modest dress for practitioners and their diverse observers, demonstrating lifestyle media's role in negotiating women's multiple relations to modest dress (however interpreted). Now that *Emel* does show heads and faces, hijab has become part of the fashion ensemble demanding context-specific sensibilities from lifestyle editor Fatema Zehra. Just as *Muslim Girl* took care to match hijab styles to appropriately ethnic models, so too does *Emel* emphasize the shared investment in hijab wearing as an authentic experience. A professional model would "be comfortable whatever I did to her, but with a real live person, they actually wear hijab, so for them it's important that they aren't revealing too much." The authenticity implicit in this image making rules out putting hijab on non-hijabi bodies: "I wouldn't ever have someone that didn't wear hijab just putting a hijab on for the fashion pages."

The emphasis on choice articulated by nearly all respondents in this study is evident on the pages of the magazines, seen in the diverse ways in which Muslim bodies, fashions, and lifestyles are represented. But a commitment to choice cannot mask the tensions faced by the editors and journalists, revealing the myriad ways in which individual, collective, and commercial choices are contingent and constrained. Like most magazines, these titles bear the imprimatur of their editor or publisher: seen in Ausma Khan's determination not to be hounded out of her open policy on hijab by conservative community critics; or in Tayyibah Taylor's commitment to representing diversity in the face of competing demands for ethnic precedence; or in Sarah Joseph's determination not to participate in the fashion industry's objectification of professional models. While all editors and contributors utilize a discourse of choice in support of individual women's decisions about self-presentation, they have constantly to moderate visual images for their audiences. This can at times conflict with the choices of magazine participants: young women photographed for features in *Muslim Girl* may be asked to alter their outfit to avoid stirring up negative responses; and at *Emel* the wardrobe choices of women in fashion page straight-ups may undergo minute digital modification to avoid similar criticisms. As innovators, all these editors are creating products subject to enormous vigilance from conservative sectors of their community at the same time as they want their magazine to be an emissary to non-Muslim society. The need to attend to this variety of external scrutiny and internal criticism while also trying to grow a new core readership loyal to the magazine creates a set of operational challenges particular to minority niche publications.

Far more than their precedents in queer lifestyle media, Muslim lifestyle titles operate with dual addressees. Just as queer cultural artifacts have long been used to signal sexual identities to in-group observers, so too converts use Muslim magazines to communicate information about Islam to friends and family; but, far outstripping the occasional external macropolitical interest in queer subjects and media, the English-language Muslim press after 9/11 encountered a significant non-Muslim readership and scrutiny, with editors in Britain and North America acting "as spokespersons for Muslim communities in condemning the act and expressing sympathy for the victims" (T. Ahmed 2005: 115). With politicians willing to be interviewed in publications newly regarded as conduits to Muslim voters, magazines became part of a wider process in which Muslim political and lobby groups in WENA are gaining political access, becoming "more visible in the European political stage, and becoming more adept at using national media and political channels to pursue a wide range of agendas" (Pew 2010: 10). For the Muslim lifestyle sector, fashion functions as a mode of engagement with the secular world that directly challenges the more extremist Manichean worldview (P. Lewis 2007).

Despite the often disproportionate difficulty of creating fashion editorial, dress does particular work in the mission of each magazine. Taking the morally didactic high ground, *Sisters* uses fashion to demonstrate that gender segregation is no obstacle to style, while titles like *Emel* and *Muslim Girl*, intent on promoting multiple interpretations of Islamic practice, use fashion to announce the flexible boundaries of behavior informed by faith. At *Alef*, a Muslim majority context defined a growing luxury market whose apparently unproblematic desire for consumption nonetheless required careful tuning, while at *Azizah* consumption is overtly politicized in a validation of women's spirituality that melds seamlessly with the self-help promotion of Muslim businesses reminiscent of anticolonial, feminist, and civil rights consumer campaigns. In a secular Muslim context, *Âlâ* promotes to producers and consumers alike the competencies needed for participation in commercial cultures as a route to social and economic progress.

The increased connectivity of digital communications that as I have discussed in this chapter are now routinely augmenting the reach of print media, with new online magazines, like English-language *Aquila*,[19] and short-lived Turkish-language *Îkrâ*,[20] providing (still mainly unwaged) professionalizing opportunities for participation. While some print titles go out of business, others appear. If market conditions allow, the ongoing development and diversification of Muslim style media and the advent of a new generation of style mediators look likely to provide a forum for the creation, expression, and contestation of Muslim identities whose dressed diversity on fashion pages will be an essential component of the varied press that minority and majority communities deserve.

PLATE 1 Romanian model on the cover of Armine autumn/winter 2009–10 catalogue. Courtesy of Armine.

PLATE 2 Tekbir, autumn/winter 2011–12 catalogue. Courtesy of Tekbir.

Y 3562 Tulum Elbise

PLATE 3 Kayra, spring/summer 2012 catalogue. Courtesy of Kayra.

Y 4156 Trench

PLATE 5 Tuğba & Venn, spring/summer 2012 catalogue, cover.
Courtesy of Tuğba & Venn.

PLATE 4 Kayra, spring/summer 2012 catalogue. Courtesy of Kayra.

الف
Alef.
magazine

SUMMER!

MUSLIM
GIRL

ALTERNATIVE
CAREERS
BEYOND DOCTOR,
LAWYER AND ENGINEER

THE LADY
CALIPHS
PLAY BASKETBALL
IN GEORGIA

PLAN

BE
FU
TIPS FOR G
& CAREER S

GROWING U
AMERICA

6 GIRLS ON BEING
IN AME

The Voice for Muslim Women

AZIZAH
VOLUME 4 ISSUE 4

Reclaiming a
Lost Tradition
Aishah bint Abu Bakr's
examination of ahadith

Defending, Litigating
Advocating
Women lawyers

Womb Wellness
No fibroids here

DOMESTIC
BLISS
Eliminating family violence

SISTERS

ISSUE 4 WINTER 2007

IN THIS ISSUE...
• A MOTHER'S ISLAMIC RIGHTS
• LOSING A CHILD – SISTERS SPEAK
• BALANCING WORK &
  MOTHERHOOD

10
THINGS
to hand down to
your daughter

HOW TO OBTAIN
THE LOVE OF
Allah

ALSO
New Muslim Tramp syndrome
– spot the symptoms!

PLUS
SUPERFOODS from the
GIFT IDEAS for new m

WIN
AN
IPHONE!

Funky Winter
Fashion Feature

15% OFF SHUKR CLOTHING
FOR EVERY READER!

emel

July 2008

{Design Style}
Fashion Four
a touch of flair

7/7 One Year On Discovering Doha
Seafood Fare Interior Inspirations Summer Florals

Âlâ
Güzel Yaşam Tarzı Dergisi

KOMBİNASYON
YARIŞMALARININ
ARDINDAN

Alkolsüz
Parfümler
Londra'dan

AŞK
GELDİ

Stilinizi
Sıcak Tutun
Elif Kavakçı

RABİA
YALÇIN

PLATE 7 *Muslim Girl*, "Eid Extravaganza," feature, September–October 2007. Photographed by Danijela Pruginic for *Muslim Girl* magazine.

PLATE 6 Magazine covers (2003–10) (*clockwise from top left*) *Alef* (summer 2008, courtesy of Roberto Ligresti); *Muslim Girl* (January–February 2007, photographed by Paul Perrier); *Sisters* (winter 2007, courtesy of *Sisters* magazine); *Âlâ* (October 2011, courtesy of *Âlâ* magazine); *Emel* (July 2006); *Azizah* (vol. 4, courtesy of *Azizah* magazine).

Âlâ *muhabbet*

Âlâ; Peki Rabia Yalçın, nasıl giyinmeği tercih eder normal yaşamında?

R.Y; Rabia Yalçın normal yaşamında ortama, olaya göre giyinir. Rahat, kendini yansıtan, mutlaka özgün kıyafetler giyer. Kıyafetlerinin mutlaka baktıkça görülen zarif detayları vardır.

Âlâ; Son olarak Ala dergi okuyucaları için gardroplarında olmazsa olmaz 3 ürün söyleyebilir misiniz?

R.Y; Siyah bir tayyör takım, beyaz bir elbise, mutlaka bordo bir pardesü...

Âlâ; Son dönemlerdeki tesettürlü bayanların giyimlerini nasıl buluyorsunuz?

R.Y; Bazılarını çok şık, bazılarını arayış içinde, bazılarını da aradığını bulamamış olarak görüyorum. Yanlış giyinen büyük bir kesim var. Giysiyi tesettüre uyarlamaya çalışmak gereksiz ve de uygun değil. Tesettüre uygun giysiler seçmek lazım. Özgüvenli, kendinden emin hissettirecek giysiler tercih edilmeli.

Âlâ; 2011 sonbahar- kış trendleri neler?

R.Y; *Renklerde kırmızının tonları, saks mavisi, mavinin tonları, siyahın tonları ve her zamanki gibi siyah ve beyaz... Puantiyeler, empirme desenler, uzun etekler, yelek stilinde kolsuz ceketler ve paltolar bu kışın trendleri içinde.*

Âlâ Ekim *aladergi.com* 26

PLATE 8 *Âlâ*, interview with designer Rabia Yalçın about her collaboration with Armine, October 2011. Courtesy of *Âlâ* magazine.

PLATE 9 *Âlâ*, reader in street style feature wearing Rabia Yalçın for Armine jacket, March 2012. Courtesy of *Âlâ* magazine.

Friday, 29 January 2010

Muslimah Style: Ghaida

Reader's Contribution

PLATE 10 *Hijab Style*, reader style feature, January 29, 2010, blog screenshot. Accessed January 29, 2010. Courtesy of Jana Kossaibati, www.hijabstyle.co.uk.

PLATE 11 Jersey skirt with camisole, *Maysaa* digital magazine, September 2010, issue 2, www.maysaa.com, screenshot. Accessed April 3, 2012. Courtesy of Hana Tajima-Simpson, www.hanatajima.com.

PLATE 12 Eva Khurshid New York, lookbook, fall 2009, photographed by Bianca Alexis. Courtesy of Eva Khurshid and Bianca Alexis Photography.

PLATE 13 Eva Khurshid New York, lookbook, fall 2009, photographed by Bianca Alexis. Courtesy of Eva Khurshid and Bianca Alexis Photography.

PLATE 14 Crossing the street to meet Dina Toki-O at Alessia Gammarota's hijab street style photo shoot, Oxford Street, London 2012 (photo: Alessia Gammarota). Courtesy of Alessia Gammarota.

PLATE 15 Taking selfies at the street style photo shoot, London 2013 (photo: Alessia Gammarota). Courtesy of Alessia Gammarota.

PLATE 16 Alessia Gammarota photo shoot for Sarah Elenany's Scout uniform designs, featuring Dina Toki-O in hijab (*second from right*). Courtesy of Alessia Gammarota.

PLATE 17 Winnie Détwa, first appearance without hijab, Tumblr, November 30, 2012, screenshot. Accessed July 1, 2013. Courtesy of Winne Détwa.

CHAPTER 4

TASTE AND DISTINCTION
The Politics of Style

The concept of choice has featured throughout this book, in understandings of religious identity as voluntaristic and achieved rather than pregiven and ascribed (chapter 1) and of how the development of the fashion industry widened people's ability to choose clothes as a core element in the expression of socially mobile identities in the development of modernities in the West and the Middle East (introduction), now being played out in the expanding and diversifying market for modest/tesettür fashion in Turkey (chapter 2) and elsewhere. Choice as a facet of lifestyle cultures formed the basis of chapter 3, which looked at how Muslims have melded the initially secular form of lifestyle media into new magazines that use fashion as one of the routes to the expression of modern Muslim identities through ethical participation in consumer culture. Throughout all of this hovers a fundamental tension that Muslim women's dress, and most especially the hijab, is presented simultaneously and often by the same people as both a religious obligation and a personal choice.

This chapter focuses on choice as a factor in the staging of contemporary forms of and debates about female Muslim embodiment. The first section reviews critiques about the contradictions inherent in the use of a choice discourse to resituate the apparently irresolvable contrariness of hijab discourse as characteristic of everyday material religion. The next section looks at the different work done by concepts of choice in the ways that women narrate their hijab stories, with attention to how women negotiate the experience of being judged and of judging other (hijabi, non-hijabi, and non-Muslim) women. The role of distinction in the creation of new Muslim and Islamic habituses is examined as a located set of experiences, contingent on internal Muslim factors such as the extension of *da'wa* obligations to guide other Muslims toward virtuous behavior and on external factors governing the majoritarian response to visibly Muslim (and ethnic) embodiment. The section following that explores fashion choices, tracking how hijabis craft modest dressing from mainstream high street and specialist diaspora and international retail offerings. I look at how the increase in revivalist concepts of modesty factors into (and influences) the cross-faith modesty provisions characteristic of British South Asian diaspora fashion design and manufacture. The final section situates Muslim youth practices in a subcultural frame to explore the extent to which new hijabi trends are differently legible to their various observers.

Choice, Politics, Fashion: Mixing It Up in the Everyday

For many Muslims under thirty (and probably now under forty, and under fifty) living in Muslim minority contexts in western Europe and North America (WENA), the practices they engage in as Muslims are increasingly understood as a matter of choice, rather than diktat. While regarded as an infidel affectation by groups like Hizb ut-Tahrir, who see submission to their interpretation of Qur'anic teaching as nonnegotiable (Tarlo 2010), other contemporary forms of Muslim habitus, such as those grouped under the umbrella of "European" or "global" Islam, are suffused with notions of choice (Mandaville 2003; Roy [2002] 2004). This is often characterized as the rejection by a younger generation of parental norms, especially those norms underwritten by ethnic conventions but, as I discussed in chapter 1, this "de-ethnicization" of religion (Göle 2011) is most often a process of negotiation between rather than a rejection of existing and localized practices. This syncretism, characteristic of contemporary "everyday" religion in other faiths (Ammerman 2007; McGuire 2008), is also the grounds on which new practices may be validated or invalidated by both conventional Muslim religious authorities and by majoritarian social and political authorities. This is true for generations of Muslim migrants to non-Muslim-majority countries and for religious Muslims in the Muslim majority context of secularized Turkey, where choice factors prominently in relation to the articulation of religious practices as a human right subject to protection under international law.

The discourse of choice deployed in relation to women's veiling can be seen as part of a religious habitus formed through the expansion and diversification of Protestant ideas of religious voluntarism in the context of globalized neoliberal consumer culture (chapter 1). Religions are often divided into those that define faith as achieved through conscious individual choice and those that define faith as ascribed through being born into religious or "tribal" communities. Muslims cross this divide. As a faith that welcomes converts (unlike Judaism) and that privileges the individual declaration of faith, Islam accords with the Protestant-inflected model of achieved religious individuated identity. Being Muslim can also be transmitted by birth (like Judaism) as an ascribed and collectivist identity that is in itself (for some) sufficient for membership. Like Judaism, Islam has been a faith that privileges forms of observance concerned with the clothing and feeding of the body. While the Protestant confessional approach is undeniably a factor in the formulation of faith as a matter of personal spiritual quest among younger Muslims, young Muslims are at the same time creating new practices through reengagement with long-standing Muslim forms of embodied faith behavior that include dress. It is not surprising that dress comes to be one of the key forms through which Muslim identities are performed and contested as part of an identity regarded as simultaneously achieved and (for nonconverts) ascribed.

Fashion often presents itself as all about choice; a binary opposition to the presumed impositions of religious dress. But, following Kaiser (2012), the dichotomized relationship between participating in "secular" or religious dressing can, as I discussed in the introduction, be reconceptualized as both/and rather than either/or. Everyone's decisions about how to dress are formed by a mixture of choice and constraint, determined by personal and social circumstances or the cycles of the fashion system.

Emphasizing (qua Bourdieu [1984] 2010) that these dispositions and the tastes they codify are embodied knowledges (learned from birth or acquired in the attempt to enter a different social group or class), Entwistle argues that by regarding subjectivity as embodied and as "active in its adaptation to the habitus," a middle way can be discerned between determinism and agency: "The notion of the habitus as a durable and transposable set of dispositions . . . enables us to talk about dress as a personal attempt to orientate ourselves to particular circumstances and thus recognizes the structuring influences of the social world on the one hand and the agency of individuals who make choices as to what to wear on the other" (Entwistle 2000: 37).

Thus it is not, as argued by Polhemus (1994), that postmodern young people can choose freely from the "supermarket of style": their range of choices and ability to pursue their desires is limited by social factors like age, gender, class, and ethnicity. Faith too is a structural influence: as a minoritizing social factor in WENA territories, being Muslim determines how young people are regarded by external observers, while the "internal" shape of existing Muslim habituses provides the ground on and through which are formed new Muslim youth cultural dispositions.

Decisions about (forms of) veiling, reveiling, and deveiling are socially and historically contingent and are variably perceived by differently positioned contemporaneous and historical observers. When at the turn of the twentieth century (mostly elite) women in Egypt and the Ottoman Empire engaged in public campaigns of deveiling, it was not simply a rejection of religion but was, as Leila Ahmed (2011) argues, also a response to the Western and colonial equation of veiling as a sign of Muslim and regional civilizational inferiority (see also chapter 1). Veiling was dispensed with by women from Druze and Jewish communities too as part of a wider regional assertion of modernity and (selective) Westernization. However, as is not commented on by Ahmed, many of these very public "deveiling" acts involved the removal only of the face veil, not the garment covering women's hair. Prominent Muslim feminists and nationalists in Egypt, such as Huda Shaarawi, and in the Ottoman Empire, such as Halide Edib, retained a head covering for years, a point lost on most Western observers (Badran 1996; El Guindi 1999; R. Lewis 2004). By the 1980s, Ahmed argues, the veil had been successfully recalibrated as both intrinsically Muslim and as the key indicator of female piety, reclassifying women who do not cover as less pious and as secular—not an identification that would have been adopted by or applied to unveiled Egyptian women in the 1940s and 1950s. The discursive impact of the global spread of Islamic revivalism thus impacts on Muslim women regardless of their personal preferences or understanding of their practices.

In what was to become a landmark case beginning in 2002, British teenager Shabina Begum took her Luton school to court after being refused permission to wear a jilbab rather than the uniform option of salwar kameez and headscarf (that had been negotiated with the area's large South Asian community).[1] Contested up to the House of Lords, where she eventually lost in 2006,[2] Begum's actions in seeking to distinguish herself from other coreligionists and coethnics (on the basis that the salwar kameez was insufficiently modest and insufficiently exclusive to Islam) through the assertive performance of a revivalist identity split Muslim opinion (Kariapper 2009). Begum's case and the attendant publicity impacted on girls in her own school and around the country. The case rested on Begum's right to express her faith as she chose and to distinguish herself through dress from other Asians (Tarlo 2010) without giving up her choice of school (itself "a key pathway to autonomy"; M. Malik 2010: 463).

It can seem a conundrum that some proponents of women's veiling present it as a religious (divine) requirement and as a choice. The political ramifications of this dual rationale are pressing and have come to preoccupy many commentators, who often see the stock responses of hijabis as evidence that they are the mere dupes of powerful male leaders (Begum indeed was known to have been advised by Hizb ut-Tahrir, with which her brother was associated). In the context of the veil's oversignification within neo-Orientalist stereotypes and especially the clash-of-civilizations rhetoric prevalent since the First Gulf War, a challenge must be mounted to the idea that Islam is uniquely and overwhelmingly oppressive to women while also supporting Muslim women in their challenges to forms of patriarchy that seek to legitimate themselves in Islamic terms (M. Malik 2010). Conversely, challenges must be mounted to Occidentalist stereotypes that construct Western women as immoral (whether as victims or agents of a uniquely sexualized society) while also pointing out that women in the secular West are subject to constant surveillance and regulation of their dress and body management. Thus, as Elizabeth Wilson notes in her revised edition of *Adorned in Dreams*, "to argue about or seek to legislate or criticize the veil is a displacement, and at the same time an expression, of the pressing issue of how different belief systems are to coexist in the contemporary world and of the unresolved status of women" (Wilson [1985] 2003: 257). One of the first to incorporate hijab debates into the wider frame of fashion studies, Wilson repudiates as "disingenuous" the attempt to defend veiling in terms of choice: "choice is surely not the point for religiously committed individuals. Rather it is obedience to a higher law. Moreover, choice, the mantra of western consumer society, cannot be the highest moral principal at the end of the day, and testifies rather to an emptiness at the heart of capitalist culture" (Wilson [1985] 2003: 262).

Secularists and feminists (Muslim and non-Muslim), she argues, should "defend women's right to wear what they like, not in terms of individual 'choice,' but as a mark of female autonomy and emancipation from patriarchal control." Although I dispute the "disingenuous"—Muslims are no more able to step outside prevailing discourses than anyone else—I agree with Wilson's argument that the veil should be deexceptionalized and placed squarely within contemporaneous discussions of fashion, gender, sexuality, and agency. For example, the uptake in hijab wearing among young women in Muslim majority Syria may be motivated less by piety than by the desire to "retreat" from the competitive consumption of global fashion endemic in the marriage market (Salamandra 2004; on Europe, see Duits and van Zoonen 2006). The inconsistencies in discussions and practices of veiling fashion are generic inconsistencies characteristic of everyday religion: "At the level of the individual religion is not fixed, unitary, or even necessarily coherent. Rather, each person's religious practices and the stories they use to make sense of their lives are continuously adapting, expanding or receding, and ever changing" (McGuire 2008: 210).

That some advocates of Islam present veiling as a requirement in contradiction to the choice discourse does not mean that those who conceptualize their veiling as a choice are wrong or are suffering from false consciousness. Lived religions are necessarily messy, contradictory, and changeable. Regarding as contingent the ways in which choice has come to predominate in the presentations and expression of religious activity does not minimize its effectiveness for different individuals and groups of women, nor need it construct Islam as homogeneous. Reflecting on responses from Muslim women in North America, Jane Smith concludes that while "many feel that the choice is *when* rather than *whether* to adopt the hijab," others resent the pressure to veil in order to prove their piety, arguing that "the mark of a good Muslim should be her behavior and not her appearance" (J. Smith 1999: 109–10). To continue to pose a binary opposition between freedom of choice and religious subjection makes it hard (Mahmood 2005) for Western-influenced feminists to recognize any agency in women choosing to veil as a form of subjection to faith, naturalizing the historically produced ethic of "freedom" that, as Nikolas Rose demonstrates, is part of the mode of governmentality of Western liberal political statehood. Whatever the actual constraints, he argues, we are required to understand ourselves as a choosing subject, so that each "must render his or her life meaningful as if it were the outcome of individual choices made in furtherance of a biographical project of self realizations" (N. Rose 1999: ix). This shift from a nineteenth-century view of the human as "a moral subject of habit" to the idea of "the autonomous subject of choice and self-realization" had come to hold sway by the end of the twentieth century (N. Rose 1999: xviii), with the narration of lives in psychological terms emerging as central to subject-formation processes. For Muslim feminists, Afshar argues, "power over the veil represents freedom of choice," using revivalist study of holy texts to assert the "basic Qur'anic ethic of the sovereign right of both women and men as human beings who have the freedom of self-determination" against anti-Muslim stereotypes and Muslim patriarchies; with the umma's potential to welcome Muslims (and especially converts) in their entirety "without excluding their race, ethnicity and nationality" (Afshar 2012: 35) providing biographical inclusiveness for narratives of identity formation.

The hijab stories that I discuss in this chapter, and that are a mainstay of the blogosphere, magazines, and social media covered in chapter 6, fit this general trend toward self-realization achieved through the narration of a history of choice, locating young Muslim women in WENA as typical of their wider social moment. In expressing their self-actualization as pious Muslim subjects as a tale of conscious individuated choice they depart from the narratives of inherited religious identity based in collective community and biraderi kinship ties characteristic of their parents and grandparents. In using clothing from the mainstream fashion industry as a mode for the expression of their spiritual selves they operate as the choosing subjects of neoliberalism, becoming "as it were, entrepreneurs of themselves," selecting from "a variety of market options that extends from products to social goods to political affiliations" (N. Rose 1999: 230; see also Grewal 2005; Secor 2007).

Women who experience and represent their religious dress as a form of subjection that is simultaneously required and willingly chosen are engaging in practices of daily religion that are (and are often understood to be) produced in conditions of social, spatial, and historical specificity.

This is why many young women when asserting their rights to choose to veil will argue that it is just as wrong to compel women to veil as to force them to uncover against their will. This definition of authentic hijab as chosen hijab rearticulates for Western modernities the argument that "imposing or banning [hijab is] a violation of women's rights" is influential among reformist Muslim thinking in the struggle over secularization and modernization in prerevolutionary and revolutionary Iran (Mir-Hosseini 2011: 19). For young women in states not governed by Islamic law (as also in Iran [Shirazi 2000]), the willingness to present their acceptance of religious prescripts as part of a personal and autonomous journey to spiritual fulfilment is in keeping with other narratives of religious quest favored by their generation (New Age, revivalist) and as such marks them as part of rather than distant from the preoccupations and modes of self-development of their generation. That many young hijabis (never mind niqabis) are going against parental and family convention (or wishes) is emblematic of the development of contemporary and multiple versions of Islam and marks participation in rather than rejection of Western neo-liberal consumer culture. That state agencies and majoritarian observers often fail to recognize this, locked into the civilizational need to protect Muslim girls and women from Muslim men (Razack 2008; Scott 2007), belies the real challenges that impede Muslim women's autonomous expression of social and religious subjectivities.

Restrictive community norms are still a factor, despite the determination of young hijabis. Writing about young women in Britain, Werbner points out that though they intend to signal their rejection of "village" Islam with their new styles of doctrinally informed hijab, "they are unable to escape its self-evident connection — at least for the older generation of immigrants — to traditional ideas about what constitutes *dishonor*" (Werbner 2007: 165). Regional rather than religious in origin, codes of honor and shame regulate gender and sexuality and govern distinctions of caste, class, and generation, disproportionately requiring women to represent family and community honor. New forms of veiling may be based in the appeal of a "deterritorialized" global Islamic umma, but they are experienced and encountered in highly localized situations governed by particular discourses about sexuality and its regulation that include Muslim community norms and prevailing secular codes of gendered sexuality.

Muslim women may make tactical use of choice-based rights arguments in their struggles against local Muslim patriarchies, using revivalist study of the holy texts to argue that local ethnic conventions contravene the inherent equality that Islam offers to women. In Britain, while this approach requires Muslim women to target both local male elders and state and municipal representatives (accustomed to male dominated modes of community representation), it also depends on women "being seen and known as 'Muslim'" in order to legitimate their claims (Brown 2006: 425). The external world might increasingly be anxious about (the still very small numbers of) women wearing niqabs, but within the Muslim community it is the hijab that is the testing ground: wearing hijab and dressing "appropriately" is often the price of admission for Muslim women who want to intervene in mosque activities or take part in theological discussions with senior men and the ulema who will otherwise refuse to meet with them (Kariapper 2009).

In this context of surveillance and judgment, taking up the veil as an assertion of individual rights and collective identifications involves the willing adoption of a dress item that is multiply stigmatized, whether in Muslim majority Turkey (chapters 2 and 3) or in Muslim minority WENA. The ability to intervene in the processes of stigmatization and the correlating "counterstigmatization of 'indecent,' 'open' clothing" is possible in the context of a new Islamist habitus that in Turkey and internationally has developed sufficient economic, cultural, and social capital to have diversified into internal hierarchies, reflecting the "countervailing interests of different religious orders, political factions, classes, and groups" (Sandıkçı and Ger 2010: 32; Secor 2002). Part of what makes these international Islamic habituses function is the range of popular cultural forms now available to support and help form preferred behaviors. The role of fashion in destigmatizing hijab and supporting choice was one of Fatema Zehra's motivations in London for working on the fashion pages at *Emel*, where, she reminds me, the banner is Muslim not Islamic: "some Islamic magazines [would] be preaching a religion I guess, whereas *Emel* doesn't preach it necessarily but it does incorporate it into a lifestyle."

Hijab Narratives: Observing and Being Observed, Da'wa and Distinction

When in 2008 I first used the term *coming-out story* to young women who were recounting to me their hijab narratives, we all laughed in recognition. It made perfect sense (to these metropolitan, educated, young British Muslims) to transpose to their experiences as a religious minority a concept developed in relation to a sexual minority. Many hijab narratives follow the classic coming-out formula of first coming out to yourself, then to your family, then to the wider community, a process of personal liberation that is intended also to be part of a larger project of social development. Today it has become commonplace to come out about many elements of identity from disability and illness to ethnicity. To come out is to embrace that which was stigmatized, to make visible that which should be hidden, to render political that which is relegated to the personal or private, to celebrate with pride that which should be shaming.

Women who decide to cover are subjected to increased scrutiny by majoritarian observers who they know compare them to other Muslim women and most especially to other hijabis. They know this because they do it too: even those committed to a voluntaristic rationale for hijab find themselves evaluating the behavior and dress of other Muslim women as cautionary tales or style inspiration. In seeking to present their choice of hijab as authentic, within a narrative genre that is invariably relational, women struggle to avoid appearing to judge or criticize the choices of others, as Razia recounts below.

Razia, whose account of shop work appears in chapter 6, describes her first day wearing hijab as challenging.[3] Presenting herself as not under any family pressure—"my mum's never pushed me . . . they weren't very religious, they weren't that strict at all"—she arrived suddenly at her decision to wear hijab, explaining, "[I hadn't] actually had a practice [at tying the hijab], so I just woke up that morning, spent like an hour in the mirror trying to fix it, and I thought, that's it, I'm going to walk out with it; if I don't walk out with it today I'll never wear it in my life. [It's] now or never." The momentousness of Razia's "sudden" decision meant that she was not able to get advice on styling from her older hijab-wearing sister, her mixed feelings prompting an almost adolescent display of show but not tell toward her (at the time) non-hijab-wearing mother: "I quickly said to my mum, 'Mum, bye, I'm going to work.' . . . She looked at me, and I slammed the door and went out before anybody else saw me. . . . I felt embarrassed, and I felt like I looked hideous in it. It didn't suit me. . . . That image thing kicks in. . . . The person in the mirror isn't me anymore, is this really me, and I felt like, did I do the right thing. And so I'm quite strong with my word, so I'm like, if I put this thing on I won't take it off again. I'll wear it properly like a 'good girl' [laughs]."

Presenting her decision as impetuous, Razia not only went out untutored in hijab wrapping, but did so on a day when she was due at work in her part-time shop job in London's West End rather than a day to be spent at home or college. Having worked at a branch of fashion jeweler Swarovski in Oxford Street for two months, Razia found that it was not only to herself that her appearance was rendered unrecognizable:

> I came into work, and I [said to my manager], "Oh hi, Jackie," and she was like, "Oh hello, darling." She didn't look at me, she just said hello because she thought someone just said hello to her. . . . And then she goes, "Oh my God, what happened?" . . . She didn't recognize me at first. . . . That day I remember was one of the worst days of my life because I went to the toilet about fifty times because I had about fifty different pins on me, and I found it really difficult [because] I couldn't put it on properly. . . .
>
> It was very uncomfortable, it was really, really difficult, and I thought no, . . . I've got to keep up, you know, I've got pride. I made a vow to myself, if I ever wear one, I'll wear it properly or I won't wear one.

Wearing it properly also meant wearing it consistently and for the right reasons. Razia contrasts her process to that of her sister who had started wearing hijab when still at school: "she wore it quite young actually, but she wore it because a friend wore it, and at that time she didn't understand it, [so] she took it on and off, on and off." Not necessarily apparent from Razia's account so far is that although she presents her Bangladeshi family as not very religious, and her decision to wear hijab as uninfluenced by others, she was in fact immersed in a Muslim habitus of modesty, experienced as understated and unproblematic: "my family wasn't really bothered either because modesty is something that I've always been bred and brought up with [so] obviously I wouldn't wear a top with my boobs hanging down or something that my mum would kill me [for], but there's certain things, like if I was to wear a skirt up to my knees it wouldn't be such a big issue." Small modifications as she grew up, substituting trousers for a too-short skirt in her store uniform, were easy to accommodate, sometimes prompted by her mum's advice that "you've got a bit more older, you should dress a bit more modestly and you should watch what you're wearing." Razia's decision to wear a hijab was thus an adaption of an existing Muslim disposition in which women understood and expected their dress and body management to be subject to internal scrutiny and regulation. What changed once she decided to wear hijab was that she knew her Muslim embodiment would now be scrutinized by majoritarian viewers, bringing a new set of subjects in relation to whom she would need to self-regulate her dress decisions. Razia's resolve to stick it out even after her first terrible day with a "head full of pins" was determined not only by a personal commitment to faith but also by an awareness of the political damage done by women who start and stop, a form of hijab that she regards as inauthentic because it signifies covering that has been imposed rather than freely chosen.

> The reason why I always said if I put it on I want to put it on properly, it's because I used to see girls at school; they used to come out the house wearing it properly, [and] soon as they get on the bus, slowly, slowly the convertible scarf used to come off—so I call it the convertible headscarf.
>
> [What, like a car?]
>
> Yeah, it eases back, so when they used to go back home, before they got off the bus, it used to slowly come back on again, and they used to walk into the house and I hated that. And I really hate the parents for forcing the child to wear it. [They are] teaching the child bad principles and the wrong way to put it on because it shows a bad reputation to the community. . . . You're automatically [seen as] a Muslim because I've got a scarf and I portray my religion to show people that I am Muslim and this is who I am. But then if I'm going out now and I wear a scarf and I go out clubbing, people are like, I thought you're not supposed to be clubbing, you're Muslim, it's not in your religion to do that. . . . So I always thought if I do it, I should wear it, give it respect, to the religion, give respect to myself, give respect to my parents.

Onjali Bodrul and Nathasha Ali, interns on the fashion pages at *Emel* (chapter 3), tell similar stories about the "freedom" of choice to wear the hijab, and about wearing it well:[4]

> **OB**: This is what I talked about in my dissertation as well; it's really funny because I see it as a freedom that we have a choice to wear it. [But] especially in the academic arena you are seen as being oppressed and brainwashed into thinking that this is a freedom. . . .
>
> I wore it trendily [until] twenty, and then I started wearing it properly. . . .
>
> I've had friends [who] as soon as their dad was round the corner they'd take off the hijab, shorten their skirt, everything. . . . It represented oppression to them, they hated it.

Wearing hijab only as far as the gates of the school may be a common practice (Morey and Yaqin 2011), but the obverse is also true, with some students at Muslim girls' schools wearing the hijab at school where it is part of the uniform but not at home or when socializing (Kariapper 2009). Razia and many other women who spoke to me took pains to avoid criticizing other women's hijab choices. By defining "free choice" rather than a particular style or degree of covering as the key indicator of authenticity, the blame is projected onto the parents who wrongly impose the hijab. This rescues from criticism the girls who wear it so casually and absolves them of appearing to judge other women.

In seeking to demonstrate understanding of how women arrived at particular veiling practices, including nonveiling or unveiling, many of the women I spoke to pointed to the significance of place and time. Onjali Bodrul and Nathasha Ali discussed personal and familial coordinates:

OB: My mum's from Bangladesh, and she's been here for twenty-six years now, [but] she didn't wear the scarf—we both wore the scarf at the same time, so she was thirty-six, and I was sixteen. And we wore it after we did our first umrah. [She said] it's only now that I can actually feel confident, I can go to work and not have people stare at me, but I would never have thought that would have been possible twenty years ago.

NA: Yeah, I think that's true. I had quite a different experience when I put on hijab because my [parents] actually had a bit of a problem with it; they were actually kind of like, why? They were brought up in India, and obviously they experienced a lot of the riots and so on, so being Muslim for my mother in particular wasn't easy; she couldn't advertise the fact that she was Muslim, and for me to come out and say no, I want everyone to know I'm Muslim was a big thing for her to swallow. . . . I couldn't understand that at first, but now I've come to terms with it as she has with my hijab. [She says] you don't understand how lucky you are [to have] everyone responding to you well with your hijab on. I didn't have that. And you have to respect the fact that I don't want to wear it right now because I was brought up in such a different environment: really, as British Muslims we're very lucky.

For Canadian doctoral student Rehanna, wearing hijab was a personal spiritual process that was experienced as unremittingly social: none of the women in her Mauritian family cover, and when Rehanna started to wear hijab at sixteen she saw dressing modestly "as a form of piety, and in terms of my relationship to God, I felt that it would facilitate that closeness in a way."[5] Dressing in hijab at home in multicultural Toronto posed few problems, but when she went away to college in a smaller university town with less visible ethnic and religious diversity she found herself re-positioned: "I was completely alone, and I felt like people were judging me based on their stereotypes about Muslims, [thinking that I would] try and proselytize to them [so] they kept their distance." Temporally, this predated a "9/11 kind of fear; it was just sort of a general kind of discomfort with someone who looked different." She came to feel overwhelmed by "the projection of other people," and, "alienated from [my] own sort of internal motivation," decided to relinquish the hijab "with the option of rewearing it afterwards." Her experimental style post-hijab was "a little bit punky," with less enveloping clothes and red, blue, and purple streaks in her hair, as part of "this whole alternative look that I was going for." Experimental as her hair colors might have been, her post-hijab makeover like Razia's entry into hijab was nonetheless mediated by a Muslim habitus of relative modesty: "the clothing I wore wasn't revealing, [for all that it] was very brightly colored [and] louder." Rehanna's style evolved again as she started to prepare herself for returning to hijab. Regretful that she had found it necessary to give up hijab, "for the pure sake of survival," part of her preparation to resume hijab, "like I'm in training, I'm practicing," merged "asexual" and "baggy" clothing with an ethical commitment to buy less and buy more carefully from brands that are "ethically conscious and socially responsible. . . . The modesty thing for me has to absolutely link with social responsibility."

In Muslim minority contexts wearing hijab produces new relationships with other Muslims, positive and negative. Many women spoke with pleasure of being interpellated into the community: Said Nathasha, "When I started wearing hijab, it was like, wow, people know I'm Muslim all of a sudden, I'm part of a bigger community. . . . I remember the first time I walked on a bus and a lady turned round to me and said, '*Assalamu Alaikum.*' I was like, oh, you know I am Muslim." Common to many hijabis' accounts, these positive interactions with other Muslims through which "the hijab acts as a collective affirmation device" (Tarlo 2010: 55) are often counterweighted by negative attention:

> **NA**: They will look twice at you, more so than maybe if you weren't wearing a hijab because they feel like they have the right almost to judge you. . . . You do get more surveillance. . . . I don't really enjoy that when people give you that second look.
> **OB**: No, no, because it's the same kind of criticism. Just as non-Muslims

are judging you on what you wear, the Muslims are doing it too. [Even] people with the complete kit get criticized.

This sort of competitive piety (common also in other religions) is seen by some to be legitimated by the Islamic injunction of da'wa. Da'wa (literally, the call or invitation), can focus outward on encouraging conversion into the faith, but also has an intra-Muslim mission in the shared obligation to "urge fellow Muslims to greater piety" and to "teach one another correct Islamic conduct" (Mahmood 2005: 57–60). Previously the preserve of the ulema, da'wa was increasingly preached in the early twentieth century, especially by the Muslim Brotherhood in the 1930s, as an obligation on all Muslims male and female to engage in everyday monitoring and guidance by ordinary Muslims of each other. Although women's da'wa was understood to be limited to other women, new veiling practices legitimate forms of female intervention in spheres not restricted to the private: enjoining a woman at work or on the bus to cover or to cover more strictly becomes a validated behavior. Within the "democratization" of da'wa in Europe since the 1980s, individuals might see the acquisition of religious knowledge as part of their cultivation of a pious self and as contributing to the wider project of building a "virtuous community," articulating new religious subjectivities in a context where Islamic values are not underwritten by the state (Jouili and Amir-Moazami 2006).

In contemporary WENA, hijab fashion is a key mode through which women communicate alternative interpretations of respectable or pious Muslim femininity. Their dressed practices and activities can be directed at other Muslim women who can be guided to virtue, at the collective Muslim community via the family, and at the non-Muslim majority. The impact of da'wa on the majority observer is not necessarily conceptualized in terms of conversion. Rather, women hope that through their exemplary behavior and presentation as modern and educated they will counteract negative Orientalist stereotypes about Muslim society as intrinsically primitive and patriarchal. Women I interviewed used similar terms to explain their personal style: looking "nice" to demonstrate that Muslims are not "dirty" or "primitive" or old-fashioned, participating in my research to contribute positive information to studies of Muslims.

Like the rapid fashion trends through which these women create their Muslim style, hijabi fashion is diversified by class and microgenerational changes. While the first tranche of second-generation South Asian Muslim young women in Britain may have established hijabi fashions as a way to emblematize their "correct" revivalist understanding of Islam against the restrictions of their parents' "ethnic" Islam (as many still do, to gain leverage in choices about education, work, and marriage), younger second- and contemporary young third-generation women may not have faced similar restrictions from their parents or come from families where mothers are uncovered (Kariapper 2009). In these instances, wearing hijab may be more about challenging negative external presumptions and creating dress cultures of religious pride as an antidote to Islamophobia.

While some young Muslims with sufficient cultural and economic capital might take up hijab as a conscious act of resistance to majoritarian stereotypes, others find themselves adopting forms of Muslim dress to avoid censure from local coreligionists, like the Bengali migrants to London's Somerstown who started to wear abayas (not something they wore in Bangladesh) to avoid accusations of impropriety on the local gossip circuit (Tarlo 2010), or the women in Tower Hamlets who find their hijab and Western fashion combination repositioned as insufficiently modest by the up-veiling norms established by the growing critical mass of jilbab- and now niqab-wearing women in their vicinity, sometimes facing threats and attacks (Sahgal 2012). In Britain, where housing stock is rarely large enough to accommodate the conventional three-generation South Asian family, the tendency of migrant South Asian and East African Asian families to cluster in adjoining houses or streets, "a distinct aspect of British Muslim subculture" (Basit 1997: 427) can saturate entire areas with potential surveillance by family members. This impacts especially on working-class women (Dwyer 1999) and extends to all (including young) Muslim men the potential to gain prestige by policing women's honor (Werbner 2007). For young hijabis in Muslim minority contexts, distinction may be based not on "belonging to a certain social class, but rather in the sense of belonging to the group of 'good' versus 'less good' Muslims" (Amir-Moazami and Salvatore 2003: 63), as also in Turkey (Sandıkçı and Ger 2010; Secor 2002).

Razia has been made uncomfortable by other Muslim women's judgments. Presenting herself as unaware of the "correct" terminology for Islamic garments like the jilbab or abaya — "because those words are quite new to me; I've only learnt those two words in the last two and a half years maybe, so even I was a bit like, you know, I didn't know what it meant properly" — Razia (by then working for Swarovski at Debenhams) was aware of other staff "who were already wearing the whole thing."

I found that there was a praying room that they built upstairs, and during Ramadan time . . . you could actually go in there, you can do your praying. So I met a few girls in there who cover more than me. They'd actually wear the full thing, and they were a bit more practicing, [had] a bit more knowledge of the religion. So you'd see them in there [and] they'd try and give you some advice and say, oh you should try and wear the full thing. . . .

I felt a bit uncomfortable because I listened to them, but I felt like I was being in denial, if you like, because I didn't feel comfortable. I couldn't . . . even yet now I couldn't, I don't feel comfortable wearing the full thing. It's probably something to do with the person I was before. I love my jeans, I love my Western clothing, I wear dresses sometimes, I have like a mixture, I like the variety in my life.

This "encouragement" to "do it the proper way, if you like," was clearly somewhat uncomfortable, but Razia found a way through: "But then I got used to them telling me these things and I said yes, thank you for the information, I really appreciate it. . . . So it didn't sort of like overdo my power of what I wanted to do." In the no doubt carefully neutral physical environment of the nondenominational prayer space provided by the store as part of their staff diversity policy (chapter 5), Razia faces the sort of Islamist progressivist narrative (first hijab, then jilbab, then niqab, then gloves) that young people more often report encountering in college and university Islam societies. In the workplace staff facility, Razia uses a pluralist conception of religious practice to find a way through an intra-Muslim border dispute about what constitutes correct, authentic hijab. Her apparent deference to the other women who are presented as having more religious capital ("more practicing," "more knowledge") allows her to demonstrate respect while rejecting their attempt to define Islam and lets her quietly continue with her "mixture" of everyday religion. It is "variety in my life," blending Western clothing, rather than a progressivist narrative toward more clearly defined Islamic dress, "the full thing," that supports her in "my power of what I wanted to do."

The reputation of some college Islamic Societies (ISOC) is common knowledge among young Muslims. Onjali and Nathasha were in the loop about different London college societies: Nathasha said, "Yeah, go to King's [College London University], there's huge pressure to be wearing, not just hijab, not just jilbab, but you know, niqab, the whole works. [But] when you come to SOAS [School of Oriental and African Studies], it's completely different, or you go to LSE [London School of Economics]—I was very lucky to have a great Islamic Society, it was very open to everyone. Hijabi, non-hijabi . . . meet all sorts of people, and it's fine as long as you keep within the borders of your Islam, your morals."

Aware that the tone of student societies change as cohorts come and go, medical student and hijabi blogger Jana Kossaibati also reported running skirmishes with "hardline" ISOC members trying to infiltrate alternative Muslim student organizations. Pointing out that many Muslim students are aware of this factionalism (see also F. Ahmad 2001), she locates the student experience within the Muslim geography of London, contrasting the (relatively) liberal tendencies of Muslim student life at Imperial College in the wealthy and more Arab west of the city to the hardliners, "Wahabi, salafi, whatever you like, they are hard-core," at Queen Mary College in the South Asian and socially deprived East End. In Canada and the United States, student societies have historically been dominated by Muslim Brotherhood, Jama'at-i Islami, and Saudi-backed Wahabi groups, with the Muslim Student Association tending to a socially segregationalist stance (Atasoy 2006). Asma T. Uddin, founder of *Altmuslimah.com* (chapter 7), had already decided to start wearing hijab at college but saw other women pressured into it by men, herself experiencing the patrolling impact of "the 'Hijab Cult,'" who with "hypocrisy [that] was stifling" were praised for their form of da'wa acted out as social ostracism and criticism toward other women (Uddin 2011: 48) in a religiously sanctified example of teen girl cliqueyness (Hermansen 2003).

Reflecting that "once you wear a hijab you're [suddenly] meant to know everything about Islam," Nathasha admits that being an "ambassador for Islam" is difficult, facing judgment from Muslims and non-Muslims. Her personal spiritual decision, "inside it's very important," requires an "outward appearance" that manifests appropriate spatialized body management; "you have to act a certain way, you have to be a certain way, you have to hang out with the right people. . . . Muslim society in particular does place that sort of pressure on you." For some women and men (and their parents) hijab can underwrite the otherwise dubious respectability of cross-sex socializing (Werbner 2007). Other groups, like City Circle and Emerald Network, conspicuously do not routinize hijab as a precursor for admittance to the new Muslim environments they are creating to meet the needs of a generation of young Muslim professionals.[6]

Finding Clothes for Hijabi Fashion: Overlapping Fashion Systems from High Street to Ethnic Street

Around the world, the outfits worn by hijabis are influenced by the changing silhouettes and aesthetics of global fashion. In Turkey, tesettür dressers report that even tesettür manufacturers are producing more form-fitting clothing because the global trend has moved into body conscious (Gökarıksel and Secor 2010a), and that some of the more conservative brands like Tekbir (chapter 2) now offer items in red, previously regarded as non-Islamic. As Wilson argues, the reach of the modern fashion system means that even those who see themselves in opposition to fashion can never really be "outside" fashion. For those who see the incorporation of hijab *into* fashion as a spiritual and political project, as well as personal style quest, it is not only the high street but also different versions of ethnic clothing that are adopted, adapted, and appropriated into new forms of Islamically related dress. In Britain, with a majority South Asian Muslim population, South Asian fashion has been predominant among the fashion systems used for fusing hijabi fashion; high street finds are combined with Asian dress sourced from home countries of family origin and from the South Asian diaspora fashion industry (far advanced in Britain compared to North America [Bhachu 2004]), which itself became newly prominent on the high street within the trend for "Asian cool" from the mid-1990s, as I discuss below.

While patterns of interpenetration between these mutually constitutive fashion systems fluctuate, including recent inroads from companies aimed specifically at hijabi and modest fashion (R. Lewis 2013a), hijabi fashionistas like other youth subcultures (Elliot and Davis 2006) continue to source garments from a mixture of high street, modest, and specialist/diaspora fashion. None of these systems entirely meets the needs of this particular style cohort, whose developing interpretation of appropriate dressing pushes against secular notions of public presentation and existing Muslim dress practice. It is not just that hijabis pounce on long-sleeved shirts when they are available on the high street, with some demonstrating a highly sophisticated eye for seeing the "layerability" of garments pictured in mainstream fashion media (Salim 2013); it is also that they are buying in bulk items of ethnic and diaspora fashion when those clothing systems feature trends that are hijab friendly. The cohort of contemporary hijabis that make up the majority of my study are forging new forms of Muslim taste that plunder the existing fashion systems with which they interact, in forms of subcultural bricolage that reposition not only mainstream fashion commodities (qua Hebdige 1979) but also the minority transnational fashion cultures to which they are connected by family, religious culture, and ideological affiliation.

Like all women, where hijabis source their clothes is dependent on income, age, and occupation. But for hijabis like Razia mainstream offerings require careful filtering across the spectrum of brands and price: "Oh, I love all the retail shops in Oxford Street; I love going into Topshop. . . . It's a fashion idol's place for everyone. I love Dorothy Perkins, there's H&M, [and] Next . . . you've got Monsoon, you've got Morgan. I used to love shopping in Morgan, but I've stopped in the recent years because all their clothes are really, really skimpy." The usual revisions to women's shopping habits and dress style that are presumed to accompany changes in age and occupation are also calibrated by faith. For Muslims in a minority context these style stages are accompanied and to some extent determined by their consciousness of the non-Muslim external observer. Razia's dress decisions are not purely personal, they are also collectively representative: "Gradually I've adjusted. . . . I've had to choose my clothes according to my scarf-wearing pattern now because if I was to walk out now with a skirt [and bare legs] and wear a scarf people would look at me and go, what a stupid idiot. What is the point of covering your head if you're not going to do [it] properly." Choosing now to reveal only her feet, hands and face, and with a personal preference for trousers rather than skirts, Razia uses her discretion in degrees of covering—"sometimes I wear a three-quarter-length [sleeve]"—and shopping savvy to find suitable garments from stores, especially now that "I can't buy those teenage fashions."

In contrast to Razia's high street melange, Sara, a senior lawyer in the British civil service, buys only premium high-end clothes and makeup.[7] Born in the UK to parents who had emigrated from Yemen (Aden) in the 1960s, Sara was raised in Bradford and is now based in London. A specialist in diversity policy, she immerses her wardrobe choices and shopping geography within a cogent account of the personal and professional intersectionality of gender, ethnic, and religious discrimination, having early in her career taken a case of gender and sexual discrimination against her South Asian male manager that brought conflict with the male elders of Bradford's biraderi networks. Professionally Sara has continued to develop and implement antidiscrimination policy, proud to have been influential at the national level (and writing a PhD on the topic). Sara feels a rarity at work, as a senior woman and as one of only two Muslims in her department. With style icons like Coco Chanel, Audrey Hepburn, and Jackie Onassis, Sara favors "classic" looks from selected design houses, "Escada, Max Mara, Dior, a bit of Aquascutum": "[I am] loyal to my brand, but it's quality. . . . I don't do this nonsense fashion, you know, the things which don't last . . . not corporate, but just really, really classic pieces which are timeless." A self-confessed fashionista—"I [save up and] spend a lot on clothes, don't mind admitting it"—like many professional women her age Sara's classic look relies on a predominantly black palette. But this shared predilection becomes indecipherable as fashion when applied to a hijab. Sara, who wears rectangular silk scarves in the Arab shayla style, finds that "when my shayla is black [people are] more on edge towards me. But when fashions changed [and I started to wear] lighter ones [the] reaction is very different. They seem to like it more, they make comments about it in a more accommodating way."

The hijab not only overrides the otherwise widely understood fashion connotation of the color black, it also renders the scarf itself illegible as a fashion commodity. This mystifies Sara, who points out that her shaylas are "all designer" and "beautiful," from global luxury brands like Dior or from top Dubai designers, purchased when visiting family members relocated to Dubai. When telling me about her clothes, Sara literally enacted how her ethnically and religiously marked body overwhelms her attempted fashion signification at work:

> There's an issue about the race, there's an issue about the gender, okay, and there's an issue about perceptions of Muslim women when they're wearing their veils. And I think that for a lot of people, especially in [my government department], they find it very, very difficult to deal with, and you're seen as either very glamorous, but you're not seen as glamorous because of this [the hijab], or you're seen as, you know, someone who's more militant. . . .
>
> I try and make sure that they see me as professional first, [that they] see *me*. But invariably they only see *that* [gestures to her hijab] and they see *this* [her skin color] as well.
>
> I think as a Muslim woman they'll view you as thick [and] they treat me differently. The organization I work in now is the most misogynistic organization ever and the fact that they can't understand that a Muslim woman can have a voice, be articulate and challenge them. [It's] too much for them to understand that you have a brain because society

says that these women are trapped and coerced and we need to liberate them, [but] no one needs to liberate me and [certainly] not them.

In a civil service office with an often casual dress code Sara stands out as expensively dressed and as a hijabi, prompting discrimination that is simultaneously religious and racial: "I'm not going to lie, I get paid well [and I think] they resent that. . . . How come these black people get whatever and we [don't earn as much]?" In describing herself as black as well as Arab, Sara returns to the language of 1980s antiracist and feminist politics whose mobilization of black as a cross-ethnic political affiliation was supplanted for many by the newly unifying identification of Muslim that emerged during and post-Rushdie (chapter 1). Framing her personal narrative and political work through the language of intersectionality, Sara melds a resistant antiracist consciousness with the assertion of religious rights: "There is loads of racism that I do suffer. I think when you're black there are issues, and when you wear this [the hijab] there are issues." This slipperiness with which her hijabi body registers in different contexts determines not only her choice of clothes but also where she shops for them. She prefers to shop in London because "they're better toward Arabs. . . . Even though in Bradford there's a wider Muslim population, there is a lot of historical tension between communities there. Every time I go back to Bradford I always have [been the] victim of quite horrendous racial abuse, even in car parks or in supermarkets." In contrast, shop assistants in London "treat me really well, with respect, I know a lot of them, they put stuff aside for me." To her exasperation, staff do not correlate promotional customer relations with concepts of modesty: "They don't understand, they're thick. . . . They bring things [that] I can't wear [because] I have to cover my arms. There is no understanding. . . . Unless they're Arab; in Escada in Harrods there's an Arab woman, she's very good, but I think she's Lebanese so she's not religious, but I think she understands what you want better than the other people."

It emerges that the "problem" with the shop assistants relates more to their inability to comprehend Sara's need for conservative workwear rather than modesty issues per se, since, as she goes on to point out, Muslim women when shopping for homewear can choose whatever they like: "my mother's friends, where they're very strict with outside wear, come to our house and they wear miniskirts, you know, pelmets. . . . My worry is workwear. [My] job demands me to be conservative in terms of what I wear."

If department stores and high-end shops show a deficiency of understanding, historically in Britain the distinctive and varied needs of many Muslim women were catered to by the thriving cross-faith South Asian diaspora fashion industry. Very often dress for Muslim women, like migrants of other faiths, was felt to express ethnic and regional identities rather than securing religious distinction. In Britain, Asian dress remains a popular choice and a sometimes required wardrobe feature for revivalist women, worn at home, at the mosque, for family events, and for weddings.

A significant factor that traverses minority and mainstream fashion cultures has been the widespread take-up through the late 1990s of Asian style, an amalgam of styles, garments, and textiles that could, however spuriously, be attributed to diverse geographic and temporal Asian cultures. While conventional accounts of fashion have tended to regard non-Western and ethnic clothing as nonfashion (introduction), it is widely accepted and expected that the styles, textiles, and garments of ethnic "costume" will be cyclically adopted/appropriated into the mainstream fashion aesthetic from couture to high street (Cheang 2013). Building on the recurrent aesthetic for Asian and "Oriental" styling, "Asian cool" became a global fashion story, integral to the long-standing boho trend of the mid-1990s and 2000s. The transformation of Asian garments and styles into fashion relied on their consecration by Western celebrities and fashion authorities, reinforcing the universality of the white body as the unmarked ground on which an Asian item could signify fashion rather than tradition (Bhachu 2003; Jones and Leshkowich 2003). However, diaspora Asian women themselves might recuperate pleasures in "images and items outside of the Orientalist matrix in which they have been marketed" (Puwar 2002: 64). Despite the considerable criticism of the mainstream appropriation of Asian culture (see also Dwyer and Crang 2002; Jackson 2002), Puwar argues that it is "the disavowal of racism" in this new form of "multicultural capitalism" that "hurts," calling for "a recognition of denigrated aesthetics before celebration" (Puwar 2002: 81) to advocate a move beyond the appropriation/authenticity binarism. The "trickle up" of Asian style (garments, colors, textiles, techniques, and embellishments) into the mainstream can reinforce social divisions between those who wear "Asian chic" as fashion or as habit and can signal the influence of diaspora street style and the vitality of diaspora fashion entrepreneurship (Dwyer and Jackson 2003; Puwar and Raghuran 2003; on the United

States, see Mani 2003; on Asian chic in Asia, see Leshkowich and Jones 2003).

The presence of Asian-inspired aesthetics in mainstream fashion especially in Britain must also be seen in the context (and as a result) of a self-generated South Asian diaspora consumer culture that operated across religious divides. At the same time as the umma was being revitalized as an affective religious identification for Muslims, the 1990s also saw a blossoming in Britain of what Werbner calls "Asian fun," a mix of South Asian popular culture imports and British Asian music, literature, food, television, comedy, and film that was embraced by many young British Muslims as being simultaneously "Islamic and culturally open," while also enjoyed by other South Asians and white Britons (Werbner 2002: 192; see also Din and Cullingford 2004; Werbner 2004), with bhangra parties providing new social spaces in which, freed from racist stigma, salwar kameez featured as cool dance attire (Bhachu 2004).

At the same time as the new assertive Asian cultural identity was celebrating ethnic affinities across religious divides, new revivalist hijab trends were being developed in order to assert specifically Muslim identities. In Britain, young adherents adapted conventional Asian clothing systems. Claire Dwyer captures the transition from the salwar kameez ensemble to hijab in her study of young British Muslim schoolgirls in 1993–94, at the end of the Rushdie affair but when there was still little political anxiety about the hijab in mainstream British political discourse. Within a shared South Asian preoccupation with dressing modestly, the three pieces of the salwar kameez (or Punjabi suit), trousers, tunic, and dupatta scarf, had previously provided sufficient scope for modest raiment for women of different faiths, albeit with religious and/or caste distinctions in style and mode of covering (Osella and Osella 2007). In Britain, school students' combinations of "Asian" and "English" items reworked "the meanings attached to different styles to produce alternative identities" (Dwyer 1999: 5). In a context where salwar kameez had become naturalized as "the assertion of 'community' identity and the maintenance of female purity" (Mohammad 2005a: 386; see also Afshar 1994; Samad 1998), the advent of hijab wearing redefined the wearer as Muslim rather than Asian in ways that were understood to impact on the other Muslim girls around her, whose own form of covering became subject to newly comparative evaluation. Pilloried by classmates who suspected the switch to hijab alibied immodest behavior, they also faced criticism from parents who equated respectable Muslim body management with Asian dress: one mother refused to be seen in local community public with her daughter in a hijab.

Twenty years later and the hijab is replacing the dupatta across the generations, with young women reporting that their mothers have altered habitual Asian clothing to accommodate a more Islamically registered form of veiling. As with microchanges seen in India, where Muslims might replace the tight midriff-baring sari blouse with a long-sleeved, loose blouse or Hindu women choose kameez in the churidor style bound tight round the lower legs (Osella and Osella 2007), in Britain too these adaptations apply to all forms of South Asian dress: Onjali's mother adds a hijab to her salwar kameez, and Razia's now augments her sari, having started to cover her head in keeping with "tradition" for married women: "now she wears it [the hijab] properly and puts a proper separate scarf on."

The Muslim family habitus that led Razia's mother to encourage her toward slightly increased modesty in her later teens has been transformed by the developing religious consciousness of her daughter that renders the mother's habitual body management (the adjustable sari [Banerjee and Miller 2003]) insufficient and in need of reform. The impact of this new religiosity is seen (if not acknowledged) both on the high street where Razia shops for her modest wardrobe combinations and in the Asian fashion industry where her mother's saris are acquired. The upward movement of hijab wearing from daughters to mothers is well documented, but there has been less discussion of the fashion implications that traverse the presumed boundaries between mainstream and ethnic fashion. Asian clothing while more likely integrally to have potential for modest body management is also found wanting, itself subject to constant processes of adjustment, negotiation, and disputes over meaning. With saris and salwar kameez now being worn with an additional scarf (and bonnet, or undercap) to form contemporary versions of hijab, veiling women are not positioned simply in a dichotomous relationship between ethnic and mainstream fashion. Rather, the "cross-fertilization" between the two (Jones and Leshkowich 2003) creates interwoven production-consumption circuits and veiling regimes.

Today's young designers in the online modest fashion market are able to build on the advances of previous generations of women in the diaspora Asian fashion industry. In Britain, while there has historically been a markedly low rate of participation in the waged economy by Asian and especially Muslim Asian women (chapters 1 and 5), fashion has long provided a source of income for women, initially as homeworkers or in minority-owned factories, and then from the 1990s as entrepreneurs (Bhachu 2004; Hardill and Raghuram 1998), often driven by their own frustrations as consumers (Essers and Benschop 2007). Home sewing skills of first-generation mothers adapted the salwar kameez suit to Western fashions for daughters, transmitting cultural pride through dress in the face of racist taunting (Bhachu 2004), with second-generation entrepreneurs further "coproducing" personalized designs in collaboration with customers. By the 2000s, with an Asian middle class growing alongside the entrenchment of British consumer culture, the trend toward luxury was supported and disseminated by the growing number of glossy Asian fashion and bridal magazines (Bhachu 2004; Dudrah 2010).

The transnational fusion of Asian fashion is not restricted to the garments but is also expressed through store location, visual merchandising, and advertising and point of sales materials (Dwyer and Jackson 2003), with the location and type of retail spaces in which people encounter and consume ethnicized commodities functioning as important "social spaces [that] are constitutive of transnationality" (Dwyer and Crang 2002: 410). Shop design and atmospherics increasingly aim for a version of Asianness that can be sold through adapted versions of globalized fashion retail, to attract younger Asian consumers accustomed to high street shopping without losing the "English" clientele seeking cultural difference, and without alienating conventional "community" customers. Shops that were once dark, crowded, and with product unavailable to the customer's touch are now bright, open, and self-service, with shop owners choosing strategically to wear Asian dress to authenticate the business's community roots (Raghuram 2003) or to sport contemporary fusion to empathize with young customers (Bhachu 2004). Long significant as spaces for community sociality, and surveillance, Asian fashion shops share street space with the Asian grocers who provided essential foodstuff for early immigrants and, as cultural intermediaries to non-Asian consumers, contributed to the "institutionalization" of regional ethnic culture (Jamal 2003). In many British cities "ethnic streets" are now incorporated into municipally funded branding initiatives that seek to maximize ethnic commodity culture for city promotion (as with the creation of "gay village" urban sectors). With British Asian fashion characterized by the in-store presence of designers, close customer relations coproduce the commercial space as an immersive part of hybrid community cultures (Bhachu 2004) that, as

I discuss in chapter 6, is now transposing to the varied intimacy of online retail relationships.

In Arinder Bhullar's store on Belgrave Road, Leicester's main destination for Asian consumer culture now branded as the "Golden Mile" by the city council, the rails of luxury garments may appear at first glance to feature a surprising number of off–the-shoulder numbers, but customers know that options for more cover up are built into their design and mode of manufacture.[8] Bhullar has her clothes made in India, with each range arriving with additional elements for in-store fitting and alterations: sleeves in the same ornate fabrics, linings to insert into panels of sheer silk chiffon or lace. Like other diaspora-based designers, Bhullar transposes to her shop the collaboration between consumer and retailer/tailor long established in South Asian fashion consumption. Describing her thriving business as a "hobby turned into a career," Bhullar, like many Muslim designers/entrepreneurs still today, was not trained in design. Opening her first boutique in 1999, Bhullar moved the business to Belgrave Road in 2005, with customers from across the UK. International customers will soon be able to order online, receiving garments ready to be altered by the skilled tailors who it is presumed will be similarly available in other diaspora communities. While 60 to 70 percent of her customers are Muslim, Bhullar's marketing visuals use a pan-Asian style rubric on the assumption that consumers know that faith-specific modifications are available, as is industry standard in high-gloss Asian wedding and fashion magazines like *Asiana Wedding* and *Viya*. Muslim readers are presumed accustomed to making a nonliteral reading, able to visualize the adaptations to featured styles that would render them suitable for their particular modesty needs. This is a far cry from the literalist and puritanical judgments that descend on the Muslim lifestyle magazines discussed in chapter 4.

Green Street in Tower Hamlets, the premier shopping street for Asian consumer culture and fashion in East London, has seen the development of several flagship stores (Dwyer 2010) including Mani Kohli's high-end Khubsoorat Collection of bespoke couture occasion and bridal wear. Indian-born and educated with a degree in economics and psychology, Kohli also is not formally trained in design but builds on home sewing techniques learned from her mother. Arriving in Britain, she started with a home-selling textile import business in 1984, building up to an international brand. Gaining huge press when she designed the costumes for *Bend It Like Beckham* (2002), she continues to be favored by Bollywood and British actors, musicians, and celebrities. Herself Sikh, Kohli's mainstay of

South and Southeast Asian British customers are of all faiths, augmented by non-Asian British bridal clients who "want the influence of the ethnic embellishment, but on a Western cut."[9]

A South Asian fashion culture means that clients are ready to collaborate with the designer on their own specification, often intending that these expensive garments (between two and four thousand pounds for a wedding outfit) will be converted into evening wear for future use. A broadly understood disposition to modesty means that young women automatically design outfits with sufficient cover-up, but whereas until the early 2000s "the seniors would come and decide for the girl," now the young women shop without "an accompaniment" and decide for themselves. This style autonomy, a "change we have seen dramatically over the years," correlates with women's increased financial autonomy: "the girls are earning well, they want to spend well, they want to make a statement."

The rise in hijab wearing among young women is impacting on the ways in which Asian fashion is styled but not so far on production and marketing.[10] The three-piece salwar kameez has not yet appeared with a fourth piece for hijab. Hijabi blogger and stylist Adviha Khan of Hijabli cious.co.uk explained the challenges of creating a functional hijab from the conventional items of salwar, kameez, and dupatta: "girls are using their dupatta and tying it as a headscarf, but of course there's so much material and it's so long and wide that it can often prove quite difficult. [Some women will] find a color in the suit which is the color of the embroidery and [match that to] a normal scarf they've got and then just wear the dupatta round their neck."

Salwar kameez consumers committed to revivalist forms of modest dressing find themselves treating the suit like any other clothing from the high street, but the add-on scarf disrupts the coherence of the suit to the extent that it no longer feels authentic: "I've tried, [if] forced by my mum when I have to go somewhere, to wear it, and if it's short sleeves and you're wearing a cardigan on top and then you've got to put another scarf with it, you just feel so disconnected and it doesn't feel right because you've had to layer it in so many ways [that] it loses its integrity, and I just say I'd rather put on a pair of jeans."

Layering might be a good way to hijabify mainstream trends, but it does not automatically translate to Asian fashion. Just as some mainstream fashion stories like layering aid modest fashion, so too can the ever more rapid trend cycles in Asian fashions provide a culturally attuned window of style opportunity: "[now in] the Pakistani fashion market, long sleeves and long dresses [are] in fashion in the salwar kameez, so it's been quite lucky for girls who wear hijab because they've automatically got Asian clothes to wear. . . . Everyone's investing in that style before it changes."

Adviya, who shares the blog and styling with her sister Samia, is aware of the sometimes determining impact of Asian dress for converts to Islam in Britain:

> I would say they have a slight vulnerability when they come into a new religion [and] there's the pressure to fit into a community that might not be your cultural community. A lot of them [might] feel they need to go towards dressing in a specific way, like a South Asian and pick up the salwar kameez and the dupatta. [So on our website] we thought it was so important to say, even if you didn't [come from] a traditional British Muslim cultural background . . . you don't need to adopt another culture from India or Pakistan; you can be who you are, you can be English, you can be British, and you can dress how you've always dressed but [with] a little bit of customizations, and you'll probably feel more comfortable.

If the hijabifying of Asian dress can transmit up to their mothers for hijabis from traditional British Muslim backgrounds like Razia and, Onjali, for another, the "conscious decision to be covered" horrified her middle-class family and her refusal to "dress up in the jinglyjangly gear" proved a deal breaker when it came to attending family functions; while the Devon family of her white (convert) husband welcomed her revivalist garb, she found herself excluded from family sociality in Birmingham, unlike her uncovered sister (WNC 2006: 26). With other revivalists in Britain spurning Asian dress as too "ethnically tainted" in favor of robes associated with the "alternative diasporic identity and heritage" of the "original" dispersal from Arabia (Tarlo 2013a:74), Adviya also notes that a convert "might have started wearing hijab and then adopted the black abaya, black scarf, [for] a good few months to a year when they finally realized actually this is not me, then they switch to being a bit more colorful and then to wearing jeans and a long tunic." This "personal journey" can "take its time" but cannot be forced. While converts to Islam may seek the camouflage of local Muslim dress cultures during the course of the modesty "journey," there can be style liberation for those with the social and cultural capital to fuse cultures to which they have no prior family connection. White American fashion design professor Heather Akou constructed her unusual hijab by wearing only one part of a combination garment:

The kind that I'm wearing now is, it's actually part of a two-piece head covering which is called the Al-Amira head covering, which means "princess." And I thought even when I was back doing my [PhD] research with Somalis I saw, especially young girls, wearing the same kind of head covering. [One piece] is a tube that covers your hair and especially it covers over your forehead . . . although it's open in the back . . . at the other end of the tube. And then there's also a second piece that goes over the top that covers up your neck. . . . I only wear the first piece [except when] I go to the mosque [when] I'll take the second piece with me and put it on before I go. [Sometimes] I'll walk around town with the second piece as well; people have seen me outside of the mosque with it.

Heather, also researching hijabi fashion (Akou 2009, 2010), drew on her professional skills in textiles and dress to formulate her cool urban look. Not wearing a jilbab or abaya, she uses shaped but looser fitting clothes (trousers but not skinny jeans), keeping "the colors pretty simple because I like to show off particular details. It could be like the head covering or a piece of jewellery . . . more like an artistic style of dress I think." While this meets with her modesty needs, observers outside the mosque do not always realize she is Muslim, "because I don't usually cover my neck." In the American context where many especially African and African American Muslim women wear hijab in a turban style that leaves their neck bare (chapter 3), "it's weird that you would think the neck is the part that signals to people that hey, I'm wearing hijab, but it is." Heather's hair is not long enough to project through the open end of the stretch fabric tube but neither is it entirely or always covered, with glimpse possible depending on viewer position. Although she started wearing hijab after a few months as a Muslim because she wanted to be able to identify her faith to others (difficult for white women in Britain facing ethnic presumptions from Muslim and non-Muslim observers [Franks 2000]), Heather positively cultivates the ambiguity of her appearance: "I teach big lecture classes so I have about two hundred students a year, [and] leading up to tenure I felt like I also didn't want to rock the boat too hard. [Although] it's technically illegal to discriminate against someone on the basis of their religion, I know that in practice it happens all the time, . . . [and I] don't want it to be a barrier for students. I want them to see me as their professor and not like, oh there's that Muslim woman who's teaching us."

Heather, as an older and white convert, is untethered by inherited ethnic dress traditions: "I don't have any kind of history to draw on, [but] I don't have any of those constraints either." She is unswayed by a progressivist discourse of ever-increasing strictness in dress: "I have this opposite reaction if someone really tells me here's the rule, well I'll find a way to break it. I don't necessarily think that rules are meant to always be followed."

Hypervisible and Illegible: The Paradox of Hijabi Styles and Subcultures

That Heather's form of hijab is sometimes indecipherable as a hijab is an asset: it suits her to have it read as arty fusion fashion. But for other women, it is frustrating that the Muslimness of their outfits swamps the fashionability of their carefully styled hijab ensemble. Contemporary hijabi fashions of all varieties nearly always suffer from a relative and located illegibility, faced with audiences unable to decode nuances of style and/or spirituality. Just as Asian women's finely tuned decisions about when and where to wear what forms of Asian dress in the era of Asian chic went largely unnoticed under the lumpen Orientalizing gaze of majority observers, so too does the legibility of religious dress depend on "who is performing, with what intentions, under what circumstances, and before what audience" (Jones and Leshkowich 2003: 8). Reliant on minority and subcultural competencies, the finessing of Asian or other ethnic or religious clothing is rarely discernible to people outside that particular community.

Caroline Evans (1997) summarizes the political issues at stake in the ability to recognize in-group distinctions in her essay on subcultures. Early academic studies conceptualized (often working-class, mainly male) youth subcultures as forms of resistance to dominant and parental culture, heroicizing forms of cultural activity that were presented as resistant to consumerism. While this might have made sense for the spectacular visibility of subcultures from the 1960s and 1970s such as mod and punk, by the end of the century it no longer adequately described youth cultures that, like the rave cultures of the 1990s (Thornton 1995), were determinedly "opaque" in their styling and seemed to be more "about finding a sense of community than about rebellion" (Evans 1997: 171). Neither can "mass" culture be regarded as a monolithic entity, with people increasingly making sense of themselves through participation in consumer culture (as indeed was often the case for earlier "classic" subcultures). Rather than seeing subcultural identities as fixed, set points in a dichotomous opposition between youth and adult, subculture and mass culture, Evans advocates they be understood as "mobile, fluid, as a 'becoming' rather than a 'being'" (Evans 1997: 179). People move through subcultures (women often more than men it seems) and subcultures themselves "mutate constantly."

In terms of youth versus parents, much hijabi styling is resistant to parental cultures as per the classic subcultural paradigm. But it differs in two keys ways: first, for hijabis in WENA the "parental" Muslim culture is also itself structurally minoritized. This lived experience of material inequality is quite distinct from the discourse of minoritization cultivated by conservative Christian subcultures (and lobby groups; see chapter 5) who "imagine themselves to be marginalized and opposed by a dominant liberal, secular culture" (Brown and Lynch 2012: 341). Second, hijabi youth culture while resistant to parental norms is also characterized by a trickle up from younger to older women, as seen in the family narratives in this chapter. In Britain this is framed within a wider experience of cross-generational consumption of South Asian ethnic cultural forms characterized by sharing and contestation (Din and Cullingford 2004). In Berlin, women youth leaders in revivalist organizations embody "exemplary practices" and provide detailed guidance on selecting high street clothes ("one size larger than their bodies") for members seeking to craft themselves as "modern religious youth" with da'wa "corrections of imperfect practice" cohering group collectivization (Bendixsen 2013: 275–78). Elsewhere, revivalist dress and related practices are being transposed and adapted by older women around the world. In Cairo, chic suburban women's study groups are held as (invitation only) salons by forty- and fifty-year-olds from the traditionally Westernized modernizing elite who know about European Islam from their foreign-educated children. Adapting elements of Islamist consumer culture, women who wore miniskirts in their youth select a loose veil that, in contrast to "full" Islamic dress, renders the hijab a "more ambiguous symbol of conservatism" rather than a "reliable marker of class or piety" (Serageldin 2005: 165), distinguishing themselves stylistically from the forms of pious dress sanctioned by the (then) culturally hegemonic Muslim Brotherhood. Writing in 2006, before the Arab Spring and electoral success and subsequent reoutlawing of the Brotherhood, Allegra Stratton describes as "muhajababes" the young women who combined bright headscarves with tight fitting clothes to assert alternative expressions of piety, part of a generational push against the boundaries of acceptable Islamic behavior (concerning smoking, clothing, music, cross-sex socializing) (Stratton 2006). Just as lesbian and gay subcultures of the 1970s and 1980s have spawned forms of queer and trans activism that counter the orthodoxies of homonormativity as well as heteronormativity (Halberstam 2005),[11] so too have long-standing Islamist subcultures seen a range of internal developments, appropriations, and resistances.

Muslim youth culture is both defined against and working in conjunction with parental cultures, characterized like other revivalist practices of global or European Islam by negotiation and accommodation with existing religious authorities and community practices. If young women are using religious knowledge to assert themselves against conventional gender roles they are also committed to spreading those knowledges and practices to others, including their family. They do want to distinguish themselves from the olds, but unlike other youth cultures that depend for their cool on keeping the olds out, this one also wants to bring them in, to help them do Islam their way. They may face interpretive challenges though, with conservative migrant mothers drafting in their own imams to counter the revivalist arguments of their daughters (Ryan and Vaccelli 2013). This gives fresh impetus to the idea of subcultural participation as part of a life project (Taylor 2012), less a passing phase than linked sequences in which personal presentation is formed in dynamic relation with prevailing cultures, also themselves in flux, and in which youth and subcultural forms and knowledges may over time be transmitted both ways across generations (Bennett and Hodkinson 2012; Hodkinson 2012; N. Smith 2012).

The ability to recognize the differences between one version of hijab and another, or to discern changes to salwar kameez combinations, requires a significant degree of subcultural competency or subcultural capital (Thornton 1995). For Thornton's club cultures this was often made possible by the mediation of in-group observers whose promotion of group activities in specialist media contributed to the discursive production of the subculture and rendered it visible to different versions of dominant culture and the market. Running the risk of losing subcultural capital by too much success ("selling out"), it was important to maintain distance from the parental/mainstream and from other "uncool" young people, with "micro-structures of power" produced by the "cultural disagreements that go on between more closely related social groups" (Thornton 1995: 163).

In the postcolonial context of revivalist Muslim youth cultures, the forms and forces in relation to which contemporary hijabi fashion is forged emphasize the importance of minority-to-minority transmissions in the construction of transnationality, disrupting previous center/periphery models (Lionnet and Shih 2005). Within the multiple relations that form contemporary diaspora and minority cultural politics, the potentially homogenizing effects of transnational consumer culture are disrupted by their localized circumstances of consumption, characterized by processes of indigenization and adaptation (Jackson et al. 2007) that apply equally to global brands and to "ethnic" commodities like Asian clothing. Asian diaspora designers and consumers know that designs from London or Leicester must measure up against the fashion capital displayed by designers and consumers in India, Pakistan, and Bangladesh (see also Tarlo 1996) as well as the competing centers of Asian style in other diasporic territories, while also seeking to commoditize British fusion fashion as a distinctive aesthetic to be marketed at home and abroad.[12] The popularity of fusion fashion leads toward subtle forms of hybridity rather than fixed ideas of cultural authenticity, in which cultural distinction may be based more in "the ways things are appropriated and used, not in where they are thought to come from and how they are produced" (Jackson et al. 2007: 921). Cool young hijabis may be creating new fashions, hijabifying the high street and ethnic brands alike, but the ability of ethnic or religious minority cool to be recognized in its own terms is entirely dependent on the localized circumstances of majority and minority viewership. When relocated to Muslim majority South Asian countries, young Londoners can find themselves pilloried, as Onjali and Natasha recount:

> **OB**: I have never, ever worn a salwar kameez. . . . I get told off for it so much.
> **NA**: Do you go back to Bangladesh very much though?
> **OB**: I have been back to Bangladesh, but I wore what I wear.
> **NA**: Really? So if I went over there, I'm more Indian than them.
> **OB**: But the thing is, when you go over there, they think you're backward for wearing the scarf. They think you're not modern, and I really, I had to fight with my family, and I got really upset because I was like, look, I'm a Muslim girl, I want to wear the hijab, what's wrong with you all, and they're like yeah, but you're so backward, you're from London, what's going on with people over there.

Similarly in the United States, African American Muslim women "resent the fact that when they dress conservatively, or sometimes even when they identify themselves as Muslim, others [Muslims] think them members of the Nation [of Islam]" (J. Smith 1999: 181; see also chapter 1). The risk of misattribution, premised on the Nation's conspicuous dress code and restrained body management (itself developed as a form of distinction from the physicality of African American Christians [Starrett 2003]), gives African American Muslim women unequal access to the use of modest dress as a form of intra-Muslim distinction, exacerbating the challenges of dealing with the generic prejudice against veiled women in Muslim minority North America. If in Muslim majority (pre–civil war) Syria, where piety might have been widely accepted as a form of symbolic capital, the consumption and display of goods coded as pious could give young and nonelite individuals the opportunity to gain otherwise denied status (Kokoschka 2009), in Muslim majority Turkey covered dress fails to register to the majority observer as modern or as fashion, disparaged as backward by a prevailing but culturally Muslim secularism. Internally, the aging of the initial Turkish Islamic youth surge produces microgenerational consumption practices that though opaque to external observers make more discernible to participants the distinctions between religious organizations or tariqats (Saktanber 2002).

In establishing hijab fashion as fashion, as style, and as modern, the modest dressing cohort addresses multiple audiences within and without their faith communities. Journalists in the new Muslim lifestyle press, bloggers, and social media contributors validate hijabi practices as a subcultural formation in ways that can support what are in many places minority and stigmatized identifications. Cumulatively, this renders hijabi and Muslim fashion visible as a potential market to minority and majority players in global consumer culture. Young Muslims who want their style innovation and distinction to be recognized as fashion, but don't want to be co-opted or trivialized, must fight simultaneously against conservative Muslims who declare embellishment contraband and a fashion world that fails to see them as style consumers and tastemakers. The relationships and contributions of young Muslim women to fashion retail form the basis of my next chapter.

CHAPTER 5

HIJABI SHOP WORKERS IN BRITAIN

Muslim Style Knowledge as Fashion Capital?

Alongside a continued relationship to "ethnic" and modest fashion (chapter 4), most young hijabis craft their look from apparel available on the high street. Concerned with how particular garments find their way to the consumer and with how particular looks are consecrated as trendy within new and diverse taste communities of Muslim modest dressers, this chapter extends the discussion of how Muslim women contribute to fashion retail by focusing on the participation of hijabi women in British high street shop work. In chapter 2, I discussed how, in the Muslim majority context of secular Turkey, shop work in the modest or tesettür fashion sector provides rare job opportunities for pious women whose "covered" presentation is seen to contravene the secular values of the nation-state, and in chapter 4, how, in Muslim minority Britain, South Asian women fashion entrepreneurs engage in collaborative design decisions within the cross-faith sociability of the diaspora store. Regarding shopping as constitutive of gendered religious and/or ethnic identities for shoppers and staff, the retail experience "does not merely reproduce identities that are forged elsewhere but provides an active and independent component of identity construction" (Miller et al. 1998: ix). Just as this book covers a period in which self-consciously Muslim styling was engaged in an accelerated interaction with mainstream fashion products and modes of mediation, so too does it chronicle a moment in which a heightened awareness of faith in employment relations was changing the experiences of Muslims at work.

As highlighted in this book's opening vignette, a quick stroll around London's Oxford Street, home to the flagship stores of many of Britain's high street fashion chains, reveals visibly Muslim young women working front-of-house—a picture echoed in high streets and malls across Britain. In most high street fashion stores (and in all those discussed here) staff are required to dress according to company criteria. Sometimes stores have their own purpose-made uniform, but often staff have to wear a selection of clothes from the store's seasonal collection: especially in stores aimed at the youth market, the staff is provided with a branded T-shirt to be worn with bottoms in a set color—mostly sourced from the employee's own wardrobe. Focusing on young women who wear hijab and who work in high street fashion retail aimed at young women, this chapter asks, what is the impact of sartorially Muslim women behind as well as in front of the shop counter?

The interviews on which this chapter is based were carried out in between 2005 and 2010, a pivotal moment during which employers, employees, and service providers were gearing up to deal with a series of legal measures that for the first time provided protection from religious discrimination to all faiths, including Islam and Muslims.

The Legal Context: Religious Rights at Work and in the Courts

Until 2003 UK employment law did not offer protection for employees in terms of religion. Previous antidiscrimination legislation covered discrimination at work or in vocational training only in terms of race or ethnicity. Based on the view that ethnicity was involuntary whereas religion was elective, religious groups had to establish themselves as an ethnicity in order to gain the right to legal protection. This status was developed incrementally with regard to Jews in British law and achieved successfully by Sikhs, able to claim that their religion was premised on an ascribed rather than achieved or chosen identification (chapter 1). Facing sustained opposition and internal disagreements (Singh 2005), Sikhs were instrumental from the 1960s in pursuing cases over religious expression that, in securing the rights of Sikhs to be protected under the then prevailing legislation (notably the 1973 Race Relations Act), effectively expanded a previously "biological" definition of race to include religion and culture (Meer 2008). Many Sikh cases centered on dress and body management as inviolable expression of Sikhness as an ethnicity and a faith. Although cases included the five mandated signs of Sikhness (including the kirpan, a ceremonial sword/dagger, and the kara, a steel bracelet), much case law also centered on the right of Sikh men to wear a turban (with workplace uniform or instead of a compulsory motorcycle helmet). Not itself obligatory, the turban was defended as a sign of collective identity because it was externally identified, and denigrated, as a sign of Sikhness (Singh 2005).

Attempting to gain religious rights via the ethnicity model was not an option for a multiethnic religion like Islam. The situation changed in 2003 when the UK Employment Equality (Religion or Belief) Regulations brought the UK in line with the European Employment Equality Directive of 2000 and extended legal protection to cover faith and belief. Applying equally to minority and majority religious populations, the new legislation required employers to permit and facilitate the expression of faith or philosophical belief as defined by the employee. The law covers discrimination "on the grounds of perceived as well as actual religion or belief (i.e., assuming — correctly or incorrectly — that someone has a particular religion or belief)."[1] The emphasis on perceived religion demonstrates state recognition of the instability and potential illegibility of performances of religious identity.

In 2010 these regulations were incorporated into and superseded by the Equality Act that unified the framework of seven "protected characteristics": religion or belief, disability, marital status, sexual orientation, gender, age, and ethnicity. The religion or belief characteristic is vaguely defined, with provision to include any religion and any religious or philosophical belief, with inclusions emerging through case law (for instance, a belief in climate change, in 2009) whose implications remain unclear. Groups like Jews and Sikhs that have been historically categorized and experienced as both an ethnicity and a religion (Woodhead and Catto 2009) are liable to call into dispute the boundaries of protected characteristics, with the law sometimes arbitrating definitions of religious or ethnic belonging as much as protecting the rights of preexistent religious subjectivities.[2]

As with the previous regulations, employees' rights are limited by provision for generic and unspecified limitations. In each case employers are required to make "reasonable adjustments," with disputes and court cases revolving around definitions of reasonable. When I spoke with the UK arbitration service Acas after the 2003 regulations for religion or belief were announced, it was anticipated that cases would focus on flexible working hours to facilitate religious observance. In the area of dress, Acas expected disputes would center on health and safety (for instance, wearing a long robe when operating machinery) rather than on corporate appearance. The Union of Shop, Distributive and Allied Workers (USDAW), who had handled many cases about flexible working hours and time off for festivals in their well-represented supermarket sector, had only one personal appearance dispute, a supermarket worker whose nose ring and connected earing contravened hygiene regulations on the food counter. On the basis of advice from the Muslim Council of Britain (MCB; see chapter 1) that the jewelry was not obligatory within Islam, the member was counseled to withdraw her case.[3] In this instance the supermarket's objection was on the basis of health and safety rather than corporate styling.

The Equality Act expanded the scope of legislation to cover protection from discrimination in the provision of goods and services. During the period in which the new diversity legislation was being introduced, advocacy and mediation structures funded by the British government were shifted from a basis in what were previously three separate equal opportunities commissions (devoted to gender, race, and disability) to a merged organization, the Equality and Human Rights Commission (established in 2007). This not uncontentious move charged a single body with advocating and protecting the rights of each diversity jurisdiction,[4] whose agendas may conflict (particularly between religion and sexuality [Cooper and Herman 2013]).

The increasing frequency with which religious rights are being asserted goes hand in hand with moves from the Blair and Cameron governments to welcome religious organizations as providers of public services and as advisors on government social and educational policy. Also receiving substantial criticism (Donald 2012), the inclusion of religion or belief in the public sector equality duty prompted fears that public bodies might come under pressure to "accept culturally relativist arguments that women from certain religious backgrounds can be treated differently from other women experiencing abuse" (EVAW 2009: 2, quoted in Donald 2012: 177; M. Malik 2012). In the general distribution of state resources and forms of political recognition, British concepts of multiculturalism have undergone a shift from concerns with race/ethnicity to considerations of difference increasingly understood in terms of faith (chapter 1), alongside an increase in religious revivalism among young Muslims asserted publically through women's dress, within a global increase in youth religiosity. For commentators on the right and left, the upscaling of hijab-related legal cases calls into question established British habits of multicultural "tolerance." In a series of landmark cases and public interventions, more stringent forms of Muslim dress are being asserted as a desired religious norm, with implications for other Muslims as for the wider society.

In the context of an escalating moral panic about Muslim veiling as a sign of a perceived lack of social integration, this chapter chronicles the thoughts and responses of Human Resources (HR) professionals as they began the organizational shift to the new diversity approach, and of shop employees at a time when hijab was visibly on the increase and often, for them unpleasantly, in the news. Many of the legal cases and public panics referred to below emerged as the research was proceeding, and although there were no cases specifically about fashion retail in the public domain at that time, HR professionals were watching keenly for legal developments.

The young British hijabi shop workers who populate this chapter were all in their twenties when they spoke to me and had attended regular state (rather than Islamic) schools during the 1990s and early 2000s. They were therefore products of a British state multicultural education system; many, like the young women whose wardrobe choices I discussed in chapter 4, subsequently attended British universities. The period between my interviews and the time of this book going to press has seen an increase in veiling disputes and a shift in British popular attitudes. When I was setting up my interviews a number of developments had recently put Muslim women's dress at the center of public controversies. Related legal processes, media coverage, and parliamentary debates were very much present in the minds of my participants. Frustration with negative stereotypes was often a reason why young Muslim women agreed to talk to me, while the desire to demonstrate that their companies were taking a level-headed approach to wardrobe issues of faith at work was a priority for HR managers aware of the potential pitfalls of this heightened rhetoric at a time when they were preparing for new legislation.

If early French attempts to ban the hijab were uniformly pilloried in Britain (introduction), by the mid-2000s this was changing with challenges to accepted UK veiling practices by young women revivalists who tested the sartorial limits of multiculturalism, beginning with the case of Shabina Begum (chapter 4). Begum's actions and the publicity given to her case had implications for other Muslim girls in the UK. Where some may have "up-veiled" in solidarity, others reported being compelled to wear an unwanted jilbab once the alibi of school uniform was eroded (Hari 2005). Since then the number and range of cases has increased, with an attendant ratcheting up of opinion and practice on all sides reflecting among other things the progressivist model of ever stricter forms of covering fostered by some Islamists.

If Begum brought the jilbab into popular consciousness, in 2006 just as I was doing my interviews, the issue of the face veil or niqab hit the British press when Jack Straw, a Labour MP and former foreign secretary, revealed that he asked women wearing a face veil to remove it during consultations in his constituency office. Briefing the national press about an article he had written for the local paper of his Midlands constituency, Straw characterized the niqab as "a visible statement of separation and difference," arguing that it was an obstacle to communication in that "the value of a meeting, as opposed to a letter or phone call, is that you can—almost literally—see what the other person means, not just hear what they say."[5] As Woodhead (2012) points out, Straw's intervention continued a British liberal tradition of tolerance in that he recognized women's right to wear a niqab if they chose, unlike the French approach of banning the hijab (and subsequently the niqab and burqa). To participate in the liberal tolerance, however, minority subjects "must be liberal in the same ways as others and can, equally, only be illiberal in the same ways as others," so that demands for "greater freedom of religious expression through clothing, are generally not seen as a liberating force" (Moosa 2010: 68). Sustained criticism of Straw's comments as themselves an obstacle to social cohesion was also directed at the many MPs and ministers who echoed his identification of Muslim women's dress as a social problem.

At the same time two court cases that questioned the ability of women in niqabs to carry out professional duties hit the news, feeding the ferment of commentary and demonstration. In one, the young teaching assistant Aisha Azmi lost her case at an industrial tribunal against the school that sacked her for wearing a niqab in the classroom. The school, which had hired her to help nonnative speakers improve their English language, claimed that the children needed to see as well as hear her forming the words. In the other, legal advocate Shabnam Mughal won a partial victory over the judge in an immigration tribunal, who suspended proceedings when she refused to remove her niqab. In an interim decision Mr. Justice Hodge, president of the Asylum and Immigration Tribunal, advised that the niqab be permitted in court unless a judge's inability to hear meant that "the interests of justice are not served."[6] Couched not in the terms of health and safety that had been expected by Acas, but in the assertion that the niqab impedes verbal and visual communication, these challenges to veiling habits normalize Western modes of body management and, in the case of Straw, naturalize culturally specific presumptions that visual expression is an accurate guide to inner feeling, as has been seen in the recurrence of courtroom niqab controversies concerning defendants in 2013.

Cases have emerged over other items in addition to Muslim dress, including crucifixes worn by medical and airline staff and chastity rings worn by school pupils (Perfect 2011), disallowed for reasons of health and safety or of compliance with school or corporate uniform codes. Two cases are especially relevant for my project. In one, British Airways check-in clerk Nadia Eweida, a (Coptic) Christian, lost her case against her employers when she had demanded the right to wear her crucifix displayed on top of, rather than concealed inside, the corporation's uniform shirt, comparing her request to the already existing uniform dispensation for Muslim women to wear a hijab. In the second case, the only so far to have rested on the requirement that an employee express the company's aesthetic ethos through her individuated rather than uniform appearance, hijabi Muslim hairdresser Bushra Noah was turned down in 2008 for a stylist position at a small independent North London salon because the owner/employer claimed that the visible hairstyles of employees were essential for advertising the work of the salon. The industrial tribunal did not uphold Noah's claim of direct religious discrimination because the employer's decision would have applied to any person who covered their hair whatever the reason. But she did win on indirect discrimination because other Muslim women who covered would similarly have been disadvantaged. Noah was awarded £4,000.00 for injury to feeling. Unlike other high-profile cases taken against public sector or large private sector employers, this case was against a small independent company unlikely to have employment procedures overseen by HR professionals.

While the numbers of discrimination cases brought to employment tribunals on the basis of religion or belief have increased since the original legislation, religion or belief remains one of the smallest categories of claims accepted compared to other protected characteristics of the Equality Act (10,800 sex discrimination cases and 4,800 race discrimination cases compared to 940 religion or belief cases in 2011–12).[7] Research commissioned by the EHRC found that most bodies and respondents concerned with discrimination on grounds of religion regarded personal dress and flexible working as areas where employers should be able to make reasonable accommodations. Exceptions were widely considered to be legitimate on grounds of health and safety and of cost, as well as where requests would impede an existing "requirement for branding and uniformity" and "the capacity to communicate" (Donald 2012: 66). Where these were known factors of employment, individuals with religious commitments should recognize their responsibility to make "sensible career choices," which might include making "personal sacrifices to avoid conflict with the law or professional guidelines" (Donald 2012: 184). The legal situation, Donald suggests, is likely to remain "unsettled," with volatile public debate often misinterpreting prominent reporting of court cases as evidence of wider religious agendas. Although minority religions have generally seen the extension of discrimination legislation as a positive factor, some Christian organizations have balked at the bracketing of religious rights as equal to sexuality rights, regarding the law as an assault on the church with a broader narrative of "aggressive" secularism and the marginalization of Christianity as a foundation of British culture. Despite organizations like the Christian Legal Centre recruiting claimants in the hope of establishing case law, it is still minority religions that make up the majority of cases. With religious discrimination melding with racial discrimination, Muslims are "disproportionately vulnerable" to religious discrimination, and most especially nonwhite Muslim women, experiencing discrimination of "greater frequency and seriousness" in Britain since 9/11 (Donald 2012: 36).

Although the increasingly well-educated second and third generations of migrant Muslims in Britain do not face the same challenges as their parents, their education achievements (with a greater percentage of Muslims in higher education than the overall or "white" population [Bunglawala 2008]) are not matched by job success, with economic disadvantage extended across generations by lack of family social capital and external prejudice. While other minority ethnic women face employment problems (Butler 2012), the intersection of gender, ethnic, and religious discrimination means that South Asian Muslim women are especially likely to be disadvantaged in all areas of the labor market. Muslims of Pakistani and Bangladeshi heritage (less so Indian Muslims) do less well than South Asians who are Sikh or Hindu and less well than working-class white women from comparable economic backgrounds, with Bangladeshi Muslim women showing markedly high rates of economic inactivity (Bowlby and Lloyd-Evans 2009; Bradley et al. 2007). While it was evident in 2001 that Muslims "consistently" reported higher levels of unfair treatment than other religious groups, any religion with "large numbers of visible minorities, such as Muslims, Sikhs, Hindus" encountered increased levels of discrimination (as also for black-led churches) (Weller et al. 2001: vii). The impact of this "visible difference" was highlighted by dress and self-presentation; Hindus "with a dot" experienced increased discrimination, and Muslims felt "instantly more vulnerable if you wore traditional dress, whether you wear it for religious or cultural reasons" (Weller et al. 2001: 14). As the numbers of young Muslim women wearing hijab have increased, so too has the sense that a widely perceived "Muslim penalty" turns wearing the hijab into an obstacle for employment success. Anecdotes abound of instances in which "Islamic garments seem to trigger off stereotypes in interviews" (Bradley et al. 2007: 20), with women failing at interviews until they reappeared without the hijab. The strong perception that wearing a hijab hinders progression once in a post (Bunglawala 2008) compounds general experiences of disadvantage in training and employment (Anwar and Shah 2000; Shah 2010; on Canada, see Persad and Lukas 2002). Although media portrayals of Muslims have contributed to a more hostile hiring climate, the hypervisibility of the hijab means that Muslim women are paying the penalty more than their male peers and face worse job discrimination than other minority ethnic women. Muslims account for half of the cases brought to employment tribunals on the grounds of religion or belief, a jurisdiction that overall shows 88 percent of cases with a secondary jurisdiction, of which 66 percent were about racial discrimination (Savage 2007).

Inside the courts and out, challenges to expressions of faith-based identities provoke widespread cultural crises for minority and majority communities. Face covering of any form is a minority practice among the UK veiling population, yet Muslims who cover in other ways along with those who do not cover at all find themselves having to defend the right of coreligionists to choose the niqab. The intense focus on the niqab has shifted the commonsense definition of the "veil" from head covering to face covering, with some revivalist young women taking up the niqab as a badge of antiestablishment honor (just as had been the case previously with the hijab after the first French bans), while the government issued guidance to schools in 2007 offering them the opportunity to ban niqabs from their premises on the grounds that it might impede safety, security, or learning (Kariapper 2009). By the mid-2000s young people in Britain were markedly more supportive of dress rights at school, regardless of uniform requirements (with 83 percent young Muslims versus 68 percent older Muslims reporting such support [Field 2011: 163]). Opinion among young Muslims against a school's right to ban the hijab increased from 57 percent in 2004 to 80 percent in 2005, while in relation to workplace dress 88 percent of young Muslims challenged the right to ban hijab (Field 2011: 163). The defense of women's rights to dress as they please does not necessarily correlate with what young people themselves actually wear: it demonstrates the prevalence of choice as the discourse through which religious identification is expressed (chapter 4).

Choice is a shared framework for young Muslims around the world, inflected with local and regional specificities. Second- and third-generation Muslims in Britain are accustomed to the British model of secularity that has been less troubled by public expressions of diversity. This is in contrast to the structural exclusion of religion from public life in the secular republics of France and Turkey, each inflected by the national religious culture of Catholicism and Sunni Islam respectively (chapter 1), or Indonesia's prohibition of hijab at school in the 1980s to prioritize youth and adult performance of loyalty to New Order national civil religion through workplace and formalwear uniform dress (Arthur 2000a). While the judgment in Britain on Begum saw it as essential to protect other Muslim girls from the potential pressure to wear a jilbab in a Muslim minority context (M. Malik 2010), the European Court of Human Rights (ECHR) upheld the Turkish ban on headscarves at a university in the Sahin case to protect the secular majority from oppression by Islam. In the context of Turkey's EU accession process, the court's willingness to maintain the veil ban was "crucial to the constitution of women as non-particularist neoliberal subjects as demanded by the EU and the global economy" (Gökariksel and Mitchell 2005: 157), further entrenching the unveiled body as the unmarked norm of secular society. Surveying the wider mix of cases in 2007, Werbner concluded that "resort to the law in France, and possibly in Germany, Belgium and the Netherlands, reveals a clear divide between French and Anglo-American legal cultures. . . . Rather than Huntington's clash of civilizations between Islam and Christianity, the civilizational clash appears to be between political cultures that tolerate visible pluralism and those that do not" (Werbner 2007: 177).

Modood suggests that, in contrast to France and Germany, whose policy on racialized minorities has always been one of integration rather than distinction, the sociality to which UK minorities are expected to cohere may be a distinctively British concept of multiculturalism that celebrates diversity as part of shared British values. The politicized advent of faith identities might thus be seen as "a rebalancing of multiculturalism rather than its erasure" (Meer and Modood 2008: 490). The increased legal protection for (variably defined) religious rights is of particular significance to young people who, like many of my respondents, are invested in the dressed expression of religiously coded forms of identification.

The ways in which individual choice in the expression of religion at work merits legal protection was significantly altered by the ECHR in 2013. In a decision on four cases, including Eiweda, brought by British Christians, the ECHR overturned the previous assumption that protection applied only to religiously required practices,[8] by ruling that protection extended to practices intimately linked to a religion or belief even if they were not usually considered mandatory. Thus Eiweda's sincere desire to manifest her faith by showing her cross was to be permitted,[9] as it did not (unlike coclaimant nurse Shirley Chaplin's dangling cross in a hospital) constitute a risk to health or safety or impinge on the rights of others (EHRC 2013a). The right of Muslim women to adopt the face veil, similarly regarded as not mandatory by many Muslims in Europe, was not protected by the ECHR however. The July 2014 decision to deny a French women's appeal against the ban on face covering (supported by British solicitors from Birmingham and British civil rights organization Liberty [Willsher 2014a, 2014b]) was denied, the court supporting the French (and Belgian) case that it was a the "legitimate aim" of the state to preserve "the conditions of 'living together.'"[10]

Unable to predict these particular judgments (passed after the interviews in this chapter, and repeatedly of interest across the hijabi blogosphere; see chapter 6), the HR professionals in this chapter were aware that the religion and belief jurisdiction was liable to be especially mutable. Their strategy of trying to anticipate and contain the potential contestations they might encounter in the domain of workplace dress builds on a long history of retail wardrobe codes and highlights the growing significance of aesthetic labor in the field of fashion (Witz, Warhurst, and Nickson 2003).

The Retail Context: Embodied Aesthetic Labor

The bodies of shop staff have always been important in retail and have become even more so with the advent of branding. Studies in consumption increasingly regard all elements of the production-distribution-consumption circuit (du Gay, Hall, Janes, Madsen, Mackay, and Negus 2013; Kaiser 2012) as important, analyzing how products come to consumers and how consumers make sense of themselves through commodities. Challenging previous approaches that focused mainly on industrial labor, studies of retail have been reanimated by recognition of its crucial role in mediating the links between products and consumers (Entwistle 2009; Wrigley and Lowe 2002).

The high street (or its corollary, the mall) is not simply an inert space in which shopping happens. Inside and outside the store, the occurrence of dress acts within relational spatial frameworks, "encompassing more than one individual body" (Secor 2002: 7), connects shopper and retailer to each other and to bodies in places beyond their particular location. The trajectories of individual shopping processes undo the apparently bounded space of a single store (carefully demarcated by the uniformed bodies of its staff) so that it loses its spatial integrity, becoming, as Louise Crewe puts it, "a tapestry of different spaces, woven together to comprise personal accumulated shopping geographies that are routinely reproduced, and extended, through practice" (2003: 356). The retail mall and the "ethnic" street become relational shopping spaces linked by the activity of the consumer. This replaces the widespread presumption that "McCulture" and mallification leads inevitably to homogenization with a recognition that local distinctiveness continues in the proliferation of "differentiated spaces of consumption" that "create and reflect cultural as well as economic processes" (Crewe and Lowe 1995: 1877–78). These different consumption spaces are also spaces of work (Pettinger 2004), knitted together by the bodily movements of shoppers and shop staff.

The insertion of the hijabi shop worker into the spaces of high street fashion retail contributes to particular forms of distinction for staff and customers within the local experience of globalized commodity culture. In fashion retail, women, and especially young women, make up a significant majority of the workforce. Always heavily dependent on labor, retail has long sought to reduce costs: an initially higher-status, male-dominated, and better-paid workforce has been feminized and casualized since the early twentieth century with a shift toward customer self-service (Winship 2000). Jobs became more often part-time, favoring the cheaper labor of those (women and young people) perceived not to be the main family wage earner. The retail revolution of the 1980s, with the pronounced consolidation of the supermarket sector and a shift into a retail-led rather than producer-led globalized supply chain, saw a vast increase in the numbers of people employed in retail (as in other service sector work). Now, retail in the UK and United States is characterized by a higher percentage of staff working not only part-time but increasingly for fewer hours per week (Wrigley and Lowe 2002).

Despite changes in work roles brought about by electronic distribution technologies, retail remains labor intensive with forms of labor (from owner/managers to warehouse staff to sales assistants) that do not simply shift product from one place to another but actively create value that adds to the meanings of products (Christopherson 1996). The journeys of fashion products from distributor/manufacturer to consumer give prominence to the bodies of shop staff modeling the products on sale (Leslie 2002). Clothes and accessories that mark the wearer as Muslim, or as belonging to any religious community, are significant in fashion retail, where front-of-house staff literally represent the company or the brand with their bodies.

Associated with the rise of women as shop workers in the last quarter of the nineteenth century, shop dress codes (and later uniforms) were designed to establish the respectability of their largely female staff. Often accompanied by strict rules about behavior, dress codes created an identity for the establishment through the regulation of employees' bodies inside and outside the store, creating "modern" gender norms that impacted on female and male employees and customers alike (Reekie 1993). Within an often paternalistic management style (especially in the large department stores [Corina 1978]), the respectability of shop work as a form of employment was one of the attractions for working-class women who saw it as a step up, and for middle-class women who were reassured that the propriety of social relations in the store would help make shop work a respectable career (Lancaster 2000). With uniforms functioning as a component of subject formation (Craik 2005), women's dress at work was a key factor in the manufacture of these decorous social relations, while association with the glamor and modernity of fashion retail was itself a lure (that continued into the twentieth century [Winship 2000]).

The public comportment of employees was rendered even more important in the 1990s by the widespread take-up of corporate branding, as marketing shifted from differentiating products to fostering distinctive identities for companies and corporations. This is significant in fashion retail where, in both luxury and mass-market sectors, one corporation, gaining "oligopolistic" power (Crewe and Davenport 1991), may own several apparently separate companies presented and marketed as distinct and competing brands. While all of the shop assistants I spoke to worked for different brands, several of them were in fact employed by the same store group or consortium. Their employment conditions would have been governed by a shared contractual framework and HR policy that would have been developed and overseen for the consortium by some of the HR directors featured in this chapter. In the UK especially, high street multiples (including department stores and supermarkets; see also Worth 2007) enjoy a larger percentage of overall apparel retail sales (near 75 percent) than is the case elsewhere in the EU (Keynote cited in Woodward 2009: 89) and are accordingly bigger employers.

Across the service sector the interactive nature of the work requires staff, whether waiters, shop assistants, or merchant bankers, to perform gendered social identities suitable to the product being sold (McDowell and Court 1994) or service being delivered (Miller et al. 1998). The retail shift into branding and lifestyle marketing made prominent the bodies and demeanor of shop staff, as the 1980s focus on innovative store design was replaced with an investment in the emotional experience of shopping (Lowe and Crewe 1996). Many employers moved toward "'customized service provision' and 'customized workers' to match" (Lowe 1991: 42; see also Crang and Martin 1991), with mid-level and high-end stores investing in staff training as a core competitive asset while the budget sector downgraded staff roles with self-service shopping systems (Lowe and Crew 1996).

The requirement of staff to engage in scripted performances of emotional authenticity further privileged those workers most able to embody the values of the brand. The American company Gap "transformed the British High Street and importantly the British shop assistant beyond all recognition" (Lowe and Crewe 1996: 207), using point-of-sales technology to free up staff time to deliver a highly developed script ensuring constant customer interaction. Staff's embodied performances have become commodified to the point where "the sales assistants . . . increasingly comprise the actual product on sale" (Wrigley and Lowe 1996: 24). As front-of-house staff became more important in communicating the value of the brand in the mid-1990s, clothing retail was characterized by "a homogenization of staffing" and "increased competition for similar and possibly smaller labor segments . . . particularly true for youth-oriented chains which employ young people (many part-time) as a marketing strategy" (Christopherson 1996: 168). In the last decade critical attention has moved from a focus on emotional labor to a concern with the embodied aesthetic labor, "the mobilization, development and commodification of embodied 'dispositions,'" required to underwrite branded service performances (Witz, Warhurst, and Nickson 2003: 37). It is not enough that workers should wear (be able to fit into) the correct uniform or dress code; they must also have the right hairstyle, demeanor, and tone of voice, all attributes of subjective embodied dispositions that are "to some extent" present preemployment and that companies seek to transform into skills for service delivery. The ability of corporations to transform workers into effective aesthetic laborers is variably enabled or restricted by the class, gender, ethnic (and, I propose, religious) embodied capacities already present within the local workforce, given increased significance with the extension of aesthetic labor as part of branding practice across the retail sector and into the high street (Pettinger 2005a).

Marked by social and aesthetic relations, the high street is a space in which styles are actively made, moderated, disseminated, and adopted. To shop, to work in a shop, to be simply perambulating in the stores, is to be part of a consumptionscape in which one sees and is seen as part of the fashion spectacle that surrounds and fosters the mechanisms of acquisition. Window display, visual merchandising in-store, ads that surround the shopper in the street or the mall, all provide tips on ways to wear current trends (see also Glennie and Thrift 1996). So do the dressed bodies of other consumers and the bodies (and sometimes the advice of) shop staff. Not surprisingly the young women who populate this study are immersed in a high street fashion culture as consumers and workers. Like many of the Muslim and non-Muslim customers they serve, their wardrobes consist of a mix of high street purchases carefully combined with items sourced elsewhere to create their own minutely differentiated look that is both "unique" to them and on trend with the dominant fashion story of the day (Woodward 2009).

Nearly all the women I spoke to were motivated to seek shop work because they were interested in fashion, often choosing where to apply on the basis of liking the store's merchandise and wanting the staff discount. In the context of low-paid fashion retail the discount can "constitute a portion of the wage" (Leslie 2002: 72), emphasizing the "fusion of consumption and employment" by which retail workers supplement the store uniform or dress code by spending their own time and money achieving the hair, makeup, and accessories "sympathetic" to brand style (Pettinger 2005a: 472). But the ability to look "right" can also allow staff to accrue forms of distinction conferred by working in fashionable brands (Crang 2004; Wright 2005), while further diminishing the servile associations of service work by breaking down the set script with the theatrical development of personalized "improvisational performances" (Crang 2004: 693).

In fashion retail the clothed bodies of shop staff signal the aesthetic vision and values of the company. Employees at all levels need to demonstrate cultural competency with the codes of fashion relevant to their sector. As Joanne Entwistle has demonstrated in her study of the women's fashion buying team at the London department store Selfridges, these senior decision makers at the top of the fashion retail hierarchy, not usually on display on the shop floor, acutely feel the need to look right in order to demonstrate "through bodily enactments and expression" their aesthetic capital to designers and competitors: "critically in this market the knowledge is worn on the body" (2009: 41).

The same requirement to have and display embodied fashion capital applies to front-of-house shop staff. Despite shop work's generically low status and low pay, staff, need to use their fashion savvy, dependent on preexisting feminine and class-specific style competencies (Pettinger 2005a), to advise customers and make sales. The rapidly changing cycles of style that characterize the industry go beyond clothes to the bodies that wear them. A new ad campaign may produce a look achievable only on certain sorts of staff bodies, posing an "employment risk" to staff (Leslie 2002: 69). In the high street this has been seen most recently in the overt flouting of equal opportunities policies by Abercrombie & Fitch, whose recruitment policy of hiring only pretty young things and buff young men regularly brings (welcome) displays of public and press condemnation and lawsuits (Craik 2012; Saner 2012). Utilizing embodied staff aesthetic labor for competitive advantage between brands, corporations display "some flexibility" in how branding strategies are implemented within the company, aware that "geography affects taste for fashion and [that] the precise market niche is subtly different in different areas"; metropolitan branches feature "a more ethnically diverse workforce [with] a style aesthetic that was more distinctive" in contrast to the coiffed chic of staff in suburban branches (Pettinger 2004: 178–79). For hijabi shop workers location is key to the ease with which they are recruited and to the capacity of shop managers and HR to grasp the potential brand value of religious cultural capacities when harnessed into aesthetic labor in the delivery of localized customer interactions.

The self-presentation of shop staff may facilitate comfortable retail geographies for Muslim consumers, as shoppers and workers circulate cultural knowledges about which stores are likely to have veiled staff and/or be Muslim-friendly employers. If, as David Gilbert (2013) argues, garments are rendered meaningful by the manner of their acquisition (shopping with friends, good advice from an assistant) as much as by their design or even their wearing, then the presence of the veiled shop assistant becomes an important element of the shopping process.

Shop Staff: Experiences at Work

The shop assistants I spoke to worked in a range of high street multiples including River Island and Next, in global brands such as Topshop and Dorothy Perkins from the Arcadia group, plus department stores like Debenhams and Selfridges, and budget store Peacocks. They came predominantly from London, Manchester, and Bradford and were all of British South Asian, mostly Pakistani, family backgrounds. While one was a childhood first-generation migrant, the others were second and third generation, heirs to the mass migration of South Asians to Britain in the 1960s (chapter 1). For young women growing up in the former textile and industrial towns of Manchester and Bradford the neighborhood often contains not just other Muslims but other members of their family and kinship or biraderi networks.

The Muslim population has been characterized historically by a low rate of female participation in the formal wage economy with many first-generation migrant Muslim women (often speaking little English) working informally in family businesses or caring for children and relatives. It is only more recently that Muslim women are entering paid employment in greater numbers and in a greater range of occupations despite the intersecting challenges of gender-, ethnicity-, and, increasingly, faith-based inequalities. The young women I spoke to are emblematic of their generation in a number of ways. They are all fluent in English and *au fait* with British cultural forms (including fashion and fashion media) as well as having varying degrees of fluency in other community languages. They are all high school graduates and are either currently at or about to start university (working in retail part-time or during the vacations), or have graduated (including one who is making a career in retail buying). Some are taking or about to start master's programs. They typify the educational achievements of the second and third generation encouraged to outstrip the often limited educational opportunities and achievements of previous generations. Reflecting how proeducation norms of British Pakistani parental ethnic capital have achieved education success for young women (Shah, Dwyer, and Modood 2010), their stories counter the commonly held presumption that Muslim parents will not let their girls go to college or work for fear of tainting family honor and indicate that these young women and their families have negotiated ways of containing potential perceived risks and gossip (Basit 1997; Dwyer and Shah 2009).

Just as some retail factors like store uniforms helped to promote the respectability of retail for female staff a hundred years earlier, for Muslim women the choice of retail as the setting for employment can itself help to make their public presence more acceptable. The disciplinary visuality of the retail space developed by stores to regulate staff labor (and maximize sales) can also be appropriated into the panoptical regime of the local community. Unlike taxi driving, which involves encounters with strangers in the closed and mobile space of the car, or the inaccessible "closed" spaces of office work, the open space of the store means that a woman's comportment with others is subject to "the disciplinary gaze of the store and the public as a whole, including parents, who can make an inspection of their daughter's performance anytime" (Mohammad 2005b: 195). In-store "CCTV cameras monitoring the activities of shoppers and staff" further assuage the intensification of community scrutiny brought about by potentially unsupervised gender mixing and contact with non-Muslim men (Mohammad 2005a: 385; see also Afshar 1994; Essers and Benschop 2007; on migrant domestic labor, see Silvey 2005), within a widespread double standard that allows boys more laxity than girls (S. Ahmed 2009; J. Smith 1999).

While the store's open spatiality might make work "safe" in community terms, the geographical location of the retail workplace is also a factor in how comfortable it is to be hijabi at work. Although Muslims in Britain often report being isolated as "other" (see Bowlby and Lloyd-Evans 2009), it is also the case, as my interviews show, that in areas with a large Muslim population and/or a cosmopolitan mix, the established familiarity of managers, coworkers, and customers with Muslims can create forms of cultural knowledge that render individual Muslim shop assistants less of a novelty and therefore easier to accommodate. In Bradford, eighteen-year-old third-generation British Pakistani AY was not even looking for work but was recruited when shopping in a branch of Dorothy Perkins because her cool ensemble, including hijab, was exactly the image the non-Muslim store manager wanted to project: "It was just one of them things. I just went into the shop, literally, and the lady said to me, oh you look like the perfect sort of person we need to be working in this branch, and they were admiring the way I looked and the way I dressed. . . . [They liked that I looked] slightly different I think."[11]

Looking "different" in this instance did not mean looking Muslim, it meant looking *trendily* Muslim. The manager's ability to recognize AY's hijab as part of her overall fashion-savvy self-stylization normalizes the hijab within a discourse of fashion innovation. This transcends an affirmative action approach in which the hijab would have registered primarily as a religious symbol. In Bradford, with a large and youthful Pakistani Muslim population, AY's modish modesty counts as cultural capital, and her boss has sufficient competency with local subcultural styles (chapter 4) to see that AY's "corporeal disposition" could provide competitive advantage (Warhurst and Nickson 2007: 107) for *her* branch of the national brand. As a cool school-leaver (having just completed her A levels with a place secured at a local university), AY's personal fashion knowledge continued to be valued by staff and customers after her arrival: soon she was promoted with extra responsibility for visual merchandising, styling the store mannequins, and was frequently asked advice by customers, who, she told me, "say I represent the shop quite well, in the sort of clothes I wear and the way I represent myself."

The capacity of the hijabi body to be a cool brand ambassador is understood by workers to be reliant on cultural competencies that are socially and spatially specific. Twenty-two-year-old graduate Naila, who worked part-time (before starting her master's) at the Bradford branch of mid-market apparel store Next, argued that this was "something that's quite specific to Bradford. . . . If somebody from out of Bradford came they wouldn't expect to see it, but I think in Bradford it's just normal to see a Muslim girl wearing headscarf. People [are used to seeing] the wide range of how Muslim girls dress."[12]

The presence of visibly Muslim staff is understood in this context as a bonus for the shop, especially when faith combines with ethnicity and multilingual Muslim staff like Naila, who is second-generation British Pakistani, can assist non-English-speaking customers. Varying by type of retail and location, interaction with shop staff can play an essential part in people's experience of shopping, helping to "construct [the] shop as a site of sociality" (Miller et al. 1998: 131). Visibly Muslim shop assistants can act as a bridge, bringing into the high street multiples elements of ethno-religious sociality more usually encountered in the ethnic retail space (chapter 4), bringing into fashion employment a linguistic capability more usually recruited in welfare work (Dale 2002).

That said, hijabi shop workers demonstrated considerable delicacy in how they negotiated processes of mutual recognition with Muslim customers. Naila is sometimes greeted with the Arabic *As-Salaamu Aleikum* [peace be with you] by "older ladies and older guys," and while she responds in kind, she doesn't herself initiate the salutation, sticking to the generic store script (here presented as entirely naturalized behavior): "I think it's just a habit of saying 'hi,' 'hello' to whoever it is. . . . I think it's an automatic thing that I say to whoever approaches a till. But, even though I can tell someone is Muslim. . . . I never say it [*As-Salaamu Aleikum*] first."

Not inaugurating the departure from store protocol, Naila can nonetheless accurately interpret the unspoken concerns about modesty that underlie some customer enquiries: "Sometimes you might get other girls in headscarves coming up to me and saying, 'Oh, does this look okay?' Or they might have a dress or something in their hand, and might say, 'Oh, do you think this is alright?' Or they might say, 'Oh, is this too see-through? What do you think? Would I need to wear something underneath it?'"

In contrast to Naila's reticence, Laila Shah, at budget brand Peacocks in Manchester, will often initiate the Islamic salutation. Currently a first-year undergraduate at a local university and herself a first-generation Pakistani migrant, she arrived in Britain with her family via Saudi Arabia. Laila links the declaration of religious identity closely to her linguistic community affiliations: "If it's a Muslim customer I would be like Islamic, I would say, you know, ['salaam']. . . . If they're speaking Urdu, I will speak Urdu with them because that's my own language as well, so they feel comfortable. People like it I think, and my manager [said] it is a positive thing."

At Dorothy Perkins AY is also seen by management as a language resource for Punjabi-speaking customers. Some of the customers also give her *salam*, but she is careful not to initiate: "I'll wait for it to come from them. . . . It's not even because I think it's rude; it's just I think it's more professional [to] wait for them to come to you. [Also, it makes it fairer] so that other staff don't think that I'm undermining anyone else or saying anything bad about another customer."

Her hesitation is a sophisticated mix of respect for customers about whose preferences she doesn't want to presume and sensitivity to how her Islamic interactions might be perceived by coworkers unable to participate in this linguistically and religiously specialized communication.

Implementing Diversity Legislation: HR and Retail Management

The willingness of companies to accommodate religious requirements from staff and even to value their religious and ethnic distinction is part of a long trajectory in which from the early twentieth century the subjectivity of the worker came to be seen less as something to be subjugated and more as something of potential value to the employer and ultimately the state. Human resources (or its predecessors such as occupational psychology) developed as new areas of professionalized expertise that produced work as an element of self-actualization for the choosing subject of neoliberal governmentality (N. Rose 1999). The extension of employment regulations to include religion or belief as a protected characteristic delineated new areas of staff individuality to be operationalized at work, with HR and employee relations (ER) managers tasked with acting to protect workers' rights as required by law and with demonstrating to internal and external audiences that the company is so doing, including creating consent among staff for processes of religious self-disclosure at work.

It was not easy to find brand HR directors to participate in this research. Their job is to protect the brand, and most requested anonymity and that their participation be kept confidential. While my interviews with UK and London regional HR directors for brands and consortia cover most but not all of the brands at which the shop assistants worked, when brands or companies are referred to in quotations or material deriving from interviews with HR professionals they are identified only by generic descriptors agreed to by the HR informants.

The senior managers I spoke to in HR and their ER colleagues were generally based at the company headquarters with overall responsibility for staffing policy that was implemented in stores by a mix of HR staff and local managers. With service delivery becoming key to retail success, store managers were, as du Gay puts it (1996: 131), "responsibilized" to achieve shop floor buy-in to brand values, "reimagined as 'inspirational leaders'" contributing to their own personal development as entrepreneurial subjects. Few stores are large enough to justify an in-house HR specialist, mostly supporting local managers through an HR helpline and training programs. Most cases would be resolved at a local level, coming to the attention of the HR team only when information or guidance was needed or if conflict had escalated. As several HR directors explained, trying to track developments via cases at employment tribunals would tell me only part of the story because most retail companies will aim to settle rather than risk bad PR even if they think the case winnable. This is common across employment sectors and across the six jurisdictions of the Equality Act. Most employment tribunal cases are withdrawn or settled (sometimes through Acas-mediated conciliation) (Perfect 2011: 18), with religion or belief cases showing a similar success rate to other strands. Litigation is regarded as a last resort by both employers and many religious advocacy groups. Strategists from HR recommend an "anticipatory approach" in preference to a "reactive one," with Donald concluding that the "most productive level of engagement" lies not in the courts but on the "front line" of decision making with "policy-makers, practitioners and workplace managers" focusing on "implementation rather than litigation" (Donald 2012: xviii). Everyday practice is likely to reveal more about how individuals negotiate the role of faith in their lives than legal challenges whose often sensationalist reporting (by lobby groups and the press) fails to explain the limited applicability of individualized case law or the full background behind the pursuance of the case (Donald). As Bond and Hollywood point out, the "emergence of Diversity Management in the 2000s reflects the growing emphasis on the business case for equality in an organizational context as opposed to the rights-based approach of 'equal opportunities,' which it has largely succeeded" (Bond and Hollywood 2009: 6).

Organizations see value in making diversity work beyond the employment issues covered by HR, needing to include (in the public sector) the diversity duty to service users and customers, and aware of the reputational value of achieving good practice status within the now proliferating range of external benchmarking schemes. These factors, as well as in some cases a personal commitment to justice, fairness, meritocracy—"HR specialists often hold these values strongly" (Bradley et al. 2007: 39)—meant that for the HR/ER managers I spoke to in 2009–10 it was a priority to get the company ready to be fully compliant with the Equality Act due to come into law within months of our interviews. They were almost unanimous in presenting their companies as already in accordance with the spirit of the new regulations. Keen, as one might expect, to give a positive rendition of company-employee relations, this narrative is also in keeping with the UK retail sector's history of anticipating government regulatory regimes in order to maintain autonomy where possible, via compliance with private (voluntary) rather than public (legally enforceable) regulatory codes (Wrigley and Lowe 2002).

Human resources policy in many stores exemplified the shift across the sector from policies based on the three areas previously covered by an equal opportunities framework to those conceptualized in terms of diversity. Company policy on religious expression was often presented as part of a wider "dignity at work" package, in keeping with the emergent inclusive diversity frame. This was often associated with codes of conduct concerned with social and environmental sustainability at home and abroad that, as a major preoccupation of popular consumer discourse (taken up as an Islamic value by many of the Muslim modest designers; see chapter 6), has become a key factor in corporate social responsibility (CSR) programs. With companies across the spectrum using CSR as part of brand messaging, staff diversity becomes a newly valuable commodity. In 2011, for example, the UK Topshop website augmented its diversity statement with a Responsibilities Report that celebrated UK staffing diversity alongside accounts of measures for ER due diligence across their global supply chain.[13] Their UK statistics reveal Asians to be the largest ethnic minority at 3.2 percent overall but do not include faith; this was typical of all the companies I interviewed in 2009–10, none of whom had yet adapted its equal opportunities monitoring forms to include religion. A time lag before faith statistics become available is to be expected: employers and employee diversity representatives are aware that is it particularly delicate to persuade staff to self-declare for the new religion or belief jurisdiction (as for sexual orientation), despite the potential gains of being able to demonstrate through numbers the need for resources and special consideration (Adams and Carter 2007; Bond and Hollywood 2009).

Other companies, like Debenhams, keep the social diversity of their staff base for the recruitment pages on which they list the six categories covered by the Equality Act alongside their commitment to recruit staff that "reflect the communities in which we provide a great customer experience."[14] This approach is common across retail, where the desire to reflect the local community makes "strong business sense," with some retailers reporting that they want to match local diversity in both "the produce they sell and in the mix of staff" (Bond and Hollywood 2009: 31; see also Bunglawala 2008), persuaded perhaps by reports that in a multicultural city "any store with an all white staff is unlikely to compete successfully for custom" (Bradley et al. 2007: 40). An appreciation of the business case does not always translate into practices that increase the recruitment of more diverse staff or their progression thereafter (Adams and Carter 2007).

Effective HR aims to preempt areas of potential conflict, often mainstreaming issues beyond the HR function by cascading down (Dickens et al. 2009) resolution tools throughout the company's lines of management. This proactive approach was taken by Helen, the ER director of the large "Company Clothing" consortium, when she realized that hijab wearing was generally on the increase and might arise as an issue in-store:

> We actually did an article recently though in our ER newsletter, just about the different types of headscarf, etc., for our HR representatives to say can you cascade this message out to stores just in case we do receive a request. But we've not had any problems with that; we've not had any employees request to wear the veil or the full coverage [of a face veil]. . . .
>
> We've had quite a bit of request in terms of the headscarves. We say that's absolutely fine. Again, as long as you're wearing clothes that reflect the brand and you're dressed comfortably and fashionably, that's absolutely fine. In terms of our dress code in our handbook, it's only a paragraph which just basically says, again, you need to reflect the brand that you work for and to dress appropriately.[15]

On the wider issue of the Equality Act, the company had by spring 2010 developed a workshop for senior HR staff to brief and lead their HR teams to be ready for the new diversity legislation due to become law in autumn that year.

In relation to store uniform codes, none of the HR professionals I spoke to saw any reason why wearing hijab should be a problem, often expecting that hijabis would be self-selecting about where they applied, just as was the case elsewhere in the fashion retail sector. Jackie, now HR director for a major UK department store chain, pointed out in relation to her previous post in the United States with a high-end designer store, that he (the unnameable American designer) would only have beautiful bodies, male and female, in his shops: "if R walked out into the store and somebody wasn't gorgeous, then heaven help you."[16] It was quite typical in retail, she noted, for bodies not considered appropriate to be "selected out" during different stages of the recruitment process, with the luxury sector and cosmetics the most notorious on this count. In the UK department store sector where she now works, the company needs staff to communicate a corporate image rather than fashion-forward bodily gorgeousness. Their black uniform includes a choice of trousers or skirt, and staff who choose "to wear a veil will be able to do so but will be expected to conform with some of the business-like requirements with regards to color, etc. . . . [So] veils are normally in black . . . in the same way [as they and all their colleagues] coordinate their shoes." Within the uniform's restricted options, the hijab can be normalized as one among other accessory choices.

The overt and covert regulation of the dressed body of the shop worker is a well-established retail industry standard. Implementation varies according to sector and location, with less employment protection in the U.S. retail sector than in the UK and the EU. To my surprise, when I spoke to Ruth, the HR manager of the London flagship store of Brand X, a major high street retailer with high-profile designer tie-ins (part of the Company Clothing group), she told me that when it came to managing uniform compliance the modest dressers were the least of her worries. At Brand X shop staff had to wear a short-sleeved T-shirt with the company name on it and plain bottoms of their own choice. If someone wanted to add a hijab, she told me,

> That's fine, we don't have any problem with it. The key thing is that they wear the branded T-shirt, so if they want to wear that under, or over their clothing, or with part of the T-shirt showing through their religious attire, then that's fine. [The T-shirt is short-sleeved], but [people can wear it with a long sleeve underneath or a cardigan on top]—as long as the [company] name is visible to customers [so that they can] find someone for help.
>
> The only problem we had with the T-shirt is people customizing them, but it's not for religious reasons. They'll just slash them and tie them in the middle and make them into bikini tops, and all sorts.[17]

Brand X, like many other retailers in the youth sector, has a staff base that closely mirrors its customer demographic, so the visibility of the branded T-shirt is crucial for distinguishing staff from customers. With both sets of young people more invested in product fashionability than customer service (Birtwistle and Shearer 2001), managers can have an uphill struggle with young secular staff desperate to customize the top. In scenes reminiscent of school, uniform and dress codes have to be monitored constantly in the face of staff noncompliance and subversion (as across the retail and service sectors; see du Gay 1996; Pettinger 2005a; Warhurst and Nickson 2007): "It's up to the managers to police that in their own teams. You have team briefs at the start of the day, and at the start of each shift, [and if] someone's not complying with the standards then they'll be challenged and asked to change."

That neoliberal enterprise culture has to "inscribe itself [upon] persons with particular biographies and upon organizations with specific histories" (du Gay 1996: 150) is evident at Brand X, where the organization's history as a fashion-forward company produces an implementation mode that allows for individual interpretation: "We're a creative industry; we like people to express their individuality; we don't want everyone to be clones. The only uniformity is those branded T-shirts; everything else [is open]." This company ethos combined with Ruth's own commitment to diversity means that she recognizes as a potential organizational asset the preexistent dispositions that incline religious employees to self-disciplined modes of comportment: "I would actually prefer to have *more* Muslim employees. . . . Younger employees who *don't* follow any particular religion and are out drinking and taking drugs every night tend to be the ones who take up most of our time in HR. So I would much rather have more religious diversity for that reason."

Muslim Bodies at Work: Contention and Cooperation

In the visually loaded climate of fashion retail any significant style change can make one feel conspicuous. But for Muslim women who decide to transform their appearance by starting to wear the hijab, the workplace can feel daunting. The ways that women deal with staging this transition at work vary enormously. In chapter 4 I recounted how Razia's "sudden" decision to wear hijab presented a surprise to her family as well as to colleagues in her part-time store job at Swarovski jewelers in the Oxford Street department store Debenhams. While her transformation meant that her manager Jackie initially failed to recognize her, the overall response was described as positive. I return to Razia's story now to explore further how HR policy is understood, implemented, and experienced by managers and Muslim employees.

When I met Razia she had just given up her part-time job in retail because of the demands of her full-time job in a west London community advocacy NGO. Now age twenty-six, she was for the first time since sixteen not working a shop job, having started as a schoolgirl with a weekend job, also in jewelry in another section of the Oxford Street Debenhams. In a pattern entirely typical of the fluid and part-time young female workforce of fashion retail, she had moved around London's West End working for a variety of brands in their own shops or in department store concessions. Having also been appointed as a weekend department manager in the Oxford street flagship store of British Home Stores (part of the Arcadia group), Razia was clearly a skillful retailer valued for her ability to cope with the pressures of a West End operation. Her talents were recognized again when Swarovski "poached" her from another fashion jewelry brand. Razia then worked for Swarovski in two other department stores until she returned with them to their branch in Debenhams for what was to become her final shop job. It was soon after she was recruited by Swarovski that she started to wear the hijab, becoming, she thought, their first hijabi employee. Her manager, who responded positively on a personal level to Razia's new appearance, contacted the head office for guidance because of the specifics of the product:

> It was a concern because Swarovski's a jewellery company. It portrays an image . . . so you show off the necklaces, you show off the earrings and it's sort of like promoting the jewellery. . . . I knew back then there was an issue with a lot of companies; they didn't favor people wearing scarves because of the company image. And I said to her, look is it okay that I've worn this, I don't want you to get in trouble. And she goes, no, no I'm sure it's okay darling, [and] I knew that she had a doubt in her head and she was trying to be really nice to me and said I will call up and I'll find out for you. . . . She goes, no, darling, it's fine. I've checked with head office, they said it's alright. They haven't had this kind of thing before, but they have said it's fine.
>
> And I was like, oh my God, phew. [If] they had turned around and said, I'm sorry, you can't, that would leave me really, really gutted and I wouldn't have known what to do and I'd be really, really cheesed off, and I thought damn, you know, what do I do. I've got religion on one side, I've got a job that I really want to do, a dream job on the other side, how do I balance it out in this Western society. . . . So I was in the clear, which was brilliant.[18]

In this instance Razia's working attire was governed by the regulations of the brand rather than those of the department store where she was physically located, and it was to brand headquarters that her manager appealed for guidance. As Razia had anticipated, her manager made the point that "we'll still need you to promote the company's jewellery," immediately offering solutions by asking, "what kind of things would you feel comfortable wearing?" Razia, who appreciated being given a choice, was happy to cooperate: "I said, I love wearing rings so I could still wear rings and bracelets, I could still show those off. . . . And before, I wasn't very fond of brooches but I wore it for the sake of doing something extra for the company . . . compensating for not wearing a necklace or earrings." Overall, her manager and the company were "fantastic": "I actually thought, wow, this company is *the* company to work for. They gave me a lot of respect, [and our] manager was brilliant, which was the best thing about the job. They were really, really good about it."

This success story relied in part on the already established good relationship between Razia and her immediate manager, augmented by a fashion brand willing to engage constructively with a previously unencountered element of employee relations. The company and Razia's manager displayed the sort of "cultural intelligence" (qua emotional intelligence) that Bradley et al. advocate as a key focus of staff development—especially for line managers who are widely acknowledged as having the "most crucial role in ensuring the development of a diversity friendly workplace" (Bradley et al. 2007: 43). In this instance the cultural intelligence of Razia's manager was not premised on learning a toolkit of items of Muslim dress but on her ability to initiate and maintain an open dialogue. This allowed the company maximum flexibility to respond to Razia's own developing understanding of how she might now dress at work and continue to perform her function as mannequin.

Having perceived her hijab as withdrawing from her employers a part of her body that had previously been available for the display of the brand's necklaces, Razia noted in her retrospective account that "I've seen girls now, as a fashion they wear the long necklace on top of the scarves." Had this development in hijabi fashion been around at the time it might have meant that Razia would have felt she could or should continue to model the necklaces. However, having never "been a necklace type" even pre-hijab, she finds the hijab and necklace combination anathema to her personal taste. "I just can't put myself to put that on." In being willing to accept Razia's own interpretation about what she could and could not wear as a hijabi the company was demonstrating good practice. But she was also their first and only hijabi worker. Would it have made a difference if they also employed other hijabis who did wear necklaces, or if the fashion for necklaces over scarves had been visible at the time? Would HR staff and management have had the subcultural competences to recognize the hijab and necklace combination as a new hijabi trend? I raise this because the decisions that employers make are structured not just by legislation but by the behaviors of staff on the ground, fitting into their lives in different ways at different times and in different ways across the lifespan of a single employee. When Razia started at Debenhams at age sixteen, for example, she wore the store uniform without any problem, describing herself as like any other teen: "I opted for the pencil skirt which was very, very fitted, very nice, quite appealing to the youngsters. I'd go for the extra, extra, extra small, size six [laughs]. I'd fit into that. So yeah, you'd just wear that with nice tights underneath, maybe some fishnets and some nice dolly shoes. That suited me for about four and a half years actually."

Her description of the tight skirt is not entirely a typical teen fashion narrative because, although Razia says that her family "wasn't very religious," this is in fact relative. As I discussed in chapter 4, she was immersed in a habitus of Muslim modesty in which as she grew older her mother gently reminded her to dress with more care, prompting in this instance a switch to longer skirts or trousers.

Whereas Razia communicated with her manager after the event, Maleeha carefully prepared the way. A twenty-seven–year-old business studies graduate, Maleeha is second-generation British Pakistani. Although she was happy in her job as assistant lingerie buyer at Selfridges, she had considered leaving and taking a new job in order to avoid staging this transformation in her current workplace.[19] In the end she decided she couldn't wait and initiated a careful and assertive public relations exercise with her colleagues:

> I was very nervous . . . because I feel the way I dress is a reflection of my personality so, you know, I like to dress nicely, I like clothes, I like fashion and [I] like to spend my time looking at fashion magazines and going shopping and things. So — and I almost felt like changing the way that I look, people will think she's changed, or whatever. . . . I'm also the kind of person that doesn't like the attention on me, I don't like people making big hoo-ha, so I sent a quick e-mail round [to my immediate team] to say that I'm going to start wearing a veil so don't be alarmed when you come in on Monday morning and see me sitting there. . . .
>
> And I did actually say in the e-mail, I don't want a big fuss. . . . And

I think I also mentioned that it was quite a big thing for me and I was feeling a bit nervous. So walking in, gosh, it was a really strange feeling walking in on Monday morning. My manager quietly said, "Oh my God, Wow! You look amazing, you look lovely," which was really nice. The rest of the team just carried on doing their work and I think because of that e-mail didn't really say much. . . . Overall everyone was amazing, everyone was like, "It suits you, you look lovely." I was asked why I did it of course, to which I was honest and just told them that it was because of my religion. I am commanded to do it.

I've been called a princess, been called romantic, a queen. . . . It's quite strange but if people say things like that it's really nice, very sweet and it does make you feel better.

Although Maleeha does not work primarily on the shop floor (the buying team make regular observational visits), her location in the open plan buying office does not reduce the significance of how she looks. While open plan offices bring into view the bodies of everyone who works there, the scrutiny of personal style and appearance that inevitably ensues (Freeman 2010; Tyler and Abbott 1998) is of particular significance in a fashion workplace. Here, Entwistle argues (coincidentally regarding the same Selfridges buying office), "high fashion style circulates visually in the fertile environment of the open plan office as a form of embodied knowledge," emphasizing the extent to which "dressing fashionably constitutes something of the 'aesthetic labor' in this employment market" (2009: 115).

For Maleeha, in the lingerie buyers' section, the need to achieve current norms of high fashion may be less pressing, but her understanding of the prevalence and power of visual scrutiny is spot on. Her e-mail to colleagues proved helpful in anticipating some of the questions that might arise in relation to her spiritually driven visual transformation. But underneath this specificity lies her tacit understanding, as a participant, of the importance of appearance in her workplace social relations. Announcing her intended change of dress makes overt the practices of visual surveillance and evaluation, gossip, rumor, and discussion that govern the sociality of the open-plan office. While all staff may feel similarly subject to the collective gaze, to announce, for example, a radical new haircut, would be perceived as inappropriately attention seeking. Maleeha's decision to wear hijab, while a private personal spiritual choice, is of such visual magnitude that it cannot be ignored and so enters a different category of communication within the visuality of the office. Here, the aesthetic labor of fashion melds with the intended spectacle of religious observance: hijab renders adherents conspicuous to a mixture of observers. While Maleeha's highly visible change in her appearance at work did as expected prompt discussions with coworkers, it is also common for Muslim shop workers who have always appeared in hijab to find their religiously inspired attire a topic of conversation and question.

The display of Muslim identities through dress factors into relations with coworkers in two key ways: generically it prompts questions about Islam and specifically it prompts implicit and explicit comparisons with other workers who are Muslim, raising questions about different types of Muslim self-presentation (as also in schools; see Dwyer 1999). Most often hijabi shop assistants are asked to explain why they cover and other Muslim coworkers don't; although to their informed eyes it might be perfectly obvious that their colleague is dressing with modesty in mind (no short skirts, long-sleeved tops), the majoritarian shop team is rarely equipped to recognize this. In these discussions and in interactions with other Muslim staff, hijabi shop workers tread carefully so as not to criticize the choices of other Muslims whose interpretation is different from their own. But not everyone is happy with relativism. In Manchester at River Island, Taslima was happy to talk about religion with a non-Muslim colleague and the other Muslim, non-hijabi young woman at the store. Coming from a devout and conservative Hanafi family, with a mother who ran Qur'an classes at home, the matter of music brought a potentially awkward dispute: "I said no, you're not allowed to listen to music and then Farida said, well course you are. And I was like, but you're not. So on that, I felt like Farida didn't really know what she was talking about. . . . Farida said her parents aren't religious, right, but because my parents, my mum's religious, I know more about certain things than say Farida does. So yeah, it felt a bit stupid me saying you can't listen to music and Farida's having an argument with me saying you can and then Darren's thinking, what are these two going on about."

Just as many hijabis often absolve other young women of blame for not wearing the hijab or wearing it the wrong way by blaming the parents for failing to educate them about Islam (remember Razia's "convertible hijab" in chapter 4), so too does Taslima temper her criticism of Farida without watering down her own convictions: "There can't be an [alternative] interpretation, you can't listen to music. . . . So she just doesn't know because she's not been taught that."

It is not only that different Muslim women have different interpretations of Islam, but that those interpretations and practices may change over the course of individual women's working lives. While Maleeha had considered leaving Selfridges in order to avoid making the transition with her existing work colleagues, Razia found herself re-presenting herself to old colleagues in her new guise as hijabi when she returned to work in Debenhams on the new Swarovski concession. This prompted less discussion than might have been anticipated: "Because I think some of them they knew me from before and they respected that I'm a Muslim girl, one time or another in life I probably would wear it eventually. They did say, oh, you know, we miss your hair [or] how does it feel . . . because obviously they will be alien to the headscarf and [not know] the moral behind it, so I was more than happy to explain to them because it just made somebody else feel comfortable around me."

Conversations with employers and employees suggest that clothing is not emerging as a key problem area in fashion retail work. At least clothing requirements seemed easy to accommodate. More challenging in terms of resources and management were requests for prayer rooms and time off for festivals. Prayer rooms were difficult in shops, especially smaller branches, where nearly all available space is devoted to front-of-house functions. For festivals, many companies have been proactive in developing "diversity calendars" so that managers can anticipate staff demands for shift changes and leave.

Time off for religious festivals is not usually a problem in the fashion retail sector, ER manager Helen claimed, because "staff working in retail know that it will involve unsociable hours" and because retail employers "favor part-time as opposed to full-time contracts." It is commonplace for company recruitment policy to ensure that retailers have a highly flexible workforce with which to respond to seasonal sales variations. In relation to diversity demands, this can allow managers to use staff flexibly not just within a given store but across the region if needed. As Helen explained, in a large flagship store with over a thousand staff, "we can easily accommodate a number of requests, but if you're in a store where you've only got twenty staff and ten of them want the same days off for Eid or Diwali . . . then it's going to affect the service and being able to actually operate the store. So you have to look [in] advance if you're going to give all those people the same time off, do you need to call in support staff from other stores or whatever that may be."

In the one instance I heard of someone being denied leave for a festival,

Taslima in River Island in Manchester encountered problems when her manager didn't understand that she needed an extra meal break for *iftar* to break her fast during Ramadan.[20] Fed up with protracted negotiations, and with a manager who couldn't believe that she didn't just eat at work and pretend to her parents that she was fasting, this twenty-two-year-old second-generation Indian local undergraduate left the job.

In contrast, in Bradford, AY's non-Muslim manager and colleagues were well informed and overtly solicitous:

> [We don't have to tell them], they already know—and a few weeks before, they're warning us, Ramadan's coming up, are you ready? Make sure you're fit and healthy.
>
> They don't give us heavy jobs, so it'll just be basically, AY, would you like to stand on the till today for a few hours instead of [doing heavier stockroom work]?

Muslim staff sometimes have to define and legitimate their forms of religious practice. In the case of disputes that actually go to arbitration, unlike Taslima who simply quit, the religious rights covered by the new legislation create opportunities for the development and exercise of new forms of religious authority as those representing employers and employees seek interpretations of doctrine to support their case. Although there is still little research on how managers are experiencing the new legislation, it is clear that religion or belief and the new sexual orientation characteristic are the areas that they feel most uncomfortable dealing with, often anxious that they lack expertise and, as covered in some of the proactive HR staff materials that I was shown, fearing that they may cause offense. Managers are often hampered by confusion between affirmative action that is legal and affirmative discrimination that is not (Bunglawala 2008). Cases get siphoned off to HR rather than dealt with locally as routine management issues (Denvir et al. 2007; Dickens et al. 2009). At the Acas helpline half of all questions about religion and belief are about Islam, mostly from employers (Savage 2007: 45). The need for guidance is increasingly met by external sources, with workplace dress featuring prominently. This is despite early research on the new regulations noting "the contrast between the absence of calls recorded in the Acas helpline survey regarding workplace dress codes, and the high profile the issue was being given in the UK media during the fieldwork period [the Jack Straw controversy and early crucifix uniform cases]" suggesting that "the issue of workplace dress codes is not of primary concern to employers or employees in the workplace," who were more worried about flexible leave arrangements (Savage 2007: 60).

With women making up only 35 percent of claimants in religion or belief cases and with Muslim women still underrepresented in the formal labor market, it is hardly surprising that Muslim women's anecdotal experience of hijab as a barrier to employment and career progression far outstrips the litigation statistics. The continued prevalence of negative stereotypes and excessive reporting of hijab and niqab cases gives Muslim women's dress a disproportionate significance in the minds of employers and employees (see also Adams and Carter 2007). For companies seeking to recruit young people this is important to address in the context of young Muslims' preoccupation with hijab and Islamic attire: "It is crucial that ethnically diverse people are visibly represented in publicity in terms of dress as well as skin color. The hijab has become a political conversation; it is important that this is normalized in the context of the workplace. . . . Dress codes should emphasize that Islamic dress may be worn and that salwar kameez and hijab is a perfectly acceptable form of professional clothing, as it is in many other countries" (Bradley et al. 2007: 69–70).

Faith and business sector organizations responded quickly to the new legislation from 2003, working with government to help prepare employers and employees and community leaders/organizations likely to be caught up in the implementation of the new regulations. As with the regularly updated guides for employers offered by the Equality and Human Rights Commission (EHRC 2013b), one of the challenges for those producing guidance and for their readers is how to avoid homogenizing religions, providing general guidance without obscuring internal diversity (Acas 2010). In relation to dress in particular, employers are advised by the Employers' Forum on Belief that proactive and consultative procedures are essential for the formulation of dress codes with sufficient clarity and maximum flexibility (Employers' Forum on Belief 2010). The MCB's *Good Practice Guide for Employers and Employees*, published in 2005, also warned that "the way that Muslims dress varies significantly," explicating that for men a beard is "considered obligatory within some strands of thought and encouraged in others" and that for women while "some Muslims may not wear the hijab (headscarf) they may feel uncomfortable wearing tight clothing or short skirts which are also discouraged in Islam" (MCB 2005: 14). This expansive definition is somewhat undermined by their subsequent guide to schools, which iterates that in public "girls should be covered except for their hands and faces" (MCB 2007: 20). On dress codes specifically, Acas advocates that employers follow the "guiding principle" of evaluating the "impact of dress upon the employee's ability to do their job" (Acas 2010: 15; M. Malik 2010). As well as providing guidance online and in publications, religious leaders and faith organizations are involved in helping employers resolve disputes and develop policy. In the retail sector the MCB has advised on the development of hijab staff uniform options for Muslim women at Next, IKEA, and the chemist Boots, with company logo incorporated into branded store-issue headscarves. Addressing coreligionists, the MCB's 2005 guide warned Muslim employees that "trivial demands and over-litigation may also lead to employer disaffection and relocation, exacerbating the unemployment problems already faced by the Muslim community" (MCB 2005: 22), with the lowest level of employment of all faith groups in Britain.[21]

Individual cases are taken to be emblematic of all Muslims or all Christians yet are often motivated by "ideological and theological disputes . . . that are also taking place *within* religious organizations" (Donald 2012: xii), and might have negative unintended consequences for coreligionists. As I discussed in chapter 4, in-group disagreements may be invisible to employers: in the prayer room at Debenhams other Muslim women made unwelcome attempts to persuade Razia to dress "more" Islamically as part of their da'wa mission to guide others to virtuous behavior. Like the off-putting judgments in Muslim student groups, the delicacies of intra-Muslim relations in the commercial space of the store escaped the well-intentioned inclusiveness that underlay the store's provision of a "neutral" multifaith, nondenominational space for prayer and quiet reflection.

If the hijab was generally presented as unproblematic in my interviews, all the HR professionals anticipated that requests to wear a niqab would be harder to accommodate. None had yet received a request, but several predicted that it would be customers rather than the brand itself that might be the source of objections. At Company Clothing, Helen and her team had again been proactive:

> We've never had the request, but we had that debate in HR to say, what are our thoughts, etc. And we decided well look, if that person was customer or client facing it may pose a bit of a challenge, so we'd have to evaluate the request first of all [and] obviously there's quite a bit of case law around that now, which is great, which has paved the way for our answer with people, but we've never received that request. . . .

[If somebody actually did turn up to interview in a niqab] we'd have to evaluate, what do you want to wear, how often do you want to wear this and what role do you actually do and what are the potential restrictions—not a risk assessment, that's the wrong word—but probably an evaluation of that person, their role and the request.

On the ground at Clothing Company, in the Brand X flagship store, Ruth the HR director had also not yet encountered a niqab wearer on the shop floor: "Mmm . . . I mean the company wouldn't have any problem with it. . . . I suppose the only concern would be how customers would react." In the department store sector Jackie also did not think it had yet arisen in recruitment but pondered, "people might take a view that customers might find it threatening."

While everyone agreed that niqab wearers might self-select out of fashion retail in their high street sector, the projection that prejudice would likely arise from customers and not the company illustrates the challenge for HR professionals in juggling legal obligations with commercial interests. It also perhaps reflects that the 2010 Equality Act extended employer obligation to include protecting employees from third-party harassment (subsequently scheduled to be repealed as part of the Enterprise and Regulatory Reform Bill in 2013). At the time of the Equality Act in 2010 however, Acas warned employers that they now became "potentially liable for harassment of their staff by people they did not employ" (Acas 2010: 2). Were they to have niqabi employees in customer-facing roles in store, the company would be obligated to protect them from any ensuing customer harassment. When asked if they had experienced prejudice from customers, none of the shop workers in my sample had any instances to share, relating perhaps to their workplace locations in cities with significant Muslim populations like Bradford, or in the diverse metropolis of London. It may be simply that customers who felt some prejudice were not moved/able to express it. But as research on women shop workers facing sexual harassment from male customers reveals, the customer-focused ethos of retail work often leaves employees feeling unable to contest harassment and managers unwilling to risk sales by confronting customers (Hughes and Tadic 1998; on the finance sector, see McDowell and Court 1994).

Professionals in HR concerned to facilitate a reasonable expression of faith and belief at work are focused on in-store facilities (for dress, prayer, and food) and relations between staff rather than between customers and staff. In this light, the identification of customers as the likely driver of any obstacles for niqab wearers is very interesting. Like the controversy raised by Jack Straw and the two court cases about the niqab at work, Jackie located communication problems as the potential issue with niqabi shop staff: "Yeah, because all our customer service training is around the nonverbal stuff of the eye contact with a customer, that first glance with a customer, engaging them, and that is, you know, less easy to do with . . . if the face is completely covered."

While the niqab has often served as the limit case in discussions about the compatibility of Islamic practice with the world of work, Alveen Malik warns against treating it as an exception, arguing that whether women wear hijab, jilbab, or niqab, "in my opinion the degree to which a woman chooses to cover up is not the issue. If any judgement is to be made it should be on her performance and ability to carry out her civic duties" (A. Malik 2010: 27). Advocating the acceptance of "the veil as part of a modern British way of life," she proposes that in return religious women who adopt the veil "must be held responsible for strengthening their civic bond with the state and the British public" (A. Malik 2010: 33). While there is much to be gained by Malik's evaluative approach, and its resonance with the MCB guidance that religious individuals should be "sensible" in their employment and civic choices, others in the Muslim community do not regard with equanimity the prospect that court cases and related publicity may validate the niqab as "Islamic," regarding it as an imported regional Saudi or Gulf cultural practice now being recategorized as religious (Kariapper 2009).

It remains to be seen how the neoliberal desire to incorporate minority identities into new forms of consumer citizenship will play out in relation to religion in fashion arenas around the world. With few notable exceptions (such as Walmart's Toronto-based "Bollywood" range and their UK Asda "Asian clothing" collection in 2009; see chapter 7), most mainstream global fashion retailers don't see ethnic or Muslim consumers as a niche market. While the globalization of fashion retail means that many of the same stores appear in malls or high streets across the world, just as local planning and employment regulations determine the commercial and industrial relations available to supranational brands in all sectors, so too will local and regional norms and legislation about the expression of religious identity determine how hijabi shop staff are valued and employed (Floor 2006). In this context, hijabi shop staff bring into the store an embodied combination of subcultural capital and consumer fashion expertise. The visible religious and/or ethnic diversity of hijabi staff that makes them vulnerable to intersecting social and employment discrimination is also—in some times and places—commodifiable as a valuable marker of British style.

Yet in parts of Britain local store managers can recognize the benefits and value of having bodies on the shop floor whose self-presentation marks them as Muslim. The ability of hijabi shop staff to act as mannequins for the store's products and for modest fashion adds to their generic value as in-store style mediators. Just as ethnic marketing has gained traction, so too, as I discuss in chapter 7, has Muslim marketing emerged as a new growth area. The enhanced value that ethnic corporate branding strategies place on staff with ethnic experiential knowledges may now transfer to Muslims. When shop customers use young women like Naila, Laila, and AY as translators of Urdu or Punjabi, the service they are providing is not only linguistic translation but also mediation between cultures, faiths, and fashions, just as their presence in hijab provides role models who, when accumulating critical mass, may mediate employment cultures for minority communities (Bowlby and Lloyd-Evans 2009).

There were lots of stories in London in the mid-2000s that Russian-speaking staff was being recruited in Knightsbridge luxury boutiques and at Harvey Nichols to serve the incoming Russian plutocracy. In the 2010s retail attention turned to Chinese luxury shopping tourists in Britain (Walker 2011) and elsewhere, with Gulf retailers recruiting staff in China.[22] By 2014 London retailers were laying on Arabic-language personal services to maximize sales from the annual pre-Ramadan "Harrods Hajj" influx of ultrawealthy Gulf shoppers (Hui 2014). If special knowledge for selling to Russians was based in language, ramped up to include body management training for the Chinese (take and return the credit card with both hands), and combining Arabic-language sales service with petrol-friendly shop-to-car portering, will stores start to value the cultural knowledges of stylish British hijabis? Valued Muslim shoppers from the Gulf tend to wear abayas and rarely engage in style innovation with hijab, but will the high street be able to recognize and harness the distinctiveness of young British hijabi fashion subcultural capital for reaching the local market of British Muslims? With the international increase in hijab wearing as part of a fashion ensemble, the embodied aesthetic knowledge of cool young hijabis could become a form of desirable economic and cultural capital for brands wanting to break into newly discernible markets.

CHAPTER 6

MODESTY ONLINE

Commerce and Commentary on the Net

his chapter looks at new routes for Muslim fashion design and discussion made possible by the Internet and related information and communication technologies (ICTs). With commercial websites joined by a proliferation of blogs, discussion forums, and social media, the design and dissemination of Muslim fashion online is inextricably linked to parallel developments among women and entrepreneurs from other religions.[1]

Because this chapter focuses on the significance of digital communications for the formation of new faith-based fashion markets and forms of mediation it looks more generally at how religions interact with developments in ICT. While the apparent newness of the Internet seemed at first to be a radical departure (whether regarded as an opportunity or a disaster), experience and scholarship now locate digital ICTs within a longer history of religious engagement with different forms of communication, each with implications for the structure of religious authority and modes of knowledge transmission. Online and digital communications in particular enable new actors to achieve prominence with rapidity previously impossible. A significant example here in relation to Islam would be the early adopter activities of online jihadists (Bunt 2009). Not surprisingly perhaps much of the early critical work on digital Islam focused mainly on men's participation. This chapter in contrast focuses not on only women but on a field of cultural and commercial activity, fashion, that is usually regarded as outside of the mainstream of religious concerns. It is my contention that the growing field of fashion online in both commerce and commentary is developing new forms of religious interpretation and knowledge transmission that have significant ramifications for women's engagement with Muslim cultural politics.

Muslim designers and bloggers from the UK were early adopters of the Internet for modest fashion. Unlike tesettür in Turkey, where most leading brands are male-dominated family businesses with some female participation, many of the British and North American Muslim brands that have sprung up in the last fifteen to twenty years are run by young women. The British Muslim designers who feature in this chapter are in many ways heirs to the previous generation of South Asian diaspora fashion entrepreneurs discussed in chapter 4, while the bloggers of today can be seen as the next phase from the print Muslim lifestyle media explored in chapter 3. The sequence is not a chronology of one form being replaced by another. It is an accretion, with older elements reappearing and longstanding challenges continuing: lifestyle magazines became active online; new designers face economic challenges like all fashion start-ups plus marginalization by the mainstream industry. Different is that digital communications make evident very quickly the microgenerations of style and mediation that characterize the contemporary Muslim consumptionscape.

British Muslim designers now work in a context that is increasingly international and cross faith. This potentially expands their customer base and complicates their design and marketing choices, requiring them to negotiate different versions of modesty. Designers and commentators must be cognizant of regional and national taste distinctions between Muslims as well as the diverse tastes and spiritual interpretations of modest dressers from other faith and secular backgrounds as they participate in the creation of a digital network of modest discourse characterized by interfaith and faith/secular connectivity.

The Internet as a New Medium for Religion and for the Spread of Modest Designs and Debates

The Internet has been indispensable to the advancement of commerce *and* commentary concerned with modest fashion. Creating opportunities for "new intermediaries to enter value chains" (French et al. 2004: 54), the Internet provides the means for the development of a niche market, growing and diversifying, which serves modest dressers around the world. The rise of online brands selling modest apparel was accompanied by the development of a lively blogosphere and social media devoted to modest styles, all foregrounding women as entrepreneurs and commentators. Starting in the late 1990s and taking off in the early 2000s, this field of online activity is characterized by fast changes in modes of address and interaction typical of markets and communications online. For the modest dressing sector, often prompted by religious motivation, the increasing overlap and fluidity between commerce and commentary is of particular significance, opening up new routes to prominence for women within and between faith communities, and between religious and secular participants.

The Internet, however, is not neutral, is not used and experienced by everyone in the same way (and is unevenly available to the world population). While the technologies of the Internet may be new, like all media forms they do not arise without history but are part of a reciprocal ongoing process of remediation between new and old media (Jensen 2011). Fashion blogs need to be seen in relation to their print antecedents in magazines and newspapers (Rocamora 2012), and for faith-based user groups digital communication technologies need to be seen in relation to existing models for the development and transmission of religious knowledge. Early research into religion and the Internet often focused on the distinction between *religion online* (understood to mean information about offline religion shared through online communication) and *online religion* (new religions developing and existing solely online, plus online-only material from offline religions [Brasher 2001; Karaflogka 2006]). Attention now focuses on the mutability of and overlap between religion online and online religion (Bunt 2009), in keeping with the porousness of online and offline experiences (Jensen 2011). Discourses about modest dress online and practices of modest dressing offline are similarly mutable. Arising primarily from existing offline religions, women's practices of and discussions about modesty are made possible, and sometimes called into being, by new modes of online merchandising and commentary.

The development of e-commerce has been one of the essential conditions for the emergence of the expanding niche market recognizable today. As for any specialist market, e-retail allows companies to reach more consumers more cheaply, across more geographical territories. For the modest fashion sector, e-retail has the potential to reach consumers outside the faith groups from which brands originate. In the first two decades of the twenty-first century the markets for modest clothing aimed at, and produced by, particular faith groups have expanded and segmented, facilitating access to modest fashion and stimulating interest in it. A new category of "modest fashion" has emerged and become legitimated over the Internet, operating through a mix of commerce and commentary that connects faith groups with each other and with the secular world. It functions simultaneously as a taste-making mechanism, an ideological category, and a marketing device.

While offline shops, and to an extent home selling or mail order, had been meeting the needs of some consumers, this often depended on living in or near an area of religious or related ethnic demographic density. As modest dressers often complain, mainstream fashion retail appears to have no interest in meeting their consumer needs (unlike the now widespread provision of "ethnic/religious" foods in supermarket chains; see chapter 7). Into these gaps rose the new online modest market and a new cohort of modest style mediators. Often themselves members of (sometimes parent to) this youthful modest style demographic, women dominate the field as designers, entrepreneurs, and opinion makers, more likely these days to perceive consumer culture as one of the means by which religious (and related ethnic [Comaroff and Comaroff 2009]) identities can be achieved and expressed than to see consumption and religion as oppositional. Rather than see commerce as the grounds against which subcultures define themselves, one can, as Sarah Thornton argues in relation to (pre-Internet) music club cultures, regard "various media and businesses as integral to the authentication of cultural practices," with niche and micromedia, like style magazines and club flyers, "construct[ing] subcultures as much as they document them" (Thornton 1995: 8, 117). This continues today in the activities of modest fashion bloggers and social media operators. But while previous club culture mediators could selectively distribute club flyers to encourage only the desired participants, today's subcultural modest media-tors rely on interactive media that limit possible gatekeeping.

In the UK, Muslim brands have led the way in the development of the niche market in modest clothing, online and offline. In the United States and Canada, Jewish and Christian faith groups with dress requirements show similar developments in the commercial production and distribu-tion of clothing. This is seen among modern orthodox and ultraortho-dox Jews as well as among different Christian groups, including the Mor-mon Church of Jesus Christ of Latter-day Saints (LDS). The accessibility of clothing matters because women's dress decisions are not arrived at in a vacuum: the historically specific ways in which women's forms of modest dress are enabled and constrained by social, cultural, and economic con-texts includes the range and availability of garments from which women can choose. While, for example, earlier generations of Islamist (some, anti-consumerist) women in Egypt had to sew their own clothes or hire seam-stresses because none were commercially available (El Guindi 1999; see also chapter 1), contemporary modest dressers from Muslim and other faith groups are able to render the body modest through its appropriate comportment in apparel that derives from *within* the mainstream fashion system. Made possible by the advent of cheaper home Internet connec-tions and broadband women can now find product designed with modesty in mind, consult style guides, and join in fashion discussions about how to style modesty just like their secular counterparts. It is not, therefore, only the processes by which the modest appearance is achieved that can be in and of themselves spiritually, socially, politically, and personally sig-nificant (qua Mahmood 2005), but also the ways in which they are repre-sented, disseminated, and discussed. Integral to the circuit of culture (du Gay, Hall, Janes, Madsen, Mackay, and Negus 2013) that characterizes the globalized fashion industry, the role of the Internet in distribution (Kaiser 2012) for modest fashion through e-retail and style mediation connects production, distribution, and consumption to processes of religio-ethnic identity formation and to related forms of regulation (and resistance) that are themselves shaped by changes in online technologies and cultures. The medium of the Internet has created opportunities for women not (or not directly) involved in commerce to publicize their ideas about modest dressing, producing new modes of fashion mediation that become a form of religious interpretation fostering women's voices and perspectives.

With nearly all the first generation of modest online retailers originat-ing from a faith community, the desire to support modest dressing and behaviors is broadly understood as part of a religious, social, and community commitment. Characteristic of the field, the distinction between the commercial and the confessional is flexible rather than fixed. Commercial websites include educational and inspirational material, glossaries of modest clothing, and international accounts of related practices. Entrepreneurs may have to be careful to avoid alienating potential consumers from outside (or from different elements within) their own communities as online shopping brings them into contact with consumers using different modesty codes. While all apparel companies need to distinguish their offering from competitors, companies in the modest sector face a challenge of considerable delicacy in advocating their style and their version of modesty. Some sites deliberately define modesty as multiple and fluid, not specific to any one faith, with some brands moderating their offering to meet the needs of consumers from a variety of other faith backgrounds (R. Lewis 2013b; Moors 2013).

The spread of social media and the blogosphere means that commercial websites are expanding their role in commentary. In just over a decade it is possible to see two if not three generations of innovation: posting educational information was fast established as a characteristic of the first generation of Internet pioneers, but few hosted a blog. Now, even small modest fashion brands run a blog and use social media like Facebook (established 2004) and Twitter (2006) to drive traffic. More recent start-ups may develop a blog and social media prior to launch, building brand awareness before products arrive. The small-scale modest fashion entrepreneur shares much with the marketing strategy of bigger companies. While corporate bloggers provide a small percentage of the overall blogger population, the use of social media had by 2010 become so common in all (commercial and independent) blog sectors that "the lines between blogs, micro-blogs, and social networks [were] disappearing" (Sobel 2010). As the need to maintain a presence on multiple digital platforms increases, more modest fashion companies are outsourcing elements of their digital communications to companies specializing in social media, sometimes from the brand originator's faith community (R. Lewis 2013e). Modest fashion brands replicate marketing practices now common in fashion and lifestyle sectors of trying to encourage consumers to identify with the brand rather than the product. In this case, the identification fostered is both with the brand and with practices of modesty, rendering corporate online presence part of a new Internet-based fashion discourse about modesty that is liable to transcend divisions of faith.

While the Internet as a new medium brings specific opportunities and challenges, the significance of new media in developing and disseminating religious ideas is not new. Neither is it new that innovations in communication technologies (like the printing press and the development of the vernacular Bible) produce changes in the interpretations and practices of the creeds that they communicate. Religious institutions and, though not always in the same ways or to the same effect, their congregations have variously repudiated, harnessed, controlled, and fought over new modes of communication and transmission. Preceding the relationships of religion to the Internet is the early adoption by Protestant evangelical churches in the United States of radio in the 1930s and television in the 1960s (Allner 1997; Brasher 2001), and the widespread use of audio cassettes in the da'wa movement in Egypt since the 1970s (Hirschkind 2006).

Women's online discourse about modesty contributes a distinctively gendered strand to the emergence online of new forms of religious discourse often regarded as a male sphere of activity. As Bunt (2009) and others have established, the Internet has facilitated the development of new forms of religious interpretation outside of the hierarchies of conventional clerical religious authority. Characterized by flat, or lateral, modes of relationship typical of early Internet pioneers, new interpretations circulate online and are implemented offline, validating new forms of religious authority. Muslims, especially Islamists, led the way among other faiths in seeing the potential of the Internet for developing and spreading ideas. The first cohort of Muslims online were often drawn from the same cadres of Western-educated engineers and techies who populated and established the protocols for the early years of the Internet (J. Anderson 2005; Bunt 2009), whereas the advent of satellite television stations like Al Jazeera provided opportunities for women news reporters (Mernissi 2004: 4–6). Just as analogue radio and television created televangelist stars and power brokers who influence American government policy, the Internet brings new groups and individuals to the fore. By the late 2000s most world religions had to some extent migrated online, disproving the anxieties of the 1990s, and revealing the extent of localization with online Islam in multicultural Muslim minority contexts being "markedly different from its manifestations in other Islamic countries" (Ess, Kawabata, and Kurosaki 2007: 952).

New forms of religious authority online also vary across faiths depending on preexistent religious structures of authority and forms of knowledge transmission and modes of ministry (Campbell 2005; Turner 2007).

The centralized transmission of religious authority that characterizes some Christian denominations contrasts to decentralization in Judaism and Islam, where clerical authority is habitually achieved through disputation. For Islam, Peter Mandaville suggests, the Internet marks "the intensification of a tendency toward decentralized authority that has always been present" (Mandaville 2007: 102; see also Volpi and Turner 2007). Building on the advent of mass literacy in the Muslim world in the late nineteenth and early twentieth centuries (still ongoing for many women), the reach of the Internet means that the debate is no longer taking place within and between religious elites and is known to a wider Muslim public, increasingly living diasporic and transnational lives in pluralistic societies. For second- and third-generation migrants, rarely fully literate in Arabic or community languages, the initial predominance of English as an online language was integral to the dissemination of the "global" or "European" Islam (chapter 1) developed by Muslim intellectuals among whom "English has emerged as a preferred medium to call attention to new ideas" (Eickelman and Anderson 2003: 8). For Islam the role of the Internet in allowing "the migration of discourse from narrower to broader, more 'public' realms" opens the space for nonelite, nonclerical participation, through a medium that "not only places messages into wider circulation but also rebalances their authority from that of sender to include the circulation itself" (J. Anderson [1999] 2003: 46). Given that the face-to-face spaces previously reserved for the formal and informal transmission of Islamic knowledge—typically the madrassa and the mosque (J. Anderson 2005) and the coffeehouse—were territories barred to women, this relocation of knowledge transmission and the opportunity to participate in its circulation cannot but be significant for women.

Across the faiths electronic and digital media has expanded and diversified existing religious publics, but there is "nothing inherently progressive about the new media" (Meyer and Moors 2006: 5–10). New modes of communication can be harnessed as easily by majority as by minority religious cultures, to develop conservative or progressive communities. Facilities like "fatwa-online" or "ask the rabbi" can build reputations for self-appointed moral guides disproportionate to their level of religious knowledge (Biala 2009) just as they can advantage clerics of both elite and minority status (Bunt 2009) and be used to create new transnational publics for campaigns by progressives and conservatives (Mandaville 2007). That digital platforms let more people express their opinions does not lead necessarily to a more tolerant public domain: for Kline, blogging has given "new voice and new reach to the extremist strain in American society" (Kline and Burstein 2005: 22). In the new intellectual elite of diasporic Islam, Turner suggests, the competition to gain followers in the context of the individualization of religiosity typical of early Internet generations often produces an "inflationary expansion of claims to purity and strictness that has a compulsory upward trajectory" (Turner 2007: 132). The opportunity to construct an identity based on ever stricter religiosity can be appealing to second- and third-generation socially excluded Muslim migrants in Europe (J. Anderson [1999] 2003; Roy [2002] 2004), as can the opportunity to regulate the behavior of others through corrective advice dispensed as part of the da'wa obligation of moral guidance that I discussed in chapter 4.

My focus on modest clothing reveals that, as early adopters of virtual communication, women entrepreneurs and style mediators are constructing innovative forms of religious discourse online, creating cross-faith interactions spanning commerce and conversation. Women's products and ideas circulate online and through sales offline, developing networks with the potential to displace discourses about modesty into arenas beyond traditional religious authority structures. While many participants are motivated to promote modesty, the field was not initially characterized by the doctrinal judgmentalism seen in other areas of religion online. Recognizing diverse modesty codes and motivations, American Muslim designers Nyla Hashmi and Fatima Monkush are not alone in arguing that, as Hashmi puts it, "it's not only about conservative women; [it's] very much a feminist movement as well."[2] For them, as for others, the assertion of multiple modesties underwrites a challenge to community conventions as well as external perceptions. This always delicate netiquette of respectful diversity has come under attack in recent years, as I discuss below, with the uptake of social media producing an increase in the volume and ferocity of hostile comment posting.

Critical surveillance notwithstanding, women have used the Internet to share ideas, rate styles, comment on mainstream provision, and intervene in debates about modest behavior, extending the opportunities for professional and quasi-professional fashion mediation offered offline by the establishment in print of faith-based style media in the first half of the 2000s. The advent of blogging software in 1999 made the personal "weblog," or blog, increasingly accessible with a concomitant expansion of the numbers and types of voices online (Kline and Burstein 2005). Dominated initially by political and technical content, fashion bloggers began

FIGURE 6.1 *JenMagazine*, "Modesty Accessory, Many Uses," blog feature, screenshot. Accessed March 25, 2013. Courtesy of Jen Loch, http://JenClothing.com.

topic-based blogs and took advantage of cheap digital camera technology to feature their own wardrobes in personal-style blog self-portraits (Roca-mora 2011). Religious fashionistas embraced the blog, with the development of the modest blogosphere matching the chronology of the medium. One year after the first fashion blog in 2003, American LDS modest blog front-runner Jennifer Loch came online with *JenMagazine.com* (see figure 6.1) in 2004, the year that saw a huge increase of blog reading (up 58 percent) and a "greater-than-average growth" in blog reading by women and minorities (Pew 2005). British Muslim trailblazer Jana Kossaibati started Hijabstyle.co.uk in 2007 (see figure 6.2). Critical mass appeared by 2009 with a second generation of modest bloggers in the United States like LDS Elaine Hearn's Clothedmuch.com (blogging until 2013; see figure 6.3) and in Britain Muslim Hana Tajima-Simpson's Stylecovered.com (see figure 6.4). By 2011, Technorati's *State of the Blogosphere* was reporting that an

Monday, 25 March 2013

Hijab Style Exclusive: Inayah Interview

Today Hijab Style brings you an exclusive interview with the founders of **Inayah**; one of the UK's leading brands for modest clothing.

Jana: How did you come to start Inayah?

The seeds of INAYAH were planted by its owners who come from a combination of fields which fuse business acumen with in-depth appreciation and understanding of wide ranging design principles and genres. INAYAH initially started off in 2010 as an accessories brand featuring a large selection of hand crafted bracelets, necklaces, and our signature hijab pins. Our desire to remain in a consistent state of development soon took over and before long plans were underway for a major expansion into the brand seen today.

Follow Hijab Style

Latest Press Features

- BBC News
- Vogue.com
- The Guardian May 2009
- The Guardian March 2009

Subscribe to Hijab Style

Your email address:

Get email updates
Powered by FeedBlitz

Blog Archive

Blog Archive

FIGURE 6.2 *Hijab Style*, blog homepage, screenshot. Accessed March 25, 2013. Courtesy of Jana Kossaibati, www.hijabstyle.co.uk.

"important trend is the influence of the women and mom bloggers on the blogosphere, mainstream media, and brands, . . . [the] blogger segment most likely of all to blog about brands" (Sobel 2010). Successful bloggers attract large numbers of followers with international commenters from a variety of faith and/or secular backgrounds.

More recent hijabi commentators have been early adopters of social media, using Facebook, Twitter, YouTube, and Instagram as core platforms. Hugely popular, by 2012 social media were being used by 67 per-

FIGURE 6.3 *Clothed Much*, blog homepage, screenshot. Accessed May 30, 2009. Courtesy of Elaine Hearn, www.clothedmuch.com.

FIGURE 6.4 *Style Covered*, blog homepage, screenshot. Accessed April 2, 2012. Courtesy of Hana Tajima-Simpson, www.hanatajima.com.

cent of all American adults, especially the eighteen-to-twenty-nine-year-olds (Duggan and Brenner 2013) in the peer group of the bloggers in this chapter. Taking American data as symptomatic, Facebook remains the most used social media at 67 percent of American adults using it, with women showing a greater participation than men, although Twitter use has doubled to 16 percent of American adults using it since 2010, heavily frequented by those under fifty and younger users. Younger users (13 percent) and women users flock to the smartphone image-sharing app Instagram (now owned by Facebook), which has become increasingly prevalent with recent hijabi bloggers. Though less prominent in the hijabi sphere, the digital scrapbooking site Pinterest achieves a 15 percent share of American adult use and, more popular with women than men, is widely used in the American (often Christian) "crafting" digital community. Only 6 percent of American adults use Tumblr, which is much more popular with eighteen-to-twenty-nine-year-olds. As with blogging, online group participation and leadership corresponds to educational achievement of college level and above (Jensen 2011; Technorati 2011) as with the hijabi commentators featured here.

The ways in which people access the Internet is also changing, with teenagers prominent early adopters of mobile connectivity as smartphone market penetration increases, and teenage girls "significantly more likely" than boys to say they access the Internet mostly using their cell phone (Madden et al. 2013: 7). The spread of phone connectivity is important for a Muslim population that is globally youthful (chapter 1) and often living in locations with poor telecoms infrastructure (Bunt 2009). In America, as elsewhere, while many young people still access the Internet on shared family computers, the ability to access the Internet in spaces away from adult monitoring adds to the sense of being at the "centre of his or her network" established by gamester online sociality in the 1980s and 1990s (Lüders 2011: 452). Different now is that while young people can curate their own image online, the much championed connectivity of Web 2.0 means that they can be judged on their online relationships ("cute" friends, other people posting photos) as well as on what they themselves post. For modest social media, the ease with which criticism, especially of hijabis' pictures, can be circulated has become significant.

While established bloggers like Kossaibati or Hearn use Twitter and Facebook primarily to publicize new blog posts (still the favored platform of digital and social influencers [Technorati 2013]), the visually led social media are favored by more recent practitioners who have come of age with

FIGURE 6.5 *Zinah*, blog homepage, screenshot. Accessed February 27, 2011. Courtesy of Zinah, www.zinahns.com.

smartphones and the ease with which images (still and moving) can be taken and posted online: by 2012, 46 percent of adult American Internet users had created original photographic or video images of themselves to post online, while 41 percent had curated photos and videos they found elsewhere (Rainie, Brenner, and Purcell 2012). With many people (32 percent) both curating and creating, 56 percent of Internet users had been involved in image contribution online. These statistics do not include teenagers, who are generally held to be highly involved in the posting of visual material, much of it self-generated and self-portraiture. Overall, curators are more often women and young people, with creators mainly under fifty showing an equal gender mix. For some, like blogger Zinah nur Sharif, the opportunity to curate visually is a welcome development.[3] Active online since 2010, she shares her style vision and nascent business ideas through a picture-led personal style blog, Zinah (see figure 6.5), as well as her active Facebook pages and Instagram, Tumblr, and Twitter accounts.[4]

The presumption that bloggers are independent commentators has changed as the blogosphere segments and professionalizes. As predicted (Kline and Burstein 2005), an A-list of "star" bloggers emerged, whose activities crossed over to other media, while corporations sought to harness the potential of virtual commentary by developing blogs and social media as an integral part of company communications policy. By 2013 Technorati was able to report that brand digital messaging "has gone social." While consumers use social media to track new products, for purchasing decisions blogs "trail only behind retail and brand sites," ranked by consumers "among the top five 'most trustworthy' sources" for information. However, brand spend is not proportionately directed at bloggers: digital still accounts for only 10 percent of overall marketing budgets, of which only 5 percent goes to blog advertisements. Recognized as influencers, bloggers lose out on marketing spend and monetary opportunities because "due to their niche size" they are often indiscernible in the industry metrics used by marketing professionals (Technorati 2013: 5). Modest and hijabi bloggers, whose relatively low audience numbers would rank even the most popular within the "long tail" of metrics, are doubly invisible as a niche within a niche. They may, however, find themselves extremely visible to brands within the modest sector, leading to specific opportunities and tensions.

Bloggers generally are increasingly able to shift across into established forms of journalism. Positioned initially as marginal or renegade voices, key bloggers have accrued cultural and political capital equivalent to their established print media counterparts: in politics think of the *Huffington Post*, in fashion of the *Sartorialist* and the other bloggers now seated front row for the catwalk shows and featuring in the print and online editions of established fashion magazines. The careful maneuvers required if bloggers are to retain integrity as independent commentators while taking up crossover opportunities in fashion public relations (PR) (Burney 2011) have particular nuance for the faith sector. Modest fashion bloggers enter a new media field characterized by intense anxieties about visual representations of the female form and rarely able to draw on the genealogy of fashion imagery and comment that makes it so easy for the *Sartorialist*'s output to cross over. This makes it harder for modest bloggers to cross over into the monetized sphere known as "pro-blogging," further complicated in the religious domain by the heightened value accorded to a convincingly authentic, uncompromised blog voice.

Writing on the development of online religious communities among different Christian denominations in 2005, Heidi Campbell could already confirm (as indicated in Pew 2001) that in contrast to initial anxieties that online connections would erode participation in offline churches, the two were most often complementary. The affordances of digital connectivity proved more likely to result in the "transformation and reconfiguration of existing practices, beliefs, and infrastructures" than in their replacement (Cheong and Ess 2012b: 2). With religious (mainly church) groups at 40 percent constituting the most popular form of community or civic organization in America, by 2011 the Internet had become a routinized adjunct to religious community life (Pew 2011e). Diaspora Muslims (as with other religions, like young Sikhs [Singh 2012]) frequently use the Internet as their first port of call for religious information.

While regulars in online discussion groups may seek a sense of community with "brothers and sisters in Christ" that can extend their communion beyond brick-and-mortar churches, for many the needs of local churches to establish at the very least a basic online informational presence provided leadership roles for "techies," with attendant opportunities to attain seniority and respect (Campbell 2005; Cheong, Huang, and Poon 2011; Emerson 2012; Thumma 2000). With information overload an inevitable part of the Internet experience, the role of the mediator and guide becomes crucial, suggesting to Bunt that "a critical area in the future of CIEs [cyber Islamic environments] is not the provision of content but the provision of guidance and information management" (Bunt 2009: 288).

Despite the religiosity of the population, the (American) mainstream media outside of religious syndicated radio and television provides little specialist coverage (Kline 2005), increasing the significance of blogs and social media. Because "bloggers have impact in aggregate" the ability to promote a religious view can come not just from the pulling power of "star" bloggers but from the quantity of small bloggers posting on the same topic (Kline 2005: 22). Participation by readers (or Twitter followers or Facebook friends) in discussion or recirculating a post can create sufficient buzz to bring a topic to an audience beyond the initially digital readership.

The hypertextuality that characterizes virtual communications means that it is rare for any website or blog to be experienced in isolation as readers click through from Internet search engines or from links on other sites. As Anastasia Karaflogka (2006) discusses, for virtual communications in the religious sector attitudes to digital traffic are telling. Official websites and social media of religious institutions may permit users to link to them but try to maintain their authorized discourse by refusing reciprocal links out. Other sites seek mutual links, and others mask institutional or political affiliations (Bunt 2009). With many Christian blogs linking more to their own "A-list" of Christian blogs and websites than to other digital sources (Cheong, Halavais, and Kwon 2008), the development of different gatekeeping practices are important indicators of attitude and presumed addressees when analyzing online content (R. Lewis 2013b).

In fashion terms this click-through culture melds mediation with sales, as readers of blog posts (or Pinterest pages) can click through to purchase on brand or retail websites in ways not conventionally possible with print magazines (Rocamora 2012). Whereas fashion magazines for much of the twentieth century had been part of a world in which "fashion has a more substantial and a more popular existence as an image on the page than it has as a set of clothes on the rail" (McRobbie 1998: 164), once dematerialized online fashion mediation is almost inevitably connected back to sites of commerce. This is not entirely the case for the modest sector. Although many modest companies rely on the reduced costs of e-commerce, their products often have a higher profile through image remediation than through actual sales. In a field where most modest dressers source most of their apparel from a mixture of high street and ethnic providers (chapter 4), augmented by the occasional "star" purchase from a modest brand, the significance of designers and brands cannot be deduced solely from the quantity of product sold. Sales are crucial to the sustainability of the company, and, like all fashion start-ups, modest brands show a high failure rate with several of the companies featured here ceasing to operate or operating on only a minimal scale during the period of my research. In this context maintaining a profile within online modest fashion discourse becomes essential to keep a brand alive, even if products are (sometimes temporarily) unavailable. With the hijabi fashionscape deriving inspiration from image as much as from product, the overlap between bloggers and producers in the circulation of names, designs, looks, and images remains key.

Challenges for Modest Fashion Bloggers: Brand Giveaways and Reader Photos

The end of the 2000s saw an increase in modest blogs of all sorts along with the expansion of designers and entrepreneurs entering the modest market. A second generation of modest designers and mediators is characterized by a less functionalist attitude to website design, visual representation (especially regarding the female form), and digital communications. This section introduces a selection of key bloggers and explores the issues raised for the modest blogosphere by two elements of the fashion blog genre: brand giveaways and the reader style photos.

Recently completing her medical training, Jana Kossaibati started her topic-based blog *Hijab Style* as an eighteen-year-old school student in 2007 because "there are so many websites and magazines out there about fashion in general, but there's nothing for us."[5] Born in London to Lebanese parents, Kossaibati, who started to wear the hijab at age thirteen, has become a highly regarded source of information for hijabis and for external observers. At first searching hard to find modest brands to announce to her readers, the blog has developed several popular formats that mix mainstream and Muslim fashion providers to create a Muslim fashionscape. "High Street Finds" reflects the shopping habits of young British hijabis with a trawl of the high street stores for seasonal highlights. "Style Inspiration" echoes the typical fashion blog mix of reports on British and international designer collections and celebrity style icons but, in Kossaibati's case, also includes international Muslim and Islamic designers and brands (including the Turkish tesettür companies discussed in chapter 2) alongside profiles on prominent Muslim tastemakers like Queen Rania of Jordan,[6] and the wives of Turkish AKP politicians.[7] For the smaller designers that Kossaibati covers, securing a profile on *Hijab Style* can be key to market success. With readers of a similar age growing up with her (at the younger end of the eighteen-to-thirty bracket, with few teens), the blog has responded to Kossaibati's own changing wardrobe needs, from student to young professional with "WorkWear Wardrobe" (see figure 6.6), and the modesty requirements of Muslim women whose preferences for jilbabs or abayas are different from her own. Kossaibati's commitment to chronicling and supporting a range of modesty interpretations is seen also in her "Modest Street Style" feature, which remediates images, including the one post to date on the *Sartorialist* (December 15, 2009) of a hijabi (hailed across the hijabisphere, and generating significantly more comments on the *Sartorialist* site than any other non-celebrity-related post that year).[8] Kossaibati's street style selection chronicles changing global hijab styles, such as the shift from the Turkish satin square to the long "pashmina style" or şal that I discuss in chapter 2.[9]

Creating product giveaways at first required Kossaibati to beg for promotional offers. Within four years the market for modest fashion had increased, and Kossaibati had more offers than she could schedule for her monthly giveaway slot. Modest bloggers must now arbitrate between the demands of companies and the ever more discerning needs of their readers. Facing an onslaught of PR demands — "can you do a post about a collection, we're a new company, we've just started, post about us" — by 2011 Kossaibati was restricting blog editorial to things she felt were "really going to be of interest," using Twitter for mundane (sales, product line) announcements. Otherwise, "I've felt that's got a little bit out of hand,

The WWW: Navy and Grey

If there's one thing I find the most difficult to find for workwear, it's tops and tunics to wear with trousers. Most are either too casual, too tight, or too short. And when you're in a hurry in the mornings, sometimes you just need to have a selection of neutral basics to put together for a 'go to' outfit. I love this tunic from Uniqlo because the fit is flattering and the fabric thin enough to layer another top underneath. I'd wear it over a pair of tailored grey trousers, and add a lighter scarf to avoid the whole outfit becoming too dark. Or add a pop of colour with bright accessories.

www.hijabstyle.co.uk

Merino Tencel Round Neck Half Sleeve Tunic £29.90, Uniqlo; Grey trousers £22, Next; Navy dip hem crew neck trimarl top £8, Dorothy Perkins; Dolce Grey scarf £13.99, Bellissima Scarves; Hematite bling rings £8.50, Dorothy Perkins; Hards bag £45, Aldo; Country Music shoe £39.99, Clarks.

FIGURE 6.6 *Hijab Style*, "WWW (WorkWear Wardrobe)," blog fashion feature, screenshot. Accessed April 15, 2013. Courtesy of Jana Kossaibati, www.hijabstyle.co.uk.

and the blog's become a bit of an advertising kind of thing, a platform for companies trying to disseminate their information," with readers quick to complain.

While the increase in modest fashion products is generally welcome, the increase in brand PR attention means that, like their nonreligious counterparts, modest bloggers face generic issues about autonomy and impartiality. As New York modern orthodox Jewish blogger Nina Cohen of *Alltumbledown* discovered after posting about her dilemma over how to review a free sample dress whose late and damaged arrival had prompted a request from the company not to refer to the problems, writing an honest but unfavorable review may go down well with readers (R. Lewis 2013e), but in relations with brands it can have consequences offline as well as online. For Kossaibati, with (by June 2011) twenty-five hundred daily visitors and upward of two thousand subscribers, it is of little significance if a poor review simply means that her write-up won't be featured on the company website. What she might lose in cross-promotional tie-in, she gains in continued respect from her readers. But she found herself "expressing mutual outrage" when counselling a newer blogger, with far fewer followers, who was intimidated and even felt "threatened" by a brand over a negative review because, as Kossaibati saw it, they felt they could—the new blogger has less clout and less evident support. Modest fashion can be a small world, connected by community contacts that can be both advantageous and discomfortingly exposing. By 2013 Kossaibati was considering dropping giveaways entirely; they drive traffic but add little value to blog content. In contrast, bloggers generally that year were enthusiastic about promotions and about monetized content (Technorati 2013).

Maintaining independence has a particular value in the modest sector where bloggers see their work as spiritually fulfilling rather than commercially driven, few earning yet more than a token amount. In the fashion field as elsewhere, the consecration of cultural capital has required its workings to be complex and covert (qua Bourdieu), with fashion industry norms obscuring the revolving door between journalists and commercial PR (McRobbie 1998) and the link between positive editorial and ad revenue. Although the further blurring of fashion roles (with stylists acting as designer "muses" and journalists) makes overt some of these relationships in the mainstream fashion field, in the modest sector, with fewer opportunities for monetized activity, independence retains its premium. In facing the changes to economic and cultural capital posed by the Internet, conventional media companies showed a similar pattern to conventional religious institutions, initially anxious about loss of authority and market share. But, as with religions, digital communications have augmented rather than replaced previous media form and content (Marshall 2011), with journalists now required to service blogs and social media for their magazine or TV station. In a gatekeeping of status that mirrors criticism within the religious field of untaught interpreters being accorded unearned authority online, the incursion of bloggers into paid fashion mediation raises journalistic and designer hackles at the perceived lack of knowledge among even celebrated bloggers.

In contrast, modest fashion is so recent a field of cultural mediation that its few years of print media magazines can hardly be said to constitute a hinterland of "old" media. Relations between print magazines and online commentators are usually cordial, with many bloggers providing guest features. Among themselves bloggers demonstrate a self-help ethos: Kossaibati responds to informal requests for blog and website advice; others develop semiprofessional service provision to train the next microgeneration, like Elaine Hearne's Mormon Fashion Bloggers network, open to all LDS bloggers willing to cross promote with a badge on websites and social media.[10] Rather than see this as self-interested reputation enhancement, Cheong et al. emphasize that the tendency to regard blogging as a "team sport" of shared enterprise in the collective growing of, in their instance, the Christian blogosphere reflects participants' understanding of blogging and now social media (Cheong 2012; Cheong, Halavais, and Kwon 2008) as a religious practice, seen also in the Muslim blogosphere. In modest fashion online this network of the committed crosses between faiths *and* between the commercial and commentary sectors. Seeing the high street rather than each other as their main competition (R. Lewis 2013c), religious entrepreneurs are happy to copublicize each other if it gains profile for the concept of modest fashion per se, and bloggers and social media players collaborate online and sometimes offline in mutual support. For social media practitioners, influence is gauged by page views and announced on screen by numbers of Facebook likes and Twitter followers, with reposting and retweeting indicating their status and that of others (Technorati 2013). Other forms of mutually beneficial cross promotion include new ratings mechanisms that validate digital modesty as a recognizable sphere of activity and endorse the social media sites of the organizers. For example, "Top 100 Muslim Women Facebook Fan Pages," compiled by *American Muslim Mom* in 2011, was widely and rapidly circulated (with Kossaibati's *Hijab Style* coming in at number 7).[11] With readers, fans, and friends following favorite bloggers when they guest post, online modest fashion discourse is now sufficiently established for content to migrate quickly across platforms and faiths.[12] Assisted by keywords and Google alerts, the zone of modest mediation extends into related popular websites, forums, and blogs concerned with sewing, crafting, homeschooling, and parenthood. Achieving modest fashionability on a budget with how-to tips and original patterns, women mix discussions of styles and textiles with debates about multiple modesty codes, the regulation of female sexuality, and women's role within conventional and "alternative" religions.[13]

Often characterized by (and moderated to ensure) respect for multiple definitions of modesty, discussion can also become heated and hostile, challenging the delicate habits of tolerance that for early participants characterized much online modesty discourse (Cameron 2013; Tarlo 2013b). As Moors notes, those bloggers and YouTubers who "firmly distinguish between what is and what is not legitimate hijab" receive less traffic than those who "refrain from strongly normative statements" (Moors 2013: 29). The ideological commitment to (and, for some, business case for) individual choice (chapter 4) in when and how to cover most especially triggers regulatory attention in the domain of the visual. Bloggers, like brands and print media, face vociferous criticism if their visuals transgress presumed community codes of dress and visual representation. The ability to move beyond literal modes of reading is essential for the development of any minority media, but the etiquette needed within the religious sphere can be especially delicate. For bloggers this comes to the fore in their handling of reader photos, a key component of the fashion blog genre, but potentially explosive in the modest domain. Unlike other fashion blogs, reader submissions to modest fashion blogs face evaluation on grounds not only of style but of modesty and appear in a segment of the blogosphere subject to hostile surveillance from community members rarely simpatico to fashion.

Surprised by how many photos she received, Kossaibati ran a very popular readers' style feature (see plate 10) but sometimes had to turn down photos of readers whose version of modesty did not meet her minimum requirements. As she explained in 2010, although it is her unspoken prerogative to define how modesty appears under her banner, she avoids injunctions or regulations: "If I set rules for myself about what I show on the website in terms of what I think is modest, so for example I won't put skinny jeans up, because for me I don't believe that's a good enough criteria, then I felt that I have to apply the same standards to readers' photos as well, because okay, sure that's the way they want to dress and that's fine, but at the end of the day it's on my website, and people look at it as if this is what I am promoting personally, even if I'm not. [I] have had to say a few times, I love your style, but I just want to promote what I feel is the best standard for hijab that I believe in. And actually people have been pretty understanding about that."

Made cautious by critical responses to previous visuals, Kossaibati aims to project modesty broadly defined and to protect her potential contributors. In the end she stopped the reader feature because arbitrating different modesty codes was "a lot of effort to curate [and] I felt so terrible [having] to tell people no." By 2013, after six years of activity, the trend to ever increasing visuality and self-imaging coupled with the faster turnaround of the new social media added to her general disenchantment with the world of blogging. By now age twenty-four, the "old" hand reflects that "there's just no more longevity with anything. [A] lot of people use Instagram and it's literally . . . outfit of the day, taken it, done, that's it, tomorrow is a new thing, even two, three times a day. And I can't keep up with that, mentally or physically." Though Kossaibati is committed to using fashion visuals that show the body and face (one of the reasons why she declined to write for *Sisters* magazine), Instagram does not work for her as a blogger who avoids showing her own picture: "Most of my Instagram is pictures of food! I don't have a problem with showing bits of me, like if I'm wearing a bracelet, but I'd rather not have my face in it."

While Kossaibati avoids featuring her own image on her blog, designer and entrepreneur Hana Tajima-Simpson always has, and specifically used her blog *StyleCovered.com* to create publicity prior to the launch of her company Maysaa in 2010. Like other second-generation modest designers able even by the late 2000s to presume a more fashion-forward audience (R. Lewis 2013c), Tajima-Simpson has always adopted and adapted the visual language of the secular fashion industry. Raised in rural Devon in southwest England by her Japanese father and English mother, when Tajima-Simpson "reverted" to Islam at age seventeen she was able from the first to craft her own form of hijab, untrammeled by family ethnic or community dress conventions and living at a distance from established Muslim populations. With two artist parents she grew up with an aesthetic disposition able to affect the "disinterest" in the market—"for me, a hundred percent, it's nothing to do with the business side, [it's] a creative outlet"[14]—characteristic of a fashion-as-art discourse that distinguishes designers from the lowering associations of trade (McRobbie 1998). Tajima-Simpson started out using three blogs to produce a differentiated web presence, "so in one way or another, what I want to say will get out there": "For *Style Covered* I have to make sure that there is [sic] elements within everything that I post that is relevant to people who do cover. . . . The *Maysaa* blog [see figure 6.7] is really difficult to write because it has to maintain a business angle, [but] it has to be interesting, and personal as well . . . [whereas] Tumblr [see figure 6.8] is much more personal and much

*Previous page: chiffon dropped
pocket tee &
This page: Sheer overlay maxi
skirt coming soon to maysaa.com*

FIGURE 6.7 *Maysaa* digital magazine, September 2010, issue 2, www.maysaa.com, screenshot Accessed April 3, 2012. Courtesy of Hana Tajima-Simpson, www.hana tajima.com.

FIGURE 6.8 Hana Tajima-Simpson, self-portrait on Tumblr, screenshot. Accessed April 2, 2012. Courtesy of Hana Tajima-Simpson, www.hana tajima.com.

less writing . . . a cross between a blog and Twitter so you can reblog other people's things. . . . It's very much a community type thing because you're following other people and they're following you."

Incorporating her self-portrait was a way to include a "visual perspective" that formed "a link with the readers." While exposing the evolution of her personal hijab style can expose "a lot of personal development," there is little that is unmediated in her image production. Tajima-Simpson dresses specifically for the camera: "unless I make a point about it, whatever I've worn in the picture is something that I have worn or will wear, but because of the time I'll tend to do a set [of] five or six outfits in a day."

Like the reader photo shoots in *Âlâ* magazine (chapter 3), bloggers and "civilians" alike know they need to be camera ready. Judgments involved in her own self-imaging are transferred to others when dealing with reader photo submissions. Tajima-Simpson's "You Wear It Well" feature on *Style Covered* started slow, but "now [November 2010] every day I'll get two or three people sending me pictures." Like Kossaibati, Tajima-Simpson must arbitrate style and morality: "It's really difficult. I mean people can wear whatever they like, I'm not at all fussed, but for me to put something on the blog I have to also be aware that other readers might make comments that aren't necessarily nice. . . . I don't want them to come under any negative scrutiny because of me, so I have to be really careful about the kind of pictures. Sometimes I'll crop it so you can't see a certain bit, something like that."

If personal style blogs are understood generally to widen the range of images of women seen in fashion media (Rocamora 2011), modest bloggers who post their own or readers' images find themselves articulating alternative versions of modish modesty against a ground not only of fashion but of competing religious and community expectation. Mormon Elaine Hearn was not surprised to receive some criticism after she featured herself in skinny jeans (see figure 6.9); "[I knew that for some] LDS people skinny jeans would also be immodest, but I feel like a lot of it came from different Christian sites."[15] These anonymous posts were especially painful "because I am also Christian and we're not taught to say negative things like that, and so it was very hurtful for me to realize the lack of Christian fellowship." Women designers/entrepreneurs and bloggers alike express a need to intervene in community definitions of modesty (whether over particular types of garments or the use of bright colors and patterns), to wrest the power to define modesty away from "conservative" women (R. Lewis 2013a).

FIGURE 6.9 Elaine Hearn, in skinny jeans on her *Clothed Much* blog, screenshot. Accessed April 15, 2013. Courtesy of Elaine Hearn, www.clothedmuch.com.

Early in her brand's history in 2009 designer Sarah Elenany reflected that "we don't get attacked from the mainstream press as much as we get attacked from our own community."[16] She explains with a rueful laugh, "my community is run by the elders . . . usually men, and I think they see anything which is promoting fashion as unwanted and unimportant." Other modest style leaders encountered the same problem: "I know that Hana gets it, even Jana who's very, very conservative, gets it." In this context, the positive coverage available in the new Muslim lifestyle magazines (see figure 6.10) was an antidote to the dismissive attitude of established Muslim community media. Bloggers, like the lifestyle magazine editors in chapter 3, are aware that criticism often comes from outside their target audience. Adviya Khan and her sister Samia at *Hijablicious* combine a personal style blog with guest posts on modest topics, "fashion fixes to bare your soul not your flesh," and learned soon after their launch in 2010 not to respond when their personal style photos (see figures 6.11 and 6.12) received negative comments: "we're not very conservative as maybe some people would like, so we do get sometimes comments that are a bit negative. . . . I think probably all hijabi bloggers and YouTubers get that at some stage. It is sometimes quite upsetting. . . . I appreciate everybody's opinion, but I think some people, especially on the Internet, because of the anonymous nature that it has, feel they can go out of their way to be nasty [whereas] they wouldn't do that in real life."[17]

Deciding not to engage was both practical because moderating took up too much time and spiritual because "we want to provide fashion inspiration not religious advice." This approach, of locating "expertise in the field of fashion rather than in that of Islam," is typical for Moors (2013: 28) of online Muslim fashion brands and mediators who by leaving decisions about proper Islamic dress to the individual and avoiding claims to religious authority are able by inference to normalize hijab fashion as part of Islamic practice. Adviya certainly wants to avoid the "black hole [of] justifying the religious credibility of your blog." Aware nonetheless that by picturing what they consider to be acceptable hijabi fashion the sisters are presenting a spiritual or religious judgment, they rely on a discourse of choice to reassure that "we don't want to impose it on anyone and say this is exactly how [it] should be." As an advocate of respect for diversity of practice, Adviya was shocked at the level of opprobrium aimed at blogger Dina Toki-O for her YouTube hijab tutorials (see figure 6.13) — "from what I've seen on the Internet, I think the YouTubers get a lot more. . . . Some of [the commenters] are atrocious, [even saying] you're a slut. . . . A lot of the funny [nasty] ones are men, Muslim men who go on there who watch women's YouTube videos about hijab and then they feel they have the right to comment after watching a video which isn't really for [them] anyway. . . . And because of the nature of YouTube you can't possibly moderate every single comment [but] some of them [I find] upsetting as a reader, so I know she would probably get quite upset. But then at the same time you've got the millions of thousands saying we want more."

When I started this research, I noted that the interactivity of the Internet could provide a supportive antidote to (often male) criticism, adding significance to the "likes" and comment streams that generically indicate

FIGURE 6.10 Sarah Elenany in *Emel* magazine, February 2012.

FIGURE 6.11 *Hijablicious*, Adviya Khan, personal style blog photo, screenshot. Accessed April 16, 2013. Courtesy of Adviya Khan, http://hijablicious .com.

FIGURE 6.12 *Hijablicious*, Samia Khan, personal style blog photo, screenshot. Accessed April 16, 2013. Courtesy of Samia Khan, http://hijablicious.com.

1:00 / 6:32

how to wear cute summer hijab tutorial and measly outfit of the day!

FIGURE 6.13 Dina Toki-O, YouTube Hijab Tutorial, screenshot. Accessed April 15, 2013. Courtesy of Dina Torkia, www.youtube.com/user/dinatokio.

status online. The spiritual uplift of online connectivity was still positive for American convert Heather Akou (chapter 4) in 2010, seeing potential "on a daily basis" to reinforce the lesson of "the scale and diversity of the umma" experienced and emblematized offline by the hajj (Akou 2010: 345). Since then, the affordances of social media have given comment streams a life of their own. While exceptionally the Vatican was able to negotiate the removal of the comments function as a precondition to their YouTube participation (Campbell 2012), most media corporations along with small-scale modest bloggers remain at the mercy of respondents.[18] By 2013 Kossaibati despaired: "it's the same old, same old. It's like the e-mails that I used to get, except now it's not one comment here or there, it's hundreds of people replying to each other and arguing and fighting. The backlash that [people] get when they post, is horrendous. It's just sickening and there are massive debates going on all the time. On Facebook and YouTube it's like a free-for-all with the comments and people will say this is not hijab [and] then people argue. . . . There's a lot of hate."

Some of this is from men, who get "shot down" with "why are you even here, it's not for you," but "the vast majority of it is other women." With surveillance and criticism endemic in offline female student life (chapter 4), online interactions further erode the sisterly ideal of avoiding judgment: "On Facebook it doesn't seem to apply at all and it's really hard. For example, [YouTuber Amenikin] will post loads of statuses saying, we shouldn't be judging each other [and] you're just driving people away from the concept of modesty. . . . It's not encouraging people to better themselves."

The harshest invective was reserved for the American Egyptian "dejabi" blogger Winnie Détwa, who chronicled her transition out of hijab. Defense, Kossaibati noted, came not only from readers and bloggers: "what's interesting, a lot of the companies are still supportive of her, which is really nice. So they still interact with her, they still will send her stuff to review." Détwa continues to post—"it might not be with her head covered but it's still modest and it's still applicable to hijabis"—and, as I discuss in chapter 7, remains part of the digital modest community. The ability to include a wide range of practices within the frame of modest fashion was initially a distinguishing feature of the subcultural capital of hijabi mediators, demonstrated in their adroit handling of finely nuanced discussion and disputation. This preferred netiquette of multiplicity and respect by which modest mediators once defined the boundaries of the field is now under erosion by the "commentariat."

The interactivity of digital media platforms affords the creation of a counterdiscourse by men and women who consistently populate media response modes. Rather than hosting their own sites, many seek to police the new practices of modest fashion through sustained attacks on the comments function of others' sites. These commenters do not patrol mainstream media to police female modesty: the modest fashion field is their chosen battleground. While the use of the Internet and social media in teen bullying and (misogynist) hate campaigns against public figures has made Internet trolls a recurrent news story in the 2010s, for the Muslim modest fashion sphere digital connectivity has expanded the reach of community, male elder, and clan regulation that women long faced offline (chapter 1). The connectivity of the Internet creates new transnational localisms in which Muslims geographically distant can intervene in local discussions. Whereas editors of Muslim lifestyle print magazines in the mid-2000s knew that their target readers were likely to be judged on the content of their magazine consumption by older or more conservative observers, for online fashion mediators today the zone of interaction and judgment is potentially limitless. This is important for modest fashion entrepreneurs and mediators because, unlike the characterization (Thornton 1995) that subcultural elites maintain subcultural capital by guarding the boundaries between the cool and the uncool, in the field of modest fashion distinction is acquired by demonstrating the opposite—by not judging others too much. The A-list of modest designers and mediators *are* consecrating hijabi looks *as* style, but heretofore have done so by exercising a recognized subcultural authority that rests on their spiritual sisterhood as guides to inclusion rather than exclusion.

The Accelerated Cycle of Modest Fashion: New Generation Designers

The need to avoid offending the most conservative elements of a given community, even if they are not the company's target demographic, was a factor for many early entrepreneurs. As the modest market expands and segments, younger designers across the faiths are increasingly able to create their own spot within the modest fashion niche. Distinctive variations in communication strategies have emerged, especially in relation to representations of the female body. New companies launched modest brands with sophisticated online marketing techniques and high production values, far less tentative about selling modesty through the visual language of secular fashion, presuming a fashion-literate viewer able to read website visuals selectively rather than literally. New forms of religious and ethnic distinction are generated by younger generations with the social and cultural capital to move between minority and mainstream fashion systems.

Most of the early modest company websites and blogs, regardless of originating faith, are notable for avoiding the sexualized imagery associated with the fashion industry. Religious delicacies about showing the human form are especially pronounced in relation to images of women and (sometimes to their own frustration [Tarlo 2010]) bring companies, designers, and communication teams up against competing regulations and practices within their own religious communities and those of others to whom they wish to sell. In particular some Muslim companies adhere to, or want to avoid offending those who do adhere to, interpretations of Islam that prohibit the representation of the human form. This has resulted in websites that crop the face and/or head from images, or that avoid showing product on bodies at all, restricting visuals to product shots or to mannequins. Companies that do use models in nearly all faiths avoid the sexualized poses that are fashion industry standard. As American modern orthodox Jewish designer Naomi Gottlieb puts it, "models don't understand. . . . 'So you don't want me to look sexy?'"[19] These same challenges were faced by the new Muslim lifestyle print media in the early to mid-2000s and continue to prompt immediate and intense feedback for independent bloggers and social media posters across the faiths. Commercial companies too are quickly criticized for their representations of women and range of garments. While bloggers might lose readers, commercial companies risk losing customers. Recent brands benefit from entering a diversified field that makes possible a greater range of imagery. The garments may have similar potential for modest outfitting, but their presentation on the body is not necessarily bound by the lowest common denominator.

In the UK this was seen when twenty-three-year-old Hana Tajima-Simpson and her business partner husband started Maysaa in 2010 after a successful prelaunch web-based media campaign. Always coding the products as modest rather than Muslim, her start-up quickly began to punch above its weight with a well-designed website and a virtual magazine showcasing its relatively few designs in a high fashion mise-en-scène. Maysaa moved distinctively away from the conservative visuals that previously characterized the sector. A jersey maxiskirt is worn on the sales page with a sleeveless top and displayed in her digital magazine (see plate 11) on a model posed raunchily with décolleté: "obviously we were aware that other people had a really strict policy on, can't show the head, can't show anything. . . . It's kind of ridiculous. [You] have to give the consumers some credit. Just because you show it a certain way doesn't mean that they're going to wear it that way. . . . These clothes aren't just meant for Muslims, also they're not just meant for when you go out wearing hijab."[20]

It would have been inconceivable even five years previous for a modest brand to risk this near-naked body; yet Maysaa did well with consumers who appreciated the value added of seeing modest clothing styled for fashion. American brand Eva Khurshid New York, launched a year earlier in 2009 (trading until 2011), is similarly committed to strong aesthetic (see plates 12 and 13), presuming a nonliteral reading mode on the part of its fashion-forward consumers.

Friends since high school, Eva Khurshid founders Fatima Monkush and Nyla Hashmi are unusual for entrepreneurs in the modest fashion sector, having both trained in fashion design, Monkush at the Fashion Institute of Technology in New York and Hashmi in Connecticut followed by graduate work at Elie Tahari. Abrogating to the kudos of their brand's namesake, New York, as a global fashion city, the partners built on the fashion capital of their training by situating their studio in New York's garment district (Rantisi 2004). Both women have American (convert) mothers and South Asian Muslim fathers and were supported by their families in their long-standing desire to start a fashion business. Taught to sew by their mothers, the young women began making clothes at school because "there was nothing that we'd just buy off the rack that we could wear without having to alter or layer."[21] Able by 2009 to choose their niche within the now larger modest sector, Eva Khurshid aimed at professional women who favor on-trend glamor and workwear. Like predecessors in diaspora fashion, Monkush and Hashmi base their designs on their own wardrobe needs: Says Hashmi, "we're half American, half South Asian, born and raised in America. . . . We're everything combined [so] we wanted to develop something that a woman will look at and won't think oh, that's for Muslim women, or that's for a conservative woman."

The duo discovered with their first season that using the words *Muslim* or *modest* hindered progress in the wholesale market, quickly realizing "[that we] had to become very creative with how we describe the brand and how we define modesty." They developed the "tagline" of "Sexy Redis-covered" to communicate their feminist ideal of "empowering women and

FIGURE 6.14 Fatima Monkush and Nyla Hashmi, Eva Khurshid New York designers, photo: Bianca Alexis. Courtesy of Eva Khurshid and Bianca Alexis Photography.

giving back control of what they define as sexy on their own terms," wanting, Hashmi says, "every woman to fall in love with our brand, whether they're Muslim, whether they're Jewish, Christian, whatever." Reviewed favorably in Muslim magazines and blogs and in Christian modest magazine *Eliza*, their website has nothing that indicates their modest or religious affiliation: As Hashmi says, "we're very proud of who we are, and we [don't want to] pigeonhole ourselves into a niche market. We want to branch out and be sold in Bergdorfs, sold in Saks and Bloomingdale's."

The field is opening up in terms both of product and address, with Eva Khurshid seeing it as their mission to promote fashionable modesty and "to push the boundaries of what people wouldn't even expect to be 'modest' [and] really come across as a fashion brand." While they personally draw the line at anything shorter than a half sleeve, the range responds to consumer demand for long-sleeved items too. Of the design duo, only Monkush wears hijab (see figure 6.14), but they decided to stop using Monkush as a "hijabi gauge" to arbitrate on modesty: says Monkush, "I'm the hijabi, so people assume that I dress more conservatively, but Nyla and I have the exact same wardrobe. [We] have the exact same views on hijab and modesty and how we design is exactly the same."

Tellingly, both the design-educated Eva Khurshid team and daughter-of-artists Tajima-Simpson have highly developed visual literacy, regarding imaging as essential to the communication of their spiritual as well as stylistic interpretations of modesty. Eva Khurshid worked with a photographer, Bianca Alexis, another school friend, to cast "curvier" models in line with their feminist commitment to make clothes for real-size women: As Hashmi explains, "In terms of how the models are posed, we're not that conservative, and so we've definitely gotten criticism for it, but it's usually from men. Women [give] 99 percent approval. It's usually very conservative men who are criticizing us, and honestly, they're not the ones buying our clothes; we're not going to kowtow to that." That their arresting images don't compromise their feminist principles further spurs male criticism: Hashmi says, "We always tell [the models] stand really confident, feel very empowered, [because] we know that really exudes sexiness. . . . There is no skin showing, [but I think men] get very uncomfortable when they see this strong woman standing with presence."

The use of what can seem to some as radically fashion-forward aesthetics is a significant intervention into the language in and through which female modesty can be defined, represented, and disputed. This moves away from the literalist modes of reading and netiquette that were previously standard practice for minority, ethnic, and religious media, indicating a growing pluralization of opinion and modes of expression.

Another designer committed to images of strong "independent" women is British designer Sarah Elenany, whose aesthetic preference for quirky street style over anything too girly means that her visual marketing is less likely to challenge conservative Muslims with revealed flesh or sexualized posing (see figure 6.15). Elenany's website disseminates her design vision with punky visuals and dynamically posed models, all showing their faces and hair (see figure 6.16). This was "a business choice because what I'm trying to do is not alienate anyone from the products. I put a scarf on the model, then automatically non-Muslims say, that's not for me . . . whereas a Muslim can look at the clothes and say yeah, I'd wear that kind of thing."

Like *Emel* magazine, Elenany avoids professional models, not because she wants to feature "real" Muslims as at the magazine (chapter 3), but because she does not want to endorse the fashion industry norm of unattainable female beauty. Real people, from different ethnicities, need to be aspirational role models, "rather than a model who just looks good as a job." Like many of the young women in this book, Elenany is committed to a nonjudgmental stance: "I don't think there's a right and wrong—oh

FIGURE 6.15 Elenany "Gym Minaret Hoody," photos by Alessia Gammarota, e-retail web page, screenshot. Accessed April 15, 2013. Courtesy of Sarah Elenany, www.elenany.co.uk.

obviously I think there's a right way and I think the way I dress is the right way, but I think it's up to the person to choose the way that they dress and I'm not going to say, you're right, you're wrong."

Growing up in the suburbs south of London, Elenany sees her approach to design as characteristically British (see also Tarlo 2010) but not her approach to Islam, which she feels is distinct from the majority South Asian Muslim culture of Britain. Connecting her "late" take-up of piety

FIGURE 6.16 Elenany "Salam Wrap Dress," photos by Alessia Gammarota, e-retail web page, screenshot. Accessed August 6, 2013. Courtesy of Sarah Elenany, www.elenany.co.uk.

to her Arab heritage from her Egyptian and Palestinian parents, Elenany explains, "I only really started practicing when I was nineteen, twenty, so I basically grew up like a normal person." Raised in a family without head covering or overt religiosity, Elenany's market research for her business start-up became a form of spiritual development learning about different Muslim dress practices. A "scruffy little tomboy" rather than a fashionista—"I struggle to see myself as a fashion designer"—Elenany's understanding of her brand as a business is the opposite of the arts ethos espoused by Hana Tajima-Simpson. Trained in product design and winning a place on a graduate enterprise scheme, Elenany, then age twenty-five, settled on apparel only after trying out other ideas. Her creativity is expressed through her Islamically inspired graphics, linking to her spiritual development. Initially intending to print scarves, Elenany realized that "there is a plethora of hijabs out there" and so diversified into a less saturated sector with a clothing range: "The garments come from the graphics [which express how] I feel about being a young Muslim. . . . But I didn't want to use traditional Islamic art because it wasn't relevant. . . . It's nice to look at but I don't understand it. [I want] to capture the feelings of Muslims in the graphics so they would look at them and understand them, say yes I do this, yes I get it."

Unusual for Muslim women designers, and the womenswear-dominated modest sector itself, Elenany also does menswear. Her graphic urban casual style suits the male skateboard market and connects to her interest in Muslim popular music. Unlike Tajima-Simpson, Elenany is not an Internet aficionado and blogs reluctantly to support the business. Producing good visuals for her marketing does interest her. In 2012–13 she collaborated with Italian fashion photographer Alessia Gammarota on shoots for her main collection and for her range for the Girl Scouts that I discuss in chapter 7.

Elenany's initial collection featured a monochrome palette—"based on the market research, Muslims wore dark colors"—with the introduction of brighter colors in the linings sometimes requiring her to persuade not only her Muslim customers but her other key demographic of "older" (thirty- and forty-year-old) "funky professional" non-Muslim working women who liked her edgy styling but found the lining "too loud, punky." With more non-Muslim than Muslim customers, most in the twenty-five-to-thirty age range, Elenany is keen to expand in both markets. But the social and gender norms of the British Muslim population can restrict sales. Muslim women in their late teens/early twenties, she explains, say they like her clothes but rarely have their own disposable income. Clothing acquisition is often dependent on parental finances (and therefore approval), because, "you finish your schooling, you get married, you have kids, that's it—there's no [opportunity to] be independent, to have a career." By the time we spoke in November 2011 Elenany was seeing more sales to women students and older Muslim women in an indication of shopping autonomy that, like the changes in the South Asian diaspora market discussed in chapter 4, correspond to advances in Muslim women's education and employment opportunities.

The British Muslim modest market, Elenany says, "is still at a very early stage," focused primarily on "how to style hijabs and how to style things that you already have" rather than on new designs; "successful Muslim blogs, even Jana's, are about styling; they're not about products." When consumers are persuaded to buy garments, cultural consumer habits can be another obstacle. As I heard elsewhere, Elenany reports that the majority South Asian Muslim population in Britain will spend money on outfits for special occasions, for instance, for weddings, from high-end Asian diaspora designers like Mani Kholi and Arinder Bhullar (chapter 4) but are unwilling to pay higher prices for regular wear. For a small company producing low-volume "limited edition and hand-printed" garments, Elenany's price points are seen by fashion industry insiders as correct, even low; but "the more expensive I make them the further I come away from my target market and what they pay for clothes." Muslim designers aiming for a Muslim market have to deviate from what might otherwise be the standard business model, a problem also for Barjis Chohan, who launched her clothing company Barjis at Dubai fashion week in 2011.

Born in Karachi to Rajastani Muslim parents, Chohan came to Britain in the mid-1970s at age three and was raised and educated in south London. With "moderately" religious parents, she had a childhood immersed in Pakistani and South Asian culture (Bollywood movies) but not revivalist religiosity. Beginning to veil when she had her first child at thirty-one, Chohan sees herself as typical of second-generation Muslims in Britain; "we're more in touch with our religion [and] far more educated [so for us it] was more about understanding our religion and trying to find our identity living in the UK."[22]

Art school was not her parents' preferred route: "Even though we're moderates, they're very conservative and traditional. They thought because I was academic [that the] medicine route would be better." Managing to persuade her reluctant parents, Chohan gained a place at the London College of Fashion, taking a two-year diploma course but leaving before completing the third year of BA-level study. A passionate advocate of access to arts education for working-class and ethnic and religious minority students,[23] Chohan knows the challenges posed when gendered cultural expectations combine with lack of social and economic capital: "in retrospect I felt completely lost because at that time I went to Pakistan for a few months and then came back, and I lived in a bubble at home, not exposed to the real world, never can go on the tube alone and everything. . . . I found it hard because I was struggling financially, and there were a lot of middle-class children, girls, studying, and it was very hard to relate to their lifestyle initially. But then eventually I thought I have to find a way of doing what I love doing. I wasn't still sure whether I wanted to go into fashion, [because] of all the pressure I had at home to get married, [having been] engaged at the age of fifteen to my cousin in Pakistan."

Though events delayed the marriage until she was twenty-nine, Chohan's early engagement was typical of other young women in her community if divergent from the social life of other students. After college she worked at Harvey Nichols to gain experience in high-end fashion retail and then took an MA at Central St. Martins, before obtaining a job in production at Vivienne Westwood. Like Elenany, the slightly older Chohan approached her design career as a business. Reversing the usual model of fashion brands diffusing into interior design, she set up first in textiles for interiors in the Gulf, raising funds for the higher-risk venture into fashion. Like Elenany she has her fashion products made in Britain, for the convenience of being close to source while raising her three children, and from commitment "to help the British manufacturing industry" (see figure 6.17).

British-designed and British-made their products may be, but British Muslim designers face unique dilemmas in the international market. On one hand, the renewed attachment to the umma characteristic of Islamic revivalism creates markets abroad and at home as young women reject the "ethnic" dress of their parents in favor of self-defined modesty dress styles (chapters 1 and 4). But on the other hand, the transnational affiliations of the umma do not necessarily transcend differences of national, regional, and local taste. The design difficulties this raises are further compounded by the constraints of marketing to diaspora and global Muslim consumers. For Western modest consumers "the perception of a high-end couture clothing is £70, yes?" whereas for her custom-made abayas and gowns for private clients in the Middle East "perceptions of couture would be £3,000, £2,000" (see figure 6.18). "A lot of the Western [Muslim] people find my clothes a bit too high. . . . They say there's no embroidery on it, how can you sell at £200? [Well], it's good quality, and there is embroidery, but it's very contemporary embroidery, and they tend to still want the decorative, traditional kind of abayas and clothing. . . . It's an obstacle for my growth because I'm trying to educate in a kind of nonpatronizing way. . . . It is high end, it is luxury, it's all made in the UK so you can't expect some-

FIGURE 6.17 Barjis, autumn/winter 2013, catwalk, Swarovski Boutique, London fashion week, February 2013. Courtesy of Barjis Chohan, www.barjis.co.uk.

thing to be selling at about £50, £60. Because the younger generation are so used to buying from Topshop and H&M."

Chohan thinks "the only way to capitalize on this huge market in the Western world like Canada or the United States, is to tie up with Topshop and H&M and produce a line for them for young Muslim girls who can actually wear Barjis at a very reasonable, affordable price." As Elenany reflected when we spoke in July 2011, while the penetration of global luxury brands and famous designers into the high street was by then well established, Elenany had pursued the self-same idea in 2009, "Topshop said we think our customers would be offended." Realizing that "there was no

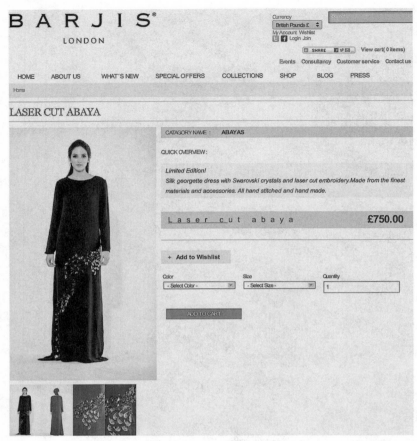

FIGURE 6.18 Barjis, "Laser Cut Abaya," e-retail web page, screenshot. Accessed April 15, 2013. Courtesy of Barjis Chohan, www.barjis.co.uk.

distribution for modest clothing" beyond the online market, Elenany specifically recruited a non-Muslim business partner with fashion industry experience. Taking professional marketing advice, they showed her first lookbook to Topshop with a pitch that she was a pathbreaker in the Muslim market; "the whole reason why if I've ever achieved anything it's because it's been new, it's because no one's doing it." Their brand "story" rang alarm bells for the retailer who had recently faced controversy for stocking Palestinian-style *kefiyah* scarves:

> They said that someone complained that those scarves were promoting terrorism so they had to take them off the shop floor, and then to make me feel a little bit better, they said that Mikey jewellery had some

smiley face jewellery and someone said that it was promoting acid, so they had to remove that from the shop floor as well. . . . But obviously what they were trying to say is, it was taking a risk basically on this very openly celebratory and Islamic brand.

I don't like to use the word *Islamophobic* because I think it's a bit unfair toward British people; I don't think British people are Islamophobic; I think they're Islamic ignorant. I just think there's a fear of the unknown, and I think it's the Muslims' fault, but I think that's a different story. It was a lot more tense back then a couple of years ago. It's okay now, or it's getting better.

I have seen a change in attitude. Why that is, I don't know. I hope it's because Muslims are reaching out to people.

Giving up on mass retailers, Elenany focused on small independent boutiques, but again "it was fine until I mentioned [that] the graphics were inspired by Islamic culture, and then they would pull funny faces."

While the mainstream remains wary, Barjis Chohan, like other Muslim designers, has discovered a significant market among modest dressers from other religions and Western converts to Islam: "I'm getting a lot of clients who are actually Jewish and very strict Christians [in] the West, so I get orders from Hannah and from Julie and from Samantha." In the inevitable chat that ensues during the consultation for made-to-order apparel it becomes clear that she is also dressing "lots of converts [to] Islam who come from an English background" as well as "a lot of American converts" and new Muslims from South Africa and France. Because her brand is "not limited to one particular country" or culture it appeals to converts who "say we want something contemporary, we want something which is understated and Western, but at the same time it's versatile enough for us to wear the hijab." Working with a different aesthetic, Elenany finds that her urban cool — "a British look just cut a bit bigger" — serves a similar purpose, providing essential social camouflage for Muslim women in Europe: "in Germany I think they get a tougher time, so there is more of a need to be like everyone else, and because the style of mine is normal and not ethnic and not floaty and feminine, it's just about pragmatic clothes [that let you fit in], especially for the French [where] you're not allowed to wear a hijab if you want to work. . . . That's really sad isn't it? But it's really great to be British."

In North America, where her quality casual offering fits national taste distinctions, Elenany's British style credentials help sales in the cross-

FIGURE 6.19 Sarah Elenany in Âlâ magazine, October 2011. Courtesy of Sarah Elenany.

faith modest fashion sector: "I think it's because modesty dressing is more of a celebratory thing over there because it's so Christian." The elements that secure success with Muslims in Muslim minority Germany and France and with non-Muslims in Canada and the United States did not translate into results in Muslim majority Turkey. Supported by interest from the nascent Turkish modest style media, with a spread in Âlâ magazine (see figure 6.19), Elenany was encouraged by young Turkish friends to visit to Istanbul. "There's a gap for young-looking clothing, because it's all old and princessy [and] we guess that [young] people who are into street culture and hip-hop music are crying out for something else." Realizing that her products would not appeal to mainstream style consumers in the conservative religious district of Fatih (chapter 2), she identified Galata as the new avant-garde fashion location, approaching top independent boutiques Laundromat and Building: "[But when] we told them it's a modest brand for Muslims, it was, well yes, we don't have those customers in these shops but we don't really care. . . . It was basically the same problem as we had in London."

If "ladylike" Turkish modest taste does not yet embrace British street style, at home Elenany struggles to break through the ethnic aesthetic tendencies of British hijabi fashion despite that South Asian British designers report a trend to fusion among younger customers: "British Muslims aren't very British, they're still very cultural, they love Asian things, and they love Arabia." Even when modest designs do transcend localized taste preferences, the materiality of the fashion commodity means that Muslim and modest early adopter e-retailers face fulfillment problems (Wrigley and Lowe 2002). In contrast to other conservative subcultures, modest fashion entrepreneurs cannot fully benefit from the potential expansion offered by online transnational community formation: unlike the commercial electronic transmission of Christian rock music (Brown and Lynch 2012), or Middle Eastern and Islamic heavy metal (Levine 2008), you can't download frocks and scarves. International success may depend on local manufacture and distribution; Maysaa, temporarily relocated to Malaysia, where Tajima-Simpson enjoyed near superstar status among consumers who welcomed her "British sensibility and aesthetic that's different from what they have."[24]

Around the world consumers follow brand Facebook and Twitter announcements to meet designers offline at the proliferating events now available for Muslims, from major annual conventions like ISNA (chapter 1) to newer fashion-themed women's gatherings, producing new offline communities and behaviors. Facebook relations have become central to the annual "Smokey not Smudged" charity fashion event started by Kossaibati and other university medical students at London's Imperial College. Now organized by younger cohorts, by 2012 the event's Facebook page, used promotionally by organizers and participating brands, was also full of messages from individual young women seeking new contacts to meet offline rather than going on their own.[25] Cautious, I hope, about sharing addresses or telephone numbers on open websites, young Muslim women presumed their online community to be a safe zone within a public Facebook page, seeming rarely cognizant like most of their generation that these are monetized platforms (Baym 2011; Jenkins 2008) intent on data mining (Montgomery 2000).

Digital connectivity brings subcultural participants into contact with style leaders, extending the social capital of who you know to include those you "know" online, creating new relationships themselves forged through the coproduction of fashion mediation. This was illustrated when I observed a hijabi fashion street shoot set up by Alessia Gammarota in 2012. A collaboration with star blogger and YouTuber Dina Toki-O, the event drew an enthusiastic crowd of young student-aged fans equally motivated by the chance to meet their blogger idol and the opportunity to dress up for a professional photo (see figure 6.20). Treating it as akin to

FIGURE 6.20 Hafsa Mia and Kashka Rowlands at the Dina Toki-O and Alessia Gammarota hijab street style photo shoot, Oxford Street, London, 2012 (photo: Reina Lewis).

a pop star's PA (personal appearance), a throng of young hijabis scoured Oxford Circus for Toki-O's arrival, hailing her with awe and rushing to be close (see plate 14). Picture taking was in no way limited to the professional photographer or bloggers (with blogger Zinah al Sharif also promoting the event). All the young women had smartphones or tablets and were snapping away so that bloggers and "civilians" alike were mutually "papped" by the excited crowd (see plate 15). Images were immediately uploaded onto Facebook and other social media platforms, adding to the increasing availability of self-generated images of hijabi bodies of unregulated construction and distribution.

This trend to self-imaging on social media has not gone without comment. While the early utopianism of online religious discourse was enhanced by the absence of "racial, gender, or class signifiers" in the initially text-based formation of online religious communities (Helland 2000: 215), this apparent invisibility is removed in the drive to self-imaging afforded by recent social media. Today, online modesty discourse is permeated with a presumption of visibility. The convergence of media forms means that visual norms of fashion editorial and celebrity culture are mimicked by young women's online self-presentation. While like many modest designers and magazine editors Barjis Chohan had to brief professional models that she did not want sexualized body management in her shoots, by 2013 she felt moved to intervene in how young women were presenting themselves online. By now this issue was not about the relatively small numbers of personal style blogger self-portraits, but about mass participation by young women in the snap-and-post culture of social media: "For me it's like educating the industry. For example, young Muslim girls, if they're taking photographs on Facebook, they've got a hijab but they're pouting. So I tend to put on my Facebook messages, no point putting the hijab on if you're pouting. . . . [You] can smile, you don't have to be a Victoria Beckham, you know?"

In this self-imaging, the consumer's "sense of self is itself being dynamically refigured as a result of engaging with the online environment" (Currah 2003: 29). In the modest fashion domain, where commentary mingles with commerce, being hailed by an e-mail or a Facebook post or tweet is about more than money; it is about being interpellated into a community of spirit.

New Forms of Religious Interpretation and Authority

Religious discourse online publicizes forms of religious interpretation not usually given prominence, challenging existing hierarchies of religious knowledge with new interpretations and new modes of transmission. The Internet tends to fragment forms of religious authority, augmenting, sometimes replacing, hierarchical clerical communications (the one to the many) with self-selecting participatory networks (the many to the many) (Bunt 2009; Eickelman and Anderson 2003; Mandaville 2007). Writing on Islam, Bunt sees an inevitable standardization of multiple interpretations; "rather than a single ummah idealized as a classical Islamic concept, in fact there are numerous parallel ummah frameworks operat-

ing in cyberspace, reflecting diverse notions of the concepts of community" and the uneven access of different Muslim sects and groups to digital technology (Bunt 2009: 31). Muslim women's online mediation about
modesty can be seen as part of one such parallel framework. Extrapolating from the Muslim context, I identify the development of modesty discourse across and between faiths and between religious and secular contributors as another set of communities or publics, in which, increasingly,
multiple interpretations of modesty are coming to be the norm.

The activation of fashion as a mode for religious knowledge construction and transmission mirrors the widening of the "religious" domain by
the first generation of (male) Muslim online communicators, "casting
[religious] talk in idioms of speech and thought previously or otherwise
allocated to separate speech communities" (J. Anderson 2003: 54–55).
Volpi and Turner suggest that in the widespread individualization of religion typical of the late twentieth century, the demonstration of "'my
religiosity' [is] perhaps most clearly expressed through personal blogs,
where ordinary [people] can record their daily activities [and share] intimate and mundane activities with the world" (Volpi and Turner 2007:
4–5). The public enactment online of this individuated religiosity, a subjectivity that has become "an important feature of modern spiritually"
(Volpi and Turner 2007: 5), creates, I argue, new witnesses and interlocutors whose mutual engagement validates the everyday fashioning of modest self-presentation *as* religious practice. In this way I insert modest fashion online discourse into Heidi Cambell's call in 2011 for research on how
"recent developments, such as religious blogging, podcasting, and online
worship . . . are creating new forms of religious outreach and reception"
(Campbell 2011: 245).

As diverse digital constituents come online, the range of discourses
previously regarded as external but now included within religious content will increase. Framed through the logic of fashion, itself usually trivialized, women's online discourse about modesty can be seen as one such
form of transmission, emerging as a predominant mode through which
women are establishing themselves as religious interpreters and intermediaries. This is not to say that participants label their activities in this
way (and many might think it presumptuous, grandiose, or downright un-
faithful, with some [Moors 2013] specifically denying claims to religious
authority). In identifying these activities as constitutive of religious interpretation, I mean no disrespect. Feminist researchers have long known
that women are likely to disparage their achievements or play down the

significance of their role, and that researchers on women's religious lives must, as Linda Woodhead advocates, be willing to see the presence of religious knowledge and authority even when women disclaim it ("Oh, I don't know anything about religion, you should ask my husband, the pastor").[26] In this vein, I assert a place for the nefarious practices that create modest dressing and body management within the frame of everyday religion that, as discussed in chapter 1, is characterized by syncretism between faiths and between faiths and secularity that often forges the spiritual from the commercial. With "public and personal" concerns appearing in religiously themed blogs just as blogs not identified as religious show evidence of being "influenced by spiritual beliefs," blogs are likely to "represent a reintegration of religious life into the practices of the everyday" (Cheong, Halavais, and Kwon 2008: x). The impact of digital discussions about modest fashion and behavior and the wider range of styles being worn as modest conjoin with the increasingly diverse modes through which modest dressing is visually represented in commerce and commentary to create new discourses about how to experience and express religion in everyday life.

The fundamental reflexivity of digital cultures operates "logics that put [religious] authority in a different place than in the past" (Hoover 2012: xii). When Muslim women in WENA assert alternative interpretations through a claim to a "true" Islam, this is most often a renegotiation of a relationship with rather than rejection of established religious authorities (Jouili and Amir-Moazami 2006; Mandaville 2007; Salvatore 2004). While some forms of media may privilege the ideas and participation of particular social groups, "messages also migrate from one medium to another," with new domains opening up in which to discuss religious ideas previously the preserve of elite clerical forms of transmission (Eickelman and Anderson 2003: 4). The rendering of blogs and social media as platforms suitable for the development and transmission of religious discourse in the form of modest fashion facilities and guidance (commercial and non-monetized) constitutes new places and new publics for religiosity dominated by women. Just as the Middle Eastern (and Western) beauty salon provided a space in which women could transmit the knowledges required to achieve "modern" body management qua the male terrain of the coffee-house or political salon (Ossman 2002), so too do digital mediators create online spaces for the transmission of training in the techniques of the modest body. These new religious publics are appearing simultaneously among Jewish, Christian, and Muslim women and show increasing potential to migrate across media platforms, between commerce and commentary, *and* across boundaries of faith and secularity.

Mainstream fashion bloggers were innovators of new genres of fashion commentary within a field already saturated by print media. That most mainstream fashion commentary ignored modesty as a fashion-related dress practice and that there was very little specialist print media provision meant that ICT was for modest fashion bloggers the means to invent not only new genres but also a new zone of fashion mediation (now itself periodically a news story for mainstream and fashion media).[27] In a sector where faith concerns bring bloggers and brands into close proximity and as multiple versions of modesty become the norm online, there will be implications for the many manufacturers and bloggers and consumers who see their participation in modest fashion as spiritually and socially motivated and fulfilling. Fashion bloggers in the mainstream who had already gained access to conventional fashion media opportunities were by autumn 2012 elevated further with the recognition that "'blogger' [style] has become a trend in its own right" (Fox 2012: 47). The once iconoclastic individualism associated with A-list personal style bloggers was to be commodified with special ranges in the high street, sanctified by celebrity blogger curation. Needless to say, this has not yet extended to even the most A-list in the modest blogosphere, but it illustrates a central conundrum for the field. An inherently ambiguous concept, modest fashion, once it is rendered viable as a fashion category, further becomes liable (like all fashion trends) to be endlessly modified, replaced, repositioned, recycled, and appropriated. The extent to which the network of the committed welcomes new forms of commodification offered by Muslim branding and practice in interfaith civic contribution forms the basis of chapter 7.

CHAPTER 7

COMMODIFICATION
AND COMMUNITY

T o evaluate the dynamic, uneven, and contested relationship between commodification and community formation this chapter
looks at the connections between commercial Muslim fashion and
three associated spheres: Islamic branding, interfaith dialogue, and new
Muslim taste communities including non-hijabi modest fashion. In the
first section I explore how fashion has come to play a belated role as the
third "F" alongside finance and food as a key market for Muslim-focused
consumption. There being a high degrees of contestation over the "Islamic-
ness" of commodities and their modes of marketing, this section provides
an early analysis of the potential opportunities and limitations that Muslim marketing offers to women entrepreneurs and participants in Muslim
fashion, including attention to how the commodification of religious iden-

tities creates opportunities for new forms of self-actualization through work for Muslim cultural mediators within the professional marketing field. Following this, I explore the opportunities and issues for commerce and community activism raised by the growth of a cross-faith modesty discourse that provides new markets for Muslim designers alongside the new interlocutors and audiences created for Muslim cultural commentators by the demand for interfaith dialogue post–9/11 and 7/7. From this consideration of the role of fashion in the construction and contestations of extra-Muslim alliances and communities, I return to intra-Muslim community formation and gatekeeping; my final section explores how the diversification of hijabi fashion into new taste communities has expanded to include "dejabi" modest dressers at the same time as its widening impact prompts a resurgence of antifashion anticommercialism.

Muslim Branding

Dating to the late 2000s, Islamic marketing is generally seen to follow the model of ethnic marketing developed in the United States from the 1970s in which increased market segmentation led to the creation of ethnic subjects as marketable consumer groups for specialist and mainstream products (Grewal 2005; Halter 2000). As third- and fourth-generation immigrants became more affluent in the context of Black Power, signs of ethnic diversity once potentially stigmatizing were transformed into potential assets, with goods marketed as authentically "ethnic" becoming central in the understanding and staging of minority identities. This identity through consumption model was extended to sexual minorities with the creation, as I discussed in chapter 3, of the gay consumer segment in the late 1980s (R. Lewis 1997; Mort 1996; Sandıkçı and Ger 2011). While the addition of Muslim commodities and consumers to marketing preoccupations may be more recent, it would be wrong to think of religion as a latecomer to the world of marketing. As seen in chapter 1, religion in WENA has long been a central, and disputed, component of marketing practice and consumer culture, exemplified by the creation of department stores from the 1850s as respectable spaces for female labor and consumption. While much religiously inflected consumer culture was normatively Christian, the nuanced localism in campaigns by retailers and marketers in their engagement with religion demonstrates, as Sean Nixon argues, that "there is no general, universal logic of consumer culture or commercial society" but rather "instead only specific commercial cultures" (Nixon

2003: 16). Commercial cultures shape and are shaped by their particular spatial-temporal moment of emergence, which for Islamic branding includes three central factors: increased spending power within the global Muslim population (second- and third-generation migrants in WENA growing more affluent and raised within the framework of consumer culture, petro-wealth in Gulf Muslim majority territories, and the increased disposable income of a growing middle class in Muslim majority countries and those with substantial Muslim populations); the increased visibility of Muslim entrepreneurs; and the foundational role of consumption in new forms of Islamist affiliation. In contrast to the anticapitalism of much early Islamic revivalism (chapter 1) in which consumption stood as contagious and corrupting signs of Western decadent immorality, contemporary Islamism adopts a model of new social movements in which "feelings of belonging happen less through formal membership in a hierarchical structure but more through engaging in shared patterns of consumption" (Sandıkçı 2011: 249), as is the case with the amorphous connected forms and practices of women's Muslim fashion and lifestyle religious cultures.

Welcome by some as an antidote to Orientalist civilizational constructions of Muslims as primitive, impoverished nonplayers in capitalist modernity, the construction of the presumed shared values of the "Muslim consumer" is also prone to essentialist homogenization that minimizes the variety of Muslim religious practices and interpretations (Sandıkçı 2011). Despite this, the experience of cultural commodification need not be only negative for minority cultures. For Muslim women, still during the course of this research feeling underserved by the mainstream fashion market, there may be benefits in being regarded as a consumer rather than marginalized as a "non-person" nonconsumer (du Gay 1996: 100), as was previously demonstrated by the double-edged experiences of ethnic cultural commodification. Writing in light of the 1990s fashion for "Asian cool" (chapter 4) Dwyer and Crang note that, while mainstream fashion discourse in its plundering of minority styles may relegate Asian dress back to the temporally alien zone of the unfashionable at the end of the season, the interaction with commodity culture can offer minority fashion designers and consumers a "matrix for the fashioning of ethnicities"; rather than see ethnic identities as essential and preexistent, commodification sits within the social processes "through which ethnicities are produced and in which ethnicized subjects actively engage with broader discourses and institutions" (Dwyer and Crang 2002: 411–12). Moving away from a critique of cultural commodification as only and always a form of appropriation, "the consumption of one ethnic group's object by another" allows for the potential consumer pleasures of ethnicized subjects and emphasizes a "transnational 'circuitry' out of which commodified cultural forms emerge—rather than 'chains' through which these commodities move" (Dwyer and Crang 2002: 417). While the commodification of ethnicity marks "the entry into the market of domains of existence that once eluded it," Comaroff and Comaroff also argue that participation in ethno-branding is not always or only negative for minority communities (Comaroff and Comaroff 2009: 28), repositioning and reanimating rather than inexorably eroding what is valued as "authentic" (see also Esman 1984). The same applies in the commodification of religious cultural forms and the production of religious and religio-ethnic subjects including the role of Muslim marketing operatives.

With ethnic marketing established by the 1990s as "an industry in its own right" (Halter 2000: 49), Muslim marketers in the 2000s entered a field in which the way was paved to target and create new niches for commodities, consumers, and marketers premised on the cultivation of faith-based subjective dispositions. As seen, for those workers who can be marked as Muslim, whether serving as a journalist or blogger cultural intermediary (chapters 3 and 6), or working in fashion retail (chapter 5), or, as here, in professional marketing, the growing, if uneven, understanding that Islam is not an ethnicity or a singular set of cultural and religious practices produces opportunities and tensions. I follow Nixon's lead in analyzing commercial culture products such as ads not only as image but as emitting from and acting on the located workplace sociality and subjective dispositions of the cultural intermediaries involved in their creation: my study of Ogilvy Noor's branding service therefore combines textual analysis of their launch materials with interview accounts from one of the marketers who produced them to track changes in workplace culture and employment opportunities for staff branded as Muslim alongside the wider impact of Islamic marketing on consumers and entrepreneurs. Historically, practices of religious and ethnic branding follow from the entrenchment of lifestyle consumer cultures in the retail revolution in the 1980s that, as I discussed in chapters 3 and 5, shifted marketing focus from commodity to brand. With programs to train employees in "living the brand," new value accrued to marketing professionals able to display the "sensitivity to meld local and subcultural behaviors central to the corporate brand" (Schultz and Hatch 2006: 15). So too marketers in non-Western contexts like India could parlay local knowledge of national markets into a "proprietary commodity called the Indian consumer" to gain leverage with multinational corporate clients (Mazzarella 2003: 250). The blended dispositions required for these forms of mediation allow ethnic or minority culture staff to use their ethnic competencies as overt cultural capital and valid insider knowledge, with brand marketing strategies moving toward an understanding of ethnicity as malleable, plural, and voluntary.

It remains to be seen the extent to which this finessing will apply in Muslim marketing, with even those Muslims involved in branding processes conflicted between anger at not previously being recognized as valuable consumers and anxiety about what it would mean for Muslims to be interpolated as faith-based consumer subjects (see also Hastings-Black 2009), as I observed when I attended the Inaugural Oxford Global Branding and Marketing Forum at the Said Business School of Oxford University in 2010.[1] Lending academic credibility to an event aimed at marketing professionals concerned with global branding practices for products, corporations, and nations, the forum contributed to the validation of the field (Sandıkçı and Ger 2011), providing a platform for marketers to pitch products and approaches. One such was the new product from global marketing and communications firm Ogilvy & Mather, who had launched Ogilvy Noor that year. Differentiating themselves from the other significant research on segmentation in the Muslim market by JWT in 2008,[2] their press release presented Noor as the "world's first bespoke Islamic Branding practice," promising to help brands "better engage with Muslim consumers worldwide" by providing "insight into Shariah values" (Ogilvy & Mather 2010). Available to prospective clients as an expensive coffee table book, *The New Muslim Consumer* was an exercise in market creation aimed at existing clients underutilizing the Muslim market and new clients seeking focused advice. To deter brands from entering this lucrative market without expert advice, the release warns of "risks of boycotting which exists when Muslim consumers are alienated." With some Islamists regarding it as a religious duty to boycott global and local "infidel" brands (Farah 2011; Izberk-Bilgin 2012), this is not an unrealistic pitch, but by placing all Muslim consumers within the boycott frame Noor risks undercutting its own claim to value as a service able to delineate the diversity of Muslim opinion.

Developed by Miles Young, Global CEO at Ogilvy & Mather and convert to Islam, the initial Ogilvy Noor marketing research focused on four Muslim majority countries, Egypt, Saudi Arabia, Malaysia, and Pakistan.

Developed over two years, the launch publication authored by Nazia Hussain (below) created a typology of Muslims consumers, ranging from older "Traditionalists" rooted in local community practice, to the younger assertive "Futurists" who, regarding themselves "as steadfast followers of Islam in a modern world," emphasized individual choice in modes of practice.[3] Marketers, Noor advocated, should focus on the Futurists, globally connected and media savvy, whose questioning of established sources of religious interpretation was creating, as discussed in chapters 1 and 6, a "flatter, wider umma."

This "New Muslim Consumer" reflects the youthfulness of the world Muslim population (chapter 1), but, like Indian marketers in the 1990s who cautioned global branding clients that "there is no GenerAsian A" (Mazzarella 2003: 246), Ogilvy Noor warns that, while "it is tempting to view younger Muslims through the Generation-Y prism so favored by global marketers," the youthful "New Muslim Consumer is fundamentally different because of a strong reliance on faith" (Ogilvy & Mather 2010). Their report challenges the temporal alterity often accorded to Muslim religious revivalism, advising that the "move towards conservatism should not be mistaken for a rejection of high-tech lifestyle or products," alert to a pattern of selective adaption of Western technologies and commodities characteristic of the formation of Middle Eastern modernities at the start of the previous century (chapter 1; see also Sandıkçı and Ger 2002). While the nascent branding industry's focus on sharia compliance risks, as Jafari (2012) warns, reducing Islam to fixed ahistorical concepts of halal/haram (despite claims by some religious authorities to do just that), Ogilvy Noor's offer to help companies track localized changes in Muslim consumer behavior moves toward an understanding of Islam as a religion defined by individual practice, to "think sharia (or halal), act local" (Prokopec and Kurdy 2011: 212). Advising that Muslim consumers will not offer an "automatic acceptance" of Western commodities "if they reject the underlying ideas and values," Noor calibrates the importance of sharia compliance according to the product's proximity to the body with a global brand index that rates halal certification for foods or cosmetics more important than for finance or travel. Emphasizing halal as a process rather than a product brings the entire commodity chain within the purview of Islamic values (Wilson and Liu 2010), situating Muslim consumers within new forms of transnationality and new imagined geographies produced by marketers seeking cross-border penetration for ethnic/

local or religious brands (on "East Asian consumer culture," see Cayla and Eckhardt 2008).

With early research suggesting that consumer behavior is determined more by degree of religiosity than by allegiance to particular faiths or denominations (Essoo and Dibb 2004; Mokhlis 2009), those focusing on selling to Muslims must find a way to maximize the religious appeal of general goods and those with an overt religious purpose. One way has been to harness a global revivalist discourse that frames Islamic values as universal human values, positing sharia compliance as a form of social and ethnic sustainability and moving halal credibility beyond certification to brand behavior and values. As seen in the preoccupation with ethical fashion in Muslim lifestyle media (chapters 3 and 6), rises in levels of education and income produce increasing interest from Muslim consumers in sustainable and ethical consumption, utilized by marketers to enhance brand value by reframing company philanthropy as a form of Islamic corporate social responsibility (Temporal 2011b, Thibos and Gillespie 2011; see also chapter 5).

To develop Noor, Ogilvy & Mather harnessed the religio-cultural capital of Muslim and Muslim acculturated managers from their worldwide staff. As Noor launched in 2010 I spoke to Nazia Hussain, who, having previously initiated the company's Cultural Strategy function, was then head of strategy at Ogilvy Noor. Of Bangladeshi Muslim heritage, Hussain's experiences of elite cross-cultural transnationality started young, as she attended the Indian international school in Saudi Arabia while her diplomat father was posted there, followed by education in China and then English at Oxford. Expert in advising clients how to accommodate cultural variance—"if I had a tagline it would be that I make ideas travel"[4]—she could now transfer her attention to faith-based communications at Ogilvy Noor, where "everything we do is Muslim informed, and that's a huge departure." Begun as an in-house, rather than client-focused (billable) project, recruitment was based on preemployment subjective capabilities that could be operationalized for company advantage, requiring team members to manifest a personal commitment, to be "not just interested [but] deeply passionate and committed to making this a success." The necessary Muslim literacy could be diversely acquired: "we have someone who's converted to Islam, someone who is a very devout Muslim, someone like me who's not an incredibly devout Muslim but my mother is a religious scholar and so I understand how important it is." The fourth, non-Muslim, team member was Lebanese with intimate knowledge of Muslim life through marriage and twenty-five years' professional experience of the Arab markets. The positive response to the project put a new premium on Muslim experience for Hussain, who "hadn't realized, to be honest, how few Muslims there were in the industry." A "barrage of e-mails" from "all the Muslims within Ogilvy" revealed an unimagined hunger for the validation of faith experiences, matched by in-house support with not "a single negative remark from anyone within Ogilvy—I'm so very proud of that." Not surprisingly, the initial staffers on Ogilvy Noor found themselves involved in the sort of capacity development that I noted in fashion design and mediation (chapters 3 and 6), confirming Temporal's observation that the "biggest requirement by Islamic brands [is not] manufacturing competency or business know-how, but branding and marketing skills and techniques" (Temporal 2011b: 296).

Despite that the Ogilvy Noor team took pains not to set themselves up as experts on Islam, Hussein's ethno-religious background became newly prominent. Having previously established as director of cultural strategy that "I am not aligned to any particular cultural or religious group in the work I do," with colleagues aware that "I'm not a practicing Muslim, [because] I go out for drinks with them," her involvement in Ogilvy Noor outed her at work as a person of Muslim heritage. Not having expected the project "to be as meaningful to me in the way that it has been," Hussein found in her reengagement with Islamic practice and her interactions with enthusiastic young respondents "a real sense of community around promoting [the] beauty of positive Muslim values in the context of the world the way it is today." Just as in the 1990s "Arab London intermediaries" were able to commodify their located hybridity into roles as "professional interculturalists" in the economic and cultural spheres of Gulf Arab transnationality (Salamandra 2005: 75), so too does Hussain's work at Noor foster a positive self-actualization as a transnational diaspora Muslim whose life choices included the "deliberate decision to live in a majority non-Muslim context."

Joining postlaunch and now Noor vice president, Shelina Janmohamed reflects three years later that Noor is still in its "start-up phase" because "we're not just growing our own business, we're growing an industry."[5] As a PR communications professional whose intervention into British Muslim cultural politics was initially through popular literature (*Love in a Headscarf*, 2009), blogging, and journalism (*Emel* and mainstream

British media), Janmohamed sees value in using "Muslim professionals as opposed to professional Muslims" and is adamant that "it's absolutely not enough to be Muslim to be leading on a creative development." While "clients feel that they're in safe hands if they're with somebody who themselves is Muslim," marketing companies must proceed with caution lest the client premium on presumed "innate knowledge" pigeonhole Muslim staffers as "the resident Muslim when actually that's not their expertise at all," restricting the opportunities for professionals "from ethnic or faith backgrounds" to work on projects of more general interest.

If global marketing to Muslims was initially focused on finance and food, by 2010 lifestyle products (Temporal 2011a) like fashion, and to a lesser extent halal beauty, had come onto the radar of global marketers with an oft-quoted report from Bloomberg valuing the global Muslim fashion industry at $96 billion (Meyer and Couch 2010), with the global Muslim spend on all (not only modest) apparel valued at $224 billion in 2012, projected to rise to $332 billion by 2018 (Thomson Reuters 2013). Published the same year as the first market estimate in 2010, the Ogilvy Noor report included a scoping exercise on Muslim fashion that name-checked the same WENA designers I had been tracking. The report also highlighted the significance of new forms of Muslim fashion mediation, citing bloggers like Jana Kossaibati of *Hijab Style* (chapter 6) and quoting editor Ausma Khan of *Muslim Girl* magazine (chapter 3). With word-of-mouth recommendation an important characteristic of the Muslim market overall, Hussain elaborates that, in a gender-segregated sociality "amongst young women who spend all their time with other young women," bloggers as "tastemakers and influencers on the Internet" have become especially important. So far, recognition of the Muslim market in the fashion industry has been sector specific: "at the very top end of the fashion market and at the very bottom end of the fashion market you have a huge amount of Muslim-friendly offering. You have sensitivity, you have understanding, you have empathy, you have all of that at the high fashion luxury end and at the Asda, Walmart end. Everything in the middle is, as you say, currently ignoring the Muslim consumer." Hussein relates the uneven market penetration of interest in Muslim consumers to Ogilvy Noor's typography:

> Like young people everywhere—[the Futurists want] good quality, very on trend, exciting, edgy, outer urbanwear that is going to make them look like they're connected to the world. [They are] knowledgeable,

educated, affluent, etc., [and they say] I want to be stylish, but I see absolutely no reason why my faith has to be compromised in that pursuit. And that's what's going to actually drive forward, in my view, the development of high street brands like Mango or Zara [who] will have to become much more cognizant of these young consumers. It won't be the people who are buying haute couture right now who are driving that, and it won't be the mums who are buying value-end school uniforms; it'll be the young, connected, Internet savvy, digital generation.

Muslim designers and brands highlighted by Ogilvy Noor such as Sarah Elenany and Eva Kurshid are themselves part of this cohort. It is not surprising that the marketing professionals alighted on the same fashion players that I had been researching; the new value attached to specific forms of minority experience by ethnic or religious marketing raises the profile across the field of the still very few Muslims able to operate professionally.

Ogilvy Noor trumpeted the prescience of their initial research as events in the Arab Spring began to unfold the following year. Hussein was lead author of an article released on February 28, 2011 that, claiming the revolutionaries as members of their Futurist consumer segment, cautions that a generation of politicians brought to power by the Traditionalists "have never before had to have the kinds of conversations they must have with the Futurists. Understanding what they stand for can therefore help us better understand the implications of what's happening today— especially since the power to shape the future lies in their hands" (Hussein et al. 2011).

Given that nation-states are often important clients for branding specialists, their forthright condemnation of the region's autocratic regimes combines display of knowledge about the younger generation of consumers (and potential future power brokers) with offers to train existing powers to communicate better with their angry populace. A follow-up piece of research published in June 2011 sought opinion from young Muslims in the MENA, Central and Southeast Asia, and WENA regions, finding an attitudinal shift in values and ideas about leadership (from benevolent, nepotistic, and feared to equal, meritocratic, and loved) that "go beyond the events of the Arab Spring": "[These are] not just political and local shifts but also commercial, social, creative, regional, even global. . . . The values of the new generation are going to shape modes of behavior with all aspects of society. . . . If global corporations are to engage successfully with them either as partners, employers, or providers of goods and services, the onus is on them to understand these values better" (N. Hussein 2011).

As an antidote to the anti-neoliberalism accompanying some renditions of regional revolt (that was to come to the fore in the Turkish events of May 2013), Hussein's 2011 report provides an Islamic justification for material success: "striving for success is inherently Islamic—commerce was a part of the Islamic nation right from the start, with Khadijah the wife of the Prophet (pbuh) as the very first businesswoman. . . . Futurists tend to quantify success not through financial measures alone, but through the leadership roles that they are able to carve out for themselves [and] the amount of greater community and social good they are able to effect." Like the diminished role accorded to the profit motive in the double narrative utilized by Islamic companies in Turkey (Demir, Acar, and Toprak 2004; see also chapter 2), Noor's validation of enterprise as part of a wider social contribution (invoking the popular archetype of Khadijah as commercial provider for early Muslim welfare) attempts to reconcile community values with the construction of Muslims as consumer subjects. Anticapitalist suspicion of consumption still prevails among some Islamists, and it is not only global brands that face challenges of religio-cultural inappropriateness. In 2008 a test case by theologians from Ankara University accused tesettür clothing company Tekbir (literally, "God is great"; see chapter 2) of accruing "income by capitalizing on religious convictions and initiating unfair competition by applying a sacred name to a brand name": the case was not concerned with the modesty of the clothes, but with the "predatory association" by which the company attempted to assume a "monopoly over the meaning of religious symbols" (Tepe 2011). Although Tekbir won the case, the theologians' jurisdictional incursion into fashion illustrates the importance of claims to religious authority through defining modest dress that, as I discussed in chapter 6, often underpin women's online discourse about modest fashion. Warning against an "Islamic brand fetishism" that aims "to convince its consumers that they will get a certain level of 'piety' status [and] fulfil transcendence of faith by just consuming the signs of Umma," Süerdem predicts that the exclusionary potential of "missionaries" for Islamic consumer culture "excommunicating the 'Other' Muslims" could be "as dangerous as Orientalist ideology [in] branding Islam as the other of the west" (Süerdem 2013: 7–8). Regarding products of the "hyperreal umma" as inherently inauthentic, his polemic that "fashionable hijab replaces the traditional symbols of modesty determined by historical contexts," with Indonesian women covering their "hair in the same way as a Turkish Muslim woman in Germany" (Süerdem 2013: 7), projects an imagined authenticity onto local forms of hijab that misrecognizes the hybridity and national, ethnic, and sectarian distinction fundamental to their development (chapter 1).

Like other forms of marketized relations, Muslim consumer cultures inevitably produce their own forms of exclusion, not least the unaffordability and aesthetic challenge of keeping up with hijab fashion trends. To some extent as I discuss in the next section, this is countered by the commitment to inclusion that characterizes the disposition cultivated by many participants in hijabi fashion, but sensitivity to the variety of coreligionist societies may not protect Muslim designers trying to break into foreign markets. I explored in chapter 6 how aesthetic taste differences among Muslim populations can impede sales, but Muslim designers also have to contend with intra-Muslim forms of distinction that go beyond product design. British designer Barjis Chohan wanted to show in London fashion week in 2013 to reinforce her brand's status as "London fashion" in order to overcome class and ethnic prejudices inherent in doing business in the Gulf: "the Middle East market is very loyal to their Middle East abaya designers. They will buy the Dior and Valentinos, but when it comes to abayas they want someone who speaks Arabic and who is Arabic. [A design by a] British Asian originally from Pakistan — they don't see that as luxury [because] their maids are Pakistani. So there is that level of . . . arrogance [that's] a big obstacle for me. . . . To be very successful in the Middle East I need to be part of London Fashion Week; I need to be part of the mainstream fashion industry."

Within WENA, enthusiasm for the Muslim market rarely translates into ad revenue for the Muslim style media with editors and bloggers routinely encountering aversion from brands worried about "extremist" content and fearful that majoritarian consumers would shun products marketed overtly to Muslims (chapter 3; see also Storey 2007). If in the predigital years of early queer consumer culture, advertisers used stealth marketing to reach queer consumers with coded subcultural references to which the non-gay literate majority viewer would be oblivious (Clark 1993), the affordances of digital communications give today's marketers opportunities to create personalized campaigns to reach Muslim groups and individuals directly (El-Fatatry et al. 2011). Although young Muslims are active builders of the online communities beloved of marketers, this has not translated into revenue for the hijabi blogosphere. At *Hijab Style*, despite that Kossaibati regularly cites high street brands (with click-through links to their e-retail webstores), when she applied to Mango in 2013 for an ad she received an automated rejection. Given that by 2015 Mango in Britain was marketing fashion for Ramadan, it is impossible to know if this was aversive or simply that her blog was too small to meet standardized marketing metrics. With metrics counting numbers (of hits, followers, friends) rather than content,[6] brands would have to be specifically targeting Muslims before they noticed Muslim media as a potential marketing destination. Even when brands do have products aimed at Muslims the marketing does not necessarily follow, as Tayyibah Taylor of *Azizah* magazine found when she approached Hallmark for an ad on the basis of their new range of Eid cards: "The right hand didn't know what the left hand was doing. . . . First we had to explain what the Eid card was, and then [it] seemed like different departments really weren't even aware of it. . . . And they said no, we're not going to advertise this product. I was like, well how do you expect people to know about them? They say, well, when they go into the Hallmark store they'll buy it, they'll see them." This apparent lack of awareness is surprising given the company's investment in ethnic marketers to grow their diversity related product line (Halter 2000).

One company who did know about Eid was the British supermarket and value clothing chain Asda (owned by Walmart; see chapter 1), who have expanded their offering to include garments aimed at the ethno-religious market. Given that the grocery sector had long led the way in stocking ethnic or religious product lines and in using point of sale to harvest customer data, Asda was already better informed about consumer demographics in relation to faith and ethnicity than most clothing retailers. A major player in the value clothing market and aware that South Asians made up their largest group of ethnic customers, the venture into clothing built on an existing range of Asian food and DVDs tested in selected British stores. In company terms, it built on the Toronto-based "Bollywood" fashion selection seen the previous year in Walmart in Canada and on the "Arabic" Walmart store set up in Dearborn, Michigan (Hastings-Black 2009), with its large Middle Eastern population. In Asda in Britain the clothing range was designed and marketed to appeal to South Asian customers of all faiths and to reach out to non-Asians interested in the ongoing boho aesthetic.[7] Launched in September 2009 to coincide with Diwali and Eid, major clothes-buying points in the South Asian calendar, the initiative gained significant press in the mainstream and community media. Not everyone welcomed the retail giant's recognition of South Asian wardrobe needs, with some Asian shopkeepers in Leicester's Belgrave Road worried that they would lose out to the cheaper prices made possible by Asda's economies of scale. While the new budget line was unlikely to impact on the higher-end luxury range retailed by designer Arinder Bhullar, featured in chapter 4, her business partner was aware that "Belgrave Road is already suffering in the credit crunch and this will make it worse for the small shops."[8]

As sources at Asda explained, the Asian collection was designed to provide budget everyday items to augment rather than replace more elaborate special occasion garments from specialist diaspora designers like Arinder Bhullar. The range aimed to accommodate the prevalent fusion style popular with Asian and non-Asian customers and the mixed-dress economy of Asian customers, many of whom, the store knew, changed into Asian ensembles such as salwar kameez when they got home from work. To maximize potential sales the range was incorporated into the main apparel offering rather than being merchandised as a subbrand in-store. In some matters the company's design team, none of them Asian, were reliant on local expertise at their regular manufacturer in India. When customer research among Asians in Britain revealed as essential that the salwar trousers should be cut according to convention as a one size fits all garment, the knowledge transfer from their Indian counterparts went beyond the aesthetic glossing signaled as a form of cultural authentification in the press information. With both Asian and non-Asian customers favoring the on-trend fusion fashion, it was often the crossover items that sold best, such as the caftan style tunic top that both groups teamed with jeans, rather than the three pieces that could be combined to form the salwar kameez suit. The success of the fusion rather than the "Asian" items with Asian consumers reinforces the waning power of older generations' equation of salwar kameez as the sole expression of ethno-religious norms of female modesty (chapter 4) and demonstrates the growing consumer and community power of younger generations. While Muslims have yet to be endowed with the sort of cultural capital accorded to (selected) African American tastemakers (Lamont and Molnár 2001), using fashion to promote dialogue outside the community remains a prevalent aim of designers and dressers within the modest sector. For marketers this is important, as emphasized in Hussain's second report for Ogilvy Noor on the Arab Spring in 2011, explaining that their Futurist generation more than the Traditionalists are focused on presenting positive images of Islam to the wider world. Premised on a generational understanding of Islamic values as universal values, "integration with the non-Muslim world, and an ability to coexist in complementary value systems, will therefore be one of the key directions in which they will want both their own lives and their leadership styles to develop in future."

Imagining New Communities: Dress as a Conduit to Intra- and Interfaith Dialogue

The urgently felt need to engage with non-Muslims after 9/11 and 7/7 led many young Muslims, as I discussed in chapter 1 (see also S. Ahmed 2009), to seek further religious education. For many in Britain and Europe, this was accompanied by the growing influence of neo-Sufi approaches that "discredit the politicization of God and umma and challenge the Salafi perception by embracing the Sufi aspiration to a state of submission to God motivated by pure love for Him" (Chapman, Naguib, and Woodhead 2012: 189). While, as discussed in chapter 4, concepts of liberation through submission may challenge liberal thinking (Jouili and Amir-Moazami 2006; Mahmood 2005), this "softer version of Islam" has accompanied and underwritten a shift in Muslim activism from "dissent to accommo-dation and from political to civic aims" (Chapman, Naguib, and Wood-head 2012: 187). Although faith-focused Muslim feminists may find their progressive exegesis dismissed by secular feminists (Muslim and non-Muslim) who "fall into the same trap as fundamentalists" in regarding Qur'anic meanings as "inviolable and fixed" (Zine 2006a: 16), in Britain as elsewhere in WENA, Muslim communities and organizations have under-stood, at times operationalized, the PR advantages of promoting women's civic participation. In Britain, government community outreach after 7/7 in 2005, despite the tendency to focus on male elders as community rep-resentatives (oblivious that some may be associated with extremist reli-gious Rights in the subcontinent [Bhatt 2012; Patel 2012]), resulted in new attention to and resources for the gendered voluntary sector networks established by older South Asian women over two generations of migra-tion (Werbner 2002), extended by the early 2010s to include profession-alized religious roles in chaplaincy work (Gilliat-Ray 2010). While these public roles may construct women as "professional Muslims" inclined or restricted to "viewing each issue through the eyes of faith" (Hakim 2010), Muslim dispositions forged through discourses of multicultural engage-ment may also reanimate minority and majority debates about the ex-panded role being given to faiths of all sorts in the organization of civic and political life. In North America and elsewhere, progressive Muslims advocate "social justice, gender justice and pluralism," critical equally of Muslim patriarchies and neoliberalism (Safi 2003: 3). Articulated more formally through organizations like ISNA, the wider promotion of ethnic and gender equality as inherent Islamic values has created new leadership roles for women but, in seeking to naturalize Muslims within an American national narrative of assimilation (L. Ahmed 2011; Grewal 2005), may obscure unresolved divides of race and ethnicity within the Muslim population (Wadud 2003).

There has emerged a cohort of hijabi activists, at "the liberal end of the conservative spectrum," whose increasing visibility at the annual ISNA convention is used by Leila Ahmed (2011: 95) to track revivalist influence in organized Muslim American life. In my research, these events and their British counterparts also indicate how commerce is being used to as a mode of intra- and extra-Muslim civic engagement. Like other young designers who take a stall at conventions, Fatima Monkush and Nyla Hashmi of New York brand Eva Kurshid were hailed as models of embodied modest presentation:

> **NH**: At ISNA Fatima was stopped multiple and multiple times—where did you get that, what are you wearing?
> **FM**: Right. CAMP—the Council for the Advancement of Muslim Professionals—was doing [an ISNA event and] the attire was semiformal, so one of our dresses was appropriate, [but] the majority of the women there were wearing traditional South Asian or Arab dresses.

Permeable online and offline sociality meant that when LA brand Vela scarves used Facebook to announce their stall it brought new attendees from among their young social media followers. Mainstream media coverage of their launch also prompted extracommunity outreach, as Tasneem Sabri explained: "I responded to a flood of e-mails, especially after the *LA Times* [piece], of American women who say I'm not Muslim but I love your pieces and I would like to buy a piece and wear it, [but] would it be offensive to the Muslim faith. And my reply was no, I think it's a great opportunity for you, if you did wear it, to bring up the topic of what the hijab is, what it means to Muslim women and . . . what it means to be modest."[9]

In Britain Sarah Elenany's business crossed into multifaith commerce when she was contacted to design uniform items (see figure 7.1) for the British Girl Scouts: "The thing that I love about it the most is that it's really positive for the British/Muslim relationship because [British] Muslims are very angsty, [with] a huge chip on their shoulder, and they think

FIGURE 7.1 Elenany designs for the Scouts, screenshot. Accessed April 20, 2012. Image reproduced by permission of The Scout Association.

everyone's against them, and I hope [this] shows them that they're not. . . . I think it's really positive in that sense, which is great because that's what Scouting's supposed to do."[10] The commission (modeled for Elenany in plate 16 by star blogger Dina Toki-O, second from right) arose because of increased Muslim participation in what has been historically a Christian, and sometimes evangelical, organization: "There are some Scout groups starting up in, I think particularly in [Muslim-populated] East London, and they were having to [create their own] customized stuff—the usual Muslim story." While the Scouts' formal uniform was fine, the short-sleeved polo shirt in the activewear uniform posed a problem; but not just for the Muslims. Her client had explained that "our non-Muslim regular Scout Explorers [age fourteen to eighteen] are always complaining about the uniform, [saying] it rides up my back, you can see my bum when I bend over, I'm not comfortable, I'm exposed." Recruited ostensibly to serve Muslim members, but made more viable by cross-faith and secular modesty needs, Elenany's designs were promoted as part of the nondenominational "i.Scout" supplementary product range, "modest and comfortable, with extended sleeves and deep pockets—handy when on camp."[11] The press-worthy collaboration provided added value to the Scouts' multifaith and multiethnic participation communications strategy.

Outside of commerce, fashion commentary has provided young women with routes to community ambassadorship through interfaith activity. Having by summer 2013 completed her medical training degree and about to commence several years of hospital work, Kossaibati was not sure whether or how to continue her blog *Hijabstyle*. Her parents, at first concerned that blogging would cause their then teenager's exam results to suffer, were now proud of the opportunities it brought for her to meet people, support charities, and represent young British Muslims, encouraging her to continue, Kossaibati said, as "good life experience."[12]

In the print sector, success at *Emel* magazine has given editor Sarah Joseph a platform on mainstream national media with a regular appearance on BBC Radio 2's spiritual slot *Pause for Thought*, reaching an audience of eight to ten million mainly mature non-Muslims. With listeners of all faiths writing in, "you feel like you impact upon people at a human level." Her ability to participate is, she knows, helped by the economic and cultural capital she brought to Islam as an educated, white, British convert: "I felt that I belonged, I knew my position." Having become a minority only through conversion, she is frustrated by the "current discourse when they say to young Muslims, do you belong, are you British? . . . You can be both simultaneously and it's all about loyalty. [At *Emel*] we try and instill amongst everybody that it's about the four 'C's: confidence, contribution, common good, and connectivity." For Joseph, connectivity goes beyond religious boundaries: "It's got to be much more about [our] common needs as human beings, as opposed to a prescriptive list of dogma." This message, typical of the European or global Islam developed in a minority context (chapter 1), is exported back to the erstwhile heartlands of Muslim majority societies: "We get a lot of messaging across the world that we need something like this [because] we are a Muslim country but [our] lifestyles aren't necessarily completely Muslim." Bringing added value to the umma, Muslims in WENA are able to "challenge modernity authentically [while] still owning it: we are the West, [this] is us."

For Joseph, part of being in and of the West is to make ethical contributions to wider society through both Muslim community capacity development and participation in formal interfaith activities. In Britain this once ad hoc field of activity has formalized and diversified from the often bilateral organizations set up between Christians and Jews in the 1940s to include other religions and combinations in response to changes in migration and perceived social and political needs. In America the events of 9/11 made the need for dialogue between Christians and Muslims feel more urgent, though American theologians for much of the 2000s remained "significantly behind their British and Continental colleagues" in finding ways to "think interfaith" (J. Smith 2007: 101), not helped by the tendency of some evangelicals to regard America as a new mission field for the conversion of Muslims. Sensitivities about the need to maintain religious distinction plus the theological challenges of which religions can be regarded as providing a route to salvation (with American Muslims more inclined than those elsewhere to recognize the salvific potential of other faiths [Pew 2013]) have led many to prefer the term *multi-* or *inter faith* dialogue to the composite *interfaith* that implies the development of a new merged spirituality. Whatever the label, many prefer to widen the scope of dialogue by taking ideas of ethical rather than theological dialogue as the basis for connections between communities.

Converts like Joseph make up high numbers of those involved in interfaith dialogue, though women have historically been less involved; despite that the push for dialogue may come from liberals, it has often been the case that dialogue partner "representatives" reproduce internal hierarchies of gender and age (Pearce 2012; J. Smith 2007) and class and ethnicity (Wadud 2003). In Britain, government attempts to expand and regularize its dealings with religious communities have given increased attention to interfaith and cross-faith organizations. This form of governmentality cannot, Linda Woodhead argues, simply graft new constellations onto an older model that regards religions as discrete bounded religious identities; instead she sees emerging a "multifaith" approach that "embraces both religious and secular commitments" (Woodhead 2012: 11); and that, with the return (or renewed visibility [Davis and Robinson 2012]) of religious actors to welfare and education provision, is increasingly "marketized" and "mediatized" within a logics of "consumer capitalism rather than national state bureaucracy" (Woodhead 2012: 20–23).

This "marketized" and "mediatized" approach to religious practice is typical of the practices in Muslim and modest fashion that I have discussed in this book, producing and legitimating forms of discourse that traverse presumed divides between faiths, between the religious and the secular, and between spirituality and the market. Reaching out to consumers from other communities is more than just good business sense for entrepreneurs in the modest fashion industry: as with bloggers and journalists, they share a mission to validate and encourage women in practices of modest dressing. Just as Paul Temporal saw the potential for Islamic marketers to leverage sharia compliance into PR value within CSR messaging, in the small-scale modest fashion sector companies can also aim at a double niche market of ethical and modest fashion consumers, with new online portals like MODSHOP, based in New York, urging Muslim dressers to develop "conscious modest fashion."[13] Curating a selection of "brands that make you feel good about what you wear," the converted Muslim founder Sadeel Allam entered in 2014 a well-established modest fashion field, able to launch with brand strapline "catering to hijab fashion and multi faith modesty" but aware that "it's going to take time" to convince Muslims that "Hey, this is important, part of your faith and you are responsible for people's lives through the clothes you wear."[14]

Sometimes support from without is a valuable antidote to criticism from within, as with the escalating social media attacks facing Muslim modest fashion mediators discussed in chapter 6. This is not to say that the modest fashion sphere is immune from concerns about evangelism and contamination as have historically dogged attempts at interfaith community dialogue; if some women delight in the bricolage of repurposing items from different faith and secular origins, others are anxious that religious distinction will be compromised if commodities are too strongly marked by exogenous origin (Cameron 2013; Tarlo 2013b). The growing activity of women's modest fashion as a mode of plural dialogue online is matched by a growth offline of women's interfaith groups, some prompted by the anti-Muslim discrimination evident after 9/11,[15] though Muslim women also report being frustrated that their clothes so often form the topic of conversation (J. Smith 2007).

If some brands learned early that they couldn't sell to mainstream store buyers with the words *Muslim* or *modesty* in their branding, others have moved away from messaging modesty to capture the widest possible market for their products, well aware that the syncretism that underlies everyday ethical practice blends and blurs distinctions between faiths and of faith. If distinctive taste communities for modest fashion are arising that transcend faith boundaries, it is not surprising, in the context of e-commerce's capacity to reach diverse consumers, that many brands are now developing marketing strategies that are not only cross-faith but also faith-free. Though maintaining brand loyalty in the face of consumer expectations both stylistic and moral may prove hard, a neutral communications strategy could well become characteristic of the sector as companies seek to establish their style vision as fashion-worthy not just morally worthy. Jewish company Kosher Casual (based in Israel, selling mainly in North America) welcomed non-Jewish customers and considered rebranding with a more neutral name (R. Lewis 2013b), while in America, Mormon designer Athelia Woolley of Shabby Apple had already decided that "the word modest is not a good word for fashion. It's why as a consumer I never bought from a modest dress company." The South Asian British diaspora "ethnic" fashion market that has long met the modesty sensibilities of multiple South Asian religio-ethnicities while also selling "fusion" fashion to Western customers is also now utilizing the potential of e-commerce for multi- and intrafaith messaging. Raishma Islam, whose designer bridal wear was innovatively merchandised in the ethnic shopping parade of Green Street with dual showrooms styled as Asian and Western (Dwyer 2010), is now online only,[16] adapting her previously high-end fusion evening range to daywear matched to midmarket price points of high street giants like Zara. Designing *churidor* tunics that can be worn as dresses, her site markets conventional ensembles ("Asian suits") as individually purchasable components with style guides on adapting Asian aesthetics to assist both the "the modern British Asian woman" and non-Asian customers.[17] Herself Muslim and not comfortable "to go sleeveless,"[18] Islam's provision of additional sleeve pieces for all tops and dresses continues the cross-faith modesty service of Asian fashion, though the presumption of the Asian and diaspora norm of consumers who can sew or have access to tailors may not work so easily for Western consumers unaccustomed to modifying through stitching.

These types of considerations about consumer segment, brand identity, and messaging are to be expected as a niche fashion field develops; reaching more consumers may be the commercial aim, and encouraging modest dressing may be for many a spiritual aim, but to what extent does success dilute the boundaries of spiritual integrity? This gatekeeping is not quite the model of subcultural cool that would frown on too much mainstream success as "selling out" (chapter 5). As the modest fashion field of production and mediation has grown in size, so too is its impact critically evaluated from within. In my final section, therefore, I look at limit cases that test and redefine the boundaries of modest dress.

Redrawing the Boundaries of Modest Presentation: Halal Celebrities and Dejabis

By 2012 the field of modest fashion had spawned a nuanced internal critical dialogue about niche commercial and media activity. American hijabi blogger and journalist Miriam Sobh posted in May 2012 on Hijabtrendz .com about the impact of slim Caucasian models on the modest catwalk and in marketing: "In an ironic twist, Hijab-wearing Muslim women are falling prey to the same thing their choice of garb ostensibly protects them from: a relentless bombardment of distorted female body images."[19]

Ranging geographically from Tekbir's catwalks in Turkey to interviews with modest dressers in Indonesia and the United States, Sobh wonders if the advantages of improved choice for hijabi consumers are being undermined by the "tricky side" of marketing that reinforces the impossible bodily ideal of the mainstream fashion industry. With a quote from Jana Kossaibati emphasizing the range of pictorial practices in Muslim fashion marketing and asserting that Muslim "consumers are savvy enough to look beyond the adverts," Sobh, who brands her site "the first fashion, beauty and entertainment site for Muslim women," concludes that "as long as we put our beauty and bodies first, we will never be happy." Debate resumed in June 2013 when the well-respected campaigning website *Muslimah Media Watch* ran an article by Izzie raising concerns about the negative impact of hijab fashion mediation. Relaying her failed attempts to follow the how-to guide of hijab tutorials, Izzie name-checks from the A-list of hijabi bloggers, bewailing that, though "of course many Muslim women don't feel they can emulate J Lo or Beyoncé [we do feel] we can emulate YaztheSpaz or Amenakin," with the impact of new "halal celebrities" who combine hijab with weight loss and perfect makeup likely to be as pernicious as mainstream fashion media.[20] While some commenters also felt overwhelmed by the new hijabi ideal, others rebutted that hijabis were capable of using the Internet discerningly, taking the tutorials as inspiration rather than instruction. When Sobh reposted the *Muslimah Media Watch* article on *Hijabtrendz*, she highlighted how the influx of social media combined with commercial endorsement to bombard Muslim women with images of "happy, smiling, seemingly, 'perfect' hijabis who are portraying this perfect life."[21] Conscious that "for most hijabi bloggers, it's not their intention to make people feel bad," Sobh warns, "we don't know what goes on behind the scenes. . . . No one can see their kids running around unsupervised because, 'hold on, mommy needs to take one more selfie.'"

Rather than see this as a backlash against the hijab fashion industry and niche media, this stream of critique is further sign of the field's maturity. The move toward greater visuality afforded by smartphones and tablets has involved more Muslim women than ever before in the construction and circulation of hijabi images. The ways in which this will self-regulate may lead to the development of new informal codes of visual respectability on the part of "civilian" contributors. I expect that these new protocols will change over time, just as had been and continues to be the case with previous forms of Muslim fashion mediation, whether in the shift to showing faces at *Emel*, the inclusion of non-Caucasian bodies in Turkish catalogues, or the incursion of hijab fashion shows into London fashion week. The take-up of visually led social media like Instagram and Tumblr excites the mainstream fashion industry because the "social curation" of fashion can be directly linked into sales sites,[22] building reputation for individual social media users and providing unpaid marketing talent for companies. Although the power of Muslim and modest bloggers and social media to drive sales is little recognized by the fashion industry that still declines to sponsor them, it is recognized within the modest domain as a form of cultural authority. In worrying that the impact of celebrity YouTuber hijabis will come to define praiseworthy hijab practice, bloggers and respondents are engaging in activities of religious interpretation in which, as has long been the case for Islam, religious authority is established through learned disputation. In this instance, disputative reputation rests on fashion capital as much as religious/spiritual capital and on the ability not only to operate but also to evaluate new modes of transmission.

The consecration of bloggers and social media hosts as style arbiters widens the field by pushing at its limits, as when Egyptian American hijabi blogger Winnie Détwa decided to stop wearing her hijab. Having started her personal style blog *Winniedetwa* in October 2011, Détwa like other recent bloggers is equally active on Facebook, Instagram, and Tumblr, where she curates a mix of visually sophisticated self-portraits (see figure 7.2) alongside remediated fashion, art, and reportage images and selected written texts from Muslim and popular cultural sources. Wearing

FIGURE 7.2 Blogger Winnie Détwa, in turban and moustache, Tumblr, February 23, 2012, screenshot. Accessed July 1, 2013. Courtesy of Winnie Détwa.

hijab, Détwa appeared in a variety of styles, with rectangular shaylas (see figure 7.3) and square silk echarpes that covered her neck and ears, but most often in her distinctive turban wraps (see figure 7.4) for which she provided popular video guides. These were not without critics ("those turbans you wear? Not hijab . . ."), but mostly her cool styling was praised and emulated. Her decision in November 2012 to stop wearing hijab was evident initially as visuals on Tumblr (see plate 17), immediately prompting text comments from followers, before she posted on her blog and Tumblr a written statement:

FIGURE 7.3 Winnie Détwa in hijab, Tumblr, July 6, 2012, screenshot. Accessed July 1, 2013. Courtesy of Winnie Détwa.

FIGURE 7.4 Winnie Détwa in turban, Tumblr, September 13, 2012, screenshot. Accessed July 1, 2013. Courtesy of Winnie Détwa.

I removed the hijab a month ago, and my biggest conflict, since then, was how I would come out to my followers about it. I'm not conflicted on how much criticism I would get, it was more so the fact that I don't want *anyone* to feel obliged to make the decision that I had made—because, as most of us know, hijab was not made to be a trend or an accessory.

I began this blog knowing that everything that was personal, to me, would be published via the internet and cyberspace, and that's a risk I had decided to take and do/will not regret. I took so many things into consideration, such as how this could [affect] the blog and how my community may react to it, but I decided that this was the decision I was going to make.

. . . I've received mild backlash from my Muslim community, but at the end, I realized that if people loved me and the person that I was merely for a head covering, then I did not need their love or respect anyhow. My followers on Tumblr were, for the most part, understanding, and that's what I had hoped for because my supporters mean *the world* to me.[23]

Détwa's dilemmas about how to handle online her transition out of hijab mirror the concerns voiced by Maleeha in chapter 5 about how to manage her transition into hijab in her job as a fashion buyer in London department store Selfridges. Offline and online, into and out of hijab, both women were aware that their personal spiritual decisions were context specific in their impact on those with whom they had professional relationships. That Détwa's work as a blogger is largely unremunerated does not stop her having a professionalized sense of obligation to her readers. Aware that "many hijabis look up to this blog for hijab inspired fashion," Détwa promised to continue to provide guidance: "I'm still a turban queen."[24] She frames her change of religious practice in marketing terms: the "brand of Winnie Détwa and the person I have become was definitely impacted by my choice to wear hijab and I am glad that I was able to experience such a beautiful element." The switch in brand messaging, so to speak, requires the market as much as her readers to expand its definition of hijab and modest fashion to include her new bare-headed presentation (see figure 7.5). It is for this reason that it is so significant, as noted by Kossaibati in chapter 6, that the Muslim modest brands continued their association with Détwa. For the religiously motivated modest niche, where community can include commerce as well as readers, the

FIGURE 7.5 Winnie Détwa, Tumblr, March 12, 2013, screenshot. Accessed July 1, 2013. Courtesy of Winnie Détwa.

potentially negative impact of commodifying oneself as a blogger brand can be transformed into an agentive practice of Islamic self-actualization. For Détwa, as for Kossaibati, the dissemination of fashion expertise can meet Islamic obligations to contribute to community well-being by assisting individuals in the personal practice of their faith, by arbitrating intra-Muslim disputes about dress and modesty, and by contributing to extra-Muslim platforms as participants in political, interfaith, and social forums.

Détwa's ongoing popularity reveals that there is an audience for versions of Muslim modesty that are not underwritten by hijab. Still a rarity in the Muslim modest blogosphere, Détwa's practice renders visible forms of religiously informed Muslim dressing that might otherwise go under the radar online, just as they do on the street. Similar, if still rare, others in the modest blogosphere are chronicling major transitions in religiously informed dress, such as American Jewish modern orthodox fashion blogger Nina Cohen of *Alltumbledown* (2009–14), whose decision in 2011 to stop covering her hair was expanded through guest posts to include Christian as well as Jewish and Muslim respondents (R. Lewis 2015).

When Muslim fashion blogs started many were driven by the near total unavailability of fashion guidance or products for women who wanted to wear hijab in the form of contemporary fashion. The field of hijabi fashion imagery and mediation as with the niche industry offering has now grown exponentially, and, though still contentious to some, hijabi dressers are increasingly able to see their style and spiritual decisions validated as fashion and as daily religious practice. If there is a shortage of image, product, and awareness today, it is in the area of Muslim (and other) modest dress that is less spectacular and hence less recognizable within and without faith communities. The growing numbers of women who are discarding the hijab (or wearing it selectively [Zine 2006b]) in keeping with their new interpretations of religious practice attract less political and style attention, as has long been the case for the many observant Muslim women who have never considered hijab to be religiously required.

If the absence of a headscarf makes Muslim women less visible as Muslims, the process of *ceasing* to wear hijab has itself begun to take on a hypervisible status in mainstream media and reportage, adding new elements to long-standing Orientalist obsessions with the "mystery" behind the veil (chapter 1). If the Muslim media want to privilege images of women donning the veil, the mainstream media seek out images of women removing the veil to confirm a civilizational index of Muslim difference and inferiority premised on saving imperiled Muslim women from oppressive Muslim men (Razack 2008; Spivak 1988).

This is not new. What is new is that after five decades of Islamic revivalism equating hijab with Muslim identity and piety, removing the veil has become important as an alternative marker of religious engagement for another generation of women. Unlike their mothers, grandmothers, or great-grandmothers who may have deveiled as a sign of (Westernized) modernity, or secularity, or class mobility, many contemporary dejabis articulate deveiling as a form of pious practice, presenting it within the same frame of hijabi fashion discourse to which many had themselves contributed. Given that the dejabbing process inevitably calls into question some of the tenets of the hijab blogosphere and that it is, equally inevitably, prone to fetishistic celebration in mainstream media and political discourse, it is not surprising that sustained consideration of de-jabi issues often clusters on sites like *Muslimah Media Watch* or *Altmusli-mah*, whose overtly political remit includes but is not primarily focused on fashion. The founder and editor in chief of *Altmuslimah*, Asma T. Uddin, had herself decided to discontinue wearing hijab, committed to a vision of Islam as a religion that, "aside from its essential core, is about inter-pretational diversity" (Uddin 2011: 49). Conscious that accounts of dejab-bing may be appropriated by majoritarian or Islamophobic commentators (feminist and nonfeminists [Zine 2006b]), many respondents nonetheless welcome coverage of dejabi stories as a corrective to the "silencing" and "shaming" of dejabis that reinscribes the hijab as the "litmus test" of being a "true Muslim."[25] With some respondents wary of going public for fear of hate mail and to avoid the deluge of invitations to join "helpful" pro-hijab conversations, it remains to be seen whether digital communications will become a predominant forum for the development of this further element of Muslim women's modest presentation.

Since this chapter was completed, global brands have begun to selec-tively target Muslims as a consumer segment: in 2014 DKNY promoted a Ramadan collection in the Gulf; and in 2015, fashions marketed for Rama-dan appeared at Hilfiger, Mango, Uniqlo (in a collaboration with Hana Tajima-Simpson, retailed in Singapore), Monsoon/Accessorize (Middle East), and at Net a Porter.

CONCLUSION

This book set out to take Muslim fashion seriously as fashion and to explore how as designers, cultural intermediaries, and consumers Muslim women were using dress to create and communicate a range of modern identities to disparate viewers and communities. I argued that the increase in Orientalist civilizational presumptions about Muslims after 9/11 has created an environment in which women (and men) whose dress and presentation marks them as Muslim face increased pressure, assault, and discrimination within a securitizing discourse that locates Muslims outside the spaces and values of secular modernity. I have shown this to be the case not only in the West (within the differently inflected Christian secularities of Europe and North America) but also in the Muslim secularity of the Turkish republic, where the commercial development of tesettür fashion links expanding retail geographies to shifts in regional post–Cold War geopolitics. I have also argued that innovations in hijabi fashion emerge as a response, a riposte, to the heightened scrutiny encountered by Muslims since 2001, with a transnational cohort of predominantly young women forging new styles of modest dressing that assert through their participation in mainstream consumer fashion cultures their place in modern society. For fashion studies, I propose that the new forms of religious interpretation and practice being forged through modest fashion design, mediation, and consumption reveal the mutually constitutive and transformative role of lived religion in the secularized world of fashion and of fashion in the contemplation and enactment of religion and religio-ethnic identifications, contributing a new element to understandings of multiple modernities and multiple fashion systems.

I have identified how Muslim modest dress formations can be regarded as a youth subculture, and shown how the structure and reach of these localized transnational practices expand definitions of subculture to include cross-generation "upward" transmission rather than only contestation. I have also explored how and where hijabi fashion dressers find their clothes, situating Muslim fashion as forged through, and impacting on, a range of multiple fashion systems. In so doing, this book has repositioned the products and retail practices of the globalized mainstream fashion industry in relation to minority fashion industries that include the well-established South Asian diaspora fashion industry and the more recent niche of Muslim and modest fashion. I have extended the field of knowledge about Muslim and modest fashion further by providing a history of Muslim fashion mediation, from the first Muslim lifestyle magazines to the expanding hijabi blogosphere and social media, analyzing the regulatory challenges faced by cultural intermediaries in dealing with an aversive fashion industry and with surveillance and criticism from coreligionists alarmed by the alignment of faith with fashion. The belated wake-up to the value of Muslim consumers seen in the development of an Islamic marketing industry in the late 2000s provides the final loop in the circuit, with a critical exploration of how religious and religio-ethnic subjective capabilities become newly valuable commodities for professional marketers. In a post-9/11 environment in which women in hijab encountered pervasive discrimination and violence in schools, playgrounds, malls, workplaces, and streets "so regularly that it was unremarkable" (WNC 2006: 26), I explore how tesettür shops in Turkey and high street fashion retail in Britain provide employment opportunities for visibly Muslim women who often face a double Muslim and ethnic "penalty" when seeking work. Regarding the spaces of fashion retail as agentive for workers and consumers, I evaluate the extent to which hijabi style knowledges can be recognized, and operationalized within service sector employment, brought into view by the formal structure of diversity employment legislation and the informal subcultural competencies or capitals of retail managers and brand directors.

With many young women mobilizing fashionable dress as an anti-Orientalist communique to majority viewers, my book evaluates the impact of hijabi copresence in contemporary visuality. As well as analyzing the hypervisibility of the veiled body, I discuss the invisibility or illegibility of the deveiled or dejabi body, coming full circle in my examination of how these recently constituted communities of modest dressers are able to encounter, countenance, and contain examples of Muslim-motivated fashion that moves away from the veil as a sign of piety or identity. The importance of commerce, in continuing to sponsor dejabi bloggers for example, and in visualizing through marketing campaigns the widest array of Muslim dressing, points to a new phase in the field. Already, as I demonstrate, strengthened by commercial and community links between faiths, the ability of the Muslim and modest fashion field to recognize faith-related body management that departs from what were central tenets of participation signals a new step in the development of a subculture able to retain currency over longer periods of women's lives.

I started this book by discussing how wearing hijab in a Muslim minority context makes women more visible, hypervisible, to majoritarian observers. It also makes non-hijabi women less visible as Muslims, sometimes to Muslims and non-Muslims alike. I wrote in chapter 6 of how, despite sometimes claims to the contrary, I think that Muslim and modest bloggers and designers are engaging in forms of religious knowledge development and transmission through the practices and discourse of modest fashion. These new forms of religious authority can also be seen in the ability of bloggers and respondents to include non-hijabi women, to make visible as Muslim elements of self-presentation that were hitherto disregarded. As the field of practice expands and as the early cohorts of hijabi fashionistas get older, it is probable that ever more variety will appear in terms of fashion and in terms of what is recognizable as consciously Muslim self-presentation. Beyond the fashionscape, this wider definition of Muslim modest fashion parallels a growing ideology of inclusion rather than exclusion (contra Wahabiist strictures [Safi 2003]) within Muslim spiritual and political thought, characterized by a commitment to dialogue within and without the faith (Hussain 2003). For modest fashion discourse, this interfaith and nonfaith dialogic frame provides a mechanism for the formation of dressed everyday religion. That validation of some practices involves judgment of others is the perennial problem for those seeking to widen the boundaries of permissibility, especially when, as I have discussed throughout this book, many young women (as also older women) see their religious practices as immersed in a world of choice and diversity. Just as it is a struggle to countenance "poor" hijab practice, whether the inauthentic "convertible" on/off hijab criticized in chapter 4 or the pouting hijabi selfies that worry Barjis Chohan in chapter 6, so too it may be contentious but not impossible to include non-hijab presentation within the frame of modest fashion.

I reported in my introduction that when I contacted people to ask them to participate in this research I was often asked if I was hostile to hijab. I should also report, as I close the book, that I was also often asked by friends and colleagues who were secularist or not religiously affiliated if I was not worried that my research might provide support for religious intolerance, probing, am I not concerned about the growth of the religious Right? The answer to that is, yes, I am concerned; despite the obvious good inclusivist intentions of many of those individuals and organizations involved, I am concerned that the increase in overt religious provision of services in welfare, education, and health will produce forms of exclusion from provision for those who do not match their religious moral codes or creeds. I am concerned that progressives within religious organizations will lose ground to well-funded, cosupporting religious Rights who (as seen in the use of employment protection for religion and belief in chapter 5) seek to advance their power through strategic use of case law. But, I say to my interlocutors, so too are many of the women with whom I have spoken. Muslim modest dressers like modest dressers in other faith groups are often just as concerned about the rise of religious Rights as I am and often more so, because their battle to define and defend their understanding of Muslim practice is waged as much and as constantly against the forces of conservatism within their religious communities as it is waged against religio-ethnic prejudice on the streets or in the media. In the securitized post-9/11 context I agree with Claire Alexander that "it may be possible to argue [that] as "the 'color line' was for the early twentieth century, 'The Muslim Question' has become the defining issue of our times" (Alexander 2013), with clothing and body management (veils and beards) augmenting and sometimes replacing skin color as key signifiers of alterity.

In this climate, the pressure not to show division can be enormous, making even more important the forms of mutual support developing within modest fashion subcultures. Formal affiliations can be supportive *and* regulatory, often using dress to "teach" women exemplary behavior, which is then policed, and the informal networks of the hijabi blogosphere and social media can be subject to hostile surveillance, increasing in venom and velocity as the technology enhances comment functions. But it also provides room for baggy, contradictory, changeable forms of solidarity that I have argued merit serious attention. Recognizing the imbrication of discourses of choice within the logic of neoliberal consumer capitalism, I have argued nonetheless that the use of choice in the assertion of veiling and modest fashion practices should not be taken as an opportunity to disregard or dismiss them. Rather, in face of constant challenges to the authenticity of intent or rendition of modesty, I agree with Carla Jones's call to recognize the "ambivalences" within Islamic consumer practices in which "power relations—transnational, national and especially those classed and gendered—influence which categories of consumption can be framed as virtuous and which cannot" (C. Jones 2010: 621). With the MCB launching a report to celebrate the power of the "the Muslim pound" and to promote London as a center for sharia finance (on the occasion of the first meeting in October 2013 of the World Islamic Economic Forum in a non-Muslim-majority country [MCB 2013]), it is worth remembering the political importance of allowing for ambiguity, so that new forms of religious interpretation, authority, and community emerging from Muslim modest fashion practices may find their way in a world where being Muslim looks set to obtain for some a commercial value. Just as the benefits and costs of the pink pound have impacted unevenly on the queer population (losing benefits because same sex relations can now be recognized by state welfare agencies as well as by a hospitality industry newly welcoming gay weddings), the participants in today's subcultures of Muslim modest fashion may find themselves rapidly repositioned by the (to some) unexpected consequences of commodification.

I don't think that the young women I spoke to for this book will look the same in ten years' time. I could barely keep up with changes and microchanges of hijabi and modest fashion while I was writing it. But I do think that hijabi and modest Muslim fashion is part of a female subcultural formation in which, as with the lesbian/gay/queer fashion subcultures I discussed in chapters 3 and 4, participation can last a lifetime. Muslim modest fashion discourse looks set to keep up with the changing world and life stages of the women who started it in their teens and twenties. As the founding generation of hijabi bloggers and designers gets older, they may find that the practices they established are called into question by new and younger subcultural members. They may find that they have more in common with women who dress modestly from other faith backgrounds or for reasons other than faith than they do with other Muslims. They may find that world events reposition the way they dress and prompt changes in how they dress, and they may find that mainstream, diaspora, and minority fashion industries provide them with better or worse resources each year or each season. They may even find that the world ceases to be so extraordinarily interested in what they wear. But for the moment, as this book goes to press, I am hopeful that the new forms of affiliation, alliance, and aesthetics being developed in the multiple modes and levels of hijabi and modest Muslim fashion, as commerce, commentary, and daily religious practice, will prove beneficial not just for those who wear the clothes but for those who live with and around them.

NOTES

Introduction

1. See Carla Jones and designer Dian Pelangi in discussion, *Faith and Fashion*, London College of Fashion, March 6, 2014, accessed May 16, 2014, http://www.arts.ac.uk/research/research-projects/current-projects/faith-and-fashion/.
2. For examples outside WENA, see Schulz 2007.
3. While *hijabi* and *niqabi* have become standard usage in English, *dejabi* and *dehijabi* have not yet gained the same currency, seen by some to imply too much a rejection, rather than a modification, of modest embodiment; personal conversation Syima Aslam and Irna Qureshi, Bradford, March 18, 2014.
4. *Young, British and Muslim: Academic Research and Real Lives*, Manchester Town Hall, November 22, 2011; see www.religionandsociety.org.uk/events/programme_events/show/young_british_and_muslim_academic_research_and_real_lives, accessed October 22, 2013.
5. *Modest Dressing: Faith Based Fashion and Internet Retail*, a research project based at the London College of Fashion; see www.arts.ac.uk/research/research-projects/completed-projects/modest-dressing/, accessed October 22, 2013.
6. Human resources managers quoted in chapter 7 spoke on condition that their names and companies be kept confidential. All nonprofessional participants appear with an alias. Further details appear in each chapter.
7. On hijab styles as visual protest in Iran, see Shirazi 2000.
8. On parallels in the hypervisibility and invisibility of British Arabs as Muslim, see Nagel and Staeheli 2008.

Chapter 1: From Multiculture to Multifaith

Epigraph: Sarah Harris, "Young. British. Female. Muslim." *Times*, May 29, 2010.

1. For a fuller discussion, see Gilliat-Ray 2010, Perfect 2011, and the findings of *British Religion in Numbers* (2008–10), a statistical research project

hosted by the University of Manchester www.brin.ac.uk/figures/, accessed October 23, 2013.

2. On the colonial role of census processes, see Appadurai 1996.

3. All 2011 census figures from the Office of National Statistics (ONS). Accessed May 28, 2013, www.ons.gov.uk/ons/rel/census/2011-census/key -statistics-for-local-authorities-in-england-and-wales/rpt-religion.html #tab-Differences-in-religious-affiliation-across-local-authorities.

4. See Atif Imtiaz's blog, *Bradford Muslim*; bradfordmuslim.blogspot.co.uk, accessed November 1, 2013.

5. As noted also by Meer and Noorani 2008.

6. See Women Against Fundamentalism. Accessed October 22, 2013, www .womenagainstfundamentalism.org.uk/.

7. See Nazli Alimen, "Faith and Consumption: The Menzil Community in Turkey." Presentation at the inaugural conference of the British Association for Islamic Studies (BRAIS), Edinburgh, April 2014.

8. Linda Woodhead, "Strategic and Tactical Religion," plenary address, Sacred Practices of Everyday Life, May 9–11, 2012, University of Edinburgh; www .religionandsociety.org.uk/events/programme_events/show/sacred _practices_of_everyday_life.

9. On the controversial evangelical Christian affiliations of the late twentieth-century fast fashion chain Forever 21, see Kaiser 2012.

Chapter 2: The Commercialization of Islamic Dress

1. In addition to sources given here and subsequent chapters, see the excellent bibliography of Banu Gökarıksel and Anna Secor's National Science Foundation research project *Veiling Fashion* at veilingfashion.unc.edu /biblio.php, accessed November 1, 2013.

2. Elif Kavakçi, personal interview, telephone, London-NYC, May 25, 2013.

3. Kadri Gursel, "Three Powerful Men Decide Turkey's Future": www.al -monitor.com/pulse/originals/2013/03/erdogan-ocalan-gulen-turkey -pkk-peace-process-presidency.html, accessed May 25, 2013.

4. I thank Nazlı Alimen for updates and related points on tariqats.

5. Mustafa Karaduman, personal interview, Istanbul, October 20, 2009, translator Leylâ Pervizat.

6. This information and all subsequent quotations are from Nilgün Tuncer, Mehmet Dursun, and Şevket Dursun, personal interview, Armine showroom, Istanbul, October 22, 2010, translator Leylâ Pervizat.

7. Türker Nart, personal interview, in store, November 8, 2010, Istanbul.

8. This and subsequent quotes are from "Bosnia Changed My Life," *Emel*, April 2012, 36–38.

9. On prewar Bosnian Muslim dress practices, see Huisman and Hondagneu-Sotelo 2005.

10. See www.kayra.com.tr, accessed July 19, 2012.

11. See www.armine.com.tr, accessed July 10, 2013.

12. See "Kayra SS/14 Backstage": vimeo.com/88995696; and www.kayra.com
    .tr/c/1/all-products, accessed July 5, 2014.
13. Mustafa Karaduman in *Yeni Bizim Aile*, July 1992, 9–11, reprinted in Kılıç-
    bay and Binark 2002.
14. See edbdesigns.blogspot.co.uk/2012/03/update-on-turkish-hijab-fashion
    -brands.html, accessed May 3, 2013.
15. So termed by Jana Kossaibati on *Hijab Style*; see "The New Face of Turkish
    Fashion": www.hijabstyle.co.uk/2012/11/the-new-face-of-turkish-fashion
    .html, accessed April 20, 2013.
16. Necip Karaduman, informal personal interview, in store, Fatih, Istanbul,
    April 22, 2008, translator Leylâ Pervizat.
17. "Fatma," informal interview, in store, Tekbir, Fatih, December 3, 2007,
    translator Leylâ Pervizat.
18. "Sophia," informal interview, in store, Tekbir, Fatih, April 22, 2008, trans-
    lator Leylâ Pervizat.
19. Personal conversation, Tempo shop, Fatih, April 22, 2008, translator Leylâ
    Pervizat.

Chapter 3: Muslim Lifestyle Magazines: A New Mediascape

1. See the website of *Bidoun* magazine, www.bidoun.org/, accessed October 9,
   2007.
2. See also "Glossy 'Jihad Cosmo' Combines Beauty Tips with Suicide Bomb-
   ing Advice," *Daily Mail*, March 13, 2011: www.dailymail.co.uk/news/article
   -1365806/Glossy-Jihad-Cosmo-combines-beauty-tips-suicide-bombing
   -advice.html, accessed March 13, 2011.
3. I am grateful to Penny Martin for her insights on this, personal conversation, May 2009.
4. I interviewed Sarah Joseph twice during this research, on September 24,
   2007 and February 21, 2012.
5. Paul de Zwart, personal interview, September 1, 2007, London.
6. "New Lifestyle Magazine Targets Muslim Girls," *VOANews.com*, February 9, 2007: www.voanews.com/english/archive/2007–02/2007–02–09
   -voa71.cfm, accessed March 22, 2010.
7. Faye Kennedy, personal interview, February 25, 2008, Toronto.
8. Ausma Khan, personal interview, February 25, 2008, Toronto.
9. Tayyibah Taylor, personal interview, April 10, 2009, Raleigh, NC.
10. Na'ima Robert, telephone interview, London-Cairo, July 15, 2008.
11. Hijab Style, "The Price Issue," June 14, 2012: www.hijabstyle.co.uk/2012
    /06/price-issue.html#.Um14cnDIaW4, accessed October 22, 2013.
12. Onjali Bodrul and Nathasha Aly, personal interview, October 23, 2007,
    London.
13. Claire Murray, personal interview, February 25, 2008, Toronto.
14. Elena Kovyrzina, personal interview, February 25, 2008, Toronto.
15. Nuzalita, "Runway 2012," *Azizah* 7, no. 2 (2012): 77–83.

16. "The Sisters Fashion Statement," *Sisters*, no. 29 (January/February 2010), 114.
17. *Sisters*, no. 29 (January/February 2010), 18.
18. Elif Kavakçi, personal interview, telephone, London–New York, May 29, 2013.
19. See www.aquila-style.com/magazine/, accessed October 22, 2013.
20. Active September 2012–January 2013, www.ikradergim.com/, accessed October 22, 2013.

Chapter 4: Taste and Distinction

1. For a full account of these and other cases, see Kariapper 2009; on Begum, see Tarlo 2010.
2. See www.publications.parliament.uk/pa/ld/ldjudgmt.htm.
3. "Razia," personal interview, September 29, 2009, London.
4. Personal interview, Onjali Bodrul and Nathasha Ali, London October 23, 2009.
5. "Rehanna," personal interview, Toronto, June 2010.
6. See www.thecitycircle.com/, accessed July 18, 2013. See also www.emerald network.co.uk/, accessed July 18, 2013.
7. "Sara," personal interview, July 31, 2009, London.
8. Arinder Bhullar, personal informal interview, in store, Leicester, May 21, 2012.
9. Mani Kohli, personal interview, June 10, 2009, London.
10. On recent trends, see podcast of *Faith and Fashion*, November 2013.
11. Reina Lewis, "Queer Visualities: Out of the Closet and into the Wardrobe," *Theorizing Queer Visualities*, conference, University of Manchester, April 15, 2005.
12. British Asian Fashion Network steering group discussion, London College of Fashion, April 2, 2014.

Chapter 5: Hijabi Shop Workers in Britain

1. See guidance from the UK's Department of Trade and Industry, "Discrimination in Employment," 2007, webarchive.nationalarchives.gov.uk/2007 0603164510/http://www.dti.gov.uk/employment/discrimination/index .html.
2. On the Jewish Free School dispute over definitions of Jewishness, see Herman 2011.
3. Jo Bird, national equality research officer, Union of Shop, Distributive and Allied Workers (USDAW), personal conversation, September 18, 2009.
4. On contention, see www.guardian.co.uk/society/2012/nov/28/herman -ouseley-equality-human-rights-failure, accessed November 29, 2012.
5. See www.telegraph.co.uk/news/main.jhtml?xml=/news/10/06/nveils106 .xml, accessed December 1, 2006.
6. *Independent*, November 10, 2006: 23.
7. Ministry of Justice, *Employment Tribunals and Employment Appeal Tribunal*

Statistics (GB) 2011–12, https://www.gov.uk/government/statistics/employ ment-tribunal-and-employment-appeal-tribunal-statistics-gb, accessed January 30, 2015.

8. Employment tribunals in the UK had historically avoided ruling on doctrine, arbitrating instead in terms of perceived social exclusion or disadvantage as a result of religious discrimination. This is in keeping with the distinction between UK equality legislation, which protects against discrimination on grounds of religion or belief, and the freedom of religious expression central to the European Convention of Human Rights (article 9) that protects against religious persecution (Donald 2012).

9. The airline had voluntarily amended its uniform policy to accommodate the crucifix before the ECHR judgement.

10. Press release, ECHR, "French Ban on the Wearing in Public of Clothing Designed to Conceal One's Face Does Not Breach the Convention," July 1, 2014, hudoc.echr.coe.int/sites/eng-press/pages/search.aspx?i=003–480 9142–5861661#{"itemid":["003–4809142–5861661"]}, accessed July 1, 2014.

11. "AY," personal interview, September 30, 2009, Bradford.

12. "Naila," personal interview, July 21, 2009, Bradford.

13. Including a *Code of Conduct Guidebook*, downloadable in English and Chinese, www.arcadiagroup.co.uk/fashionfootprint/code-of-conduct-and -guidebook, accessed November 26, 2012. See also www.arcadiagroup.co .uk/fashionfootprint/downloads, accessed November 26, 2012.

14. See debenhams-jobs.com/our-people-and-culture/your-contribution. aspx, accessed November 26, 2012.

15. "Helen," interviewed, April 13, 2010, London.

16. "Jackie," interviewed October 27, 2009, London.

17. "Ruth," interviewed October 29, 2009, London.

18. "Razia," interviewed September 29, 2009, London.

19. "Maleeha," interviewed January 1, 2009, London.

20. "Taslima," interviewed March 3, 2009, Manchester, and personal correspondence.

21. See www.ons.gov.uk/ons/rel/census/2011-census/key-statistics-for-local -authorities-in-england-and-wales/rpt-religion.html#tab-Differences-in -religious-affiliation-across-local-authorities, accessed May 28, 2013.

22. Mortimer Singer, "Why Luxury Brands Should Still Believe in the UAE": www.businessoffashion.com/2013/07/op-ed-the-resurgence-of-the -united-arab-emirates.html, accessed July 10, 2013.

Chapter 6: Modesty Online

1. This chapter is informed by the research project "Modest Dressing: e-Commerce and Modest Fashion," which was funded in 2010–11 by the Arts and Humanities Research Council/Economic and Social Science Research Council Religion and Society Programme, and in 2011–12 by the London College of Fashion. I am grateful to my coinvestigator Emma Tarlo

and the project researcher Jane Cameron. For a fuller account of related issues in cross-faith modesty, see the essays in Lewis 2013e.

2. Fatima Monkush and Nyla Hashmi, personal interview, July 12, 2010, New York.

3. Zinah nur Sharif, personal interview, March 26, 2013, London.

4. For Zinah nur Sharif's official online presence on her website, Facebook, Twitter, and Tumblr, see www.zinahns.com/; www.facebook.com/zinah blog; twitter.com/zinahns; and zinahns.tumblr.com/.

5. I interviewed Jana Kossaibati formally three times during this research and met her informally on several other occasions. Interview dates are given below with reference to dates incorporated as needed in the main text. Jana Kossaibati, personal interviews, November 6, 2008, October 14, 2010, and April 8, 2013, London.

6. See www.hijabstyle.co.uk/2009/06/style-inspiration-queen-rania.html# .UYJsYqKccZk, accessed May 2, 2013.

7. See www.hijabstyle.co.uk/2012/06/style-inspiration-zeynep-babacan .html#.UYJr-6KccZk, accessed May 2, 2013.

8. December 16, 2009: www.hijabstyle.co.uk/2009/12/muslimah-on-sartori alist.html, accessed April 30, 2013.

9. "The New Face of Turkish Fashion": www.hijabstyle.co.uk/2012/11/the -new-face-of-turkish-fashion.html, accessed April 20, 2013.

10. See www.clothedmuch.com/p/mormon-fashion-bloggers.html, accessed May 2, 2013.

11. See americanmuslimmom.com/top-100-muslim-women-facebook-fan -pages, accessed July 7, 2011.

12. I thank Sue Ryan for sending me links.

13. My thanks to Melissa Esplin, Janine Goodwin, and Laura Lewis for sending me links.

14. I interviewed Hana Tajima-Simpson twice for this research, dates below, with dates indicated in main text as necessary. Hana Tajima-Simpson, personal interview, November 3, 2010, and June 17, 2011, London. References to which interview is under discussion have been incorporated as necessary in text or notes.

15. Elaine Hearn, personal interview, November 22, 2010, Los Angeles.

16. I interviewed Sarah Elenany four times for this research, dates below, and met informally on several other occasions. Dates are given in main text as required. Sarah Elenany, personal interview, July 8, 2009, July 5, 2011, November 16, 2011, and June 19, 2014, London. References to which interview is under discussion have been incorporated in text or notes.

17. Adviya Khan, personal interview, May 25, 2012, London.

18. Chris North, BBC social media manager, personal conversation, November 16, 2011, London.

19. Naomi Gottlieb, interviewed by Jane Cameron, July 14, 2010, New York.

20. Hana Tajima-Simpson, personal interview, November 3, 2010, London.

21. Nyla Hashmi and Fatima Monkush, personal interview, July 1, 2010, New York.

22. Barjis Chohan, personal interview, January 17, 2013, London.

23. Chohan in discussion, June 25, 2013, www.arts.ac.uk/research/research -projects/current-projects/faith-and-fashion/, accessed October 22, 2013.

24. Hana Tajima-Simpson, personal interview, June 17, 2011, London.

25. See www.facebook.com/events/396601833729680/, accessed September 20, 2012.

26. Linda Woodhead, "Strategic and Tactical Religion," plenary address, Sacred Practices of Everyday Life, May 9–11, 2012, University of Edinburgh, May 2012: www.religionandsociety.org.uk/events/programme_events/show /sacred_practices_of_everyday_life.

27. See, for example, www.dailymail.co.uk/femail/article-2049283/High -necklines-low-hemlines-The-rise-Mormon-modesty-blogs—fashion -bang-trend.html, accessed February 14, 2012; see also www.styleite.com /media/mormon-modesty-fashion-blogging/, accessed February 14, 2012.

Chapter 7: Commodification and Community

1. For the organizers' executive summary, see Temporal 2011b.

2. See Temporal 2011b.

3. Miles Young, CEO, Ogilvy & Mather Worldwide, "Keynote Address," Oxford Global Islamic Branding and Marketing Forum, Said Business School, Oxford, July 26, 2010.

4. Nazia Hussain, personal interview, September 23, 2010, London.

5. Shelina Janmohamed, personal interview, March 12, London.

6. I am grateful to Chris North for his insights on social media and metrics.

7. See Asda's blog announcement of their Asian clothing range, September 14 2009, your.asda.com/news-and-blogs/george-launches-first-asian -clothing-range-on-high-street, accessed June 10, 2013.

8. Rajinder Bhullar in *This Is Leicester*, September 15, 2009, www.thisis leicestershire.co.uk/Leicester-traders-fear-Asda-s-Asian-range-hit-sales /story-12094814-detail/story.html#axzz2Vpp4SKrG, accessed June 10, 2013.

9. Tanseem Sabri, personal interview, November 23, 2010, Los Angeles.

10. Sarah Elenany, personal interview, November 16, 2011, London.

11. See shop.scouts.org.uk/p-6827. i.aspx, accessed July 7, 2013.

12. I am indebted also to Mrs. Kossaibati for her insights. Personal conversation, June 25, 2013.

13. This and all other quotations: www.modshop.us/modern-modest-clothing -fair-labor-jewelry-modest-wedding-dresses, accessed April 11, 2014.

14. Sadeel Allam quoted in Hafsa Ahmad, "Is Modesty Enough: How about Fair Labour," *Altmuslimah*: www.altmuslimah.com/b/mca/4935, accessed April 9, 2014.

15. See, for example, the British organization Women's Interfaith Network:

www.wominet.org.uk/, accessed July 7, 2013. In discussion: www.fashion
.arts.ac.uk/research/faith-fashion/, accessed July 7, 2013.

16. With Mani Kohli closing her Green Street store the same season, in favor
of an appointment-only showroom in an affluent Redbridge suburb.

17. See www.raishma.co.uk/, accessed June 2, 2014.

18. Raishma Islam, personal conversation, London, May 15, 2010.

19. Mariam Sobh, "Modernizing Modesty: The Hijab and Body Image": boing
boing.net/2012/05/11/modernizing-modesty-the-hijab.html, accessed
July 9, 2013.

20. Izzie, "On (Not) Living Up to the Hijab Tutorial Ideal": www.patheos.com
/blogs/mmw/2013/06/on-not-living-up-to-the-hijab-tutorial-ideal/,
accessed July 9, 2013.

21. Miriam Sobh, "Not Living Up to the Online Hijab Fashion Ideal": www
.hijabtrendz.com/2013/06/24/living-online-hijab-fashion-ideal/, accessed
July 9, 2013.

22. Vikram Alexie Kansara, "Social Curation Start-ups Target Fashion Industry": www.businessoffashion.com/2011/04/fashion-2–0-social-curation
-start-ups-target-fashion-industry.html, accessed July 10, 2013.

23. Winnie Détwa, "The Girl with the Elephant in the Room: Removing the
Hijab": winniedetwa.blogspot.co.uk/2012/11/the-elephant-in-room
-removing-hijab.html, accessed July 9, 2013.

24. Winnie Détwa Tumblr, November 4, 2012: winniedetwa.tumblr.com
/archive, accessed July 12, 2013.

25. Nicole, "NPR's Dejabbing Sideshow": www.patheos.com/blogs/mmw/2011
/04/nprs-well-intentioned-hijabophobia/, comments by Dina and
Humayra. See also "Why I Chose to Take Off My Hijab: Four Women
Speak," parts 1 and 2: www.altmuslimah.com/b/wba/3676, accessed July
10, 2013; and www.altmuslimah.com/b/wba/3677, accessed July 10, 2013.

REFERENCES

Abaza, Mona. 2007. "Shifting Landscapes of Fashion in Contemporary Egypt." *Fashion Theory* 11, no. 2/3: 281–99.

Abu-Lughod, Lila. 2002. "Do Muslim Women Really Need Saving?" *American Anthropologist* 104, no. 3: 783–90.

Abu-Lughod, Lila. 2013. *Do Muslim Women Need Saving?* Cambridge, MA: Harvard University Press.

Acas. 2010. *A Guide for Employers and Employees: Religion or Belief and the Workplace.* London: Acas.

Adams, Lorna, and Katie Carter. 2007. *Moving On Up? Ethnic Minority Women and Work: Black and Asian Women in the Workplace; The Employer Perspective.* Manchester, UK: Equal Opportunities Commission.

Afshar, Haleh. 1994. "Muslim Women in West Yorkshire: Growing Up with Real and Imaginary Values amidst Conflicting Views of Self and Society." In *The Dynamics of "Race" and Gender: Some Feminist Interventions*, edited by Haleh Afshar and Mary Maynard, 127–50. London: Taylor and Francis.

Afshar, Haleh. 2012. "Secularism, Racism and Contemporary Politics of Belonging: Muslim Women in the UK." In *Secularism, Racism and the Politics of Belonging*, edited by Nira Yuval-Davis and Philip Marfleet, 33–37. London: Runnymede.

Ahmad, Ali Nobil. 2010. "Is There a Muslim World?" *Third Text* 24, no. 1 (January): 1–9.

Ahmad, Fauzia. 2001. "Modern Traditions? British Muslim Women and Academic Achievement." *Gender and Education* 13, no. 2: 137–52.

Ahmad, Fauzia. 2013. "Gendering the Muslim Question." In *The New Muslims*, edited by Claire Alexander, Victoria Redclift, and Ajmal Hussain, 13–5. London: Runnymede.

Ahmed, Leila. 2011. *A Quiet Revolution: The Veil's Resurgence from the Middle East to America.* New Haven, CT: Yale University Press.

Ahmed, Sughra. 2009. *Seen and Not Heard: Voices of Young British Muslims.* Markfield, UK: Islamic Foundation, Policy Research Centre.

Ahmed, Tahira Sameera. 2005. "Reading Between the Lines: Muslims and the

Media." In *Muslim Britain: Communities under Pressure*, 2nd ed., edited by Tahir Abbas, 109–26. London: Zed Books.

Akçaoğlu, Aksu. 2009. "The Shopping Mall: The Enchanted Part of a Disenchanted City, the Case of ANKAmall, Ankara." In *Muslim Societies in the Age of Mass Consumption: Politics, Culture and Identity between the Local and the Global*, edited by Johanna Pink, 53–72. Newcastle upon Tyne, UK: Cambridge Scholars Publishing.

Akou, Heather Marie. 2009. "Is There an 'Islamic Dress'? Evidence from the Internet Generation." *Khil'a: Journal for Dress and Textiles of the Islamic World* 3 (January): 1–16.

Akou, Heather Marie. 2010. "Interpreting Islam through the Internet: Making Sense of the Hijab." *Contemporary Islam* 4, no. 3 (January): 331–46.

Alexander, Claire. 2013. "The Muslim Question(s): Reflections from a Race and Ethnic Studies Perspective." In *The New Muslims*, edited by Claire Alexander, Victoria Redclift, and Ajmal Hussain, 5–7. London: Runnymede.

Allner, Michel. 1997. "Religion and Fashion: American Evangelists as Trendsetters and Innovators in Marketing and Communications." *Mode/Modes* 2, no. 1: 145–55.

Al-Qasimi, Noor. 2010. "Immodest Modesty: Accommodating Dissent and the 'Abaya-as-Fashion' in the Arab Gulf States." *Journal of Middle East Women's Studies* 6, no. 1 (winter): 46–74.

Altınay, Rüstem Ertuğ. 2013a. "From the Daughter of a Republic to a Femme Fatale: The Life and Times of Turkey's First Professional Fashion Model, Lale Belkis." *Women's Studies Quarterly* 41, nos. 1 and 2 (spring/summer): 113–30.

Altınay, Rüstem Ertuğ. 2013b. "Sule Yuksel Senler: An Early Style Icon of Urban Islamic Fashion." In *Islamic Fashion and Anti-Fashion: New Perspectives from Europe and North America*, edited by Emma Tarlo and Annelies Moors, 107–22. London: Bloomsbury.

al Yafai, Faisal, ed. 2010. *Women, Islam and Western Liberalism*. London: Civitas.

Amir-Moazami, Shirin, and Armando Salvatore. 2003. "Gender, Generation, and the Reform of Tradition: From Muslim Majority Societies to Western Europe." In *Muslim Networks and Transnational Communities in and across Europe*, edited by Stefano Allievi and Jorgen S. Niessen, 52–77. Leiden: Brill.

Ammerman, Nancy T. 2007. "Introduction: Everyday Religion: Observing Modern Religious Lives." In *Everyday Religion: Observing Modern Religious Lives*, edited by Nancy T. Ammerman, 3–18. Oxford: Oxford University Press.

Anderson, Benedict. 1983. *Imagined Communities: Reflections on the Origin and Spread of Nationalism*. London: Verso.

Anderson, Jon W. [1999] 2003. "The Internet and Islam's New Interpreters." In *New Media in the Muslim World: The Emerging Public Sphere*, 2nd ed., edited by Dale F. Eickelman and Jon W. Anderson, 45–60. Bloomington: Indiana University Press.

Anderson, Jon W. 2005. "Wiring Up: The Internet Difference for Muslim Networks." In *Muslim Networks from Hajj to Hip Hop*, edited by miriam cooke and Bruce B. Lawrence, 252–63. Chapel Hill: University of North Carolina Press.

Anwar, Muhammad, and Firsila Shah. 2000. "Muslim Women and Experiences of Discrimination in Britain." In *Multi-level Discrimination of Muslim Women in Europe*, edited by Jochen Blaschke, 217–64. Berlin: Edition Parabolis.

Appadurai, Arjun. 1996. *Modernity at Large: Cultural Dimensions of Globalization*. Minneapolis: University of Minnesota Press.

Appadurai, Arjun. 2001. "Grassroots Globalization and the Research Imagination." In *Globalization*, edited by Arjun Appadurai, 1–21. Durham, NC: Duke University Press.

Arat, Zehra F., ed. 1999a. *Deconstructing Images of "the Turkish Woman."* New York: Palgrave.

Arat, Zehra F. 1999b. "Educating the Daughters of the Republic." In *Deconstructing Images of "the Turkish Woman,"* edited by Zehra F. Arat, 157–80. New York: Palgrave.

Archer, Louise. 2002. "'It's Easier That You're a Girl and That You're Asian': Interactions of 'Race' and Gender between Researchers and Participants." *Feminist Review* 72: 108–32.

Archer, Louise. 2007. "Race, 'Face' and Masculinity: The Identities and Local Geographies of Muslim Boys." In *Muslims in Britain: Race, Place and Identities*, edited by Peter E. Hopkins and Richard Gale. Edinburgh: Edinburgh University Press.

Argun, Betigül Ercan. 2003. *Turkey in Germany: The Transnational Sphere of Deutsch*. London: Routledge.

Arthur, Linda B. 2000a. "School Uniforms as Symbolic Metaphor for Competing Theologies in Indonesia." In *Undressing Religion: Commitment and Conversion from a Cross Cultural Perspective*, edited by Linda B. Arthur, 201–16. Oxford: Berg.

Arthur, Linda B., ed. 2000b. *Undressing Religion: Commitment and Conversion from a Cross Cultural Perspective*. Oxford: Berg.

Asad, Talal. 2003. *Formations of the Secular: Christianity, Islam, Modernity*. Stanford, CA: Stanford University Press.

Aslanbay, Yonca, Özlem Hesapçı Sanaktekin, and Bekir Ağırdır. 2011. "Lifestyles of Islamic Consumers in Turkey." In *The Handbook of Islamic Marketing*, edited by Özlem Sandıkçı and Gillian Rice, 129–46. Cheltenham, UK: Edward Elgar.

Atasoy, Yildiz. 2006. "Governing Women's Morality." *European Journal of Cultural Studies* 9, no. 2: 203–21.

Badran, Margot. 1996. *Feminists, Islam, and Nation: Gender and the Making of Modern Egypt*. Princeton, NJ: Princeton University Press.

Bălăşescu, Alexandru. 2003. "Tehran Chic: Islamic Headscarves, Fashion Designers, and New Geographies of Modernity." *Fashion Theory: The Journal of Dress, Body and Culture* 7, no. 1: 39–56.

Bălășescu, Alexandru. 2005. "After Authors: Sign(ify)ing Fashion from Paris to Tehran." *Journal of Material Culture* 10, no. 3: 289–310.

Banerjee, Mukulika, and Daniel Miller. 2003. *The Sari*. Oxford: Berg.

Barnes, Ruth, and Joanne Bubolz Eicher. 1992. *Dress and Gender: Making and Meaning*. Oxford: Berg.

Baron, Beth. 1994. *The Women's Awakening in Egypt: Culture, Society and the Press*. New Haven, CT: Yale University Press.

Barton, Michael. 1989. "The Victorian Jeremiad: Critics of Accumulation and Display." In *Consuming Visions: The Accumulation and Display of Goods in America, 1880–1920*, edited by Simon J. Bronner, 55–73. New York: W. W. Norton.

Basit, Tehmina. 1997. "'I Want More Freedom, but Not Too Much': British Muslim Girls and the Dynamism of Family Values." *Gender and Education* 9, no. 4: 425–40. doi: dx.doi.org/10.1080/09540259721178.

Baym, Nancy K. 2011. "Social Networks 2.0." In *The Handbook of Internet Studies*, edited by Mia Consalvo and Charles Ess, 384–405. Chichester, UK: Wiley-Blackwell.

Belk, Russell, and Rana Sobh. 2011. "Gender and Privacy in Arab Gulf States: Implications for Consumption and Marketing." In *Handbook of Islamic Marketing*, edited by Özlem Sandıkçı and Gillian Rice, 73–96. Cheltenham, UK: Edward Elgar.

Bendixsen, Synnøve K. N. 2013. "'I Love my Prophet.' Religious Taste, Consumption and Distinction in Berlin." In *Islamic Fashion and Anti-fashion: New Perspectives from Europe and North America*, edited by Annelies Moors and Emma Tarlo, 272–90. London: Bloomsbury.

Bennett, Andy, and Paul Hodkinson. 2012. Introduction. In *Ageing and Youth Cultures: Music, Style and Identity*, edited by Andy Bennett and Paul Hodkinson, 1–6. London: Bloomsbury.

Benson, Susan Porter. 1988. *Counter Cultures: Saleswomen, Managers, and Customers in American Department Stores 1890–1940*. Champaign: University of Illinois Press.

Bhachu, Parminder. 2003. "Designing Diasporic Markets: Asian Fashion Entrepreneurs in London." In *Re-Orienting Fashion: The Globalization of Asian Dress*, edited by Sandra Niessen, Ann Marie Leshkowich, and Carla Jones, 139–58. Oxford: Berg.

Bhachu, Parminder. 2004. *Dangerous Design: Asian Women Fashion the Diaspora Economics*. London: Routledge.

Bhatt, Chetan. 2012. "Secularism and Conflicts about Rights." In *Secularism, Racism and the Politics of Belonging*, edited by Nira Yuval-Davis and Philip Marfleet, 6–9. London: Runnymede.

Biala, Tamar. 2009. "To Teach Tsni'ut with Tsni'ut: On Educating for Tsni'ut in National-Religious Schools." *Meorot* 7, no. 2: 1–13.

Birtwistle, Grete, and Linda Shearer. 2001. "Consumer Perceptions of Five UK

Fashion Retailers." *Journal of Fashion Marketing and Management* 5, no. 1: 9–18.

Black, Ian. 2010. "Al-Qaida Puts Celebrities and Bombs Online with Inspire Magazine." *Guardian*, July 1. Accessed July 1, 2010. www.guardian.co.uk /world/2010/jul/01/al-qaida-online-inspire-magazine.

Blaschke, Jochen, and Sanela Sabanovic. 2000. "Multi-level Discrimination of Muslim Women in Germany." In *Multi-level Discrimination of Muslim Women in Europe*, edited by Jochen Blaschke, 35–147. Berlin: Edition Parabolis.

Bond, Sue, and Emma Hollywood. 2009. *Equality and Human Rights Commission Research Report* 36, *Integration in the Workplace: Emerging Employment Practice on Age, Sexual Orientation and Religion or Belief* (autumn). Manchester, UK: Equality and Human Rights Commission.

Boubekeur, Amel. 2005. "Cool and Competitive: Muslim Culture in the West." *ISIM Review: International Institute for the Study of Islam in the Modern World* 16 (autumn), 12–13.

Bourdieu, Pierre. 1994. "Structures, Habitus and Practices." In *The Polity Reader in Social Theory*. Cambridge: Polity Press.

Bourdieu, Pierre. [1984] 2010. *Distinction: A Social Critique of the Judgement of Taste*. Translated by Richard Nice. London: Routledge.

Bowlby, Sophie, and Sally Lloyd-Evans. 2009. "'You Seem Very Westernised to Me': Place, Identity and Othering of Muslim Workers in the UK Labour Market." In *Muslims in Britain: Race, Place and Identities*, edited by Peter E. Hopkins and Richard Gale, 37–54. Edinburgh: Edinburgh University Press.

Bradley, Harriet, Geraldine Healy, Cynthia Forson, and Priyasha Kaul. 2007. *Workplace Cultures: What Does and Does Not Work*. Manchester, UK: Equal Opportunities Commission.

Brasher, Brenda B. 2001. *Give Me That Online Religion*. San Francisco: Jossey-Bass.

Breward, Christopher, Philip Crang, and Rosemary Crill, eds. 2010. *British Asian Style: Fashion and Textiles/Past and Present*. London: V and A Publishing.

Brown, Callum, and Gordon Lynch. 2012. "Cultural Perspectives." In *Religion and Change in Modern Britain*, edited by Linda Woodhead and Rebecca Catto, 329–51. Oxon, UK: Routledge.

Brown, Katherine. 2006. "Realising Muslim Women's Rights: The Role of Islamic Identity among British Muslim Women." *Women's Studies International Forum* 29, no. 4: 417–30.

Brügger, Niels. 2011. "Web Archiving—Between Past, Present, and Future." In *The Handbook of Internet Studies*, edited by Mia Consalvo and Charles Ess, 24–41. Chichester, UK: Wiley-Blackwell.

Buchanan, Elizabeth. A. 2011. "Internet Research Ethics: Past, Present, and Future." In *The Handbook of Internet Studies*, edited by Mia Consalvo and Charles Ess, 83–108. Chichester, UK: Wiley-Blackwell.

Bunglawala, Zamilla. 2008. *Valuing Family, Valuing Work: British Muslim Women and the Labour Market*. London: Young Foundation and the London Development Agency.

Bunt, Gary R. 2009. *iMuslims: Rewiring the House of Islam*. London: C. Hurst.

Burney, Ellen. 2011. "Blog Party." *Sunday Times*, July 17, 16–17.

Butler, Vicki. 2012. *All Party Parliamentary Group on Race and Community: Ethnic Minority Female Unemployment; Black, Pakistani and Bangladeshi Heritage Women* (first report of session 2012–13). London: Runnymede.

Cameron, Jane. 2013. "Modest Motivations: Religious and Secular Contestation in the Fashion Field." In *Modest Fashion: Styling Bodies, Mediating Faith*, edited by Reina Lewis, 137–57. London: I. B. Tauris.

Campbell, Heidi. 2005. *Exploring Religious Communities Online*. New York: P. Lang.

Campbell, Heidi. 2007. "Who's Got the Power? Religious Authority and the Internet." *Journal of Computer-Mediated Communication* 12, no. 3: 1043–62.

Campbell, Heidi. 2011. "Internet and Religion." In *The Handbook of Internet Studies*, edited by Mia Consalvo and Charles Ess, 232–50. Chichester, UK: Wiley-Blackwell.

Campbell, Heidi. 2012. "How Religious Communities Negotiate New Media Religiously." In *Digital Religion, Social Media, and Culture: Perspectives, Practices, and Futures*, edited by Pauline Hope Cheong, Peter Fischer-Nielsen, Stefan Gelfgren, and Charles Ess, 81–96. New York: P. Lang.

Cavanagh, Allison. 1999. "Behaviour in Public? Ethics in Online Ethnography." *Cybersociology*, no. 6 (August). Accessed October 20, 2013. www.socio.demon .co.uk/magazine/6/issue6.html.

Cavendish, Julius. 2011. "Al-Qa'ida Glossy Advises Women to Cover Up and Marry a Martyr." *Independent*, March 14. Accessed March 14, 2011. www.inde pendent.co.uk/news/world/asia/alqaida-glossy-advises-women-to-cover-up -and-marry-a-martyr-2240992.html#dsq-comments.

Cayla, Julien, and Giana M. Eckhardt. 2008. "Asian Brands and the Shaping of a Transnational Imagined Community." *Journal of Consumer Research* 35 (August): 216–30.

Chaney, David. 1996. *Lifestyles*. London: Routledge.

Chapman, Mark, Shuruq Naguib, and Linda Woodhead. 2012. "God-Change." In *Religion and Change in Modern Britain*, edited by Linda Woodhead and Rebecca Catto, 173–95. Oxon, UK: Routledge.

Cheang, Sarah. 2013. "'To the End of the Earth': Fashion and Ethnicity in the *Vogue* Fashion Shoot." In *Fashion Media: Past and Present*, edited by Djurdja Bartlett, Shaun Cole, and Agnès Rocamora, 35–45. London: Bloomsbury.

Cheong, Pauline Hope. 2012. "Twitter of Faith: Understanding Social Media Networking and Microblogging Rituals as Religious Practices." In *Digital Religion, Social Media, and Culture: Perspectives, Practices, and Futures*, edited by Pauline Hope Cheong, Peter Fischer-Nielsen, Stefan Gelfgren, and Charles Ess, 191–206. New York: P. Lang.

Cheong, Pauline Hope, and Charles Ess. 2012a. "Foreword: Practice, Autonomy and Authority in the Digitally Religious and Digitally Spiritual." In *Digital Religion, Social Media, and Culture: Perspectives, Practices, and Futures*, edited by Pauline Hope Cheong, Peter Fischer-Nielsen, Stefan Gelfgren, and Charles Ess, vii–xii. New York: P. Lang.

Cheong, Pauline Hope, and Charles Ess. 2012b. "Introduction: Religion 2.0? Relational and Hybridizing Pathways in Religion, Social Media and Culture." In *Digital Religion, Social Media, and Culture: Perspectives, Practices, and Futures*, edited by Pauline Hope Cheong, Peter Fischer-Nielsen, Stefan Gelfgren, and Charles Ess, 1–24. New York: P. Lang.

Cheong, Pauline Hope, Alexander Halavais, and Kyounghee Kwon. 2008. "The Chronicles of Me: Understanding Blogging as a Religious Practice." *Journal of Media and Religion* 7: 107–31.

Cheong, Pauline Hope, Shirlena Huang, and Jessie P. H. Poon. 2011. "Religious Communication and Epistemic Authority of Leaders in Wired Faith Organizations." *Journal of Communication* 61, no. 5 (October): 939–58. doi: 10.1111/j.1460-2466.2011.01579.x.

Christopherson, Susan. 1996. "The Production of Consumption: Retail Restructuring and Labour Demand in the USA." In *Retailing Consumption and Capital: Towards the New Retail Geography*, edited by Neil Wrigley and Michelle Lowe, 159–77. London: Longman.

Clark, Danae. 1993. "Commodity Lesbianism." In *The Lesbian and Gay Studies Reader*, edited by Henry Abelove, Michèle Aina Barale, and David M. Halperin, 186–201. London, Routledge.

Clifford, James. 1986. "Introduction: 'Partial Truths.'" In *Writing Culture: The Poetics and Politics of Ethnography*, edited by James Clifford and George E. Marcus, 1–26. Berkeley: University of California Press.

Cohen, Nick. 2012. "Keep Corrupt Regimes out of British Culture." *Observer*, March 18. Accessed April 15, 2012. www.guardian.co.uk/commentisfree/2012/mar/18/nick-cohen-british-museum-hajj-saudi.html.

Coleridge, Nicolas. 1988. *The Fashion Conspiracy*. London: Heinemann.

Comaroff, Jean. 1996. "The Empire's Old Clothes: Fashioning the Colonial Subject." In *Cross-Cultural Consumption: Global Markets, Local Realities*, edited by David Howes, 19–38. London: Routledge.

Comaroff, John L., and Jean Comaroff. 2009. *Ethnicity, Inc.* Chicago: University of Chicago Press.

Cooper, Davina, and Didi Herman. 2013. "Up against the Property Logic of Equality Law: Conservative Christian Accommodation Claims and Gay Rights." *Feminist Legal Studies* 21, no. 1: 61–80.

Corina, Maurice. 1978. *Fine Silks and Oak Counters: Debenhams 1778–1978*. London: Hutchinson.

Cotton, Charlotte. 2009. "Process, Content, and Dissemination: Photography and Music." In *Words without Pictures*, edited by Charlotte Cotton, Alex Klein, and Los Angeles County Museum of Art, 1–12. London: Aperture.

Craik, Jennifer. 1993. *The Face of Fashion: Cultural Studies in Fashion*. London: Routledge.

Craik, Jennifer. 2003. "The Cultural Politics of the Uniform." *Fashion Theory: The Journal of Dress, Body and Culture* 7, no. 2: 127–48.

Craik, Laura. 2005. *Uniforms Exposed: From Conformity to Transgression*. Oxford: Berg.

Craik, Jennifer. 2009. *Fashion: Key Concepts*. Oxford: Berg.

Craik, Laura. 2012. "My Day as a Hollister Sales Girl." *Times Magazine*, May 5, 16–21.

Crang, Philip. 2004. "It's Showtime: On the Workplace Geographies of Display in a Restaurant in Southeast England." *Environment and Planning D, Society and Space* 12, no. 6: 675–704.

Crang, Philip, and Ron Martin. 1991. "Mrs Thatcher's Vision of The 'New Britain' and the Other Sides of the Cambridge Phenomenon." *Environment and Planning D, Society and Space* 9: 91–116.

Crewe, Louise. 2003. "Geographies of Retailing and Consumption: Markets in Motion." *Progress in Human Geography* 22, no. 3: 352–62.

Crewe, Louise, and Jonathon Beaverstock. 1998. "Fashioning the City: Cultures of Consumption in Contemporary Urban Spaces." *Geoforum* 29, no. 3: 287–308.

Crewe, Louise, and Eileen Davenport. 1991. "The Puppet Show: Changing Buyer-Supplier Relationships within Clothing Retailing." *Transactions of the Institute of British Geographers* 17, no. 2: 183–97.

Crewe, Louise, and Michelle Lowe. 1995. "Gap on the Map? Toward a Geography of Consumption and Identity." *Environment and Planning A* 27, no. 12: 1877–98.

Currah, Andrew. 2003. "The Virtual Geographies of Retail Display." *Journal of Consumer Culture* 3, no. 1: 5–37.

Dale, Angela. 2002. "Social Exclusion of Pakistani and Bangladeshi Women." *Sociological Research Online* 7, no. 3: 1.1–11.2. Accessed November 30, 2011. doi: 10.5153/sro.741.

Davidman, Lynn. 2007. "The New Voluntarism and the Case of Unsynagogued Jews." In *Everyday Religion: Observing Modern Religious Lives*, edited by Nancy T. Ammerman, 51–68. Oxford: Oxford University Press.

Davie, Grace. 2007. "Vicarious Religion: A Methodological Challenge." In *Everyday Religion: Observing Modern Religious Lives*, edited by Nancy T. Ammerman, 21–36. Oxford: Oxford University Press.

Davis, Nancy Jean, and Robert V. Robinson. 2012. *Claiming Society for God: Religious Movements and Social Welfare*. Bloomington: Indiana University Press.

D'Emilio, John. 1993. "Capitalism and Gay Identity." In *The Lesbian and Gay Studies Reader*, edited by Henry Abelove, Michele Aina Barale, and David M. Halperin, 467–76. London: Routledge.

Demir, Ömer, Mustafa Acar, and Metin Toprak. 2004. "Anatolian Tigers or Islamic Capital: Prospects and Challenges." *Middle Eastern Studies* 40, no. 6: 166–88.

Demiralp, Seda. 2012. "White Turks, Black Turks? Faultlines beyond Islamism versus Secularism." *Third World Quarterly* 33, no. 3: 511–24.

Denvir, Ann, Andrea Broughton, Jonny Gifford, and Darcy Hill. 2007. *Research Paper: The Experiences of Sexual Orientation and Religion or Belief Discrimination Employment Tribunal Claimants*. London: Acas.

Dickens, Sarah, Martin Mitchell, and Chris Creegan. 2009. *Research Paper: Management Handling of Sexual Orientation, Religion and Belief in the Workplace*. London: Acas.

Din, Ikhlaq, and Cedric Cullingford. 2004. "Boyzone and Bhangra: The Place of Popular and Minority Cultures." *Race, Ethnicity and Education* 7, no. 3 (September): 307–20.

Domosh, Mona. 1996. "The Feminized Retail Landscape: Gender Ideology and Consumer Culture in the 19th Century." In *Retailing, Consumption and Capital: Towards the New Retail Geography*, edited by Neil Wrigley and Michelle Lowe. Harlow, UK: Longman.

Donald, Alice. 2012. *Religion or Belief, Equality and Human Rights in England and Wales*. Manchester, UK: Equality and Human Rights Commission.

Duben, Alan, and Cem Behar. 1991. *Istanbul Households: Marriage, Family and Fertility, 1880–1940*. Cambridge: Cambridge University Press.

Dudrah, Rajinder. 2010. "The Media and British Asian Fashion." In *British Asian Style: Fashion and Textiles/Past and Present*, edited by Christopher Breward, Philip Crang, and Rosemary Crill, 136–45. London: V and A Publishing.

du Gay, Paul. 1996. *Consumption and Identity at Work*. London: Sage.

du Gay, Paul, Stuart Hall, Linda Janes, Anders Koed Madsen, Hugh Mackay, and Keith Negus. [1997] 2013. *Doing Cultural Studies: The Story of the Sony Walkman*. 2nd ed. Milton Keynes, UK: Open University.

Duggan, Maeve, and Joanna Brenner. 2013. *The Demographics of Social Media—2012*. Washington, DC: Pew Research Center.

Duits, Linda, and Liesbet van Zoonen. 2006. "Headscarves and Porno-Chic: Disciplining Girls' Bodies in the European Multicultural Society." *European Journal of Women's Studies* 13, no. 2: 103–18.

Dumas, Daisy. 2012. "High Fashion CAN be Modest, Says Founder of a New Modelling Agency for Muslim Women." *Daily Mail*, February 9. Accessed February 9, 2012. www.dailymail.co.uk/femail/article-2097977/Underwraps -Muslim-model-agency-founder-Nailah-Lymus-says-high-fashion-CAN -modest.html.

Durakbaşa, Ayşe. 1993. *Reappraisal of Halide Edib for a Critique of Turkish Modernization*. PhD diss., University of Essex.

Durakbaşa, Ayşe, and Dilek Cindoğlu. 2002. "Encounters at the Counter: Gender and the Shopping Experience." In *Fragments of Culture: The Everyday of Modern Turkey*, edited by Deniz Kandiyoti and Ayşe Durakbaşa, 73–89. New Brunswick, NJ: Rutgers University Press.

Dwyer, Claire. 1999. "Veiled Meanings: Young British Muslim Women and the

Negotiation of Differences." *Gender, Place and Culture: A Journal of Feminist Geography* 6, no. 1: 5–26.

Dwyer, Claire. 2006. "Fabrications of India: Transnational Fashion Networks." In *Fashion's World Cities*, edited by Christopher Breward and David Gilbert, 217–33. Oxford: Berg.

Dwyer, Claire. 2010. "From Suitcase to Showroom: British Asian Retail Spaces." In *British Asian Style: Fashion and Textiles/Past and Present*, edited by Christopher Breward, Philip Crang, and Rosemary Crill, 148–59. London: V and A Publishing.

Dwyer, Claire, and Phillip Crang. 2002. "Fashioning Ethnicities: The Commercial Spaces of Multiculture." *Ethnicities* 2, no. 3: 410–30.

Dwyer, Claire, and Peter Jackson. 2003. "Commodifying Difference: Selling EASTern Fashion." *Environment and Planning D, Society and Space* 21, no. 3: 269–92.

Dwyer, Claire, and Bindi Shah. 2009. "Rethinking the Identities of Young British Pakistani Muslim Women: Educational Experiences and Aspirations." In *Muslims in Britain: Race, Place and Identities*, edited by Peter E. Hopkins and Richard Gale, 55–73. Edinburgh: Edinburgh University Press.

EHRC (Equality and Human Rights Commission). 2013a. *Religion or Belief in the Workplace: An Explanation of Recent European Court of Human Rights Judgments*. Manchester, UK: Equality and Human Rights Commission.

EHRC (Equality and Human Rights Commission). 2013b. *Religion or Belief in the Workplace: A Guide for Employers Following Recent European Court of Human Rights Judgments*. Manchester, UK: Equality and Human Rights Commission.

Eicher, Joanne Bubolz, and Barbara Sumberg. 1995. "World Fashion, Ethnic, and National Dress." In *Dress and Ethnicity: Change across Space and Time*, edited by Joanne Bubolz Eicher, 295–306. Oxford: Berg.

Eickelman, Dale F., and Jon W. Anderson. [1999] 2003. "Redefining Muslim Publics." In *New Media in the Muslim World: The Emerging Public Sphere*, 2nd ed., edited by Dale F. Eickelman and Jon W. Anderson. 1–18. Bloomington: Indiana University Press.

Eisenstadt, S. N. 2000. "Multiple Modernities." *Daedelus* 129, no. 1 (winter): 1–29.

Eldem, Edhem. 2007. *Consuming the Orient*. Istanbul: Ottoman Bank Archive Research Centre.

El-Fatatry, Mohamed, Stephen Lee, Tariq Khan, and Vili Lehdonvirta. 2011. "A Digital Media Approach to Islamic Marketing." In *The Handbook of Islamic Marketing*, edited by Özlem Sandıkcı and Gillian Rice, 338–60. Cheltenham, UK: Edward Elgar.

El Guindi, Fadwa. 1999. *Veil: Modesty, Privacy and Resistance*. Oxford: Berg.

Elliot, Richard, and Andrea Davis. 2006. "Symbolic Brands and Authenticity of Identity Performance." In *Brand Culture*, edited by Jonathon E. Schroeder and Miriam Salzer-Mörling, 138–52. London: Routledge.

Emerson, Bo. 2012. "Pastors Use Social Media to Reach Congregations." *Online Athens: Athens Banner-Herald*, July 4. Accessed July 6, 2012. onlineathens .com/local-news/2012-07-04/pastors-use-social-media-reach-congregations.

Employers' Forum on Belief. 2010. *Employer Guides: An Employer's Guide to Dress Codes*. London: Employers Forum on Belief.

Entwistle, Joanne. 2000. *The Fashioned Body: Fashion, Dress and Modern Social Theory*. Cambridge: Polity Press.

Entwistle, Joanne. 2009. *The Aesthetic Economy of Fashion: Markets and Value in Clothing and Modelling*. Oxford: Berg.

Esman, Marjorie R. 1984. "Tourism as Ethnic Preservation: The Cajuns of Louisiana." *Annals of Tourism Research* 11, 451–67.

Ess, Charles, Akira Kawabata, and Hiroyuki Kurosaki. 2007. "Cross-Cultural Perspectives on Religion and Computer-Mediated Communication." *Journal of Computer-Mediated Communication* 12, no. 3: 939–55. doi: 10.1111/j.1083-6101.2007.00357.x.

Essers, Caroline, and Yvonne Benschop. 2007. "Enterprising Identities: Female Entrepreneurs of Moroccan or Turkish Origin in the Netherlands." *Organization Studies* 28, no. 1: 49–69.

Essoo, Nittin, and Sally Dibb. 2004. "Religious Influences on Shopping Behaviour: An Exploratory Study." *Journal of Marketing Management* 20, nos. 7–8: 683–712.

Evans, Caroline. 1997. "Dreams That Only Money Can Buy . . . Or, The Shy Tribe in Flight from Discourse." *Fashion Theory: The Journal of Dress, Body and Culture* 1, no. 2: 169–88.

Evans, Caroline. 2013. *The Mechanical Smile: Modernism and the First Fashion Shows in France and America, 1900–1929*. New Haven, CT: Yale University Press.

EVAW (End Violence Against Women). 2009. *Memorandum Submitted by End Violence Against Women to the Public Bill Committee*. Accessed January 28, 2015. www.publications.parliament.uk/pa/cm200809/cmpublic/equality/memos /ucm1502.htm.

Fabian, Johannes. 1983. *Time and the Other: How Anthropology Makes Its Objects*. New York: Columbia University Press.

Farah, Maya F. 2011. "The Arab Consumer Boycott of American Products: Motives and Intentions." In *The Handbook of Islamic Marketing*, edited by Özlem Sandıkcı and Gillian Rice, 393–417. Cheltenham, UK: Edward Elgar.

Farrar, Max. 2012. "Multiculturalism in the UK—A Contested Discourse." In *Islam in the West: Key Issues in Multiculturalism*, edited by Max Farrar, Simon Robinson, Yasmin Valli, and Paul Wetherly. London: Palgrave.

Fernie, John, and Stephen J. Arnold. 2002. "Wal-Mart in Europe: Prospects for Germany, the UK and France." *International Journal of Retail and Distribution Management* 30, no. 2: 92–102.

Field, Clive. 2011. "Young British Muslims since 9/11: A Composite Attitudinal Profile." *Religion, State and Society* 39, nos. 2–3: 159–72.

Floor, Ko. 2006. *Branding a Store: How to Build Successful Retail Brands in a Changing Marketplace*. London: Kogan Page.

Fox, Imogen. 2012. "Boldly Go." *Guardian Weekend*, September 8, 47–49.

Franks, Myfanwy. 2000. "Crossing the Borders of Whiteness? White Muslim Women Who Wear the Hijab in Britain Today." *Ethnic and Racial Studies* 23, no. 5 (September): 917–29.

Freeman, Carla. 2010. "Designing Women: Corporate Discipline and Barbados's Off-Shore Pink-Collar Sector." In *Perspectives in the Caribbean: A Reader in Culture, History and Representation*, edited by Philip Scher, 283–96. Chichester, UK: Blackwell.

French, Shaun, Louise Crewe, Andrew Leyshon, Peter Webb, and Nigel Thrift. 2004. "Putting e-Commerce in Its Place: Reflections on the Impact of the Internet on the Cultural Industries." In *Cultural Industries and the Production of Culture*, edited by Dominic Power and Allen J. Scott, 54–71. London: Routledge.

Friedman, Susan Stanford. 2007. "Unthinking Manifest Destiny: Muslim Modernities on Three Continents." In *Shades of the Planet: American Literature as World Literature*, edited by Wai Chee Dimock and Lawrence Buell, 62–100. Princeton, NJ: Princeton University Press.

Frierson, Elizabeth B. 2000. "Mirrors Out, Mirrors In: Domestication and Rejection of the Foreign in Late-Ottoman Women's Magazines." In *Women, Patronage, and Self-Representation in Islamic Societies*, edited by Dede Fairchild Ruggles, 177–204. New York: State University of New York Press.

Geertz, Clifford. 1984. *Local Knowledge: Further Essays in Interpretative Anthropology*. New York: Basic.

Geertz, Clifford. 2000. *Available Light: Anthropological Reflections on Philosophical Topics*. Princeton, NJ: Princeton University Press.

Ger, Güliz, and Özlem Sandıkçı. 2006. "Doing Research on Sensitive Topics: Studying Covered Turkish Women." In *Handbook of Qualitative Research Methods in Marketing*, edited by Russell W. Belk, 509–20. Cheltenham, UK: Edward Elgar.

Gilbert, David. 2013. "Urban Outfitting: The City and the Spaces of Fashion Culture." In *Fashion Cultures Revisited*, edited by Stella Bruzzi and Pamela Church Gibson, 11–30. London: Routledge.

Gilliat-Ray, Sophie. 2010. *Muslims in Britain: An Introduction*. New York: Cambridge University Press.

Glennie, Paul, and Nigel Thrift. 1996. "Consumption, Shopping and Gender." In *Retailing Consumption and Capital: Towards the New Retail Geography*, edited by Neil Wrigley and Michelle Lowe, 221–37. Harlow, UK: Longman.

Göçek, Fatma Müge. 1999. "To Veil or Not to Veil: The Contested Location of Gender in Contemporary Turkey." *Interventions* 1, no. 4: 521–35.

Goffman, Erving [1956] 1990. *The Presentation of Self in Everyday Life*. London: Penguin.

Gökarıksel, Banu. 2007. "A Feminist Geography of Veiling: Gender, Class and

Religion in the Making of Modern Subjects and Public Spaces in Istanbul." In *Women, Religion and Space: Global Perspectives on Gender and Faith*, edited by Karen M. Morin and Jeanne Kay Guelke, 61–80. Syracuse, NY: Syracuse University Press.

Gökarıksel, Banu. 2012. "The Intimate Politics of Secularism and the Headscarf: The Mall, the Neighbourhood, and the Public Sphere in Istanbul." *Gender Place and Culture* 19, no. 1 (February): 1–20.

Gökariksel, Banu, and Katherine Mitchell. 2005. "Veiling, Secularism, and the Neoliberal Subject: National Narratives and Supranational Desires in Turkey and France." *Global Networks* 5, no. 2: 147–65.

Gökarıksel, Banu, and Anna J. Secor. 2009. "New Transnational Geographies of Islamism, Capitalism and Subjectivity: The Veiling-Fashion Industry in Turkey." *Area* 41, no. 1: 6–18.

Gökarıksel, Banu, and Anna J. Secor. 2010a. "Between Fashion and Tesettür: Marketing and Consuming Women's Islamic Dress." *Journal of Middle East Women's Studies* 6, no. 3: 118–48.

Gökarıksel, Banu, and Anna J. Secor. 2010b. "Islamic-ness in the Life of a Commodity: Veiling Fashion in Turkey." *Transactions — Institute of British Geographers* 35, no. 3: 1–21.

Gökarıksel, Banu, and Anna J. Secor. 2013. "Transnational Networks of Veiling-Fashion between Turkey and Western Europe." In *Islamic Fashion and Anti-Fashion: New Perspectives from Europe and North America*, edited by Emma Tarlo and Annelies Moors, 157–67. London: Bloomsbury.

Göle, Nilüfer. 1996. *The Forbidden Modern: Civilization and Veiling*. Ann Arbor: University of Michigan Press.

Göle, Nilüfer. 2003. "The Voluntary Adoption of Islamic Stigma." *Social Research* 70, no. 3 (fall): 809–28.

Göle, Nilüfer. [2005] 2011. *Islam in Europe: The Lure of Fundamentalism and the Allure of Cosmopolitanism*. Translated by Steven Rendall. Princeton, NJ: Markus Wiener.

Grewal, Inderpal. 2005. *Transnational America: Feminisms, Diasporas, Neoliberalisms*. Durham, NC: Duke University Press.

Grewal, Inderpal, and Caren Kaplan, eds. 1994. *Scattered Hegemonies*. Minneapolis: University of Minnesota Press.

Gül, Songül Sallan, and Hüseyin Gül. 2000. "The Question of Women in Islamic Revivalism in Turkey: A Review of the Islamic Press." *Current Sociology* 48, no. 2: 1–26.

Hakim, Faz. 2010. "A Discussion of the Underlying Conflict That Exists between the Public and Private Lives of Muslim Women in Britain." In *Women, Islam and Western Liberalism*, edited by Faisal Al Yafai, 19–26. London: Civitas.

Halberstam, Judith. 2005. *In a Queer Time and Place: Transgender Bodies, Subcultural Lives*. New York: New York University Press.

Halter, Marylin. 2000. *Shopping for Identity: The Marketing of Ethnicity*. New York: Schocken.

Hardill, Irene, and Parvati Raghuram. 1998. "Diasporic Connections: Case Studies of Asian Women in Business." *Area* 30, no. 3 (September): 255–61.

Hari, Johann. 2005. "Multiculturalism Is Not the Best Way to Welcome People to Our Country." *Independent*, August 5, 35.

Harris, Sarah. 2010. "Young. British. Female. Muslim." *Times*, May 29. Accessed December 9, 2011. www.thetimes.co.uk/tto/faith/article2522634.ece.

Hastings-Black, Michael. 2009. "American-Muslim Identity: Advertising, Mass Media and New Media." In *Muslim Societies in the Age of Mass Consumption: Politics, Culture and Identity between the Local and the Global*, edited by Johanna Pink, 303–24. Newcastle upon Tyne, UK: Cambridge Scholars Publishing.

Hebdige, Dick. 1979. *Subculture: The Meaning of Style*. London: Methuen.

Heffernan, Teresa. 2011. "Travelling East: Veiling, Race, and Nations." In *The Poetics and Politics of Place: Ottoman Istanbul and British Orientalism*, edited by Zeynep İnankur, Reina Lewis, and Mary Roberts, 157–65. Istanbul: Suna and İnan Kıraç Foundation.

Hélie-Lucas, Marieme. 2012. "The Struggle of French Women of Migrant Muslim Descent in the Defence of Secular State Schools." In *Secularism, Racism and the Politics of Belonging*, edited by Nira Yuval-Davis and Philip Marfleet, 47–52. London: Runnymede.

Helland, Christopher. 2000. "Online Religion/Religion-Online and Virtual Communitas." In *Religion on the Internet: Research Prospects and Promises*, edited by Douglas E. Cowan and Jeffrey K. Hadden, 205–24. New York: JAI Press.

Hennessy, Rosemary. 2000. *Profit and Pleasure: Sexual Identities in Late Capitalism*. London: Routledge.

Herman, Didi. 2011. *An Unfortunate Coincidence: Jews, Jewishness, and English Law*. Oxford: Oxford University Press.

Hermansen, Marcia. 2003. "How to Put the Genie Back in the Bottle? 'Identity' Islam and Muslim Youth Cultures in America." In *Progressive Muslims: On Justice, Gender and Pluralism*, edited by Omid Safi, 306–19. Oxford: Oneworld.

Heydra, Natasa. 2007. *MSLM*. Exhibition catalogue. Rotterdam: MAMA, Showroom for Media and Moving Art.

Hine, Christine. 2000. *Virtual Ethnography*. London: Sage.

Hirschkind, Charles. 2006. "Cassette Ethics: Public Piety and Popular Media in Egypt." In *Religion, Media, and the Public Sphere*, edited by Birgit Meyer and Annelies Moors, 29–51. Bloomington: Indiana University Press.

Hirschkind, Charles, and Saba Mahmood. 2002. "Feminism, the Taliban, and Politics of Counter Insurgency." *Anthropology Quarterly* 75, no. 2: 339–54.

Hodkinson, Paul. 2012. "The Collective Ageing of a Goth Festival." In *Ageing and Youth Cultures: Music, Style and Identity*, edited by Andy Bennett and Paul Hodkinson, 133–45. London: Bloomsbury.

Hoggard, Liz. 2013. "Modesty Regulators: Punishing and Rewarding Women's Appearances in Mainstream Media." In *Modest Fashion: Styling Bodies, Mediating Faith*, edited by Reina Lewis, 175–89. London: I. B. Tauris.

Hoover, Steward M. 2012. "Foreword: Practice, Autonomy, and Authority in the Digitally Religious and Digitally Spiritual." In *Digital Religion, Social Media, and Culture: Perspectives, Practices, and Futures*, edited by Pauline Hope Cheong, Peter Fischer-Nielsen, Stefan Gelfgren, and Charles Ess, vii–xii. New York: P. Lang.

Hopkins, Peter, and Richard Gale, eds. 2009. *Muslims in Britain: Race, Place and Identities*, Edinburgh: Edinburgh University Press.

Hughes, Karen D., and Vela Tadic. 1998. "'Something to Deal With': Customer Sexual Harassment and Women's Retail Service Work in Canada." *Gender, Work and Organization* 5, no. 4: 207–19.

Hui, Sylvia. 2014. "Ramadan Super-Luxury Shoppers Descend on London for Pre-Fast Splurge." *Huffington Post*. June 26. Accessed January 25, 2015. www.huffingtonpost.com/2014/06/27/ramadan-shopping-london_n_5536721.html.

Huisman, Kimberly, and Pierrette Hondagneu-Sotelo. 2005. "Dress Matters: Change and Continuity in the Dress Practices of Bosnian Muslim Refugee Women." *Gender and Society* 19, no. 1: 44–65.

Hussain, Amir. 2003. "Muslims, Pluralism, and Interfaith Dialogue." In *Progressive Muslims: On Justice, Gender and Pluralism*, edited by Omid Safi, 251–69. Oxford: Oneworld.

Hussein, Nazia. 2011. "Muslim Youth Redefining Leadership." Ogilvy & Mather. Press release. June. Accessed October 23, 2011. www.ogilvynoor.com/wp-content/uploads/2011/06/Lets-Do-It-Our-Way-Muslim-Youth-Redefining-Leadership.pdf.

Hussein, Nazia, with Simin Radmanesh and Tanya Dernaika. 2011. "The Future Rises in the Middle East." Ogilvy & Mather. Press release. Accessed October 23, 2013. www.ogilvy.com/On-Our-Minds/Articles/The-Future-Rises-in-the-Middle-East.aspx.

Izberk-Bilgin, Elif. 2012. "Infidel Brands: Unveiling Alternative Meanings of Global Brands at the Nexus of Globalization, Consumer Culture, and Islamism." *Journal of Consumer Research* 39, no. 4 (December): 663–87.

Jackson, Peter. 2002. "Commercial Cultures: Transcending the Cultural and the Economic." *Progress in Human Geography* 26, no. 1 (February): 3–18. Accessed February 27, 2007. doi: 10.1191/0309132502ph254.

Jackson, Peter, Nicolas Thomas, and Claire Dwyer. 2007. "Consuming Transnational Fashion in London and Mumbai." *Geoforum* 38, no. 5 (September): 908–24.

Jacobs, Alexandra. 2010. "Fashion Democracy: The World of Virtual Anna Wintours." *New Yorker*, March 29. Accessed January 28, 2015. www.newyorker.com/magazine/2010/03/29/fashion-democracy.

Jafari, Aliakbar. 2012. "Islamic Marketing: Insights from a Critical Perspective." *Journal of Islamic Marketing* 3, no. 1: 22–34.

Jamal, Ahmad. 2003. "Retailing in a Multicultural World: The Interplay of

Retailing, Ethnic Identity and Consumption." *Journal of Retailing and Consumer Services* 10, no. 1: 1–11.

Jenkins, Gareth. 2012. "Islamism in Turkey." In *Routledge Handbook of Political Islam*, edited by Shahram Akbarzadeh. Abingdon, UK: Routledge.

Jenkins, Henry. [2006] 2008. *Conference Culture: Where Old and New Media Collide*. 2nd ed. New York: New York University Press.

Jensen, Klaus Bruhn. 2011. "New Media, Old Methods — Internet Methodologies, and the Online/Offline Divide." In *The Handbook of Internet Studies*, edited by Mia Consalvo and Charles Ess, 43–58. Chichester, UK: Wiley-Blackwell.

Jivraj, Stephen. 2013. "Muslims in England and Wales: Evidence from the 2011 Census." In *The New Muslims*, edited by Claire Alexander, Victoria Redclift, and Ajmal Hussain. London: Runnymede.

Jobling, Paul. 1999. *Fashion Spreads: Word and Image in Fashion Photography since 1890*. Oxford: Berg.

Jones, Carla. 2010. "Images of Desire: Creating Virtue and Value in an Indonesian Lifestyle Magazine." *Journal of Middle East Women's Studies* 6, no. 3 (fall): 91–117.

Jones, Carla, and Ann Marie Leshkowich. 2003. "Introduction: Re-Orienting Fashion or Re-Orientalizing Asia?" In *Re-Orienting Fashion: The Globalization of Asian Dress*, edited by Sandra Niessen, Carla Jones, and Ann Marie Leshkowich, 1–48. Oxford: Berg.

Jones, Carla, and Ruth Mars. 2011. "Transnational Conceptions of Islamic Community: National and Religious Subjectivities." *Nations and Nationalism* 17, no. 1: 2–6.

Jones, Glynis, ed. 2012. *Muslim Women's Style in Australia: Faith Fashion Fusion*. Sydney: Powerhouse Museum.

Joseph, Sarah. 2010. "Are Liberalism and Islam Compatible?" In *Women, Islam and Western Liberalism*, edited by Faisal Al Yafai, 11–18. London: Civitas.

Joseph, Sarah. 2013. "The Power of Fashion." *Emel*, January, 48–49.

Jouili, Jeanette S., and Schirin Amir-Moazami. 2006. "Knowledge, Empowerment and Religious Authority among Pious Muslim Women in France and Germany." *Muslim World* 96, no. 4 (October): 617–42.

Kaiser, Susan B. 2012. *Fashion and Cultural Studies*. London: Bloomsbury.

Karaflogka, Anastasia. 2006. *e-Religion: A Criticised Appraisal of Religious Discourse on the World Wide Web*. London: Equinox.

Kariapper, Ayesha Salma. 2009. *Walking a Tightrope: Women and Veiling in the United Kingdom*. London: Women Living under Muslim Laws.

Karim, Jamillah. 2005. "Voices of Faith, Faces of Beauty: Connecting American Muslim Women through Azizah." In *Muslim Networks: From Hajj to Hip Hop*, edited by miriam cooke and Bruce B. Lawrence, 169–88. Chapel Hill: University of North Carolina Press.

Kılıçbay, Barış, and Mutlu Binark. 2002. "Consumer Culture, Islam and the Politics of Lifestyle: Fashion for Veiling in Contemporary Turkey." *European Journal of Communication* 17, no. 4: 495–511.

Killian, Caitlin. 2003. "The Other Side of the Veil: North African Women in France Respond to the Headscarf Affair." *Gender and Society* 17, no. 4 (August): 567–90.

Kline, David. 2005. "Toward a More Participatory Democracy." In *Blog! How the Newest Media Revolution Is Changing Politics, Business, and Culture*, edited by David Kline and Dan Burstein, 3–24. New York: CDS Books.

Kline, David, and Daniel Burstein, eds. 2005. *Blog! How the Newest Media Revolution Is Changing Politics, Business, and Culture*. New York: CDS Books.

Kokoschka, Alina. 2009. "Islamizing the Market? Advertising, Products, and Consumption in an Islamic Framework in Syria." In *Muslim Societies in the Age of Mass Consumption: Politics, Culture and Identity between the Local and Global*, edited by Johanna Pink, 225–40. Newcastle upon Tyne, UK: Cambridge Scholars.

Köni, Hakan. 2012. "Saudi Influence on Islamic Institutions in Turkey Beginning in the 1970s." *Middle East Journal* 66, no. 1 (winter): 97–110.

Lamont, Michèle, and Virág Molnár 2001. "How Blacks Use Consumption to Shape Their Collective Identity: Evidence from Marketing Specialists." *Journal of Consumer Culture* 1, no. 1: 31–45.

Lancaster, William. 2000. *The Department Store: A Social History*. Leicester: Leicester University Press.

Larsen, Elena. 2001. *Cyber Faith: How Americans Pursue Religion Online*. Washington, DC: Pew Research Center. December 23. Accessed October 25, 2013. www.pewinternet.org/Reports/2001/CyberFaith-How-Americans-Pursue -Religion-Online.aspx.

Leach, William. 1980. *True Love and Perfect Union: The Feminist Reform of Sex and Society*. New York: Basic.

Leach, William. 1989. "Strategists of Display and the Production of Desire." In *Consuming Visions: Accumulation and Display of Goods in America, 1880–1920*, edited by Simon J. Bronner. New York: W. W. Norton.

Lemire, Beverly, and Giorio Riello. 2006. *East and West: Textiles and Fashion in Eurasia in the Early Modern Period*. Working Papers of the Global Economic History Network (GEHN) 22/06. London: Department of Economic History, London School of Economics and Political Science.

Leshkowich, Ann Marie, and Carla Jones. 2003. "What Happens When Asian Chic Becomes Chic in Asia?" *Fashion Theory: The Journal of Dress, Body and Culture* 7, no. 3/4: 281–300.

Leslie, Deborah. 2002. "Gender, Retail Employment and the Clothing Commodity Chain." *Gender, Place and Culture—A Journal of Feminist Geography* 9, no. 1: 61–76.

Levine, Mark. 2008. *Heavy Metal Islam: Rock, Resistance and the Struggle for the Soul of Islam*. New York: Three Rivers.

Lewis, Philip. 2007. *Young, British and Muslim*. London: Continuum.

Lewis, Reina. 1996. *Gendering Orientalism: Race, Femininity and Representation*. London: Routledge.

Lewis, Reina. 1997. "Looking Good: The Lesbian Gaze and Fashion Imagery." *Feminist Review* 55 (spring): 92–109.

Lewis, Reina. 2004. *Rethinking Orientalism: Women, Travel, and the Ottoman Harem*. London: I. B. Tauris.

Lewis, Reina. 2013a. "Establishing Reputation, Maintaining Independence: The Modest Fashion Blogosphere." In *Fashion Media: Past and Present*, edited by Djurdja Bartlett, Shaun Cole, and Agnes Rocamora, 165–74. Oxford: Berg.

Lewis, Reina. 2013b. "Fashion Forward and Faith-tastic! Online Modest Fashion and the Development of Women as Religious Interpreters and Intermediaries." In *Modest Fashion: Styling Bodies, Mediating Faith*, edited by Reina Lewis, 41–66. London: I. B. Tauris.

Lewis, Reina. 2013c. "Hijab on the Shop Floor: Muslims in Fashion Retail in Britain." In *Islamic Fashion and Anti-Fashion: New Perspectives from Europe and America*, edited by Annelies Moors and Emma Tarlo, 181–97. Oxford: Bloomsbury.

Lewis, Reina. 2013d. "Insider Voices, Changing Practices: Press and Industry Professionals Speak." In *Modest Fashion: Styling Bodies, Mediating Faith*, edited by Reina Lewis, 190–219. London: I. B. Tauris.

Lewis, Reina, ed. 2013e. *Modest Fashion: Styling Bodies, Mediating Faith*. London: I. B. Tauris.

Lewis, Reina. 2015. "De-veiling Modesty: Dejabis and Dewiggies Expanding the Parameters of the Modest Blogsphere." *Fashion Theory*, 19, no. 2 (April).

Lewis, Reina, and Nancy Micklewright, eds. 2006. *Gender, Modernity and Liberty: Middle Eastern and Western Women's Writings: A Critical Sourcebook*. London: I. B. Tauris.

Lionnet, Françoise, and Shu-mei Shih. 2005. "Introduction: Thinking through the Minor, Transnationally." In *Minor Transnationalism*, edited by Françoise Lionnet and Shu-mei Shih, 1–23. Durham, NC: Duke University Press.

Lowe, Michelle S. 1991. "Trading Places: Retailing and Local Economic Development at Merry Hill, West Midlands." *East Midland Geographer* 14: 31–49.

Lowe, Michelle, and Louise Crewe. 1996. "Shop Work: Image, Customer Care and the Restructuring of Retail Employment." In *Retailing Consumption and Capital: Towards the New Retail Geography*, edited by Neil Wrigley and Michelle Lowe, 196–207. London: Longman.

Lucas, Becky. 2007. "'From A to B' (Interview with Paul de Zwart)." *Time Out Dubai*, September 27–October 4, 59.

Lüders, Marika. 2011. "Why and How Online Sociability Became Part and Parcel of Teenage Life." In *The Handbook of Internet Studies*, edited by Mia Consalvo and Charles Ess, 452–69. Chichester, UK: Wiley-Blackwell.

Lury, Alison. 1981. *The Language of Clothes*. New York: Random House.

Macdonald, Myra. 2006. "Muslim Women and the Veil: Problems of Image and Voice in Media Representations." *Feminist Media Studies* 6, no. 1: 7–23.

MacLeod, Arlene. 1991. *Accommodating Protest: Working Women, the New Veiling, and Change in Cairo*. New York: Columbia University Press.

Madden, Mary, Amanda Lenhart, Maeve Duggan, Sandra Cortesi, and Urs Gasser. 2013. *Teens and Technology 2013*. Washington, DC: Pew Research Center. March 13. Accessed January 23, 2015. www.pewinternet.org/files/old-media//Files/Reports/2013/PIP_TeensandTechnology2013.pdf.

Madood, Tariq. 2007. "Muslims and the Politics of Difference." *Political Quarterly* 74, no. 1: 100–115.

Madood, Tariq, and Fauzia Ahmad. 2007. "British Muslim Perspectives on Multiculturalism." *Theory, Culture and Society* 24, no. 2: 187–213.

Mahmood, Saba. 2005. *Politics of Piety: The Islamic Revival and the Feminist Subject*. Princeton, NJ: Princeton University Press.

Makdisi, Ussama. 2002. "Ottoman Orientalism." *American Historical Review* 107, no. 3 (June): 768–96.

Malik, Alveena. 2010. "Religious Symbols and the Notion of Public Faith in Britain Today." In *Women, Islam and Western Liberalism*, edited by Faisal al Yafai, 27–37. London: Civitas.

Malik, Iftikhar H. 2004. *Islam and Modernity: Muslims in Europe and the United States*. London: Pluto.

Malik, Maleiha. 2010. "Progressive Multiculturalism: Minority Women and Cultural Diversity." *International Journal on Minority and Group Rights* 17, no. 3: 447–67.

Malik, Maleiha. 2012. *Minority Legal Orders in the UK: Minorities, Pluralism and the Law*. London: British Academy.

Mandaville, Peter. 2003. "Towards a Critical Islam: European Muslims and the Changing Boundaries of Transnational Religious Discourse." In *Muslim Networks and Transnational Communities in and across Europe*, edited by Stefano Allievi and Jørgen S. Nielsen, 127–45. Leiden: Brill.

Mandaville, Peter. 2007. "Globalization and the Politics of Religious Knowledge: Pluralizing Authority in the Muslim World." *Theory, Culture and Society* 24, no. 2: 101–15.

Mani, Bakirathi. 2003. "Undressing the Diaspora." In *South Asian Women in the Diaspora*, edited by Nirmal Puwar and Parvati Raghurum, 117–35. Oxford: Berg.

Marshall, David. 2011. "Newly Mediated Media: Understanding the Changing Internet Landscape of the Media Industries." In *The Handbook of Internet Studies*, edited by Mia Consalvo and Charles Ess, 406–23. Chichester, UK: Wiley-Blackwell.

Masood, Ehsan. 2006. *British Muslims Media Guide*. London: British Council.

Massey, Doreen. 1994. *Space, Place and Gender*. Cambridge: Polity Press.

Mauss, Marcel. 1973. "Techniques of the Body." *Economy and Society* 2, no. 1: 70–88.

Mazzarella, William. 2003. *Shoveling Smoke: Advertising and Globalization in Contemporary India*. New Delhi: Oxford University Press.

MCB (Muslim Council of Britain). 2005. *Good Practice Guide for Employers and Employees*. London: Muslim Council of Britain. Accessed October 22, 2013. www.mcb.org.uk/faith/approved.pdf.

MCB (Muslim Council of Britain). 2007. *Meeting the Needs of Muslim Pupils in State Schools: Information and Guidance for Schools*. London: Muslim Council of Britain. Accessed October 22, 2013. www.mcb.org.uk/downloads/School infoguidance.pdf.

MCB (Muslim Council of Britain). 2013. *The Muslim Pound: Celebrating the Muslim Contribution to the UK Economy: The Muslim Council of Britain at the 9th World Economic Islamic Forum 2013*. London: Muslim Council of Britain. Accessed November 1, 2013. www.mcb.org.uk/uploads/The%20Muslim%20Pound-final .pdf.

McDowell, Linda, and Gill Court. 1994. "Performing Work: Bodily Representations in Merchant Banks." *Environment and Planning D, Society and Space* 12, no. 6: 727–50.

McGuire, Meredith B. 2008. *Lived Religion: Faith and Practice in Everyday Life*. Oxford: Oxford University Press.

McRobbie, Angela. 1998. *British Fashion Design: Rag Trade or Image Industry?* London: Routledge.

McRobbie, Angela, and Judith A. Garber. [1975] 2006. "Girls and Subcultures: An Exploration." In *Resistance through Rituals: Youth Cultures in Post-war Britain*, 2nd ed., edited by Stuart Hall and Tony Jefferson, 172–84. London: Routledge.

Medina, Jameelah Xochitl. 2011. "The University of Life." In *I Speak for Myself: American Women on Being Muslim*, edited by Maria M. Ebrahimji and Zahra T. Suratwala, 57–63. Ashland, OR: White Cloud Press.

Meer, Nasar. 2008. "The Politics of Voluntary and Involuntary Identities: Are Muslims in Britain an Ethnic, Racial or Religious Minority?" *Patterns of Prejudice* 42, no. 1 (February): 61–81.

Meer, Nasar, and Tariq Modood. 2008. "The Multicultural State We're In: Muslims, 'Multiculture' and the 'Civic Re-balancing' of British Multiculturalism." *Political Studies* 57, no. 3: 473–97.

Meer, Nasar, and Tehseen Noorani. 2008. "A Sociological Comparison of Anti-Semitism and Anti-Muslim Sentiment in Britain." *Sociological Review* 56, no. 2: 195–219.

Mernissi, Fatema. 1985. *Beyond the Veil: Male-Female Dynamics in Muslim Society*. 2nd ed. London: al Saqi Books.

Mernissi, Fatema. 2004. "The Satellite, the Prince, and Scheherazade: The Rise of Women as Communicators in Digital Islam." *Transnational Broadcasting Studies* 12 (spring/summer). Accessed July 11, 2011. www.tbsjournal.com /Archives/Spring04/mernissi.htm.

Meyer, Birgit, and Annelies Moors. 2006. Introduction. In *Religion, Media and the Public Sphere*, edited by Birgit Meyer and Annelies Moors, 1–25. Blooming-ton: Indiana University Press.

Meyer, Henry, and Heidi Couch. 2010. "Harrods Sees Profit from Islamic Fashion as Qatar Takes Control." *Bloomberg News*. July 12. Accessed October 24, 2013. www.bloomberg.com/news/2010-07-12/harrods-sees-profits-in-islamic -fashion-as-qatari-owners-showcase-abayas.html.

Micklewright, Nancy. 2000. "Public and Private for Ottoman Women of the Nineteenth Century." In *Women, Patronage, and Self-Representation in Islamic Societies*, edited by Dede Fairchild Ruggles, 155–76. Albany: State University of New York Press.

Miller, Daniel, Peter Jackson, Nigel Thrift, Beverley Holbrook, and Michael Row-lands. 1998. *Shopping, Place and Identity*. New York: Routledge.

Mir-Hosseini, Ziba. 2011. "Hijab and Choice: Between Politics and Theology." In *Innovation in Islam: Traditions and Contributions*, edited by Mehran Kamrava, 190–212. Berkeley: University of California Press.

Mirzeoff, Nicholas. 2002. *The Visual Culture Reader*. 2nd ed. London: Routledge.

Modood, Tariq. 2010. "Muslims and the Politics of Difference." In *Muslims in Britain: Race, Place and Identities*, edited by Peter Hopkins and Richard Gale, 193–209. Edinburgh: Edinburgh University Press.

Modood, Tariq, and Fauzia Ahmad. 2007. "British Muslim Perspectives on Multiculturalism." *Theory, Culture, and Society* 24, no. 2: 187–213.

Mohammad, Robina. 2005a. "British Pakistani Muslim Women: Marking the Body, Marking the Nation." In *A Companion to Feminist Geography*, vol. 6, edited by Lise Nelson and Joni Seager, 379–97. Malden, MA: Blackwell.

Mohammad, Robina. 2005b. "Negotiating Spaces of the Home, the Education System, and the Labour Market: The Case of Young, Working-Class, British Pakistani Muslim Women." In *Geographies of Muslim Women: Gender, Religion, and Space*, edited by Ghazi-Walid Falah and Caroline Nagel, 178–202. New York: Guilford.

Mokhlis, Safiek. 2009. "Relevancy and Measurement of Religiosity in Consumer Behaviour Research." *International Business Research* 2, no. 3: 75–84.

Moll, Yasmin. 2007. "'Beyond Beards, Scarves and Halal Meat': Mediated Con-structions of British Muslim Identity." *Journal of Religion and Popular Culture* 15, no. 1 (spring).

Montgomery, Kathryn. 2000. "Youth and Digital Media: A Policy Research Agenda." *Journal of Adolescent Health* 27, no. 2 (August): 61–68.

Moors, Annelies. 2007. "Fashionable Muslims: Notions of Self, Religion, and Society in San'a." *Fashion Theory: The Journal of Dress, Body and Culture* 11, no. 2/3: 319–46.

Moors, Annelies. 2009. "'Islamic Fashion' in Europe: Religious Conviction, Aesthetic Style, and Creative Consumption." *Encounters* 1, no. 1: 175–201.

Moors, Annelies. 2013. "'Discover the Beauty of Modesty': Islamic Fashion Online." In *Modest Fashion: Styling Bodies, Mediating Faith*, edited by Reina Lewis, 17–40. London: I. B. Tauris.

Moors, Annelies, and Emma Tarlo. 2013. "Introduction: Islamic Fashion and Anti-fashion: New Perspectives from Europe and America." In *Islamic Fashion and Anti-Fashion: New Perspectives from Europe and America*, edited by Emma Tarlo and Annelies Moors, 1–30. Oxford: Bloomsbury.

Moosa, Zohra. 2010. "Western Liberalism's 'Problem' with Muslim Women." In *Women, Islam and Western Liberalism*, edited by Faisal Al Yafai, 63–74. London: Civitas.

Moreton, Bethany. 2009. *To Serve God and Wal-Mart: The Making of Christian Free Enterprise*. Cambridge, MA: Harvard University Press.

Morey, Peter, and Amina Yaqin. 2011. *Framing Muslims: Stereotyping and Representation after 9/11*. Cambridge, MA: Harvard University Press.

Mort, Frank. 1996. *Cultures of Consumption: Masculinities and Social Space in Late Twentieth-Century Britain*. Abingdon, UK: Routledge.

Nagel, Caroline, and Lynn Staeheli. 2008. "British Arab Perspectives on Religion, Politics, and 'the Public.'" In *Muslims in Britain: Race, Place and Identities*, edited by Peter Hopkins and Richard T. Gale. Edinburgh: Edinburgh University Press.

Nava, Mica. 2007. *Visceral Cosmopolitanism: Gender, Culture and the Normalisation of Difference*. Oxford: Berg.

Navaro-Yashin, Yael. 2002. "The Market for Identities: Secularism, Islamism, Commodities." In *Fragments of Culture: The Everyday of Modern Turkey*, edited by Deniz Kandiyoti and Ayşe Saktanber, 221–53. New Brunswick, NJ: Rutgers University Press.

Niessen, Sandra. 2003. "Afterword: Re-Orienting Fashion Theory." In *Re-Orienting Fashion: The Globalization of Asian Dress*, edited by Sandra Niessen, Ann Marie Leshkowich, and Carla Jones, 243–65. Oxford: Berg.

Nixon, Sean. 2003. *Advertising Cultures*. London: Sage.

Nye, Malory, and Paul Weller. 2012. "Controversies as a Lens on Change." In *Religion and Change in Modern Britain*, edited by Linda Woodhead and Rebecca Catto, 34–54. Oxon, UK: Routledge.

Ogilvy & Mather. 2010. "Ogilvy & Mather Launches World's First Bespoke Islamic Branding Practice." Press release. June 8.

Okin, Susan Moller. 1999. "Is Multiculturalism Bad for Women?" In *Is Multiculturalism Bad for Women?*, edited by Joshua Cohen, Matthew Howard, and Martha C. Nussbaum. Princeton, NJ: Princeton University Press.

O'Neil, Mary Lou. 2010. "You Are What You Wear: Clothing/Appearance Laws and the Construction of the Public Citizen in Turkey." *Fashion Theory: The Journal of Dress, Body and Culture* 14, no. 1: 65–82.

Ong, Aihwa. 1995. "State versus Islam: Malay Families, Women's Bodies and the Body Politic in Malaysia." In *Bewitching Women, Pious Men: Gender and Politics in South East Asia*, edited by Aihwa Ong and Michael G. Peletz, 159–94. Berkeley: University of California Press.

Ong, Aihwa. 1999. *Flexible Citizenship: The Cultural Logics of Transnationality*. Durham, NC: Duke University Press.

Osella, Caroline, and Filippo Osella. 2007. "*Muslim Style in South India.*" *Fashion Theory: The Journal of Dress, Body and Culture* 11, no. 2/3: 235–52.

Ossman, Susan. 2002. *Three Faces of Beauty: Casablanca, Paris, Cairo*. Durham, NC: Duke University Press.

Özyürek, Esra. 2006. *Nostalgia for the Modern: State Secularism and Everyday Politics in Turkey*. Durham, NC: Duke University Press.

Patel, Pragna. 2012. "Faith Organisations and Migrants Today: The Gender Question?" In *Secularism, Racism and the Politics of Belonging*, edited by Nira Yuval-Davis and Philip Cohen, 23–30. London: Runnymede.

Peach, Ceri. 2006. "Muslims in the 2001 Census of England and Wales: Gender and Economic Disadvantage." *Ethnic and Racial Studies* 29, no. 4: 629–55.

Pearce, Brian. 2012. "The Inter Faith Network and the Development of Inter Faith Relations in Britain." In *Religion and Change in Modern Britain*, edited by Linda Woodhead and Rebecca Catto, 150–55. Oxon, UK: Routledge.

Peirce, Leslie. 1993. *The Imperial Harem: Women and Sovereignty in the Ottoman Empire*. Oxford: Oxford University Press.

Perfect, David. 2011. *Equality and Human Rights Commission Briefing Paper 1: Religion or Belief* (spring). Manchester, UK: Equality and Human Rights Commission.

Persad, Judy Vashti, Salome Lukas, and Women Working with Immigrant Women. 2002. *"No Hijab Is Permitted Here": A Study on the Experiences of Muslim Women Wearing Hijab Applying for Work in the Manufacturing, Sales and Service Sectors*. Toronto: Women Working with Immigrant Women (WWIW).

Pettinger, Lynne. 2004. "Brand Culture and Branded Workers: Service Work and Aesthetic Labour in Fashion Retail." *Consumption, Markets and Culture* 7, no. 2 (June): 165–84.

Pettinger, Lynne. 2005a. "Gendered Work Meets Gendered Goods: Selling and Service in Clothing Retail." *Gender, Work and Organization* 12, no. 5 (September): 460–78.

Pettinger, Lynne. 2005b. "Representing Shop Work: A Dual Ethnography." *Qualitative Research* 5, no. 3: 347–64.

Pew Research Center. 2001. *CyberFaith: How Americans Pursue Religion Online*. Washington, DC: Pew Research Center. December 23. Accessed October 2, 2011. www.pewinternet.org/Reports/2001/CyberFaith-How-Americans-Pursue-Religion-Online.aspx.

Pew Research Center. 2005. *The State of Blogging*. Washington, DC: Pew Research Center. January 2. Accessed June 16, 2015. www.pewinternet.org/2005/01/02/the-state-of-blogging/.

Pew Research Center. 2007. *Muslim Americans: Middle Class and Mostly Mainstream*. Washington, DC: Pew Research Center. May 22. Accessed November 1, 2013. www.pewresearch.org/2007/05/22/muslim-americans-middle-class-and-mostly-mainstream/.

Pew Research Center. 2009a. *Many Americans Mix Multiple Faiths*. Washington,

DC: Pew Research Center. December 9. Accessed November 1, 2013. www.pew
forum.org/2009/12/09/many-americans-mix-multiple-faiths/.

Pew Research Center. 2009b. *Mapping the Global Muslim Population: A Report on the Size and Distribution of the Worlds*. Washington, DC: Pew Research Center. October. Accessed November 1, 2013. www.pewforum.org/files/2009/10/Mus limpopulation.pdf.

Pew Research Center. 2010. *Muslim Networks and Movements in Western Europe*. Washington, DC: Pew Research Center. September 15. Accessed November 1, 2013. www.pewforum.org/files/2010/09/Muslim-networks-full-report.pdf.

Pew Research Center. 2011a. *The American-Western European Values Gap*. Washington, DC: Pew Research Center. November 17. Accessed November 1, 2013. www.pewglobal.org/2011/11/17/the-american-western-european-values -gap/.

Pew Research Center. 2011b. *The Future of the Global Muslim Population: Projections for 2010–2030*. Washington, DC: Pew Research Center. January 27. Accessed November 1, 2013. www.pewforum.org/2011/01/27/the-future-of -the-global-muslim-population/.

Pew Research Center. 2011c. *Muslim Americans: No Signs of Growth in Alienation or Support for Extremism*. Washington, DC: Pew Research Center. August 30. Accessed November 1, 2013. www.pewforum.org/2011/08/30/muslim-ameri cans-no-signs-of-growth-in-alienation-or-support-for-extremism/.

Pew Research Center. 2011d. *Muslim-Western Tensions Persist*. Washington, DC: Pew Research Center. July 21. Accessed November 1, 2013. www.pewglobal .org/2011/07/21/muslim-western-tensions-persist/.

Pew Research Center. 2011e. *The Social Side of the Internet*. Washington, DC: Pew Research Center. January 18. Accessed October 2, 2011. pewresearch.org/pubs /1861/impact-internet-social-media-facebook-twitter-group-activities -participation.

Pew Research Center. 2012. *The World's Muslims: Unity and Diversity*. Washington, DC: Pew Research Center. August 19. Accessed January 23, 2015. www .pewforum.org/files/2012/08/the-worlds-muslims-full-report.pdf.

Pew Research Center. 2013. *The World's Muslims: Religion. Politics and Society*. Washington, DC: Pew Research Center. April 30. Accessed January 23, 2015. www.pewforum.org/files/2013/04/worlds-muslims-religion-politics-society -full-report.pdf.

Philips, Richard, and Jamil Iqbal. 2009. "Muslims and the Anti-war Movements." In *Muslim Spaces of Hope: Geographies of Possibility in Britain and the West*, edited by Richard Philips. London: Zed.

Polhemus, Ted. 1994. *Streetstyle: From Sidewalk to Catwalk*. London: Thames and Hudson.

Poulsen, Michael, and Ron Johnston. 2008. "The 'New Geography' of Ethnicity in England and Wales?" In *New Geographies of Race and Racism*, edited by Claire Dwyer and Caroline Bressey, 157–78. Aldershot, UK: Ashgate.

Prokopec, Sonja, and Mazen Kurdy. 2011. "An International Marketing Perspective on Islamic Marketing." In *The Handbook of Islamic Marketing*, edited by Özlem Sandįkcį and Gillian Rice, 208–25. Cheltenham, UK: Edward Elgar.

Puwar, Nirmal. 2002. "Multicultural Fashion . . . Stirrings of Another Sense of Aesthetics and Memory." *Feminist Review* 71: 63–87.

Puwar, Nirmal, and Parvati Raghuram, eds. 2003. *South Asian Women in the Diaspora*. Oxford: Berg.

Raghuram, Parvati. 2003. "Fashioning the South Asian Diaspora: Production and Consumption Tales." In *South Asian Women in the Diaspora*, edited by Nirmal Puwar and Parvati Raghuram, 67–85. Oxford: Berg.

Raghuram, Parvati, and Irene Hardill. 1998. "Negotiating a Market: A Case Study of an Asian Woman in Business." *Women's Studies International Forum* 21, no. 5: 475–84.

Rainie, Lee. 2005. *Data Memo: The State of Blogging*. Washington, DC: Pew Research Center. January 2. Accessed October 25, 2013. www.pewinternet .org/Reports/2005/The-State-of-Blogging.aspx.

Rainie, Lee, Kristen Purcell, and Aaron Smith. 2011. *The Social Side of the Internet*. Washington, DC: Pew Internet and American Life Project. January 18. Accessed October 25, 2013.www.pewinternet.org/Reports/2011/The-Social -Side-of-the-Internet.aspx.

Rainie, Lee, Joanna Brenner, and Kristen Purcell. 2012. *Photos and Videos as Social Currency Online*. Washington, DC: Pew Research Center. September 13. Accessed October 25, 2013. pewinternet.org/Reports/2012/Online-Pictures. aspx.

Rantisi, Norma. 2004. "The Designer in the City and the City in the Designer." In *Cultural Industries and the Production of Culture*, edited by Dominic Power and Allen J. Scott, 91–109. London: Routledge.

Razack, Sherene. 2008. *Casting Out: The Eviction of Muslims from Western Law and Politics*. Toronto: University of Toronto Press.

Reekie, Gail. 1993. *Temptations: Sex, Selling in the Department Store*. St. Leonards, NSW, Australia: Allen and Unwin.

Riello, Giorgio, and Peter McNeil, eds. 2010. *The Fashion History Reader: Global Perspectives*. London: Routledge.

Roberts, Mary. 2007. *Intimate Outsiders: The Harem in Ottoman and Orientalist Art and Travel Literature*. Durham, NC: Duke University Press.

Robins, Kevin, and Asu Aksoy. 1995. "Istanbul Rising: Returning the Repressed to Urban Culture." *European Urban and Regional Studies* 2, no. 3: 223–35.

Rocamora, Agnès. 2011. "Personal Fashion Blogs: Screens and Mirrors in Digital Self-Portraits." *Fashion Theory: The Journal of Dress, Body and Culture* 15, no. 4: 407–24.

Rocamora, Agnès. 2012. "Hypertextuality and Remediation in the Fashion Media." *Journalism Practice* 6, no. 1: 92–106. Accessed April 4, 2012. doi: 10.1080/17512786.2011.622914.

Rocamora, Agnès, and Alistair O'Neill. 2008. "Fashioning the Street: Images of the Street in the Fashion Media." In *Fashion as Photograph*, edited by Eugenie Shinkle. London: I. B. Tauris.

Rogerson, Eleanor. 2010. "Gina Khan: 'My Experiences of Islam in Britian.'" In *Women, Islam and Western Liberalism*, edited by Faisal Al Yafai, 51–62. London: Civitas.

Rooks, Noliwe M. 2004. *Ladies' Pages: African American Women's Magazines and the Culture That Made Them*. New Brunswick, NJ: Rutgers University Press.

Rosaldo, Renato. 1993. *Culture and Truth: The Remaking of Social Analysis*. London: Routledge.

Rose, Gillian. 2012. *Visual Methodologies: An Introduction to Researching with Visual Materials*. London: Sage.

Rose, Nikolas. [1989] 1999. *Governing the Soul: The Shaping of the Private Self*. 2nd ed. London: Free Association Books.

Roy, Olivier. [2002] 2004. *Globalised Islam: The Search for a New Ummah*. London: C. Hurst.

Ryan, Louise, and Elena Vacchelli. 2013. "'Mothering through Islam': Narratives of Religious Identity in London." *Religion and Gender* 3, no. 1: 90–107.

Safi, Omid. 2003. "Introduction: 'The Times They Are a-Changin': A Muslim Quest for Justice, Gender, Equality and Pluralism." In *Progressive Muslims: On Justice, Gender and Pluralism*, edited by Omid Safi, 1–32. Oxford: Oneworld.

Sahgal, Gita. 2012. "The Return of the Grand Narrative—Relating Secularism to Racism and Belonging." In *Secularism, Racism and the Politics of Belonging*, edited by Nira Yuval-Davis and Philip Marfleet, 53–56. London: Runnymede.

Said, Edward W. 1978. *Orientalism*. London: Routledge.

Saktanber, Ayşe. 2002. "'We Pray Like You Have Fun': New Islamic Youth in Turkey between Intellectualism and Popular Culture." In *Fragments of Culture: The Everyday of Modern Turkey*, edited by Deniz Kandiyoti and Ayşe Saktanber, 254–76. London: I. B. Tauris.

Salamandra, Christa. 2004. *A New Old Damascus: Authenticity and Distinction in Urban Syria*. Bloomington: Indiana University Press.

Salamandra, Christa. 2005. "Cultural Construction, the Gulf and Arab London." In *Monarchies and Nations: Globalisation and Identity in the Arab States of the Gulf*, edited by Paul Dresch and James Piscatori, 73–95. London: I. B. Tauris.

Salih, Ruba. 2004. "The Backward and the New: National, Transnational and Post-national Islam in Europe." *Journal of Ethnic and Migration Studies* 30, no. 5 (September): 995–1011.

Salim, Dega. 2013. "Mediating Islamic Looks." In *Islamic Fashion and Anti-Fashion: New Perspectives from Europe and North America*, edited by Emma Tarlo and Annelies Moors, 209–24. Oxford: Bloomsbury.

Salvatore, Armando. 2004. "Making Public Space: Opportunities and Limits of Collective Action among Muslims in Europe." *Journal of Ethnic and Migration Studies* 30, no. 5 (September): 1013–31. doi: 10.1080/1369183042000245679.

Samad, Yunus. 1998. "Media and Muslim Identity Intersections of Generation and Gender." *Innovation* 11, no. 4: 425–38.

Sandıkçı, Özlem. 2011. "Researching Islamic Marketing: Past and Future Perspectives." *Journal of Islamic Marketing* 2, no. 3: 246–58.

Sandıkçı, Özlem, and Güliz Ger. 1997. "Constructing and Representing the Islamic Consumer in Turkey." *Fashion Theory: The Journal of Dress, Body and Culture* 11, no. 2: 189–210.

Sandıkçı, Özlem, and Güliz Ger. 2001. "Fundamental Fashions: The Cultural Politics of the Turban and the Levi's." *Advances in Consumer Research* 28: 146–50.

Sandıkçı, Özlem, and Güliz Ger. 2002. "In-between Modernities and Postmodernities: Theorizing Turkish Consumptionscape." *Advances in Consumer Research* 29: 465–70.

Sandıkçı, Özlem, and Güliz Ger. 2005. "Aesthetics, Ethics and Politics of the Turkish Headscarf." In *Clothing as Material Culture*, edited by Susanne Küchler and Daniel Miller, 61–82. Oxford: Berg.

Sandıkçı, Özlem, and Güliz Ger. 2007. "Constructing and Keeping the Islamic Consumer in Turkey." *Fashion Theory: The Journal of Dress, Body and Culture* 11, no. 2/3: 189–210.

Sandıkçı, Özlem, and Güliz Ger. 2010. "Veiling in Style: How Does a Stigmatized Practice Become Fashionable?" *Journal of Consumer Research* 37, no. 1: 15–36.

Sandıkçı, Özlem, and Güliz Ger. 2011. "Islam, Consumption and Marketing: Going beyond the Essentialist Approaches." In *The Handbook of Islamic Marketing*, edited by Özlem Sandıkcı and Gillian Rice, 484–502. Cheltenham, UK: Edward Elgar.

Saner, Emine. 2012. "Abercrombie & Fitch: For Beautiful People Only." *Guardian*, April 28. Accessed January 23, 2015. www.theguardian.com/fashion/2012/apr/28/abercrombie-fitch-savile-row.

Savage, Ben. 2007. *Research Paper: Sexual Orientation and Religion or Belief Discrimination in the Workplace*. January. Accessed January 23, 2015. www.acas.org.uk/media/pdf/g/s/01-07_1.pdf.

Schlereth, Thomas J. 1990. "Country Stores, Country Fairs and Mail-Order Catalogues: Consumption in Rural America." In *Consuming Visions: Accumulation and Display of Goods in America, 1880–1920*, edited by Simon J. Bronner. New York: W. W. Norton.

Schulz, Dorothea E. 2007. "Competing Sartorial Assertions of Femininity and Muslim Identity in Mali." *Fashion Theory: The Journal of Dress, Body and Culture* 11, nos. 2–3: 253–79.

Schultz, Majken, and Mary Jo Hatch. 2006. "A Cultural Perspective on Corporate Branding: The Case of LEGO Group." In *Brand Culture*, edited by Jonathon E. Schroeder and Miriam Salzer-Morling, 13–29. London: Routledge.

Scoble, Robert, and Shel Israel. 2006. *Naked Conversations: How Blogs Are Changing the Way Customers Talk with Businesses*. Hoboken, NJ: John Wiley.

Scott, Joan Wallach. 2007. *The Politics of the Veil*. Princeton, NJ: Princeton University Press.

Secor, Anna. 2002. "The Veil and Urban Space in Istanbul: Women's Dress,

Mobility and Islamic Knowledge." *Gender, Place and Culture: A Journal of Feminist Geography* 9, no. 1: 5–22.

Secor, Anna. 2004. "'There Is an Istanbul That Belongs to Me': Citizenship, Space, and Identity in the City." *Annals of the Association of American Geographers* 94, no. 2: 352–68.

Secor, Anna. 2005. "Islamism, Democracy, and the Political Production of the Headscarf Issue in Turkey." In *Geographies of Muslim Women: Gender, Religion, and Space*, edited by Ghazi-Walid Falah and Caroline Nagel, 203–25. New York: Guilford.

Secor, Anna. 2007. Afterword. In *Women, Religion, and Space: Global Perspectives on Gender and Faith*, edited by Karen M. Morin and Jeanne Kay Guelke, 148–57. Syracuse, NY: Syracuse University Press.

Serageldin, Samia. 2005. "The Islamic Salon: Elite Women's Religious Networks in Egypt." In *Muslim Networks from Hajj to Hip Hop*, edited by miriam cooke and Bruce B. Lawrence, 155–68. Chapel Hill: University of North Carolina Press.

Shah, Bindi, Claire Dwyer, and Tariq Madood. 2010. "Explaining Educational Achievement and Career Aspirations among Young British Pakistanis: Mobilizing 'Ethnic Capital'?" *Sociology* 44, no. 6: 1109–27.

Shah, Saeeda. 2010. "Muslim Women in the West: Understanding the Challenges." In *Women, Islam and Western Liberalism*, edited by Faisal Al Yafai, 38–50. London: Civitas.

Shields, Rob. 1992. *Lifestyle Shopping: The Subject of Consumption*. London: Routledge.

Shinkle, Eugènie. 2008. *Fashion as Photograph: Viewing and Reviewing Images of Fashion*. London: I. B. Tauris.

Shirazi, Faegheh. 2000. "Islamic Religion and Women's Dress Code: The Islamic Republic of Iran." In *Undressing Religion: Commitment and Conversion from a Cross-Cultural Perspective*, edited by Linda B. Arthur, 113–30. Oxford: Berg.

Shissler, Holly. 2004. "Beauty Is Nothing to Be Ashamed Of: Beauty Contests as Tools of Women's Liberation in Early Republican Turkey." *Comparative Studies in South Asia, Africa, and the Middle East* 24, no. 1: 109–26.

Shively, Kim. 2005. "Religious Bodies and the Secular State: The Merve Kavakçi Affair." *Journal of Middle East Women's Studies* 1, no. 3 (fall): 46–72.

Silvey, Rachel. 2005. "Transnational Islam: Indonesian Migrant Domestic Workers in Saudi Arabia." In *Geographies of Muslim Women: Gender, Religion, and Space*, edited by Ghazi-Walid Falah and Caroline Nagel, 127–46. New York: Guilford.

Singh, Gurharpal. 2005. "British Multiculturalism and Sikhs." *Sikh Formations: Religion, Culture, Theory* 1, no. 2: 157–73.

Singh, Gurharpal. 2012. "Sikhism." In *Religion and Change in Modern Britain*, edited by Linda Woodhead and Rebecca Catto, 100–110. Oxon, UK: Routledge.

Slater, Don. 1997. *Consumer Culture and Modernity*. Cambridge: Polity.

Smith, Jane I. 1999. *Islam in America*. New York: Columbia University Press.

Smith, Jane I. 2007. *Muslims, Christians, and the Challenge of Interfaith Dialogue.* New York: Oxford University Press.

Smith, Nicola. 2012. "Parenthood and the Transfer of Capital in the Northern Soul Scene." In *Ageing and Youth Cultures: Music, Style and Identity*, edited by Andy Bennett and Paul Hodkinson, 159–72. London: Bloomsbury.

Sobel, Jon. 2010. *State of the Blogosphere 2010.* Technorati Media. November 3. Accessed October 20, 2013. technorati.com/social-media/article/state-of-the -blogosphere-2010-introduction/.

Somers, Meredith. 2014. "New Group Aims to Conduct Census of Muslim Americans." *Washington Times*, March 12. Accessed March 15, 2014. www .washingtontimes.com/news/2014/mar/12/new-group-aims-to-conduct -census-of-muslim-america/.

Spivak, Gayatri Chakravorty. 1988. "Can the Subaltern Speak?" In *Marxism and the Interpretation of Culture*, edited by Cary Nelson and Lawrence Grossberg, 271–316. Champaign: University of Illinois Press.

Starrett, Gregory. [1999] 2003. "Muslim Identities and the Great Chain of Buying." In *New Media in the Muslim World: The Emerging Public Sphere*, 2nd ed., edited by Dale F. Eickelman and Jon W. Anderson. Bloomington: Indiana University Press.

Stokes, Martin. 2000. "'Beloved Istanbul': Realism and the Transnational Imaginary in Turkish Popular Culture." In *Mass Mediations: New Approaches to Popular Culture in the Middle East and Beyond*, edited by Walter Armbrust, 224–42. Berkeley: University of California Press.

Storey, Louise. 2007. "Rewriting the Ad Rules for Muslim-Americans." *New York Times*, April 28. Accessed May 1, 2007. www.nytimes.com/2007/04/28/busi ness/28muslim.html?pagewanted=all.

Stratton, Allegra. 2006. *Muhajababes: Meet the New Middle East — Cool, Sexy and Devout.* London: Constable.

Süerdem, Ahmet. 2013. "'Yes, My Name Is Ahmet, but Please Don't Target Me.' Islamic Marketing: Marketing Islam™?" *Marketing Theory*, August 8, 1–11.

Swartz, John. 2013. *Technorati Media: 2013 Digital Influence Report.* Technorati Media. Accessed October 20, 2013. technoratimedia.com/wp-content/uploads /2013/02/tm2013DIR.pdf.

Tarlo, Emma. 1996. *Clothing Matters: Dress and Identity in India.* London: C. Hurst.

Tarlo, Emma. 2010. *Visibly Muslim: Fashion, Politics, Faith.* Oxford: Berg.

Tarlo, Emma. 2013a. "Landscapes of Attraction and Rejection: South Asian Aesthetics in Islamic Fashion in London." In *Islamic Fashion and Anti-Fashion: New Perspectives from Europe and North America*, edited by Emma Tarlo and Annelies Moors, 73–92. London: Bloomsbury.

Tarlo, Emma. 2013b. "Meeting through Modesty: Jewish-Muslim Encounters on the Internet." In *Modest Fashion: Styling Bodies, Mediating Faith*, edited by Reina Lewis, 67–90. London: I. B. Tauris.

Tarlo, Emma, and Annalies Moors. 2013. *Islamic Fashion and Anti-Fashion: New Perspectives from Europe and North America*. London: Bloomsbury.

Taylor, Jodie. 2012. "Performances of Post-youth Sexual Identities in Queer Scenes." In *Ageing and Youth Cultures: Music, Style and Identity*, edited by Andy Bennett and Paul Hodkinson, 24–36. London: Bloomsbury.

Taylor, Lou. 2002. *The Study of Dress History*. Manchester, UK: Manchester University Press.

Technorati Media. 2011. *State of the Blogosphere 2011*. November 4. Accessed June 15, 2015. www.technorati.com/state-of-the-blogosphere-2011.

Technorati Media. 2013. *Digital Influence Report*. Accessed October 22, 2013. technorati.com/business/article/technorati-medias-2013-digital-influence -report/.

Temporal, Paul. 2011a. "The Future of Islamic Branding and Marketing: A Managerial Perspective." In *The Handbook of Islamic Marketing*, edited by Özlem Sandıkçı and Gillian Rice, 465–83. Cheltenham, UK: Edward Elgar.

Temporal, Paul. 2011b. *Islamic Branding and Marketing: Creating a Global Islamic Business*. Singapore: John Wiley and Sons (Asia).

Tepe, Sultan. 2011. "Serving God through the Market: The Emergence of Muslim Consumptionscapes and Islamic Resistance." In *The Handbook of Islamic Marketing*, edited by Özlem Sandıkçı and Gillian Rice, 363–92. Cheltenham, UK: Edward Elgar.

Thibos, Cameron, and Kate Gillespie. 2011. "Islam and Corporate Social Responsibility in the Arab World: Reporting and Discourse." In *The Handbook of Islamic Marketing*, edited by Özlem Sandıkcı and Gillian Rice, 300–318. Cheltenham, UK: Edward Elgar.

Thompson, Paul. 2012. "My Body Is Only for My Husband: U.S. Christian Model Kylie Bisutti Quit Victoria's Secret Because It Clashed with Her Faith." *Daily Mail*, February 8. Accessed February 8, 2012. www.dailymail.co.uk/femail /article-2097793/Kylie-Bisutti-quit-Victorias-Secret-clashed-Christian-faith .html.

Thomson Reuters. 2013. *State of the Global Islamic Economy: 2013 Report*. Accessed January 28, 2015. www.iedcdubai.ae/assets/uploads/files/tr-state -of-islamic-economy-2013.pdf.

Thornton, Sarah. 1995. *Club Cultures: Music, Media and Subcultural Capital*. Lebanon, NH: University Press of New England.

Thumma, Scott. 2000. *Report of Webmaster Survey*. Hartford Institute for Religion Research. Accessed July 22, 2011. hirr.hartsem.edu/bookshelf/thumma _article3.html.

Toledano, Ehud R. 1982. *The Ottoman Slave Trade and Its Suppression: 1840–1890*. Princeton, NJ: Princeton University Press.

Tulloch, Carol. 2010. "Style-Fashion-Dress: From Black to Post-black." *Fashion Theory* 14, no. 3: 361–86.

Tunç, Tanfer Emin. 2009. "Between East and West: Consumer Culture and Identity, Negotiation in Contemporary Turkey." In *Muslim Societies in the*

Age of Mass Consumption: Politics, Culture and Identity between the Local and Global, edited by Johanna Pink, 73–86. Newcastle upon Tyne, UK: Cambridge Scholars.

Turam, Berna. 2013. "The Primacy of Space in Politics: Bargaining Rights, Freedom and Power in an Istanbul Neighborhood." *International Journal of Urban and Regional Research* 37, no. 2: 409–29.

Turner, Bryan S. 2007. "Religious Authority and the New Media." *Theory, Culture and Society* 24, no. 2: 117–34.

Tyler, Melissa, and Pamela Abbott. 1998. "Chocs Away: Weight Watching in the Contemporary Airline Industry." *Sociology* 32, no. 3: 433–50.

Uddin, Asma T. 2011. "Conquering Veils: Gender and Islams." In *I Speak for Myself: American Women on Being Muslim*, edited by Maria M. Ebrahimji and Zahra T. Suratwala, 45–50. Ashland, OR: White Cloud Press.

Volpi, Frédéric, and Bryan S. Turner. 2007. "Introduction: Making Islamic Authority Matter." *Theory, Culture and Society* 24, no. 2 (March): 1–20. doi: 10.1177/0263276407074992.

Wadud, Amina. 2003. "American Muslim Identity: Race and Ethnicity in Progressive Islam." In *Progressive Muslims: On Justice, Gender and Pluralism*, edited by Omid Safi, 270–85. Oxford: Oneworld.

Walker, Peter. 2011. "Britain's Stores Tempt Chinese Shoppers." *Guardian*, December 27. Accessed October 22, 2013. www.theguardian.com/business /2011/dec/27/britain-stores-tempt-chinese-shoppers.

Warhurst, Chris, and Dennis Nickson. 2007. "Employee Experience of Aesthetic Labour in Retail and Hospitality." *Work, Employment and Society* 21, no. 1: 103–20.

Weinzierl, Rupert, and David Muggleton. 2003. "What Is 'Post-subcultural Studies' Anyway?" In *The Post-subcultures Reader*, edited by David Muggleton and Rupert Weinzierl, 3–23. Oxford: Berg.

Weller, Paul, Alice Feldman, Kingsley Purdam, et al. 2001. *Religious Discrimination in England and Wales*. London: Home Office, Research, Development and Statistics Directorate.

Werbner, Pnina. 2002. *Imagined Diasporas among Manchester Muslims*. Suffolk, UK: James Currey.

Werbner, Pnina. 2004. "Theorising Complex Diasporas: Purity and Hybridity in the South Asian Public Sphere in Britain." *Journal of Ethnic and Migration Studies* 30, no. 5: 895–911.

Werbner, Pnina. 2007. "Veiled Interventions in Pure Space: Honour, Shame and Embodied Struggles among Muslims in Britain and France." *Theory, Culture and Society* 24, no. 2: 161–86.

White, Jenny B. 2002. "The Islamist Paradox." In *Fragments of Culture: The Everyday of Modern Turkey*, edited by Deniz Kandiyoti and Ayse Saktanber, 191–220. London: I. B. Tauris.

White, Jenny B. 2013. *Muslim Nationalism and the New Turks*. Princeton, NJ: Princeton University Press.

Willsher, Kim. 2014a. "France's Burqa Ban Upheld by Human Rights Court." *Guardian*, July 1. Accessed July 1, 2014. www.theguardian.com/world/2014 /jul/01/france-burqa-ban-upheld-human-rights-court.

Willsher, Kim. 2014b. "French Muslim Women on Burqa Ban Ruling: 'All I Want Is to Live in Peace.'" *Guardian*, July 1. Accessed July 1, 2014. www.theguardian .com/world/2014/jul/01/french-muslim-women-burqa-ban-ruling.

Wilson, Elizabeth. [1985] 2003. *Adorned in Dreams: Fashion and Modernity*. London: I. B. Tauris.

Wilson, Jonathon A. J., and Jonathon Liu. 2010. "Shaping the Halal into a Brand." *Journal of Islamic Marketing* 1, no. 2: 107–23.

Winship, Janice. 2000. "Culture of Restraint: The British Chain Store 1920–39." In *Commercial Cultures: Economies, Practices, Spaces*, edited by Peter Jackson, Michelle Lowe, Daniel Miller, and Frank Mort. Oxford: Berg.

Winter, T. J. 2009. "The Poverty of Fanaticism." In *Islam, Fundamentalism, and the Betrayal of Tradition, Revised and Expanded*, edited by Joseph E. B. Lumbard, 301–13. Bloomington, IN: World Wisdom.

Witz, Anne, Chris Warhurst, and Dennis Nickson. 2003. "The Labour of Aesthetics and the Aesthetics of Organization." *Organization* 10, no. 1: 33–54.

WNC (Women's National Commission). 2006. *She Who Disputes: Muslim Women Shape the Debate*. London: Women's National Commission.

Woodard, Jennifer Bailey, and Teresa Mastin. 2005. "Black Womanhood: *Essence* and Its Treatment of Stereotypical Images of Black Women." *Journal of Black Studies* 36, no. 2: 264–81.

Woodhead, Linda. 2012. Introduction. In *Religion and Change in Modern Britain*, edited by Linda Woodhead and Rebecca Catto, 1–33. London: Routledge.

Woodhead, Linda, and Rebecca Catto. 2009. *Equality and Human Rights Commission Research Report 48, "Religion or Belief": Identifying Issues and Priorities* (winter). Manchester, UK: Equality and Human Rights Commission.

Woodhead, Linda, and Rebecca Catto, eds. 2012. *Religion and Change in Modern Britain*. Oxon, UK: Routledge.

Woodward, Sophie. 2007. *Why Women Wear What They Wear*. Oxford: Berg.

Woodward, Sophie. 2009. "The Myth of Street Style." *Fashion Theory: The Journal of Dress Body and Culture* 13, no. 1: 83–102.

Worth, Rachel. 2007. *Fashion for the People: A History of Clothing at Marks and Spencer*. Oxford: Berg.

Wrelton, Steve. 2007. "Lifestyle Magazine to Be Middle East Ambassador." *Campaign*, February 14, 7.

Wright, David. 2005. "Commodifying Respectability." *Journal of Consumer Culture* 5, no. 3: 295–314.

Wrigley, Neil, and Michelle Lowe. 1996. *Retailing Consumption and Capital: Towards the New Retail Geography*. Harlow, UK: Longman.

Wrigley, Neil, and Michelle Lowe. 2002. *Reading Retail: A Geographical Perspective on Retailing and Consumption Spaces*. London: Arnold.

Yeğenoğlu, Meyda. 1998. *Colonial Fantasies: Towards a Feminist Reading of Orientalism*. Cambridge: Cambridge University Press.

Yuval-Davis, Nira, Floya Anthias, and Eleonore Kofman. 2005. "Secure Borders and Safe Haven and the Gendered Politics of Belonging: Beyond Social Cohesion." *Ethnic and Racial Studies* 28, no. 3: 513–35.

Zabaza, Mona. 2007. "Shifting Landscapes of Fashion in Contemporary Egypt." *Fashion Theory: The Journal of Dress, Body and Culture* 11, no. 2/3: 281–98.

Zine, Jasmin. 2006a. "Between Orientalism and Fundamentalism: The Politics of Muslim Women's Feminist Engagement." In *(En)Gendering the War on Terror: War Stories*, edited by Krista Hunt and Kim Rygel, 27–50. Aldershot, UK: Ashgate.

Zine, Jasmine. 2006b. "Creating a Critical Faith-Centred Space for Anti-racist Feminism: Reflections of a Muslim Scholar-Activist." *Journal of Feminist Studies in Religion* 20, no. 2: 167–87.

Zine, Jasmin. 2006c. "Unveiled Sentiments: Gendered Islamophobia and Experiences of Veiling among Muslim Girls in a Canadian Islamic School." *Equity and Excellence in Education* 39: 239–52.

Zine, Jasmin. 2012. "Introduction: Muslim Cultural Politics in the Canadian Hinterlands." In *Islam in the Hinterlands: Exploring Muslim Cultural Politics in Canada*, edited by Jasmin Zine, 1–38. Vancouver: University of British Columbia Press.

INDEX

Page numbers followed by *f* denote illustrations.

Cacharel, 79, 93

Campbell, Heidi, 251, 284

Canada, 42, 180, 241, 280, 299. *See also* *Muslim Girl* magazine

Carly, Jean François, 141

çarşaf, 17, 98, 98f, 106

Catholics and Catholicism, 47, 55, 208, 266

catwalk shows. *See* fashion (catwalk) shows

Cengiz Arjuk (store), 104

Central Asian republics, 74–75, 80, 81–82, 99

chador, 17, 69, 71

Chaplin, Shirley, 209

chastity rings, 205

Chechnya, 80, 82, 99

Cheong, Pauline Hope, 257

China, 75, 236

Chohan, Barjis, 275–77, 277–78f, 279, 283, 298

choice, discourses of: blogosphere and, 263; choice as contingent and constrained, 161, 165–67, 168; defined, 18; and global Islam, 164–65; hijab rights and, 56, 170; lifestyle magazines and, 120, 159–61, 162; and modesty, multiple definitions of, 258; narratives of choice to wear hijab, 14, 171–80; neoliberal choosing subject, 18, 23, 117, 159–60, 169, 170, 219, 321; and religious voluntarism, 165; and rights discourse, 165, 170; and the right to consume, 117; segmentation of the market and, 18; and state-imposed veiling regimes, 82; and the umma, 164–65; veil wearing as female agency, 18, 62, 167–71

Christians and Christianity: as achieved/voluntary identity, 57, 58, 165; centralized control and, 55, 244; and choice/free religious will, 56, 165; Christian Right, 9, 320; commerce and commodification and, 64–65, 288; everyday religion (syncretism), 57; interfaith dialogue and, 305, 307; minoritization of, 47, 194; modest

fashion and, 241, 246, 248f, 257, 261, 262f, 270, 279–80, 285–86, 314; as normative underpinning of Western secularism, 8–9, 10, 11, 115, 288; online communities and presence, 251–52, 257, 261, 262f, 281, 285–86; and religion and belief employment regulations, 205; and religious vs. national identity, 48; revivalism of, 55; and sexual orientation, objections to employment protections for, 206; and social media, 249, 314

churidor, 307

circuit of culture model, 5–6, 66, 187, 210, 241, 290, 318

City Circle, 180

class: identity through consumption and, 23, 62; Islamic branding and distinctions of, 298; and legitimization of business, 75; "new veiling" as leveling, 61–62; segmentation of, in UK, 39–40; tesettür and distinctions of, 76, 77, 82, 107–8

Clothedmuch.com (blog), 246, 248f

club culture, 240–41

Cohen, Nina (blogger), 255–56, 314

college and university Islamic societies (ISOC), 179–80

Collezione (brand), 103

Comaroff, Jean, 290

Comaroff, John L., 290

Company Clothing (store), 233–34

consumer culture: department stores and, 64–65, 223, 288; ethical consumerism, 132–33, 293, 304–6; gendered development of, 64; identity formation and, 19, 117, 240, 288, 289; indigenized, 14, 65–67; inequities of, 19; and Islamic principle forbidding waste, 85, 153; and lifestyle media, 124–25, 132–33, 162, 293; as localized, 288–89; mail order, 64–65; and malls, 104–6, 210; massification of, 110; "Muslim pound," 321; neoliberal choosing subject and, 18, 23, 117, 159–60, 169, 170, 219, 321; politicization of, 116, 162; religion, commerce, and commodification, 64–

65, 288; reluctance to see Muslims as consumers, 117–18, 235, 295–96, 298–300; rights-based social movements and, 117; of South Asian diaspora, 186, 188–90; and transnational circuitry, 289–90; and Turkey, 72, 75; Turkish Islamists and anticommercialism, 84, 85, 152–53, 297; and youth subcultures, 193–94. *See also* choice, discourses of; individuality; queer politics; sustainability

convergence culture, 109–10, 283

converts and conversion to Islam: and choice, discourses of, 165; demographics and, 38, 41; and ethno-religious norms, distance from, 53, 259; as exemplifying chosen religious identity, 58; fusion styling and, 191–92; and interfaith dialogue, 304–5; lifestyle magazines as started by, 53, 119, 129; as modest fashion consumers, 279

corporate social responsibility (CSR), 221, 293, 296–97

Craik, Jennifer, 12–13

Crang, Philip, 289

Crewe, Louise, 210

critical Islam, 52–53

Critical Muslim, 53

cross-faith. *See* interfaith and cross-faith dialogue

crucifixes, 205

cultural capital: defined, 110; and independence of bloggers, 256; of marketing staff, 290–91; and massification of consumer society, 110–11; and minority or nonelite groups, 111–12; respect for diversity as, 266, 267; of retail staff, 65, 214, 217–18, 235–36, 319. *See also* cultural mediation

cultural intelligence of managers, 217, 226

cultural mediation, 110–13. *See also* cultural capital; fashion mediators and mediation; Internet-based modest fashion; lifestyle magazine genre; lifestyle magazines, Muslim

Dadswell, Beth, 141

Debenhams, 178, 215, 221–22, 224–25, 230, 233

de-ethnicization of Islam. *See* ethno-religious/cultural community norms

dehijabi, as term, 323n2

dejabi: Winnie Détwa, 266, 309–13, 310–11f, 313f, *color plate 17*; process of, as hypervisible, 314–15; as term, 18, 323n2

demographics, 37–43. *See also* youth demographic of Muslims

Denmark, tesettür and, 82

Deobandi Islam, 44, 50

department stores, 64–65, 223, 288

Détwa, Winnie, 266, 309–13, 310–11f, 313f, *color plate 17*

de Zwart, Paul, 112, 121, 122, 133, 141

digital modification of images, street fashion, 158, 161

Dior, 183

discrimination and Islamophobia: African American Muslims and, 42; and changing political discourse, 44, 45; ethnicity and racialization, 54, 55; and hijab worn in workplace, 183–84, 192, 207; in hiring, 40, 206–7, 214, 318–19; and ignorance about Muslims, 279; increase in, post-9/11, 206, 306; relegation of Islam to the nonmodern, 54. *See also* employment antidiscrimination regulations; negative stereotypes of Muslims

dishdash garment, 121–22, *122f*

dishonor, 170, 178

Diva magazine, 113, 118, 132, 134

diversity: Internet netiquette as respectful of, 245, 258, 266; Muslim lifestyle magazines and ethnic, 129, 131, 139, 144–46, 147, 161; as operationalized by employers, 219; of Ottoman Empire, 96; shift to, from equal opportunities framework, 221–22; subculture and respect for, 266, 267; of the umma, 97, 169. *See also* employment antidiscrimination regulations; human resources (HR) and employee relations

diversity (*continued*)
(ER); individuality; modesty codes as multiple and fluid; retail staff
Domosh, Mona, 64
Donald, Alice, 206, 220
Dorothy Perkins (stores), 106, 182, 215, 217, 218–19
Douglas, Sukina, 35–36
Druze community, 166
Dubai, 121
du Gay, Paul, 219–20
Dursun, Mehmet, 78
Dursun, Şevket, 78, 87
Dwyer, Claire, 186, 289

Edib, Halide, 166
education: in the arts, 40, 275; bans on niqab, 208; economic disadvantages, 206–7; educators and hijab, 192; of girls, 40, 216; and needs of youth following 9/11 and 7/7, 44, 301; and participation in Internet, 249; of retail staff, 216; school uniforms/religious dress, 167, 186, 204, 205, 208, 232–33; of second- and third-generation migrants, 40, 41, 274–75; Turkey and, 72, 73
Egypt, 50, 56, 62, 65–67, 166; and modest fashion, 194–95, 241
Elenany, Sarah: and the body, representation of, 271–72, *272–73f*; Girl Scout uniforms designed by, 302–4, *303f*, *color plate 16*; and marketing, 272–75, 277–81, 296; menswear, 274; in Muslim lifestyle magazines, 262, *264f*; and negative feedback, 262; and social media, 274
Eliza magazine, 270
Embox (digital supplement), 139–40, *140f*
Emel magazine, 53, 85, *119f*, *color plate 6*; and advertising, 118, 133; and anticommercialists, 85; and the body, representation of, *135f*, 136–39, *137–38f*, 141, 160, 309; and Bosnia, 80–81; and calling in product, 134–36; circulation and readership of, 114, 118, 141; and diversity, 139, 160, 162; and ethical consumerism, 132–33; and faith as focus of fashion, 134, *135f*, 171; and hijab inclusion, or not, 139, 140, *140f*, 160–61; and interfaith dialogue, 304; and links with designers, 262, *264f*; Muslim identity and, 131–32; online supplements of, 139–40, *140f*; as politically unaligned, 118–20, 131; street style and, 158, 161
Emerald Network, 180
Employers' Forum on Belief (UK), 232
employment: discrimination at work (hijab), 183–84, 192, 207; discrimination in hiring, 40, 206–7, 214, 318–19; individuality/diversity of workers operationalized for, 219–24, 319; lifestyle magazines/media providing, 124, 128, 131, 154–55, 162; modest fashion suitable for, 76, 182–84; Muslim women underrepresented in, 215, 232, 233; South Asian diaspora fashion and, 187–90. *See also* aesthetic labor; employment antidiscrimination regulations; retail staff; tesettür retail staff
employment antidiscrimination regulations (UK): branding and uniform requirements and, 205, 206; communication requirements and, 204–5, 206, 235; court cases, 204–6, 207, 208–9, 220; dress, 202, 224–30, 231–35; employers' reasonable accommodations, 202, 206; Equality and Human Rights Commission, 202, 232; expansion of protections of, 201–2, 209, 326–27n8; flexible working hours for religious observance, 202, 230–31, 232; health and safety requirements and, 202, 205, 206, 208, 209, 233; implementation guidance, 232–33; increasing strictness of Muslim dress and, 203; legislation covering, 201–2, 206, 220–21, 222, 234; and multiculturalism, 202–3; religious authorities and, 231; shift from focus on ethnic groups to religion and belief, 43–44, 97, 200–201; third-party harassment, 234–35; and youth, importance to, 209. *See also* human re-

identity (*continued*)
achieved vs. ascribed, 57–58, 165; shops and shopping and, 200; terminology and, 32, 54. *See also* individuality; Muslims, religious identity of

IKEA, 233

Îkrâ magazine, 162

imperialist nostalgia, 66

India: adaptations of traditional clothing, 187; as emerging market, 75; and marketing, 290–91, 292, 300; migration from, 39, 207; as source of fashion, 196

individuality: lifestyle magazines and, 113; operationalized for employment, 219–24, 319; religiosity and, 284; revivalism and, 55; of veil, 11. *See also* diversity

Indonesia, 4–5, 43, 115, 156, 208

information technologies. *See* Internet

Inspire magazine, 117

Instagram, 247, 249, 259. *See also* social media

interfaith and cross-faith dialogue: Christianity and, 305, 307; Christian/Jewish organizations, 305; converts and, 304–5; and ethical consumerism, 305, 306; and Girl Scout uniforms (Sarah Elenany, designer), 302–4; government and, 305; and inclusion, ideology of, 319–20; Internet-based modest fashion and, 238–39, 240, 241, 242, 245, 274, 285–86, 302–5, 307; Sarah Joseph and, 118–19, 304–5; Judaism and, 305, 307; marketing and, 279–80, 306–7; and modesty, 319; 9/11 and need for, 305; print media and, 304; social media and, 304; and visibility of hijabi activists, 302

Internet: English as language of, 49, 244; and ethnicity, 49; extremism as fostered by, 244–45; gatekeeping practices and, 240–41, 252; hate campaigns, 267; Islamist movements and, 49–50, 238; lifestyle media and marketing on, 115; links in and out of websites, 252–53, 257; netiquette

of respectful diversity, 245, 258, 266; religions and, 237–38, 243–45, 283; religious authority structures and, 243–45, 256, 283–84, 285; religious community life and, 239, 244–45, 251–52, 283–84, 285–86; and tesettür in Turkey, 83, 85; and transnational policing of local discussions, 267; uneven access to, 83, 239, 241, 249, 284; and women, significance to, 244; youth demographic and, 49. *See also* blogs and blogging; Internet-based modest fashion; social media

Internet-based modest fashion: accessibility and, 241; as accretion from older forms, 238, 239; and the body, representation of, 267–69, 271, 283, *color plates 11–13*; brand survival and, 253; click-through culture to drive sales, 252–53, 309; commerce and commentary overlap in, 239–40, 241–42, 245, 252–53, 283, 285; consumer culture and identity formation and, 240–41; as cross-faith and international, 238–39, 240, 241, 242, 245, 274, 285–86, 302–5, 307; and e-commerce, development of, 240, 241; expansion and segmentation of markets, 240; feminism and, 245; fulfillment problems, 281; models and, 268, 271, 283; and modesty codes as multiple and fluid, 238, 242, 245, 257–59, 261, 263, 266–67; pricing, 275, 276–77, 307; religious interpretation and, 238, 241, 283–86, 297, 309; shopping autonomy and, 274–75; smartphones and, 249–50; street shoots associated with, 281–83, *282f, color plates 14, 15*; style mediators and, 240, 241, 245, 281–82, 286; women as foregrounded in, 238, 239, 240, 245. *See also* blogs and blogging; social media

Ipekyol (brand), 75, 102–3, 159, *160f*

Iran, 41, 42, 74, 78, 82; and choice, discourses of, 170; tesettür industry and, 75, 79, 82

Iraq, tesettür and, 82

Iraq War, 73–74

Islam, Raishma, 307

Islam, Yusuf, 52–53

Islam: da'wa mission of, 177, 180, 194, 233, 243, 245; morality, 62; seen as resistant to modernity, 3, 10, 54, 317–18; and spiritual authority, 55–56, 244, 309; and spiritual authority, Internet and, 243–45, 256, 283–84, 285. *See also* converts and conversion to Islam; global (European) Islam; Islam, religious interpretation (itjihad); Islamic branding; Islamic revival and revivalists; Islamic values; Islamist movements; Muslims, religious identity of; piety; umma

Islam, religious interpretation (itjihad): as changing over time, 229–30; everyday religion and, 318; hijabi fashion and, 177, 319; and inclusion, ideology of, 319–20; Internet-based modest fashion and, 238, 241, 283–86, 297, 309; and Jama'at-i Islami, 50–51; mixing of garment sources and, 181; Muslim lifestyle magazines and, 125, 131, 162; revivalists and open and flexible, 53, 71

Islamic (green) capitalism, rise of, 4, 71–75

Islamic branding: ambivalence about, 291; conditions of emergence of, 289; corporate responsibility/sustainability and, 296–97; and cultural capital of (Muslim) marketing staff, 290–91, 293–97, 300, 318; demographic statistics as important to, 37–38; and ethnic branding, 289–90; and exclusion, 297–98; homogenization of Muslims and, 291; and identity through consumption, 289; and interfaith dialogue, 306–7; legitimization of business and, 296–97; and lifestyle magazines, 117–18; and localism, 292; nation-states and, 296–97; Ogilvy Noor (Islamic branding practice), 25, 196, 290, 291–97, 300–301; religiosity and, 293; risks of alienating Muslim consumers, 291, 292; and spending power of global Muslim population, 289; as term, 31; tesettür companies and, 78, 85, 106–7, 156–57, *color plates 8, 9*; and uneven interest in the Muslim consumer, 117–18, 295–96, 298–300; and values, Islamic, 291, 292–93, 296–97, 300–301

Islamic fashion, as term, 32. *See also* Muslim modest fashion

Islamic revival and revivalists: anticonsumerist vs. commercial styles of veiling, 61–62; converts and, 53, 191–93; core constituency of, 70–71; and dress, 165; and Islamic branding, 292–93, 296; and personal choice/interpretation, 53, 71; and religious vs. ethnic identity, 53, 177–78; and religious vs. national identity, 47–48; and South Asian diaspora fashion, 185; visibility of the veil as goal of, 11, 61–62, 167. *See also* ethno-religious/cultural community norms, detachment from (de-ethnicization of Islam); everyday religion; personal spiritual quest

Islamic Society of North America (ISNA), 51, 124, 129, 302

Islamic State (ISIS), 74

Islamic values: and business, legitimization of, 71–72, 75, 296–97; ethnic and gender equality, 302; Islamic branding and, 291, 292–93, 296–97, 300–301; sustainability and, 19, 85, 153, 221, 293, 296–97

Islamist movements: information and communication technologies and, 49–50; lifestyle magazines attributed to, 116–17; progressivist discourse of stricter dress, 179–80, 193, 204; women's agency found in conspicuous dress codes of, 50. *See also* extremism/radicalization/jihadization; Islamic revival and revivalists; Turkish Islamists

Islamophobia. *See* discrimination

ISNA, 51, 124, 129, 302

ISOC, 179–80

Israel, 74, 82

Istanbul, as center of tesettür industry, 75–76, 79, 89, 97–99, 106, 159

itjihad. *See* Islam, religious interpretation

"Jackie" (ER director), 222–23, 234, 235

Jafari, Aliakbar, 292

Jama'at-i Islami, 50–51, 180

Janmohamed, Shelina, 294–95

Jenkins, Henry, 109–10

JenMagazine.com (online magazine), 246, 246f

jewelry, 192, 202, 205, 225–26

Jews and Judaism: anti-Semitism, 65; as ascribed/inherited identity, 57, 165; blogs and blogging, 255–56, 314; as ethnic group, 43, 200–202; everyday religion (syncretism), 56–57; interfaith communities, 305; modest fashion and, 241, 255–56, 268, 270, 279, 285–86, 307, 314; and Ottoman Empire, 71–72; population in U.S., 41; spiritual authority, 55, 244

jihad, 18. *See also* extremism/radicalization/jihadization

jilbab, 16–17, 50, 167, 178, 179, 204, 208, 235, 254

Jones, Carla, 115, 321

Joseph, Sarah, *119f*; and *Âlâ*, 152; as convert, 53, 118, 119, 304–5; and ethical consumerism, 132, 304–5; and interfaith dialogue, 118–19, 304–5; and Muslim identity, 131–32; and objectification of models, 134–36, 161; as politically unaligned, 118–20

Kaiser, Susan B., 6, 13, 165

Karaduman, Mustafa, 77, 78, 80, 82, 83, 85, *85f*, 101, 106

Karaduman, Necip, 99, 100

Karaflogka, Anastasia, 252

Kavakçi, Elif, 73, 153, 155

Kavakçi, Merve, 72–73

Kayra (tesettür company), 70, 83, 93, 108, 155, *156f*; catalogues of, 93–96, *94–95f, color plates 3, 4*

Kazahkstan, 82

Kemal, Mustapha (Atatürk), 67, 72, 105

Kennedy, Faye, 124, 143

Khadijah (wife of the Prophet), 297

Khan, Adviya, 190, 191, 263, *264f*

Khan, Ausma, 122, 124, 125, *126f*, 143, 146, 161, 295

Khan, Samia, 191, 263, *265f*

Khubsoorat Collection (brand), 189

Kılıçbay, Barış, 85

Kline, David, 244–45

Kohli, Mani, 39, 189–90, 275

Kosher Casual (brand), 307

Kossaibati, Jana, 27, 28; and advertising, 298–99; and the body, 259, 308; as community ambassador, 304, 313; content of blog, 254, *255f*, 258–59, *color plate 10*; and ethical consumerism, 132; and modesty codes, 258–59; and negative feedback, 266; product giveaways and, 254–56; readership of, 254, 256, 257; recognition of role of, 295; start in blogging, 246, 253–54; and student organizations, 180

Koton (brand), 103, 159

Kovyrzina, Elena, 144–45, 146

Kurds, 73

Kuwait, 82, 114, 120–21, 133

laïcité, 8, 9, 10, 67. *See also* secularism and secular states

LDS. *See* Mormon Church of Jesus Christ of Latter-day Saints

Lebanon, 42, 78, 121

lesbians. *See* queer (lesbian and gay) subcultures

lifestyle magazine genre: and advertising/editorial relationship, 133; and body management, 111, 112–13; as cultural intermediary, 110–11; emergence of, 110, 112; readers of, 115, 154; and taste community, 110, 112, 113. *See also* queer (lesbian and gay) lifestyle magazines

lifestyle magazines, Muslim: advertising and, 117–18, 133, 141, 143, 155–56, 298–99; aspirational consumer mode of, 124–25, 162; and calling in (pulling

Max Mara, 183

Maysaa (brand), 259, 268–69, 281

Maysaa (digital magazine), 259, 260*f*, 268–69, *color plate 11*

media: Asian fashion and bridal, 188; and hijab and niqab cases, 232; hostility to Muslim lifestyle magazines, 152; liberalization in Turkey and, 152; as mining Muslim lifestyle media, 114; and tesettür, 71, 84–85, 85*f*, 86–87, 155. *See also* Internet; lifestyle magazine genre; news media; radio; style media; television

Medina, Jameelah Xochitl, 54–55

Meer, Nasar, 54

men: beards, 139, 232, 320–21; commodification of bodies of, 112; dress/body management of, 61, 201; dress reform for, 66, 67; hostile comments in social media, 263, 266, 267, 271; male gaze, 8–9; menswear, 121–22, 274. *See also* gender

Mernissi, Fatima, 60

migration, demographics and, 38–42

minority relations, multiculturalism and, 44–45, 46–47

Mitchell, Katherine, 10

models: for catwalk shows, 87; impossible beauty ideals and, 138–39, 271, 308; for Internet-based modest fashion, 268, 271, 283; for lifestyle magazines, 136, 138–39, 144–45, 146, 147, 150, 160–61; modest modeling agencies, 147; for tesettür catalogues, 87, 92, 96–97, 309, *color plate 1*

modernity and modernizing: and fashion, 3, 36; imperialist nostalgia and, 66; and indigenization of Western commodities, 14, 65–67; Islam seen as resistant to, 3, 10, 54, 317–18; Ottoman Orientalism and, 67; tesettür catalogues and association with, 85; Turkey and, 9–10, 67–68, 96–97, 104–5; and veiling, deveiling, 10, 63–64, 66–68, 69–70, 314. *See also* secularism and secular states

modest fashion: antifashion discourse and, 19; market for, 135–36; rapid changes of, 15–16, 19, 321; as term, 32–33, 240. *See also* fashion mediators and mediation; hijabi fashion; interfaith and cross-faith dialogue; Internet-based modest fashion; Muslim modest fashion

modesty codes as multiple and fluid: dejabis and, 313–15; designers and, 271–72; hostile criticism of, 266–67; interfaith dialogue and, 319; Internet-based fashion and, 238, 242, 245, 257–59, 261, 263, 266–67; Muslim lifestyle magazines and, 125, 140–41, 143, 159–61; as online norm, 286

modesty codes, women as bearing burden of, 61

Modestyle (digital supplement), 139

Modood, Tariq, 44, 53, 209

MODSHOP (online portal), 306

Mohamad Ali (r. 1805–49), 65

Mohammed, Warith Deen, 42, 51

Monkush, Fatima, 245, 269–71, 270*f*, 302

Monsoon (brand), 182

Moors, Annelies, 36–37, 258, 263

Morey, Peter, 59

Morgan (brand), 182

Mormon Church of Jesus Christ of Latter-day Saints (LDS), 241, 246, 248*f*, 257, 261, 262*f*

Morocco, 42

Mostar bridge scarf design, 81–82

MSA, 51, 180

mslm Fashion Magazine (museum art project), 116

Mughal, Shabnam, 205

"muhajababes," 194–95

Muhammed, Elijah, 42

multiculturalism: the Balkans and, 80; failure of (UK), 44–45, 53; and gender, 46, 47; progressive, 47, 301–2; as secular, 44; United States, 53–54

multiple fashion systems, 13–15, 181–82, 187, 318; defined, 6–7, 12–13

Murray, Claire, 135, 146

Muslimah Media Watch, 308, 315

elite of, 71–72; demographics of, 43; education and, 72, 73; EU accession of, 11, 31, 73, 208; Islamism of, 51–52; liberalization of economy of, 69, 72, 152; migrants from, 40–41; military coup of 1980, 72; neo-Ottomanism, 73–75, 76, 81–82, 89, 105, 107–8; and racialized Turkish ethno-national identity, 96–97; and state control of religious domain, 10, 51, 67, 72; street fashion and, 280; urbanization of population, 75; and the veil as threat, 10. *See also* *Âlâ* magazine; Ottoman Empire; tesettür (covered fashion) industry (Turkey); Turkey and secularism; Turkish Islamists

Turkey and secularism: banning of the veil, 9–10, 67–68, 72–73, 76–77, 208; founding of Turkish republic and French model of laïcité, 9–10, 67; Kemalist nostalgia, 105; male dress reform, 66, 67; malls and, 104–5; nationalist Turkism of, 74; and politicization of tesettür, 60–70, 76–77, 84–85, 105, 107–8, 152, 154, 158–59; relegation of Islam to the nonmodern, 54, 107, 197; "white Turk"/"black Turk" division, 107–8

Turkish Islamists, 51–52, 77, 108; anticommercialism of, 84, 85, 152–53, 297; consumption practices, 197; and liberalization of economy, 72; neo-Ottomanism, 73–75, 76, 81–82, 89, 105, 107–8; student societies and, 51–52; and veiling regulations, 72–73; youth and malls, 105–6. *See also* AKP (Justice and Development Party) government of Turkey; tesettür (covered fashion) industry (Turkey)

Turkmenistan, 82

Turner, Bryan S., 245, 284

Twitter, 247, 249, 254, 257, 281. *See also* social media

Uddin, Asma T., 180, 315

UK Employment Equality (Religion or Belief) Regulations (2003), 201

umma (supranational community of Muslim believers): cosmopolitanism and, 59; defined, 21; ethnic diversity of, 97, 169; and forms of exclusion, 54–55, 171; information and communication technologies and, 49–50; and local norms, 170, 267, 276; and markets for modest fashion, 276; Muslim lifestyle magazines and, 131; and Muslim politics in UK, 43–44; and new forms of Islam, 37; and new Muslim publics, 48–49, 54–55; Turkish Islamism and, 74. *See also* personal spiritual quest

uniforms: corporate codes, 205, 223; Girl Scouts, 302–4, *303f, color plate 16*; school, 167, 186, 204, 205, 208, 232–33. *See also* retail staff dress codes and uniforms

United Arab Emirates (UAE), 121

United Kingdom. *See* Britain

United States: census of, 37; demographics of Muslims in, 37, 41–42, 43; hijab tying style in, 95; lifestyle magazines and, 116, 125; percentage of women wearing hijab, 48, 125, 143; secularity of, 8; as tesettür market, 78. *See also* African American Muslims; *Azizah* magazine; *Muslim Girl* magazine

Vakko (brand), 79

the veil and veiling: anticonsumerist "new veiling," 61–62, 69, 76; and body management, 59–60, 61, 62; definition of, 16; discourse of ever-increasing strictness in, 179–80, 193, 204; diversity of types of, 16–17; and gender segregation, 60–61; history and traditions of, 16–17; as inimical to fashion, 3; as outerwear, 17, 141, 150; piety, pressure to wear veil as proof of, 166–67, 168; and the pious self, construction of, 61, 62, 169; as refusal of male gaze, 8–9; the right to wear, 48, 56, 170; as sign of resistance, 56; as spatialized practice, 60–61; stigmatization of, 63, 67–68, 171; as threat to secular government, 10. *See also* bans